THESES ON THE METAPHORS OF DIGITAL-TEXTUAL HISTORY

THESES ON THE METAPHORS OF DIGITAL-TEXTUAL HISTORY

MARTIN PAUL EVE

Stanford University Press
Stanford, California

Stanford University Press
Stanford, California

Printed in the United States of America on acid-free, archival-quality
paper

Library of Congress Cataloging-in-Publication Data
Names: Eve, Martin Paul, 1986- author.
Title: Theses on the metaphors of digital-textual history / Martin Paul
  Eve.
Other titles: Text technologies.
Description: Stanford, California : Stanford University Press, 2024.
  | Series: Stanford text technologies | Includes bibliographical
  references and index.
Identifiers: LCCN 2024003650 (print) | LCCN 2024003651 (ebook) |
  ISBN 9781503614888 (paperback) | ISBN 9781503639393 (ebook) |
Subjects: LCSH: Metaphor. | Word processing. | Text processing
  (Computer science) | Computer science—Language. |
  Technology—Language.
Classification: LCC P325.5.M47 E94 2024 (print) | LCC P325.5.M47
  (ebook) | DDC 401.43—dc23/eng/20240205
LC record available at https://lccn.loc.gov/2024003650
LC ebook record available at https://lccn.loc.gov/2024003651

Cover design: Aufuldish & Warinner

To my wife, Helen Eve, with all my love

CONTENTS

ACKNOWLEDGMENTS

This work was made possible through the award of a Philip Leverhulme Prize by the Leverhulme Trust, grant number PLP-2019-023. I would like to thank Erica Wetter, Caroline McKusick, and Chris Peterson at Stanford University Press for all their help in getting the manuscript this far. My gratitude goes to Adriana Smith for her most excellent effort copyediting this work and to Simon Davies for the index. My thanks also to the series editors, Elaine Treharne, Ruth Ahnert, and Roopika Risam for their interest in and encouragement of this work.

My thanks to John E. Warnock for insights into the early resistance to the PDF format; to Steven Bagley, David Brailsford, and Jeanine Finn for sources for early criticisms of PDF pagination and transmedia constraint; and to Nelson H. F. Beebe and Karl Berry for documentation of TEX and pagination standards therein. David McKitterick and Richard Fisher helped with my inquiries on the rise to prominence of white paper and made suggestions about the title. My thanks also to the readers and editors at *Book History*, and particularly Beth le Roux and Thomas Todarello, for their incisive and helpful comments during peer review and editing. I owe thanks to Roopika Risam and Alex Gil for my section on shadow libraries and digital preservation and for the special issue of *Digital Humanities Quarterly* that they edited, in which some of the ideas in this book have previously appeared. Thanks also to Melissa Terras and Paul Gooding for the invitation to speak at the University of Cambridge on digital legal deposit, the text of which talk grew into the final chapter of this book.

I am grateful to Catherine Grant, Rose Harris-Birtill, Sam Moore, and Jane Winters for their comments on the draft manuscript of the chapter on the virtual page. Bronać Ferran provided me with links to recent copyright rulings around machine-generated artforms. I am grateful for the work of Matthew Kirschenbaum, to whom much of this book is indebted and who helped me think through the title, and for the work of Alan Liu and Kathleen Fitzpatrick.

A number of friends and colleagues have sustained me in personal ways throughout this project, which was written in the isolation of ongoing Covid shielding over a four-year period owing to my continued vulnerability, immunocompromised status, and total kidney failure. Greetings to all at A Love From Outer Space. My special thanks to Janneke Adema, Siân Adiseshiah, Juan Pablo Alperin, Tina Atlagić, James Baker, Anthony Bale, Caroline Bassett, Heike Bauer, Kaveh Bazargan, David Berry, Geoff Bilder, Mark Blacklock, Brett Bobley, Josh Bolick, Mark Bould, Peter Boxall, Peter Brennan, Nikola Brigden, Joe Brooker, Carolyn Burdett, Jack Butters, Andy Byers, Luisa Calè, Jamie Campbell, Jane Campbell, Ruth Charnock, Bryan Cheyette, Peter Christian, Roland Clare, Linda Clare, Paula Clemente Vega, Poppy Corbett, Ryan Cordell, Julian Cottee, Holly Crow, James Crow, Adam Crymble, Helen Cullyer, James Cummings, Stephen Curry, Isabel Davis, Lianne de Mello, Joe Deville, Sarah Dillon, Bob Eaglestone, Caroline Edwards, Simon Everett, Alison Finlay, Hilary Fraser, Jo Freer, Jon Fugler, Melonie Fullick, Brian Gallagher, Rupert Gatti, Matt Gold, Alex Goy, Hilary Goy, Tom Grady, Duncan Gray, Jonathan Gray, Bas Groes, Richard Hall, Clare Hankey, Anna Hartnell, Jane Harvell, Doug Haynes, Alastair

Horne, Alyson Jakes, Ben Johnson, Sean Johnston, Lloyd Jones, Alexa Joubin, Helen Karamallakis, Micki Kaufman, Wendy Kettle, Erik Ketzan, Caroline King, Sharla Lair, Rich Lane, Stuart Lawson, Doireann Laylor, Mark Leach, Lennard Lee, Esther Leslie, Liz Lightstone, Melanie Lockett, Roger Luckhurst, Al Mackenzie, Caroline Magennis, John Matthews, Caroline Matthews, Phil Mays, Zena Mays, Shamira Meghani, Kay Mendlson, Lucy Montgomery, Will Morton, Ross Mounce, Mpalive-Hangson Msiska, Joe Muller, Yvonne Nobis, Mark Oakley, Amy Pajewski, Katherine Parker-Hay, Lee Perry, Mark Pimm, Frances Pinter, Sascha Pöhlmann, Ernesto Priego, Joshua Pugh, Mark Ratcliff, Andrée Rathemacher, Jennifer Richards, Albert Rolls, Johan Rooryck, Rick Rylance, Bob Salmond, Mauro Sanchez, Melanie Selfe, Iain Robert Smith, Julie-Ann Smith, Ronald Snijder, Graham Stone, Joe Street, Duncan Stringer, Helen Stringer, Claire Sugden, Simon Tanner, Sam Thomas, Ted Underwood, Hazel Vanderhoeven, Michael Vanderhoeven, Don Waters, Charles Watkinson, Angela Waugh, Stewart Waugh, Peter Webster, Scott Weingart, John Willinsky, Jake Wilson, Jo Winning, Agnes Woolley, and Warren Young.

My sincere thanks to the medical teams at the Royal Free Hospital and the Kent and Canterbury Hospital who have saved my life, especially Dr. Chiara Giacomassi, Professor Richard Stratton, Dr. Katie Townsend, Dr. Simon Black, Professor Chris Farmer, Dr. Alex Riding, Dr. Nasir Abbas, Dr. Rupert Beale, and the entire staff of the Thomas Becket Haemodialysis Unit.

With thanks to my family, Gill Hinks, Rich Gray, Alyce Magritte, Nova Gray, Mina Gray, Sue Eve, Sam Jones, Carin Eve, Anthony Eve, Julia Eve, Juliet Eve, and Lisa Holloway. Thinking fondly, always, of the memory of Nan and John. Thanks also to Toby and Luka, our boys, for the welcome distractions.

This book is dedicated to my lifelong love, Helen Eve.

THESES ON THE METAPHORS OF DIGITAL-TEXTUAL HISTORY

THESES ON THE METAPHORS OF DIGITAL-TEXTUAL HISTORY

ONE OF THE MOST CELEBRATED, and therefore over-remarked upon, of Jorge Luis Borges's short stories is his 1941 "The Library of Babel."[1] In this tale, there is, perhaps unsurprisingly given the title, a library. However, the library is extraordinary. The library is the entirety of the universe. Composed of an infinite number of hexagonal pillars, each of which contains five shelves of thirty-two books, each of which is 410 pages in length, the library contains every work ever written and every work that could possibly exist. When the library is discovered, it triggers celebration and joy. Everything that could be known is now possible to know!

Nevertheless, notably and problematically, the library contains much that is useless rubbish. Most books contain arbitrary strings that are neither words nor mathematical formulas.[2] Certainly, actual knowledge and wisdom are within the library. The problem is how to sort it out. Borges's library appears, then, as a model of reality, narrated by an unreliable figure who embodies these paradoxes of totality.[3] Everything we could know is, of course, presented to us in the form of the totality of existence. The "only" challenge is sifting the wheat from the chaff, sorting illusion from actuality, and separating idealism from the material.[4] Without curated metadata and discoverability, knowledge and noise can be difficult to tell apart.

Readers assume, as I just have, that the Library of Babel is the universe, the one-to-one map of reality about which Borges quipped elsewhere.[5] However, what if the library did exist in a form that was not just the sum of all existence? In computing systems, we use numeric representations to create digital sound files, movies, pictures, and text. Indeed, all computer files are, at heart, vast numbers. For example, let us say that we represent the letters a, b, and c by the familiar childish gamelike code of the numbers 1, 2, and 3. In this case, in binary, a would be "01," b would be "10," and c would be "11." A system that puts these together might write "1110" for cb. Clearly, computer file formats are more complex than this extremely basic cipher. However, it demonstrates the point: "1110" is the binary for the number 14. Any computer file, then, can be expressed as a number.

Irrational numbers such as π, which expresses the ratio of a circle's circumference to its diameter, contain every possible number that could ever exist within their infinitely long sequences. In formal terms, this is because mathematicians conjecture that π is normally distributed, which means that it is a *disjunctive sequence*. This distribution means that every digital file that could ever possibly exist—and, hence, every textual document that has been written, that has not been written, and that could be written—can be found at some point within π's unending string of numbers. Our cb number, 14, is relatively trivial to find, occurring immediately after the first decimal place: 3.14. However, even if one wanted to find abc in our code, one would not have to look far. Under our system, "011011" comes to 27. One only has to search twenty-eight digits after the decimal place to come across the digit that one needs: 3.141592653589793238462643383327. Irrational numbers, in digital contexts, are the real-world Library of Babel.

This may all sound very hypothetical. However, Philip Langdale has created a (satirical) computing filesystem—dubbed πfs—that uses π to store (or, really, to compute) its data. Indeed, when one wishes to save or retrieve a file, the πfs filesystem calculates and searches through π until it finds the numbers that express the data in question. "πfs is a revolutionary new file system," claims Langdale jokingly, "that, instead of wasting space storing your data on your hard drive, stores your data in π! You'll never run out of space again—π holds every file that could possibly exist! They said 100% compression was impossible? You're looking at it!"[6]

Of course, πfs is pragmatically useless and not a serious undertaking; it is geek humor.[7] To calculate π to enough digits to find extremely long binary numbers, equivalent to files, would take a very long time. πfs works by substituting space and storage for time, in essence recomputing files every time a user wishes to access them. The πfs filesystem derives from a joke made around 2001 by Keith F. Lynch. As Lynch noted, if one calculates and stores π in binary, in addition to all of the benefits of the Library of Babel, one would be guilty of the following:

Copyright infringement (of all books, all short stories, all
    newspapers, all magazines, all web sites, all music, all
    movies, and all software, including the complete Windows
    source code)
Trademark infringement
Possession of child pornography
Espionage (unauthorized possession of top secret information)
Possession of DVD-cracking software
Possession of threats to the president
Possession of everyone's SSN, everyone's credit card numbers,
    everyone's PIN numbers, everyone's unlisted phone
    numbers, and everyone's passwords
Defaming Islam. Not technically illegal, but you'd have to go
    into hiding along with Salman Rushdie.[8]

As Lynch went on to joke, "Also, your computer will contain all of the nastiest known computer viruses. In fact, all of the nastiest POSSIBLE computer viruses."[9] Indeed, the Library of Babel also contains every piece of malicious computer code and all dangerous knowledge and wisdom that could ever exist, assuming that one believes that we can represent all epistemic artifacts in digital form. In addition to being the font of all wisdom, it is also a dark archive that contains humanity's (and every other possible species in the universe's) worst.

I have chosen to open this volume with remarks on πfs and the Library of Babel because this book is about digital-textual histories and metaphors. What πfs shows us is a more basic premise of digital textuality: that text and numbers are indistinguishable from one another in the computational era and that to study electronic text implies a need to examine the numerical, digital, and computerized contexts and environments within which they are fashioned.[10] In the contemporary period, the "history of text" we are writing is also the "history of computers" and the "history of numbers" because, in the present day, everything written can be represented numerically. Hence, while it is tempting, given the small Venn-diagrammatical overlap between brilliant writers and brilliant mathematicians, to think that the space of writerly quality and the arena of mathematical/computational quantity must sit at opposite poles, this is not true. No matter how many liberal humanist defenses we make of writing, πfs reminds us that all text can be refactored to numbers and some numbers contain all text that can ever possibly be written, if we only choose to calculate them. To understand contemporary digital textuality and its metaphors, we must also work to understand the technical components that sit beneath them and the computer-scientific principles that have conditioned their development.

Digital Book History

By now, the study of the history of books and their materialities is so old that the field of the history of books has its own history.[11] Ever since Robert Darnton famously asked, "What is the history of books?" so the mythology goes, the field has burgeoned.[12] In our digital and globalized era, though, the recent trajectory of material-textual studies has had an outward, planetary focus. As Dennis Duncan and Adam Smyth note,

we have moved "away from bibliography's historical focus on the Western codex, towards a global study of the materials and practices of reading and writing from scrolls and tablets to inscriptions on shells and
bones."[13] This world-literary focus has diffused the scholarly practices
marching triumphantly under the banner of "bibliography." Indeed, at
this point in their life cycles, textual scholarship and the study of material texts have become highly diverse fields of endeavor. Researchers
in these fields focus on various global media over an extended period,
covering the prehistory of the printing press to the resurgent orality
of the digital audiobook.[14] Such disparity has led Wim van Mierlo to
ask whether any continuity even "exists in the methodological, conceptual and theoretical underpinnings of the discipline," positing that we
might speak instead of "discontinuity and diversification or fragmentation of methods and frameworks."[15] The histories of the histories of
books proliferate.

This book, the product of a decade of thinking about critical approaches to text technology, continues this proliferation and dispersion
by focusing on metaphor's role in digital-textual production history.[16]
The book is wide-ranging in its subject and approaches. Some chapters
of this book examine the historical evolution of digital-textual metaphorical concepts (such as "whitespace"), while other parts conduct
sociological readings and interpretations of the metaphors that we use
(such as "home" in computing contexts). Sometimes, the remarks are
simply about technological and computing environments—all of which
have a relevance for digitally consumed contemporary text. However,
as a unifying feature, this is a book about the messy *digital-linguistic*
frames that condition our current reading and writing practices in an
era when virtually all texts are "born-digital" and most are disseminated via the web. As of the early 2020s, the vast majority of the world's
novelists, poets, dramatists, and even MFA students begin their writing
days by settling down not with a pen in their hand but instead in front
of the familiar blinking vertical line of a computer cursor and the latest
version of Microsoft Word. There are exceptions. Don DeLillo and Jennifer Egan claim to resist the lure of the digital machine and conduct
their initial drafting using pens, paper, and typewriters.[17] George R.

R. Martin sticks to the earlier, but nonetheless digital, technology of WordStar.[18] In general, though, it is not possible comprehensively to understand the environment from which contemporary literature and text emerges without heed to the digital sites of their production, commodification, dissemination, and reception. In turn, paying attention to the environment entails a focus on cognitive metaphor, which tells us how to understand an aspect of a concept.[19]

Specifically, I hypothesize that digital-textual (and other computational) metaphors often move through three phases: they are initially descriptive, then they encounter a moment of fracture or rupture, and finally they go on to have a prescriptive life of their own that conditions future possibilities, even though they no longer seem to function as we might expect. This book looks for the moments when digital-textual metaphors *break*, because these instances show us how the possibilities for our future text environments have become constrained by metaphors that are untethered from their original intent. This book focuses on the ways that digital-textual metaphors do *not* work in order to uncover how our textual softwares become locked into paradigms that no longer make sense. This is important because, as Stuart Hall showed us, "metaphors are serious things. They affect one's practice."[20] In a different context, but also stressing the importance of metaphor, Jacques Derrida writes that "metaphor is never innocent. It orients research and fixes results."[21] We are, therefore, right to pay heed to such digital metaphors. This degradation of digital-textual metaphor has also been noted by Jeff Jarvis, who charts it as part of the so-called Gutenberg Parenthesis theory, which posits that the age of print was merely a bracket of history from which we are now departing in the internet age. For, "in the simplest expression," writes Jarvis, "it will become progressively less meaningful to say that we 'turn a page' in our lives, that our transparent selves are 'open books,' even that we have the 'complete story' when we read on screens in scrolls that never end."[22]

This book also marks the first time I have written about textuality without *reading* a set of texts, instead focusing on the surrounding para-apparatuses that are the conditions of possibility for digital text. This book is an attempt to interpret the environments of digital textuality and text editing through their metaphors and histories. If it is true that paratexts in the physical space can be read, examined, and analyzed, then it is also true that the same can be said for the "metadata"—as we might term such para-apparatuses—of digital-textual objects.[23] Indeed, other projects have also been invested in such work and have led the way. The legacy MONK project even stood for "Metadata Offer New Knowledge." Yet when I talk about the analysis of "metadata" here, I am not referring to the traditional elements that might be bracketed under such an approach. I do not mean the titles of works, their ISBNs, and their DOIs, for example. Instead, I analyze a broadened scope of "metadata" that includes the digital paratextual contexts that condition electronic text production. These range from actual technologies and their implementations, such as Unicode or the history of white paper, to metaphors of "vision" in our operating systems. Language and technology become hybrid forms of metadata that influence how we understand text in the twenty-first century.

This attention to metaphor has been the focus of other studies, most notably Marianne van den Boomen's 2014 *Transcoding the Digital: How Metaphors Matter in New Media*. Crucially, for van den Boomen, building on Lev Manovich's idea of "transcoding" as a process of "'conceptual transfer' from the computer world to culture at large," metaphor saturates all of our interactions with contemporary computation.[24] As she points out, "we barely realize" the extent to which most of our digital terms "are metaphorical."[25] This idea of "transfer" or "transport" has long been central to our understanding of metaphor. Indeed, the etymology of the term is what allows Marshall McLuhan to state that all media are metaphors. As he put it: "The word 'metaphor' is from the Greek *meta* plus *pherein*, to carry across or transport."[26] Whether it is "mailing," "chatting," or "searching," whenever we describe the things we do on computers, we usually use metaphors that "carry over" from other domains. (Although, as I will go on to discuss, this may, in fact, be the case with *all* language.) Reading such metaphors, as I do in this book, requires a delicate balancing act. On the one hand, in a point to which I will return, we must be able to recognize what van den Boomen calls the "compressed metaphoricity that stands in for a complex dynamic machinery" while seeing, on the other, that metaphor is grounded in real "things in itself."[27] The balance is between how we *do* still understand metaphors, even when they do not wholly "work" and have gone past the "break" point, while pointing out the limitations of just how literally we can take them.

In focusing on language and metaphor, I do not mean to understate these digital spaces' crucial materiality. Computer systems are distinguished, argues Matthew G. Kirschenbaum, "not by virtue of their supposed immateriality but by virtue of their being material machines conceived and built to sustain an *illusion* of immateriality."[28] In Friedrich Kittler's extreme formulation, all computing systems— all digital spaces—boil down to just "signifiers of voltage differences" within hardware circuits.[29] Hence, despite our investment in the idea of the virtual as "unreal," we are also finely attuned to the interplay of the real and the virtual. For example, the most significant contemporary spokescorporation of internet retail, Amazon, is dedicated to the process of making something tangible from seemingly nothing. That is, perhaps the most prominent emblem of the virtual space would mean far less if, when one clicked "Buy now," nothing physical turned up on one's doorstep (although in recent years, the sales of virtual servers through Amazon's AWS business have been a major boon for the company). As we will see over the next few years as artificial intelligence (AI) language models gain access to real-world systems and become fully-fledged "agents," the interplay between virtuality and materiality is where computational power resides.

However, the metaphors that we use to describe digital environments (as this sentence demonstrates, there is no way of not doing it) impute a materiality to the simulated interaction with the machine. Even to refer to the digital "realm" or "environment" as a virtual "space" of sorts is already falsely to hypostatize its existence as an immaterial other-*place* (perhaps the hideously overused Foucauldian concept of "the heterotopia").[30] Virtual reality becomes, in such language, at once a reality and only *virtual*, a word that—aptly, given Kirschenbaum's repetition of "virtue"—comes to us from the late fourteenth-century Medieval Latin *virtualis* and *virtus*, meaning "excellence, potency, efficacy" but also, literally, "manliness" and "manhood." We arrive at the contemporary meaning of "virtual" in the sense of having a true essence (nonreality) that is separate from a surface effect (solidity/reality) around the middle of the fifteenth century, probably from the meaning of "capable of producing a certain effect."[31] However, to understand the impact of the disjunct between the virtual's surface effect and its true nature on contemporary textual production, we must examine the masking effects of the metaphorical language we use to speak of "the digital" and its implications.

In this book I rewrite a set of our digital-textual histories around the following seven theses—theses on the metaphors of digital-textual history, if you will—which correlate to each of its chapters:

1. The virtual page almost never existed.
2. The history of digital whitespace is the seriality of musical silence.
3. Digital text is geopolitically structured.
4. Digital text is multidimensional.
5. Windows are allegories of political liberalism.
6. Libraries are assemblages of recombinable anxiety fragments.
7. Everything not saved will be lost.

Each of these theses focuses on a metaphorical grounding: the idea of the "page" or "whitespace," for instance, using these concepts as earthing points to reappraise the concrete historical unfolding—and breakage—that resulted. Some of the chapters are very much historically rooted. In the chapter on the history of the virtual page, I interview the creators of the PDF format to rewrite this format's story. In other chapters, the debate is much more conceptual or focused on language. For example, I examine the history of the term "safety" in text processing and argue for the multiple axes across which this metaphor operates. In these senses, while some portions of this book concern new histories of digital text, other parts aim more simply to fracture and pull apart—or read and interpret—the metaphors that underpin our digital text processing.

But is "metaphor" even the correct term? A great deal of this book shows how and why our computational metaphors fall short (and analyzes the implications of this). It unpicks how we can explain particular metaphors to new users. (For instance, I ask at one point why a "menu" is called a menu, given that no food is involved, and why a "window" is called a window, given that you cannot see "through" it, although it is "framed.") However, this problem has plagued computer designers since the 1960s; it is not a new challenge. Indeed, as Thierry Bardini put it, as just one example, "The virtual desktop was not a mere metaphor, since the user did not identify the false residual of the metaphor."[32] In other words: users took only the parts that held, ignoring the points where the metaphor fell short. We can best see this challenge when software designers do not know which metaphors they should use. Take, for example, the well-known metaphor that interface design is a "conversation" between the designer and the user. John Walker, of Autodesk Inc., poured scorn on this approach: "I believe that conversation is the wrong model for dealing with a computer—a model that misleads inexperienced users and invites even experienced software designers to build hard-to-use systems. When you're interacting with a computer, you are not interacting with another person"—an interface-to-face—"you are exploring another world."[33] However, "exploring another world" is another metaphor that does not wholly hold. Computational metaphors involve selecting and judging parts that work and parts that do not. There are good and bad computational metaphors, but no metaphor is a direct one-to-one correlation with reality because, at that point, the metaphor would not be a substitution for the thing but the thing itself.

Perhaps the best indication of the contested status of "metaphor" in computer interface design was set out by Alan Kay, the noted computer scientist who worked at Xerox PARC in the 1970s and within several prestigious university computer science departments. For Kay, "One of the most compelling snares is the use of the word *metaphor* to describe a correspondence between what the users see on the screen and how they should think about what they are manipulating. My main complaint is that *metaphor* is a poor metaphor for what needs to be done. At PARC, we coined the word *user illusion* to describe what we were about when designing user interface."[34] Contrary to metaphor, which provides a substitutive context on which users can base their operational premises, illusions, of course, are meant to trick the viewer, although they are usually done, like fiction, with the consent of a willing and disbelief-suspending audience. For Kay, though, this illusory context is how we end up with supercharged analogous digital objects. There is no point, in his view, in creating digital paper that is "as hard as paper to erase and change." Instead, we take the parts of the metaphor that we like and imbue the digital copy with magical (or "illusory") powers: "But it is the magic—understandable magic—that really counts. . . . If it is to be like magical paper, then it is the *magical* part that is all-important and that must be most strongly attended to in the user interface design."[35] In reality, though, even using such terms as "interface" or speaking of the "boundary" between humans and machines operates, as does all language, through metaphor.[36]

The type of metaphor to which this book specifically refers is conceptual metaphor, stemming from the work of George Lakoff and Mark Johnson in the early 1980s. The fundamental premise behind their research is that "our ordinary conceptual system, in terms of which we both think and act, is fundamentally metaphorical in nature."[37] For Lakoff and Johnson, "the essence of metaphor is understanding and experiencing one kind of thing in terms of another," and, at its heart, almost all of what we do, say, and understand uses a relational approach to definition.[38] Importantly for this early work on conceptual metaphor, "metaphorical entailments can characterize a coherent system of metaphorical concepts and a corresponding coherent system of metaphorical expressions for those concepts."[39] Put otherwise, metaphors must remain coherent and consistent in their usage. Lakoff and Johnson postulated that, in most cases, even where there are overlapping metaphorical referents, such language systems do retain consistency and coherence.

Metaphors are also, though, only ever partial. "If," write Lakoff and Johnson, "it were total, one concept would actually *be* the other, not merely be understood in terms of it."[40] For instance, the metaphors of "the mind is a machine" and "the mind is a brittle object" give us "different metaphorical models for what the mind is and thereby allow us to focus on different aspects of mental experience."[41] In more recent parlance, different metaphors "afford" us different comprehensive capabilities for understanding an object's workings. These metaphors become "stacked" atop one another, usually because "two purposes cannot both be served at once by a single metaphor."[42] Each separate metaphor then "allows us to get a handle on one aspect of the concept."[43] This means that there can be a temptation, when designing a new environment from scratch, to multiply the number of metaphorical referents used to explain a system. As Douglas Kellner puts it, "Dominant [digital] metaphors draw from the human body, everyday life, home and business, nature, travel, technology, and the military and space travel."[44] As a result, we are furnished with windows, menus, status bars, pointers, sites, homes, wallpapers, desktops, check boxes, text boxes, spreadsheets, pages, icons, shortcuts, notepads, files, folders, trash cans, hourglasses, pings, dragging, dropping, clicking, right-clicking, scrolling, deleting, writing, redacting, signing, zooming, calling, playing, working, mailing, cutting, copying, pasting, snipping, screenshotting, saving, archiving, backing up, powering on, shutting down, spooling, buffering, loading, and downloading.[45] And what sort of coherence or consistency do we imagine might sit at the intersection of the overlap of these terms?

Indeed, Jingfang Wu and Rong Chen have partially set out how cognitive metaphors operate across a set of nonconsistent metaphorical contexts in the computational domain.[46] For instance, "a computer is a person" is a common framework in which the "CPU [Central Processing Unit] is the brain." At the same time, a "computer is a factory" in which the operating system must "schedule computational activities to ensure good performance." Concurrently, "a computer is an office" in which there are "notepads" that are "dropped" into "folders." But our computers are also "containers" of "folders" that can be "emptied" from the "recycle bin." Wu and Chen further detail the terminologies we use to describe the internet: We have "highways" carrying cyber "tourists" and "digital natives" even while the internet is also personified as "born in America." Even as the internet is a "cyberspace," it is a "sea" on which we "surf," and it is a "community," although this community space is also a "library" and a "market."[47]

However, as I will detail in the section below on cultural phenomenology, an essential part of comprehending metaphor is that it cannot be divorced from the experiential encounter with contextualized language. Hence, "no metaphor can ever be comprehended or even adequately represented independently of its experiential basis."[48] This experiential encounter is broken down into ideas of prototypical primitives that exemplify the difference between definition and metaphorical explanation. While such prototypes remain contextually grounded and their properties are hardly inherent—the prototypical "chair" will depend on the context, say whether it is a formal dinner or a more casual affair—the metaphor must be understood in terms of the chairness of the chair in specific contexts.[49]

One of the core objections that a skeptical reader might mount to much of this book is anticipated by Lakoff and Johnson. Namely, that "it is easy to find apparent incoherences in everyday metaphorical expressions."[50] In other words, the accusation (especially by those with a disdain for analytical/language philosophy) will be that such needling is more nit-picking than new knowledge. However, as Lakoff and Johnson showed, most metaphors they examined "turned out not to be incoherent at all."[51] Yet the question remains: Are the metaphorical aspects that I am extracting and here tormenting incoherent, inconsistent, or merely partially focused? Or is it, in fact, the case that we do not "understand concepts of one kind in terms or concepts of another kind at all" but instead "only that we can perceive similarities between various concepts and that such similarities will account for the use of the same words for the concepts"?[52] For example, as I will discuss, the "window" of a computer system is neither transparent nor fixed, but it is openable and framed. These windows also appear, apparently, on a "*desk*top" which, paradoxically, has been "*wall*papered." As Theodor Holm Nelson memorably put it as far back as 1990, "I have never personally seen a desktop where pointing at a lower piece of paper makes it jump to the top, or where placing a sheet of paper on top of a file folder causes the folder to gobble it up."[53]

Indeed, computational metaphors usually "form no single image," but they do somehow, within their own logics, rather than the logics to which they refer, "fit together" with a type of coherence until they hit the "break" point.[54] The consequence of this "metaphoric ideology," as Nelson terms it, is that "first, these mnemonic gimmicks are not very useful for presenting the ideas in the first place; second, their resemblance to any real objects in the world is so tenuous that it gets in the way more than it helps; and third . . . *the metaphor becomes a dead weight*" in which "once the metaphor is instituted, *every related function has to become a part of it.*"[55] The question then becomes one of transference: What is carried across in the sharing of metaphorical terms between real-world and prototypical objects and the computational environment that we aim to make hospitable? Moreover, how might it become possible to stem the harmful proliferation of functional association to which Nelson gestures? The investigation of broken metaphor gives us scope to investigate the histories of digital-textual interfaces and whence they originate in material circumstances.

This partiality of metaphor returns us to Kay's points about illusion and to note that "only *part* of [a metaphor] is used to structure our normal concepts . . . they go beyond the realm of the literal."[56] Yet, when metaphors are extended in ways that go beyond our regular, day-to-day comprehension of the referents to which they gesture, they become "idiosyncratic, unsystematic, and isolated."[57] At least part of my contention in this book is that this adjectival trinity serves as a good description of much of our computational metaphor. We have, in many ways, built entirely separate systems of language and domains of practice that do little but reenforce idiosyncratic, unsystematic, and isolated rituals of digital reperformance. Importantly, these rituals of reperformance in the computational domain reflect the original metaphorical contexts and their points of divergence. As a result, as we shall go on to see, older technologies begin retroactively to be described in terms of the digital. We say that old printed papers are "like the scrolling computer screen," when really the likeness travels the other way.[58] Indeed, as Lakoff and Johnson claim, "new metaphors have the power to define reality"; and that includes past realities and history.[59] Alternatively, as Susan Leigh

Star has put it, these battles about metaphor matter, because "power is about *whose* metaphor brings worlds together, and holds them here."[60] New computational metaphors end up being how we conceptualize extant and past technologies. At the same time, these metaphors often end up being a long way from any correlated reality.

One way we can comprehend this independence from reality is through the lens of structural metaphor. Ontological metaphors are those that impute a state of being to noninstantiated concepts. For example, in Lakoff and Johnson's example, "Time is a substance" and "Labor is a substance" are ontological metaphors that denote both time and labor as sharing a material state. Because the shared object state is the same, the two conceptual domains are made commensurate. By contrast, structural metaphor asks us to "induce similarities" between areas. Lakoff and Johnson's example is that "ideas are food" so you can digest, swallow, and devour both of these terms. Notably, while "the concept of swallowing food is independent of the metaphor," by contrast, "the concept of swallowing ideas arises only under the metaphor."[61]

Similar probings might well be applied to our experience of computational interface elements. For example, the framed rectangles that contain (another metaphor) our user interfaces are windows that can be "opened" and "closed" purely because we think of the ingrained "window" metaphor, even though, in reality, such virtual windows might more accurately be said to appear and disappear. The "frame" of the window may constitute the content-surface that allows for cross-domain substitutability. However, the structural-comparative metaphorical elements allow us to transfer function between these areas. They "arise out of orientational and ontological metaphors," as Lakoff and Johnson put it.[62] Yet again, though, the substitution of function is idiosyncratic, unsystematic, and isolated.

Whether metaphor or magically augmented illusion, user interface design fought in the battle between two competing cultures in the 1960s and 1970s. On the one hand, some developers felt that digital technologies should be "user friendly" and easy to learn. This group included Larry Tesler, who would go on to be responsible for our "copy and paste" metaphorical paradigm, and Jeff Rulifson, who worked on

ARPANET, the precursor to the internet. On the other hand, though, was the paradigm pioneered by Douglas Engelbart, one of the inventors of the computer mouse. For Engelbart, user interface design was a way to *modify users* rather than being something that should fit users' expectations. Engelbart saw, in computer interface design, a way to improve humanity by training it afresh. Tesler and Rulifson, by contrast, planned, from humanity, how to improve their user interfaces.[63]

This conflict came to a head under the leadership of Butler Lampson at PARC in the 1970s, who insisted on a "new ethic" where every product had to be "engineered for a hundred users" to give a broadly applicable design paradigm.[64] Such a paradigm was about "tailoring the user interface to what designers could find out about or imagine about how people actually do their work" instead of using the interface to "force people to learn to do it in a new and better way."[65] This approach sounds the most obvious of methods; we should make our technologies easy to grasp and use. However, it was by no means a sure thing at the outset of computational design history. Instead, the battle was between one ideology that thought computers might improve the way we do things and another that thought we do things pretty well already and should make computers conform to existing practices.

"Practice" is an apt term to explore at this point. Talk of metaphor often moves us into conceptual and cognitive arenas. Metaphor is how we translate between an observed practice (what people do) and a cognitive frame (how they think about and understand it). However, the aforementioned debate about the role of metaphor and the place of interface design in shaping or being shaped by the user shows us the value of N. Katherine Hayles's notion of an "incorporating practice." Hayles sets out a system in which "inscription" is the opposite of "incorporation." In this model, abstract signs, when written down, are given an independent existence from the writer. Written forms exist independently, but with traces, of the incorporated form that produced them. On the other hand, an incorporated gesture "such as a good-bye wave cannot be separated from its embodied medium, for it exists as such only when it is instantiated in a particular hand making a particular kind of gesture."[66]

Computer user interfaces straddle this inscription-versus-incorporation boundary and must consider the interplay between cognitive and bodily actions. As Hayles defines it:

> I mean by an incorporating practice an action that is encoded into bodily memory by repeated performances until it becomes habitual. Learning to type is an incorporating practice, as both Connerton and Merleau-Ponty observe. When we say that someone knows how to type, we do not mean that the person can cognitively map the location of the keys or can understand the mechanism producing the marks. Rather, we mean that this person has repeatedly performed certain actions until the keys seem to be extensions of his or her fingers. Someone can know how to type but not know how to read the words produced, such as when a typist reproduces script in a language that the typist does not speak; conversely, just as someone can be able to read a typescript without knowing how to type.[67]

Hence, the argument above is a debate about the *site* of inscription and the inscribability of the body. Those who wanted user interfaces to be easy to use saw the body as an inscribing agent, etching its incorporated practices onto machine interfaces. By contrast, the second school of thought saw the human body as inscribable, as quarried rock awaiting the sculpting influence of the interface designer. It is convenient for the subject of this book—writing with computers—that our comprehension of interface metaphor has been couched, previously, in terms of inscription. Because the question then becomes: Do we write with computer interfaces, or do computer interfaces write on us?

Given the aforementioned remarks on the maturation of this disciplinary area, it is unsurprising that I am hardly the first to explore such terrain. Indeed, this book is perhaps most indebted to the work of Matthew G. Kirschenbaum, whose *Mechanisms: New Media and the Forensic Imagination* (2008) and *Bitstreams: The Future of Digital Literary Heritage* (2021) inspired the mode of formal and forensic material thought that informs my analyses. In particular, this work takes a cue from Kirschenbaum's consistent attention to specifics: specific technologies, specific authors, specific actants.[68] I also bring to the table a work that is interested in computationally specific technicalities refracted through a cultural-studies (or cultural-phenomenological) lens.

As were Kirschenbaum's, this book is also an attempt to move away from the phenomenon that Nick Montfort has dubbed "screen essentialism," the tendency that we have to privilege only the final stage in the translation of digital texts into photonic forms.[69] Certainly, in this work, I examine the role of visual display units. Such an angle enables my query of why whitespace is white in chapter 3. We cannot overlook the ways in which many digital technologies continue to privilege the visual mode, an aspect to which I turn in chapter 6. However, I am also concerned by the extent to which screen essentialism obscures the underpinning historical and other-material realities, which often work in contradiction to the metaphors on our screen. Whitespace, for instance, wasn't white in the earliest forms of papermaking or in early display technologies. Further, I show, on the one hand, how the development of specific screen ideologies and metaphors—such as the virtual page— have been historically conditioned by unexpected material correlates. On the other hand, I also show how material correlates are often less predeterminate than we might expect.

What will this book examine? Many branches of literary criticism focus on narrative, style, and interpretative effect.[70] Material-textual studies further abstract this, inquiring about the enframing conditioning textual-materialities that alter our understanding of a work. For example, how and why does it matter that a scribe was left-handed and left a different mark down the left side of a manuscript? What does the particular degradation of paper tell us about the historical worth accorded to a particular text and its preservation economics? Digital-material textual studies move one step further in this dialectic and ask similar questions of computerized objects. The questions I ask include: How does the term "whitespace" relate to the fact that early computer monitors were black? How and when was the virtual "page" born? What relation does that page have to the history of print pages? Are they the same histories? Should we preserve computer viruses when storing digital text, and how are they like real viruses? How did the concept of a "code library" emerge from real-world library (that is, text-lending) systems? These metaphors condition how we think of the pasts and futures of digital text technologies.

A final reflection for this section: Many of the observations about digital *text* in this book could be said to apply to computational systems more broadly. Indeed, text is so central to "what we do" with digital systems that you can find it in almost all corners of the virtual world. However, by using the frame of digital text, we gain a narrower entry point for such investigations while refraining from overly broad claims. I believe, though, that the wider arguments herein about computational metaphor are transapplicable beyond the limits of digital text.

Cultural Phenomenology

In addition to interacting with book history, this work deploys some of the methods that Steven Connor has grouped under the name "cultural phenomenology." Connor has, on several occasions, articulated what this model means for his work. Perhaps most notably, in 1999, he wrote:

> Cultural phenomenology would aim to enlarge, diversify and particularise the study of culture. Instead of readings of abstract structures, functions and dynamics, it would be interested in substances, habits, organs, rituals, obsessions, pathologies, processes and patterns of feeling. Such interests would be at once philosophical and poetic, explanatory and exploratory, analytic and evocative. Above all, whatever interpreting and explication cultural phenomenology managed to pull out would be achieved by the manner in which it got amid a given subject or problem, not by the degree to which it got on top of it.[71]

Cultural phenomenology is the same as neither cultural studies nor cultural materialism. It instead has several characteristics that make it useful for a study of digital textuality:

1. Phenomenology is a useful starting point as it "begins and renews itself in the resolve to resist abstraction, reduction and ideal simplification." At the same time, Connor's approach asks us to reject

the "mystical or neo-religious cast of some of the work practised in its name." It is a rigorously materially and experientially grounded approach to the "shared conditions of making" that constitute culture.[72] This point guides my exploration of computational environments, with a promise never to make sweeping gestures to "the algorithm" or other nonspecific technological bogeymen.

2. Cultural phenomenology is interested in how lived and embodied practices reflect back on representations, not just on how representations refract life. That is to say that "modes of life— collective as well as individual modes—are more important and interesting . . . than styles, texts, images, discourses, and other modes of collective representation."[73] In digital-textual studies such as this, this means returning to the dialectic of design versus incorporated practice and how computers "write back" upon their users. It also involves the interchange of real-world and digital forms, bound together in metaphor.

3. Histories of technology are explicitly among those that Connor lists as potential beneficiaries of such a model and may already, albeit implicitly, be using cultural-phenomenological tactics. Tracing this back to Walter Ong's 1967 *The Presence of the Word*, Connor writes that "contemporary work on the history of technology, spurred clearly by our own curiosity, concern and intoxication with the fate of the body in the world of information technology, probably also belongs to a historicising mood concerning the body, which in itself may instance a kind of unconscious turn to the phenomenological disposition."[74]

4. Cultural phenomenologies weave together disparate areas within "a series of inveiglings" rather than "following a series of methods or frameworks."[75] Indeed, while this can lead, not least in Connor's own works, to a sometimes-meandering structure, it allows for the emergence of patterned webs of interrelation, often taking the form of unusual parataxis generated by etymological conjunction. In this book, for example, I move swiftly from analyzing the geopolitical structures of digital text and the internet to exam-

ining the political metaphors of vision and "windows." These areas may seem far removed from one another, or at a challenging distance. However, they are all linked by the overarching theme of digital textuality and a metaphor of political liberalism. This sometimes-jarring movement can force us to see new connections that were not, before, obvious.

5. Cultural phenomenology seeks a "lexical vigilance" that avoids the routinized phrasings of critique. As controversial as Rita Felski's recent interventions on postcritique may be, in which she tells us that many of the political formulations of literary criticism are predictable and ineffectual, Connor appears to agree, exhorting us to avoid the now-clichéd terminological terrains of critical theory.[76] So no "performance-enhancing terms and metaphors: boundaries, sites (as in 'site of struggle'), transgression, discourse, hybridity, subject-position, the gaze, identity, alterity, subversion, dominance, marginality, diaspora, decentring, totalising, foreclosure, undecidability (especially 'radical undecidability')," and perhaps, challengingly for my introduction already: "inscription."[77] Indeed, given the strictures of disciplinary norms, such freedom from the regularized language of literary studies and book history can be difficult to purchase. Hence, while I do not always succeed in this domain, I here aspire to such lexical vigilance.

6. Cultural phenomenology is careful about its political claims. Connor was anxious articulating this in 1999 and it is perhaps even more difficult now, but he contentiously asks: "What in measurable terms . . . has critical theory, however 'radical,' contributed to the problems of poverty, ignorance, starvation, racism, Third World debt, enforced displacement of peoples, environmental poisoning and genocide?"[78] While not disregarding the importance of politics and of seeking radical theoretical perspectives that begin from the perspectives of injustice, there is also space for cultural-phenomenological investigations that begin from a different point than the issues of "distributive justice" that lurk below the surface of almost all of our contemporary political iniquities. This book,

then, does not *begin* with questions of intersectional politics, such as Safiya Umoja Noble's important "Why are search engines racist and how can we make them less so?" or Mar Hicks's crucial "Why were women eradicated from the industry of computer science?"[79] But this does not mean that there are no political implications to this work (it is not possible to discuss the history of public libraries without the history of the British Empire, as just one example, and it is not possible to write about whitespace without considering its links to racial discourses).

Each of these elements informs the analysis in this book, even when I do not adopt the mode in totality, and provides a framework for thinking about the histories of digital-textual metaphor.

The "So What?" Question

Finally, for this introduction: the relationship between structuration and digitality is unclear (i.e., it is not obvious that studying the digital production of text *is* just a further abstraction of conditioning possibilities). It would be convenient, but perhaps wrong, to be able to claim that somehow the design of word processing software or the texture of computer mice influences the types of literatures and texts that we produce and consume. Perhaps these elements may have some bearing, but it is subtle and far from straightforward. In chapter 3, I explore this variant of what is known in linguistics as the Sapir–Whorf hypothesis (or the "hypothesis of linguistic relativity") and its translation into technological determinism. In the world of language, the Sapir–Whorf hypothesis proposes that our language determines what we can think. In material-textual studies and its digital correlate, the thesis would insist that our digital systems determine what we can write. Indeed, were this the case, it would make the arguments in this book and the rationale for its existence more compelling. This is also the basic premise of Eric Chown and Fernandos Nascimento's recent work, in which they posit that technology and its metaphors "are changing how we think," and that "technological metaphors fundamentally alter cognitive models and meaning."[80]

However, the relationship between our word processors and the text we produce on them is more complex than this. Kirschenbaum traces it elsewhere in the works of George R. R. Martin:

> But knowing [which word processor Martin uses], even know-ing something about its particular features and affordances as a word processing program, is at best a dim pretense for any real illumination of his fiction. . . . It would take a lot of convincing for me to believe that Martin's sentence structures (for example) are tied in any significant degree to the specifics of WordStar's keyboard commands.[81]

However, Kirschenbaum goes on to redeem such idiosyncratic knowl-edge: "Any analysis that imagines a single technological artifact in a position of authority over something as complex and multifaceted as the production of a literary text is suspect. . . . [Hence,] we don't know why it is important to know these things, but we would rather know them than not."[82] The situation is akin to a famous question posed in Shakespearean studies, when W. W. Greg rhetorically asked, and an-swered, of his own findings of the falsification of several dates of a quarto: "What is the literary bearing of these new facts? . . . Practically none."[83] Yet we would rather know them than not.

That said, these investigations into metaphor do have a concrete purpose and outcome. In asking where metaphors decompose, we pin-point moments, or periods, of historical rupture and epistemic break. The transition that digital-textual metaphors make from partial mime-sis to disconnected symbolism yields a way of understanding seemingly discontinuous historical change within a continuous framework. As a type of Foucauldian genealogy, such an approach works alongside the many other scholars in this domain who toil to ensure that we do not lose sight of the histories of technology that constitute our present.

This is all to say that, like much history, there is a type of nonutility to the knowledge imparted by this book, even while it enriches our understanding of histories of technology. Knowing, for instance, that Adobe almost canceled the virtual pagination of the PDF will not tell us anything directly about how people write or about the impact that the virtual page has had on the reception of texts disseminated in this form. I do not doubt that this internal argument had effects. But those effects are diffuse, multidimensional, and nearly impossible to tease apart. This evolution of the digital page is nonetheless part of contemporary digital-textual history. Further, investigating this change allows us to examine past imaginations of the future and to understand how material correlates interact with the development of new digital tech. Science fictions of the past can become histories of the present.

What, then, is the overall argument of this book? Do these theses on the metaphors of digital-textual history add up to a coherent whole? Each chapter in this work contributes a new understanding of its topic on the principle of metaphorical movement from description, through a "break," to a prescriptive stance. In chapter 2, I turn to the history of the digital page, demonstrating how our metaphors of print are by no means guaranteed a digital afterlife. While we like to think that metaphors of print directly condition digital-textual interface design, the illusory imagination that imbues interfaces with magic properties is stronger. In this chapter, I argue for the hybridity of metaphors in our understanding of digital pagination.

Chapter 3 extends this thinking further to examine the history of the term "whitespace" (a word used to mean empty space in text processing.) This chapter sprang from a straightforward historical question to which I wanted an answer: Why is whitespace called whitespace when most early computer monitors contained a black background with green text? The obvious answer that one might expect is: because paper is white. But this answer is wrong. The earliest surviving paper fragments are not white; they are stained due to insecticides. The story of how white paper came to be valued is linked to periods of iconoclasm and issues of religious virtue. However, it is also tied to ideas of "nothingness" and what constitutes emptiness. As such, there is not only a parallel racial politics of paper coloration but also a curious link between the earliest punched cards and whether white background paper represents a positive or negative binary sign. As a result, the whiteness of whitespace can be traced back to player pianos and ideas of serial processing in computing systems. To mix a hybrid metaphor that will become clear in the chapter itself, whitespace's whiteness becomes the seriality of musical silence.

If the first of these two content chapters deals with such mixed models, chapter 4 handles the international character of digital-textual systems and the ways that metaphors and practices have to traverse national boundaries. In this chapter, I draw on the historical operation of the Unicode consortium to show how the demands of international representation have placed strains on the organizational tenets of digital-textual organizations. This includes the introduction of the *kokuji* (a Japanese kanji character) *taito*, the most graphically complex character in the Han system. Writing this character by hand requires eighty-four separate strokes, and hence one would expect it to be an early candidate for computational representation. However, it took until 2020 for this character to be introduced, demonstrating a strong Anglocentric bias in the main operations of the Unicode consortium. By contrast, there is also a character in the Unicode specification for which nobody knows the use: ꝸ. In a sense, "ꝸ" serves as a metonym for this book's theme: a character that at one time must have had meaning but whose meaning is now lost to time. In this case, the documentation of a single, unified character code specification has left much to be desired, and, in an international environment, digital history is seeping away before our eyes, even as it appears fresh and new.

Drawing on the work in chapter 4 on Unicode, chapter 5 extends this thinking further by examining how digital text can be considered multidimensional. It is, of course, evident that all writing has depth. The complex inscription of graphical marks on a substrate that translates into meaningful, ambiguous, polysemous communication and mental representation contains multitudes. Digital representations of text multiply the layers of dimensionality but also ask us to consider what we mean by the metaphor of "reading" in this space. The software that transforms digital numbers into textual representations is a standardized "reader" that must "interpret" the underlying bitstream. As such, in some ways, a web browser is a type of "reader" that we should consider within the various paradigms of literary interpretation. Web browsers, though, can be good or bad readers, and there are different commercial and software reasons why they may "behave" within a particular readerly paradigm. This chapter then examines how we moved from the ideals of standards-based "good" readers to corporate-influenced misreading systems.

As chapter 5 ends with political remarks on why some companies design software to read badly on purpose, chapter 6 opens by inviting the reader to consider the politics of digital-textual interface design. Most notably, this chapter asks and addresses the questions, What is the tension between standardization and idiosyncrasy, and how does this map onto a politics of individualism? The complexities of these questions lie in their entanglement with the history of digital accessibility and the relatively late emergence of legislative and social demands for standardization for disability access to web texts. However, then questions arise as to where "freedom" sits. What "freedom" have designers to implement new models for digital text versus the need for standardization so as not to disadvantage users with disabilities/disabled users? As a quite seriously disabled individual myself, with multiple complex long-standing chronic health problems that impede my day-to-day activities, I struggle, personally, with the tensions inherent in viewing digital windows as allegories of political liberalism.

Yet political liberalism also conditions how we think of "libraries" in a computing sense, as I go on to detail in chapter 7. It is curious that we should "borrow"—to use another library term—this metaphorical terminology for the way that code is reused between applications ("dynamic link *libraries*," "shared object *libraries*," and "static *libraries*"). The reason this is important is that the originary functions and states of libraries have been sculpted into a false cultural imaginary that obscures a great deal of their actual political history. Libraries have not always been *public* libraries from which anyone could borrow. Some are, indeed, not even lending libraries. As such, this chapter explores how this metaphor has influenced our programming and writing practices to the present day and how the library metaphor is influenced by the wrongly imagined history.

Finally, to conclude this book, I close in chapter 8 with remarks on the preservation, access, and use of our digital-textual resources.

Following on from chapter 7's notes on the role and functions of libraries, I note how international legal statute is not keeping pace with the
requirements of access for preserved digital-textual material. Indeed,
in the space of digital preservation and digital archives we encounter
the strangeness of digital time (how curiously quickly unused digital
artifacts become unpreserved) but also the oddness of the digital archival genre. For, in preserving malware alongside text, we can see how
the archive serves multiple audiences across multiple axes. This poses
questions for the intermedia-ness of the material stored in such digital
archives in a way that is not seen in conventional archives. For instance,
nobody would suggest that a book containing smallpox virions should
be stored in the British Library and that it is essential for historians
to see the lethal virus spreading over the text, reliving the process of
dying by reading it. However, the equivalent formulation *is* made for
the preservation of computer viruses in digital-textual contexts, albeit
with less severe biosecurity consequences. Again, the argument here is
about how the metaphor of "virus" accurately (or otherwise) captures
the same malign agents across spaces and becomes decoupled from
real-world pathogens. Some computer viruses are, after all, lethal if
they infect hospital equipment. However, in calls for their preservation,
we see a strong divergence from print-preservation paradigms.

Throughout its eight chapters, this book asks the reader to question the metaphors that partially condition our digital-textual interfaces. It is easy to be (overly) pedantic about where metaphor fails. But
metaphor is simply a tool for understanding one domain in terms of
another. To pick holes in metaphor endlessly is to ignore the fact that,
as (ir)rational animals, we *are* capable of (arbitrarily) simply discarding
parts of the metaphor that do not work. There does not have to be a
guiding logic behind this process of picking and choosing. However,
by asking such questions of these metaphorical constructs, we better
understand the conditions under which all contemporary writing is
produced, erased, and edited. By examining how, where, and why these
metaphors "break" from their original contexts, we gain a historical
understanding of how we become tied to digital-textual metaphors that
no longer seem to work.

TWO

THE VIRTUAL PAGE ALMOST NEVER EXISTED

"Page space isn't a given, an a priori static entity."
  —JOHANNA DRUCKER, "Graphesis"

"NLS files were described as early as 1962 as 'scrolls.'"
  —THIERRY BARDINI, *Bootstrapping*

CONTEMPORARY COMPUTING TEEMS WITH PHYSICAL metaphors and analo-gies.[1] It is a virtual *space* of web*sites*, windows, menus, icons, and *point-ers*. Our internet resources, though, are *pages*. Our word processors open onto A4 *sheets*. Our scholarly articles are rectangular to mirror the common-book form of the *Philosophical Transactions*.[2] The metaphor of the page, in particular, proliferates. There is an apparent reason for such prevalence of pagination metaphors in digital-textual production and reception. Even while we may smile as first-time users of a com-puter mouse are confused about why lateral should translate to vertical motion, it is too easy to assume that digital interfaces are transparent and obvious.[3] Such assumptions lead to the well-known paradigm of supposedly intuitive interface designs, when really what is meant by "intuitive" (or, more correctly, "intuitable") is learned behavioral patterns. As Jeff Raskin puts it, "intuitive" means "familiar."[4] This is why computer interfaces become "*more* intuitive" as we use them more— for metaphor pertains to a familiar relationship that grows stronger through repetitive encounters.[5] This trope of relation provides a way for new users to imagine how a digital interface might work compared to its physical correlate.[6] Hence, through digital metaphor, we have virtual pages. Digital pages serve, then, in this mythology, as tokens of familiarity, habituating users to the electronic reading environment through analogy with known material forms.

However, the digital page has found many detractors. When thinking in the digital realm, commentators imagine that the page's visual metaphor is damaging and that we must overcome its domination. Digital formats, writes Johanna Drucker, have a persistent yet frustrating "need to acknowledge the historical priority of books and to invoke a link with their established cultural identity." At the same time, critics assume that "electronic 'books' will 'supersede the limitations' and overcome the 'drawbacks' of their paper-based forebears," as Drucker again puts it.[7] The metaphor, thinkers tell us, has become a constraint that limits computational potential. The "Beyond the PDF" conference and subsequent series of events are evidence that there is frustration in some quarters at how physical pagination is "artificially" sustained in the digital realm.[8] (As though anything in the digital space is *not* artificial . . .)

Indeed, there is a prevalent antipagination discourse that sees pages as domineering, even in the physical world of print. Pages, asserts Alberto Manguel, exert a "tyranny" of format over the text they contain, a tyranny that we must resist: "The shape of a page," he writes, "seems to cry out for counter-action."[9] Despite the very "idea of the book" being "the presentation of material in relation to a fixed sequence that provides access to its contents (or ideas) through some stable arrangement," Henry Burton wrote, in 1636, to his readers of his frustration with ordered pagination.[10] For him, pages created a situation where "the foregoing Examples are not orderly placed. Indeed it was the authors minde that they should have beene otherwise."[11] For Shane Butler, the page is "conspicuous for the impertinence and arbitrariness with which it repeatedly barges into the text, chopping up stories, sentences, and even words where it will."[12]

This assault on the paginated digital document is long-standing and ongoing. Indeed, the aftermath of the battle among Novell's Envoy, No Hands Software Inc's Common Ground, and Adobe's PDF format brought intense anxiety about enforcing the transmedial constraints of paper on digital forms.[13] As early as 1993, Pete Dyson, who edited an influential report in the late 1980s on the state of desktop publishing, voiced his worry: "My biggest concern with all of these document viewers is that they start with a printed-page image.... I believe documents should be formatted for the medium that they are intended for."[14] This principle appears in many user interface design documents, which stress that "designers will be most effective when they design online manuals to fit the electronic medium" rather than pagination.[15]

Antipagination sentiment has only grown since that time and now predominantly takes the form of attacks on the PDF format. The largest employer in Europe, the United Kingdom's National Health Service, for instance, has a policy to "avoid PDFs" and their transmedia pagination.[16] Reasons given to dodge this format include that paginated files "cannot meet the range of users' accessibility needs." Such formats, it is claimed, "give people a poor user experience, especially on mobile." PDF files are also apparently "hard to maintain and update, so users may get out of date and unreliable content." The files are also difficult to track, which means that "it's difficult to collect data on how people use PDFs, and that makes it difficult to identify problems."[17]

Further, Guido van Rossum, the creator of the Python programming language, declared in 2014 that "PDF Must Die," claiming that "bills, scientific papers, everything in PDF is harder to read than web pages." The list goes on. By 2001, the critique of PDF and its pagination had gone mainstream, with prominent commentators such as Jakob Nielsen remarking on the format's unsuitability for long-form digital reading.[18]

Despite these criticisms, the rise of digital pagination continues unabated, with the persistent artificial enforcement of the page's "extrinsic boundaries."[19] However, notwithstanding the proliferation of the digital page, the argument that I will advance here is that such computational pagination was, at one point, far from certain. Indeed, the oN-Line System (NLS), created by Douglas Engelbart in 1962, used a totally different set of metaphorical coordinates, referring to its files as "scrolls" and moving between scrolls as "jumping"; this was a far cry from pages and turning.[20] There are also better media-historical forebears for the digital page than its print correlate. Wendy Hui Kyong Chun has rightly cautioned us that analogy is not a singular, one-to-one relationship but provides for messy and perspectivized lineages.[21] Some commentators, then, see a pathway from print media to digital forms, while others believe the route to be more meandering. For instance, Roger Chartier wrote of "the revolution that has been predicted, ... which transforms the book (or the written object) as we know it—with its quires, its leaves, its pages—into an electronic text to be read on a screen."[22] This "substitution of screen for codex," writes Chartier, "is a far more radical transformation" than that instigated by Gutenberg "because: it changes methods of organization, structure, consultation, even the appearance of the written word."[23] Nonetheless, the question that this raises is whether it was ever a "substitution of screen for codex" in the virtual page's lineage.

The remainder of this chapter performs a historical reinterrogation of three interrelated phenomena on the background of the digital page:

1. Digital pages do not behave as do their physical correlates but instead mimic earlier historical forms of print that fused pagination, scrolling, and the tablet form.

2. The relatively late development of PDF, now the most widespread transmedia digital pagination format, was almost abandoned by Adobe's board of directors, who could see no audience for it.

3. There are other more robust lineages of constraint for digital pages that come from cinema and television.

Drawing on new correspondence with the PDF's creators, the argument that emerges from these historical tracings is that nothing was sure about the development of pagination in the digital space. The digital page almost never came to the prominence that is now presumed.

The Metaphor of the Page

"It cannot be assumed that a reader will properly
understand what is presented on screen."
  —DAVID McKITTERICK, *Old Books, New Technologies*

Metaphors of pagination are omnipresent in computation. These metaphors also overlap with nineteenth-century cognitive analogies of memory (supplementing the long-standing biological analogies between reproduction and the printing press).[24] To understand this, one must know a little about the workings of most contemporary computers. At base, contemporary classical (as opposed to quantum) computing systems work thus: a central processing unit (CPU) performs calculations on stored binary digits (bits) in its registers. Various layers of software and hardware then translate these bits into human-readable forms. The low-level hardware storage of these bits varies (among the most usual forms at the time of writing is the metal-oxide-semiconductor cell) but is called main memory or random-access memory—a neurocognitive metaphor ("memory"). The premise is that this fast and uniform-access-time recall unit can most quickly transfer its bits into a CPU's "registers," the place where the actual arithmetic takes place. Hence, digital data move from the slowest media (say, hard drives) into random-access or main memory and then into the CPU's registers.[25]

However, as with many computational metaphors, the analogy to "memory" is textual as well as mental. Software can "read" the contents of memory via the CPU. It can also "write" to this memory space. These inscriptive cognitive metaphors may seem flawed. We do not usually think of our brains as mediately reading or writing to our memory to conduct calculations but instead consider the mind in much more holistic terms of unmediated access. Nonetheless, reading and writing are omnipresent throughout the history of mental metaphor. As far back as Plato, with Homeric and Aristotelian resonance, the mind was viewed as (or in opposing relation to) a wax tablet or a blank slate—inscriptive technologies.[26] In the sixteenth century, as the printing press proliferated across Europe, a print-culture equivalent—the "blank page"—became prevalent in Western cultures for considering memory's operation.[27] By the time of Locke's *Essays on the Laws of Nature* (c. 1660–1664), it was common to mix cognitive metaphors of tablets and paper within the same disjunctive clauses.[28] The realist novel's early history also advanced the march toward neural metaphors of legibility and inscription, combining narratorial claims for mental interiority with metatextual depictions of reading and writing. The prominent phenomenon of mind "reading" is another instance of such metaphorical incursion.[29]

Yet it is matters of timing that mark the emergence of the pagination metaphor in computer memory management. Because of the relative descending speeds of access (from register to main memory to secondary storage), computers address memory in discrete units called . . . "pages." Moving data from main memory to secondary storage to circumvent memory limitations is called "paging." To ensure that programs can only access their own "pages," computers create a "page" table as a security measure that raises a "page" fault when violated. (This is the equivalent of ensuring that one does not find oneself inside a different novel when one turns a book's pages. It is a little like imagining pages as "force fields," as Johanna Drucker encourages us to do, holding their contained elements in a dynamic tension of relation.[30])

Pages in computer memory management unite two differing etymologies of "page." In the first case, paging means "fetching" from storage. This use most likely comes from the sense of a page(boy), who would fetch someone.[31] Pager technology also derives its name from this meaning of messaging and summoning.[32] In the second context, computers frame, bind, read from, and write to pages. This meaning comes from *pagina*, derived from the notion of "fixing" or binding.[33] The latter meaning is associated with the leaves and quires of the codex.

Computational memory "pages" share many features with their print cousins within codices. They are of a uniform size (the page "dimensions"), we can access them at random (we can "flip to" them), and the content within the page runs contiguously in sequence (the "words"— another inscriptive term in computer memory management—are in the right order). In an instructive example, though, the metaphor only goes so far. The physical contiguity of memory pages to one another is not guaranteed. The ordering is more akin to a "choose-your-own-adventure" or hypertext construction than a novel. This noncontiguity is a mode in which a chunk of "narrative" within a page is linear and contiguous. However, each page ends with an instruction to jump to a different location in the "book," and it is impossible to read, cover to cover, in order.

The virtual address of a computational memory page (imagine this as its page number) is distinct from its "page frame" (where you will find it in the "book"/main memory). Indeed, there may not even be a page frame if the computer has offloaded the data to secondary storage. Like the scattered pages of B. S. Johnson's book in a box, *The Unfortunates* (1969), there is no guarantee of finding a page in order in computer memory, or even necessarily of finding it "in the box" at all.

Dennis Tenen has encouraged us to think of such ubiquitous computational metaphors under the rubric of "speculative formalism," which helps us understand "pagination" in the digital space.[34] Speculative formalism is a model that recognizes the mediation and friction of such metaphors. It is a framework that sees the Saussurean arbitrariness of skeuomorphic metaphors such as the computer "trash can," which does not in reality "trash" the data on the hard drive. Moreover, it is a strategy that follows in N. Katherine Hayles's footsteps, calling for analyses of material metaphors.[35]

Speculative formalism, then, is a model that acknowledges that "simulations ultimately embody specific power structures in an economy of exchange between physical and mental resources."[36] In other words, these metaphors are a compromise between pragmatic ease and the transparency of machine operation. Yet "what does it mean," asks Tenen, "to turn a page in a medium that sustains neither turning nor pages?"[37] What historical conditioning has led to the prevalence of the page's visual metaphor in contemporary computing culture? What are the virtual page's actual histories as a visual form separate from its nominal presence as a metaphorical digital touchstone?

Despite this prevalence of the metaphor in the computational environment, pages are among the "most dramatically overlooked graphical forms" in Johanna Drucker's appraisal.[38] Critics note the deceptive classification of pages as "apparently self-evident graphical features of any textual work."[39] Bonnie Mak's 2011 *How the Page Matters*, which conducts a material-textual reading of the fifteenth-century treatise *Controversia de nobilitate*, agrees. For Mak, "we have read the page"—and perhaps opposition to it—"too quickly," and we are overly keen to see both the "print revolution" and the "digital revolution" as "discontinuities in the history of books and reading."[40] However, what even are the characteristics of a virtual page? Can we define such an entity in terms of its print predecessor? Writeable digital pages, for example, behave differently from those that are only readable.

That virtual pages have a direct ancestry to physical pages is an increasingly less common view. However, the word processor, historically charted in recent days by Matthew G. Kirschenbaum, is designed, at least in part, to mimic book (codex) construction, even while augmenting traditional text-creation procedures. It seems logical that such a system would yield to the architect a virtualized model of the physical artifact that it will produce. However, due to different fonts, text sizes, page dimensions, screen resolutions, zooms, and functional paratools (scrollbars), the content and flow layout of pages can be (re)written. These pages will *not* be the same across devices. Such shifting pagination gives the lie to the idea that software might be What You See Is What You Get (WYSIWYG). For instance, Xerox's Bravo document creation software in the 1970s had a disparity of resolution between the Alto machine on which it ran (which had a portrait screen orientation) and its printer output.[41] Hence, the system became What You See Is Not What You Get (WYSINWYG). PDF explicitly aimed to address these problems of write flexibility, scrolling flow, and the disparity between display and print. However, early inscribable digital "pages" do not exhibit the basic definition of "boundness" to which I gestured above. Hence, these pages are hardly pages at all.

Instead, one of the most critical metaphorical incursions to recognize amid calls to vanquish the digital page is the well-recognized and conjoined role played by the *scroll* and the *tablet*. To begin with the scroll, as far back as 1999, Michael Heim noted that computing systems had adopted metaphors of "scrolling" as their primary descriptions of reading, a metaphor that, for Heim, "takes us back centuries."[42] At the same time, newer old habits die hard. Even while computer systems deploy the scroll metaphor, they also slide between this mask of unending seamless movement and that of discrete, discontinuous "pagination." This perpetuation of the metaphors of older text technologies is part of the impulse charted by Jeff Jarvis in which "a first, sensible reflex when faced with something so new is to try to adapt what came before, to revise and redesign old forms."[43]

Thus, while the history of printing shows a long-standing movement from continuity to the discrete, the metaphors become mixed: pages that scroll. Lev Manovich indeed famously noted that, in such a system, "cultural interfaces stretch the definition of a page while mixing together its different historical forms."[44] However, such an assertion is not strictly true; it is another instance of "the habituated conflation between the page and the page of the codex."[45] This is because there is a similar story of mixed ancestry within the history of the material codex. As Manuel Portela writes, "One of the basic dualities of codex semiotics is the duality between flow (the scroll-like continuous reading surface) and break (the discontinuity between pages)."[46] Hence, there was, historically, already an overlap in the metaphors of pagination and scrolling.

Superseding but overlapping with the scroll for both random and sequential access (and portability and economy), early Christianity adopted the codex as a marker of distinction from the familial Judaic scroll.[47] Nonetheless, the digital coexistence of scrolling and pagination has parallels with this earliest form of the Biblical codex. Early Bible codices featured "a four-column page layout resembling a section of unfurled scroll," mirroring the earlier *paginae*.[48] While Isidore's (c. 560–636 CE) influential *Etymologies* gives separate definitional histories for codex, and scroll, in reality the codex page was itself once a new media form that mixed its histories, inheriting its plural lineages from the intermediate stitched *rotulet* or roll form that is part book, part scroll.[49] It is the case that all old media formats "persist into the new medium before being modified and replaced with new, better adapted, forms."[50] Indeed, all subsequent combinations were "always already new," to appropriate Lisa Gitelman's wording.[51] For it should not be forgotten that "the page offers a vertical continuity" akin to scrolling and has done so since its inception, an evident fact in the embodied encounter with the codex.[52] Of course, such periods of fusion and overlap are symptomatic of introducing any new (bookish) technology.

Scrolling occurs when the user amplifies a portion of a virtual "page," making the page itself a continuous entity. Hence, a bounded continuity of the discrete page is born, in which scrolling—which is, after all, akin to the sequential and often continuous nature of reading— finds itself juxtaposed with discontinuous turns and breaks. These conjoined metaphors are now firmly ingrained within our techno-cultural imaginations. Indeed, critics retroactively describe the reorientation from lateral to mesial inscription (the change wrought by the codex in the scroll's directional orientation) as "like the scrolling computer screen."[53] That is, earlier technologies are described in terms of those that came later, as would be describing a sundial as "like a wristwatch." It is precisely because of digital scrolling that we now see something new in pagina or print columns.

The perhaps most essential key to understanding the strange (un)materiality of the virtual page, though, is grasping that its counterpart, scrolling, was viewed as an unnatural or counterintuitive digital metaphor upon its introduction. As Kirschenbaum points out, the 1982 Perfect Writer software manual contains a diagram to explain scrolling to the user. This manual shows portions of rolled parchment inside the machine, behind the screen.[54] Ryan Cordell and Elika Ortega also showed me that the 1983 Apple IIe personal computer manual had to explain scrolling. Apple showed users the supposedly off-screen, "invisible" portions of the document moving "beyond" the visual display unit.

Supplementing this messy history, contaminated by scrolling, is the digital page's shared common ancestor, the wax tablet.[55] This erasable form offered many more opportunities than its fixed, inked cousins. As Butler notes, such erasability played a large part in the political economy of ancient Rome. In particular, Romans conveyed social standing through nominal legibility and erasure. "No Roman citizen," he writes, "was so insignificant that he did not sometimes need his name to be written, and none was so powerful that his name could not one day be erased."[56] The digital page reinscribes this power of erasure and re-writing atop a form—the printed page—that was supposed to provide a fixity (palimpsests notwithstanding). Indeed, we do not have "page computers" but "tablet computers." We have tabular scrolling, pages that scroll, and paginated tablets.

Digital pages, then, like their print counterparts, are not one thing. Some possess the infinite rewritability of the wax tablet, while others attempt to enforce a write-once, read-many (WORM) paradigm akin to the preprinted page. When we open our word processors, we assume the former; we see a sequence of editable pages between which we scroll. When we read a preformatted PDF, say of a book, we assume the latter; we expect the content to remain consistent and disseminable. However, WORM in this context is not genuinely immutable. Instead, PDF software acts as a type of technological protection measure, pre-venting changes. Consequently, read-only digital pages appear more artificially constrained than their editable counterparts.

Hence, it is the friction of the metaphor that is of historical sig-nificance for the presumed victory of the digital page. Despite our imaginations of familiar intuition, in the mid-1980s world of books in which personal computing emerged, it was "not a straightforward or speedy translation from original to screen," as David McKitterick puts it.[57] Nonetheless, despite D. F. McKenzie's assertion that the lossiness of virtual books represents a "theft of evidence" in which too much valuable information was jettisoned, the problem for the transition was instead an overload of metaphorical evidence: of scrolling, pagination, and tablet forms.[58] Thus, the virtual page required explication to users upon its introduction. Indeed, because of their messy metaphorical his-tories, digital pages were hardly intuitive at all.

The Late Development and Cancellation of PDF

One of the reasons for a new history of digital pages is that it took a long time to adopt read-only electronic pagination, which contradicts the more widely known account and seeming common sense, from our contemporary vantage point. There was, in fact, no enforcement of pagelike representation implemented at the outset of computational writing and reading. In actuality, it took until the 1990s to develop PDF, the software technology that would enable this transmedia substitutability. This delay was because computing software technologies were explicitly *not* designed to replicate pages between devices.

Early computing systems developed in a distributed, piecemeal fashion with little coordination between manufacturers.[59] Hardware and software makers rarely collaborated to pursue the reliable reproduction of precisely paginated documents. Hence, homogenized page representation in the digital environment arrived belatedly due to the limitations of early computing systems. This reliance on material infrastructures sits at odds with the flawed logic of the digital imaginary, which is one of abundance. As I have put it elsewhere, we sometimes erroneously believe "born-digital literatures [to be] abundant and overflowing, disseminable *ad infinitum*" merely due to their technological nature.[60] However, the ability to reproduce digitally paginated artifacts between systems relies on the scarce underpinning resources of hardware and software development. It relies on scarce labor.

Nevertheless, even this imagined abundance contains the seeds of scarcity. Consider, for instance, the material prerequisites for the procurement of documents over the internet. Both parties must own a computing system with a visual display unit. Both parties must have the physical infrastructure necessary to access the internet. Upon a document request from a client, a server must fetch the document from secondary storage, move its contents into primary storage, then modulate the bits into a binary form for cabled transmission. The client, meanwhile, will perform the inverse operation, demodulating the pulses into primary and then perhaps secondary storage. The software will then decode the received binary object into pixels on the screen or waveforms through speakers, ready for human consumption.

We call such transmission mechanisms, to which I will return in a later chapter, "nonrivalrous" because often, in transferring a digital artifact to another site, the original remains with the sender without degradation or loss.[61] Like ideas, we can copy digital media indefinitely;

we do not contest their ownership through material rivalry.[62] However, the nonrivalry of the digital depends upon material economies of computing and networking equipment. Indeed, "in practice," as Hartley et al. put it, "there is always a limit to non-rivalrousness."[63] Without the owned, singular, and rivalrous artifacts—monitors, keyboards, speakers, computers—it would not be possible to reproduce copies in this way.

However, critical in such systems is that the material items maintain substitutability, a type of rivalrous nonrivalry. It does not matter that two visual display units are not the same material object. What is essential is the malleability of the material object and its ability to reproduce represented forms nonrivalrously. Contrary to the established narrative, this is not strictly a new phenomenon in the digital age. Admittedly, preprinted books do not possess such malleability, but blank paper and a Xerox machine do, albeit with the associated unit and time costs.[64] Pre-inscribed scrolls did not yield nonrivalrous malleability, but the erasable wax tablet could. The rivalry of these predigital inscription surfaces is not different in *type* to the rivalry of a computer screen—a malleable surface capable of reproducing forms without the loss of the original. What has changed is a difference in the degree of fidelity and speed. This change in degree has been underway for well over a century. As Walter Benjamin remarked in an over-cited passage, "In principle a work of art has always been reproducible. Man-made artifacts could always be imitated by men. . . . Around 1900 technical reproduction had reached a standard that . . . permitted it to reproduce all transmitted works of art and thus to cause the most profound change in their impact upon the public."[65] Nonetheless, it was still difficult to introduce such frictionless technology even after the advent of the computer screen.

Digital pagination in the form of a PDF introduced a transmedia substitutability to malleable digital surfaces for the first time, even while it brought a read-only paradigm within the page context itself.[66] Indeed, the initial iteration of PDF, the Camelot Project, specifically aimed to solve two fundamental problems in the world of computer graphics and typography: (1) "how to build a computer representation, in a resolution-independent way, of any printed page"; and (2) "how to represent text, and typefaces, that are compatible with a solution to the first problem."[67]

At heart, the problem was one of substitutability. The laser printers that John E. Warnock (a later founder of Adobe, the original developer of PDF) used at Xerox PARC ran at 240 dots-per-inch (DPI). Meanwhile, computer monitors at the time used a 72 DPI format.[68] To solve this initial problem of scalability, Warnock and his team developed the page-description language PostScript (initially called JaM after John Gaffney and Martin Newell, who worked on the project alongside Chuck Geschke and Doug Wyatt).[69] PostScript replaced the earlier manual system in which researchers at PARC had "laboriously crafted type designs for each font size." This earlier approach meant that "complete type libraries would have to be constructed," by hand, "for every new, different-resolution device that might be invented."[70]

The earlier manual approach created a situation where it was possible to display documents in a unified way across different devices, but only on the prerequisites of much tedious background labor and foreknowledge of future device specifications. Such a situation is akin to having wax tablets of five different sizes and knowing how accurately to replicate an image across only those five, provided one has undertaken extensive preparatory work. Another good analogy is the "progress" of inventing manual printers' typesetting blocks. Such an advance moved from a situation where scribes could "vary the size of their scripts at will to conform to the format of the page they write on, just as they [could] vary script styles" to one where "typesetters [could] do neither of these things."[71] The analogous manual approach to computational typesetting, in which fonts were created one size at a time, barely seemed an advance at all.

PostScript overcame the limitations of this more manual approach. However, PostScript was a Turing-complete programming language, bundling full-featured variable calculation that required a heavy-duty interpreter to sit on top of the file format. This fulsome feature set brought several drawbacks for the use of PostScript as a typographic and page-layout system:

1. The transmission of executable programs carries significant security risks in networked computing environments.

2. Using complete programming languages to generate documents can result in infinite loops and indeterminate pagination.

3. It is impossible to "jump" to an arbitrary point in the page sequence without a total recalculation of the preceding elements.[72]

Most detrimentally, though, PostScript was slow. Indeed, Warnock had a contract with Steve Jobs at Apple to build the implementation for the LaserWriter, announced in January 1985.[73] However, the examples that Warnock built "took over two minutes to execute on the LaserWriter," and Jobs did not want to demonstrate this on stage in front of an audience.[74]

Adobe developed PDF as an enhancement of this earlier PostScript format. PDF solved the problem of viewing and printing the "same" document anywhere.[75] Billed initially as Interchange PostScript (IPS), this format restricted some of the more outlandish and computationally intensive components of PostScript and instead created a device-independent system that ran a purely graphical subset of the language. As Warnock describes it, he "went to work and used a trick [he] had developed that would flatten all the loops and subroutine calls in the program into a file that would contain only graphics calls. This trick reduced the computation time from over 2 minutes, to 22 secs. After doing this Steve [Jobs] demonstrated the file at the announcement."[76]

To be clear, although subsequently enshrined as an open standard, PDF and Camelot were corporate and profit driven. Adobe worked to "[consider] all the requirements of corporations regarding documents" and "to structure Camelot components so that they can be sold in ways that are useful to the corporations." Thus, the institutional office environment drove pagination in the digital space as much as did a digital fidelity to codex construction. PDF and Camelot also used a WORM-like, write-once-by-one, read-many-times-by-many paradigm of consumption, a model in which "the distribution of information is to many people."[77] At this early point, Adobe did not mention mass peer-to-peer dissemination or the facility for many creators to send to many receivers; they were still thinking in a print paradigm.[78] They envisaged the early dissemination network as a spoke system that radiates outward from a relatively small number of hubs.

Critics have often assumed, given their contemporary prevalence, that PDF and digital pagination took off immediately. John B. Thompson, for instance, notes that "PDF quickly established itself as the de facto standard in publishing and in the graphic arts."[79] In reality, it did not. Warnock and Geschke write that they were "surprised" by PDF's "slow growth."[80] In fact, in Warnock's view, PDF was widely misunderstood at the time of its inception: "Quite frankly," he writes, "the industry 'did not get it.'"[81]

Most shockingly, despite some limited early adoption by the IRS and the US Centers for Disease Control, the Adobe board of directors suggested that Warnock abandon PDF development. "I remember speaking with an analyst at the Gartner Group," notes Warnock, "and she said: Why would anyone use this instead of just sending around 'word' files and 'lotus 123' files. She obviously did not understand the issues." Warnock believes that the early problem with PDF adoption "was to charge for the reader" instead of focusing on the creator side. Nonetheless, alongside the "explosive growth of the use of the internet," Adobe's commensurate success with PDF led to the de-skilling of the compositing profession but also to the persistence of the digital page.[82]

The significance of this new history is that writable pagination arrived well before WORM-paginated formats such as PDF. While the former appeared early, PDF did not emerge until 1993. When PDF did arrive, Adobe almost canceled it for being commercially unviable and technologically undesirable. Despite the importance of such pagination in a transition from hot lead to computerized production, the publishing industry did not grasp its potential at the time. The most widely used computer file format for document dissemination nearly never existed.

New Resolutions

Several social and material suppositions lie beneath the creation of the PDF and other transmedia pagination formats. These assumptions have profoundly influenced our digital world. However, Adobe viewed them as mere engineering problems in the Camelot specification. The first is the assumption that "view and print anywhere" means that the digital document must have transmedia compatibility with print. As one example of this paradigm, Kathleen Fitzpatrick accurately writes that most e-book texts result from "simply translating texts from paper to screen."[83] In this respect, critics assert that the digital will never truly be "paperless" if it maintains the inflexible boundedness of digital pagination. For instance, in academic publishing circles, one of the core arguments that continues to maintain the supremacy of the PDF is the use of page numbers in citation styles. One can easily imagine any number of alternatives to pagination for reference purposes, some of which are already in use, such as paragraph enumeration. Nevertheless, almost all academic citation styles insist on a consistent page number between an electronic edition and its print-material relation.[84] In this way, the metadata specification constrains the type of object that can be cited and locks supposed intellectual legitimacy to format. However, I argue that it is not only this transmedia oscillation between print and digital that has most conditioned the virtual page.[85]

For example, consider that a particular page aspect ratio has come to dominate the virtual landscape of text production outside of the continental Americas: the ISO 216 A4 standard at an aspect ratio of 1:1.414.[86] At 210mm × 297mm, this sizing maintains the same aspect ratio as neither the UK A-format paperback (110 mm × 178 mm; 1:1.618) nor the B-format (129 mm × 198 mm; 1:1.534).[87] Digital pages, then, at this ratio do not usually map onto the two most common sizes for trade book sales. The digital space must also accommodate the architectures of toolbars, scrollbars, and other functional apparatuses. This accommodation again reduces the screen space given to the actual page. The ANSI Letter format used in the United States and elsewhere uses 215.9mm × 279.4 mm, introducing another aspect ratio that is not the default for the digital page (1:1.2941), although it was replicated by the original Alto display.[88] As a result, the pagination displayed in word processors and then most commonly output into PDF format is an abstract rectangle, rather than any precise geometric equivalent of its usual print correlates.[89] Most authors use a layout to write that is not the same spatiality as many printed outputs. Hence, Butler is only partially correct to note that "all that remains consistent from author to reader is the page's basic geometry; its coordinates and dimensions, by contrast, inevitably shift."[90] For what is the basic geometry if not determined by coordinates and dimensions, which are varied?

The history of this choice of paper sizing can be traced back to 1786, when Georg Christoph Lichtenberg proposed, in a letter on October 25 that year to Johann Beckmann, a system of paper sizes based on the square root of two (the A-series of paper sizes).[91] This ratio has distinct commercial advantages when producing paper because the linear sub-division allows for the least waste when cutting.[92] Of course, given how, in Mark Bland's terms, "we commonly sublimate the physical form of the book and suppress the connections between format and design and the history of their meanings," this lineage has repercussions for the digital space.[93]

However, this matter of aspect ratios comes into conflict with the history of display technologies. Various aspect ratios have evolved and seen widespread adoption throughout visual display unit development: 4:3, 5:4, 3:2, 16:10, 16:9, 21:9, and 32:9. Of these, 4:3, 3:2, 16:9, and 16:10 are the closest to the A4-page aspect ratio of 1.414:1. These latter ratios, adopted in contemporary widescreen monitors, allow for the simultaneous display of two A4 sheets side by side, except without the need for a zero-waste economy present in physical paper production's folding and cutting. That said, as John Dagenais reminds us, one of the defining remaining features of the virtual, as opposed to printed or codex, page is that it is usually seen in isolation as a single sheet, rather than as part of a dual verso and recto layout.[94]

There are, in fact, two primary historical determinants of aspect ratio sizes for visual display units: the print and the photonic. Early machines used line printers to produce a hard-copy output of their programming on the former front. In this sense, all current computing systems have a print legacy to their graphic display outputs. However, the paper form used by such systems was continuous (i.e., it was a type of scroll or *rotulet* rather than leafed paper) and it ran at 215.9 mm × 279.4 mm. Therefore, there is greater continuity for this form with the scroll than the default A4 or Letterform of later word processing. The latter of these types—the visual display that we use now—is descended from early computational systems that used light bulbs to indicate internal register state. As the television took hold of home entertainment in a broader context, the earliest computer monitors adopted the aspect ratio from this popular entertainment form (4:3, from the arbitrary Academy Ratio of 1.33:1 standardized in 1932).[95] Although this ratio is close to many paper forms, its development had no predication on document production and consumption in A4/Letter or any other medium.[96]

A series of conflicting determiners and predecessors of current display technology and norms around digital pagination now come into view:

continuous paper through line-printing output akin to the scroll

A4-paper sizing based on root-two economies of physical paper slicing

4:3 aspect-ratio display technologies from television and film environments

Importantly for the latter two ancestors, the relationship to economy is the inverse of the material paper environment. In the paper environment, the goal is to ensure that we waste no space when folding and cutting. By contrast, in the virtual environment, designers use spacing to alleviate eye strain and cognitive burden. Such spacing also, though, ensures that the perception of the virtual page is A4 or Letter. For, were the zoom to fill the entire screen, the rectangular nature of the virtual page would disappear.

We should also consider how the histories of the term "format" work in the space of digital pagination. Gérard Genette noted that "over time, the meaning of this word ['format'] has changed."[97] The original terms of paper format referred to the folding techniques that would distinguish the folio from the quarto, octavo, duodecimo, sexto-decimo, and octodecimo. The name of the format "became a shorthand way of estimating" the "flat dimensions of a book." However, the term "format" shifts in the paperback, or *livre de poche*, era. At this point, it begins to represent notions of mass reproducibility and accessible reprinting.[98] That is, the term "paperback" comes with connotations of mass accessibility—of an era when books are available to everyone. Page dimensionality and format then take on a political economy of demography, denoting the format's reach in terms of class and wealth.[99]

File formats, by contrast, are not usually thought to refer to dimensional size, although compression formats relate to storage space (a type of size that also comes with a cost). They instead refer to layout in memory of interpretable bits and bytes and the decoding routines required to render their contents legible to human users. Such thinking holds until we return to PDF and its multiple scaled resolutions that attempt to make discontinuous histories of visual display units work as a homogenized format size, for a mass audience, on the World Wide Web. Visual display unit technologies condition the sizes of virtual pages. Hence, printed pages are not the determining ancestors of the formats of virtual pages. Instead, printed pages are just one competing influence among many on the size and dimensions of digital pages.

Critics have long asserted that the persistence of the page in the digital era is due to a desire or need to replicate print. Indeed, this is the traditional way in which we conceive of all digital metaphors: they give us something from the material to supposedly recognize in the virtual. In some instances, such as newspaper production and other environments where the digital setup is there only to facilitate the production of print, this thinking holds. Digital files that maintain this transmedia pagination, harmonizing between digital and material, often continue to dominate for reasons of practicality, prestige, or encapsulation and portability, all of which are imported from print.

At the same time, seeking such continuity from the material to the virtual can mislead us.[100] I have shown how pagination metaphors are more diluted, how format histories are more convoluted, and how the display media forms involved are more varied than the conventional argument can accommodate. In the new history that I have traced, the path forks and winds a great deal more than might be expected, and the lineages, histories, and functions of these virtual pages are heterogeneous. A range of objects and forces condition the virtual page beyond its print correlate.

The prevalence of digital pagination—albeit in its estranged form—has also influenced other hardware designs. We have PgUp (page up) and PgDown (page down) keys on almost all computer keyboards worldwide that signify a movement through the document in the unit of a page (although this distance can vary). Note, though, that this is not "flip left" or "flip right," as we would in a book with pages, but more of the conjoined logic of discrete, rather than continuous, scrolling to which I referred earlier. Pages continue to flow, albeit top to bottom, not left to right (or right to left), in discrete yet continuous modes. One page after another is stacked in a vertical form. However, it is also worth noting that we also have a ScrLk (scroll lock) button on most keyboards. This key is part of a legacy function of alternation between controlling the cursor with arrows and controlling the movement of text flow. We further have the PrtSc (print screen) button that now captures a screenshot. That is to note that screens and scrolls have as significant a metaphorical impact on our keyboard technologies as do material or digital pages.

E-reading forms also continue to evolve in ways that go beyond the traditional page and that are determined by different material hardwares. New location markers in formats such as the Kindle untether reading experiences from the page's traditional language and symbolic imaginary.[101] This rootedness in text rather than page itself has possible precedent in biblical and philosophical discourses (such as the Bekker numbering used in scholarship on Aristotle or the Stephanus pagination for Plato). However, the proprietary nature of the Kindle's location function has come in for critique on accessibility grounds.[102] Such devices also attempt to give a virtual sensation of relative placement, with their "progress" marker indicating the read percentage of a text. Such an indicator intends to replicate the haptic sensation of progression through a printed book. However, the inextricable imaginary interlock between computer progress bars and the tedium of waiting for a task to complete lends an uneasy air to such an approach. Reading fiction, for example, has a progress bar in the same way as does submitting your taxes digitally. Without care, reading becomes converted into a mere process to be completed.

There are also, though, retroactive questions to be asked of our print cultures from these divergent digital forms. As Jerome J. McGann puts it, we need "a thoroughgoing re-theorizing of our ideas about books and traditional textualities in general."[103] One of the questions we might ask from this work is: Do digital pages behave as material pages would if they could? Or is it more likely that material pages were always themselves trying to harmonize rival technologies of tablets and scrolls into new forms subject to incommensurable read/write demands? From the messy metaphors, hacked histories, and strained syntheses that sit behind our histories of digital pagination, a more careful interrogation of such features shows always-hybrid entities that emerge from complex conjunctions rather than singular historical inheritance. Turning over a new leaf is more complex than it sounds.

THREE

DIGITAL WHITESPACE IS THE SERIALITY
OF MUSICAL SILENCE

MUSIC IS SOMETIMES DEFINED AS a rhythmic blend of sound and silence.[1] Similarly, in information transmission, we must distinguish signal from background noise.[2] And, in systems of writing and reading, whether electronic or manual, the graphic mark must be distinguished from the whitespace against which it derives its form. Yet how do we understand this metaphor of digital "white" "space"? How did whitespace, this term that denotes digital emptiness, even become *white*? Does it matter? Is it a coincidence that the often most prominent keys on the computer keyboard—the space bar, return, backspace, and delete buttons, which take up the most *space*—are all concerned with creating blankness, with the generation of negative visual page space? This chapter thinks about emptiness, its digital whiteness, and its relation to digital typography.

At least one school of typography, derived from Beatrice Warde, has claimed that the role of typography should be to obviate itself—to be "transparent" in some ways, leading back to a type of blankness. "There is nothing," writes Warde in her relatively famous essay "The Crystal Goblet," that is "simple or dull in achieving the transparent page."[3] In Warde's thinking, the layout on the page, the formatting of letters, and other typographical features should be made "transparent" to the reader and offer instead a direct portal to the mental effect of words. Warde believes that the good typographer should disintermediate print with forms that draw no attention to themselves. In her view, the media form should appear transparent, even if it might still have complex subliminal effects. This chapter seeks to do the precise opposite with respect to blankness itself. I wish to highlight the mediality of blank space and to undo the logic of transparency promulgated by this school.

Blank space, despite its blankness, is *structured* and *functional*. As a result, whole books, such as Laurie E. Maguire's *The Rhetoric of the Page*, have been devoted to the "positive, creative potential of the blank in printed texts."[4] At the most binary taxonomic level, we might distinguish between a metaphorical blankness that is empty substrate (a blank page without ink or markings) and a blankness that is an absence of that substrate (say, a hole in paper where pages have been bound into a book).[5] Adding a third party to this binary, in poetry, Emily Dickinson's dashes have been construed as various types of nontextual/ nonlinguistic "blank," despite their obvious textual presence and differentiated weights. Dickinson's "blanks" are differentiated from one another and have their own unique characters. They are also a "blankness" signaled by a presence, instead of merely an absence. Further, in this vein, Heather Wolfe, the curator of manuscripts at the Folger Shakespeare Library, has cataloged the different types of holes that survive to this day in Early Modern English manuscripts.[6] There is even, it turns out, a volume dedicated to categorizing the forms of emptiness in damage entitled *Catalogue of Damage Terminology for Works of Art and Cultural Property: Paper*.[7]

For the reader curious about how a *Celestial Emporium of Benevolent Knowledge* for holes might appear, Wolfe is instructive:

Human-caused, pest-caused, holes formed through errors in the production stage and at the use stage, holes caused by the passage of time and exposure to the elements, holes caused by wear and tear and rough and tumble, holes intentional and unintentional, holes created for authentication, obliteration, binding, and filing. Wormholes, rodent nibbles, burn holes, letterlocking slits, pin holes, pricking holes for drawing straight lines, pouncing holes for tracing and drawing, sewing and stitching holes, volvelle holes, holes caused by the breaking of seals when unlocking letters, "casement" holes in templates. . . . Holes as apertures, holes as damage. Holes as information management, holes as information mismanagement.[8]

Paul Reynolds also provides a "glossary of holes," although his definitions seem more poetic than factual.[9]

Blankness, in its many forms, also holds historic economic and cultural import. As Henry R. Woudhuysen notes, there were many reasons to leave a leaf or page empty even in the early modern period, when this was an expensive business. Indeed, given that paper was the most costly material in the printing process and because compositors were paid "proportionately the same amount for 'setting' a blank page as for a page crowded with justified type," blank pages might seem to be profligate lunacy.[10] However, this is not really the case, as blank pages at either end of a volume served to "stop damage to a book's vulnerable ending."[11] Empty pages worked as safety buffers for the print within, justifying their economic merit. Of course, empty space was never *just* for protection, and there are instances of it as waste. David McKitterick, for example, has charted instances where typesetters left space for illustrations that were never provided.[12] Also, every page has a margin, an officially empty/blank space framing its content, which seemingly invites readers to make their own mark on the work.[13]

Several authors have also considered what it means to write in the same color as a background page—that is, writing that is not distinct from the substrate. Tangentially, when expressing the difficulty of writing without suffering, the controversial (for his antifeminism) Henry de

Montherlant famously put it that "happiness writes in white ink on a white page."[14] This reflection has even prompted an entire work of philosophy dedicated to understanding the role of pain in the production of artistic creativity titled *Does Happiness Write Blank Pages?*[15] While the default backing color here is assumed to be white—the perennial signifier of absolute emptiness—Teju Cole is among a group of writers who nimbly invert this schema. For Cole, the quintessential black undersurface is "carbon paper," which sits between white sheets but conveys a copy of the message.[16] However, Cole notes that while most users of carbon paper believe that they end up with two copies, there are in fact three. Cole writes, "What I had not noted at the time was that on the black paper there was a third copy of whatever had been written. The black paper was ridged and marked with all the original handwriting. Black on black, full of meaning, but shaped by absence. The black paper was the ghostly record. Black on black, secretly sensible."[17]

From a work about the meetings of cultural and racial blacknesses, Cole asks us not to discount the intermediate black paper as a transparent medium involved merely in the transposition of white culture to white culture. Also important, of course, for this metaphor is that the material brought across the carbon-paper color divide (for it is at the same time a separator) is black. Carbon paper does not transport whiteness from one sheet to another; it transports black marks, even if the underlying surface on which the now-agential carbon paper "writes" must be white.

However, such a separation of text from background strata is the mainstay of most contemporary digital image/text processing. For example, for optical character recognition to work, the software must distinguish text from whitespace. Hence, while, as I noted in chapter 2, the history of the page in digital reading and writing took a winding and forking path, recent scholarship on graphical approaches to the page has recognized this digital-visual complexity. Andrew Piper, Chad Wellmon, and Mohamed Cheriet, for instance, have highlighted the importance of the page's visuality. In their work, they draw the attention of contemporary book historians to the field known as document image analysis (DIA). DIA is a discipline that, in contrast to at least some bibliographic work, views the page as a more holistic *image*, an approach that moves "away from a text-centric understanding of the page."[18] Nonetheless, the very purpose of DIA is, in some senses, to return to a text-centric understanding. For instance, in their detection of footnotes, Piper et al. look to measure "the relationships between lines and white space as a way of identifying the location and presence of footnotes."[19] Thus, while, in some particular ways, this approach is not *text* focused, the breakdown of the page's visuality into a binary of "a single vector of black/white pixels" has but one function: to separate text and other semantic markings from whitespace in a binary fashion. Indeed, the technical paper behind the method notes that "each document image is represented by a concatenated image of its two top textlines and two bottom textlines," which nonetheless has a textual (if not linguistic) centricity.[20] The basic fact of the matter is that, at heart, we usually want to "detect" whitespace only to discard it in favor of text.

Such discarding of whitespace forms part of the lossy culture of digitization that many book historians have decried. As Piper puts it elsewhere, "The losses that accompany scanning, not only to the textual integrity of the book through optical character recognition and its many errors, but also to the historical knowledge that such objects convey," can make all digitization "seem like a threat or endangerment to knowledge."[21] Examples of such losses include stain marks, creases, bleed-through, and other cues that can serve as clues for the book historian. By treating such space as uncontoured whiteness in the transition from physical to digital, we lose a great deal of valuable historical information about textual production. This also exposes another important distinction. Physical whitespace is detailed and readable. Digital whitespace aims at homogeneity and genericity.

There is, however, potential creativity in our processes of digitization; it is not all negative. Ryan Cordell, for instance, asks whether it is "reasonable to say that machines can *compose*—in the bibliographic rather than authorial sense." That is, we should consider whether machines can be considered fallible typesetters, thought of as "a species of compositor."[22] I have made a similar argument in my study of the compositing of Jennifer Egan's first collection of short stories where it seems that optical character recognition (OCR) errors crept into the second printed edition.[23] Nonetheless, a crucial but assumed function of this OCR typesetting process is distinguishing marks on the page from the page itself. Hence, when Rose Holley describes the function of OCR as dividing "the page into elements such as blocks of texts (columns), tables, images, etc.," there is an even more fundamental underlying divisive process. OCR must separate the "whitespace" of the page from all other elements. As Holley notes, "OCR software is still reliant on there being a clear contrast between black and white to be able to distinguish what is text and what is background page."[24]

Importantly, in many OCR contexts, a computational compositor cannot always easily distinguish text from the whitespace background. While it is usually easy for humans to tell whitespace and text apart, page bleeds, "dirt specks, stains," and variable inking weights make this classification process more computationally difficult than might conventionally be assumed.[25] If whitespace were unequivocally empty in the physical domain, this distinction would be a simple task. However, whitespace is not empty.

While I will consider and query the term "whitespace," there is another vital point to consider for meaning and overload. When printed on white paper, black textual characters add semantic depth to the sheet. As words and characters appear, they bring meaning. Even when we overprint multiple text strings atop one another, there is a growth in semantic context and understanding. As the words proliferate, ever greater possibilities for meaning emerge, as seen in the works of various typographer-poets, such as Hansjörg Mayer.[26] However, at a certain point in an overprinting process, as words become indistinguishable from one another, the printed letters return the textual surface to an originary state of disarray. There is a point beyond which overprinting no longer conveys new meaning but instead "blanks" the canvas space. This overload is a return to whitespace in a different color from the original page space. That is to say, absence and total saturation are two poles that meet in a horseshoe topology rather than two ends of a straight-line spectrum of opposition.

From these initial remarks, and leading on from the discussion of visual display units at the close of chapter 2, this chapter interrogates the histories, conventions, namings, and uses of negative space in computational-textual environments. This chapter sequentially examines three aspects of whitespace and the physical metaphors/constraints that play in this area:

1. The transition from white paper page surface to black-background terminal visual display units

2. The composition and display of margins, tabs, and other whitespace

3. The Unicode system's variable characters for different whitespace widths, including analogies to em- and en-spaces but documenting and noting the twenty-five different types of whitespace characters provided for within the specification

This chapter touches on many aspects of the neglected importance of whitespace. For whitespace is significant. Indeed, one of the most prevalent, and possibly among the most important, computer programming languages of the past decade—Python—uses whitespace as its distinctive syntactical marker that determines logical code flow. Further, nondisplay control characters—a kind of "negative space"—such as the LTR (Left to Right) and RTL (Right to Left) characters—are crucial for the correct display of languages beyond the Anglocentric defaults of computational character flow. While much other work has examined the idea of the blank—in, say, "missing words, empty brackets, censored lines," or the use of "etc."—this chapter focuses on the background space of the page that is omnipresent as a textual precondition.[27] For our computational whitespaces contain depths that may lie invisible but that can nonetheless be [].

Why Is Space White?

Part way through his 1850 epic *Moby-Dick; or, The Whale*, Herman Melville's narrator, Ishmael, famously reflects on the color white:

Or is it, that as in essence whiteness is not so much a color as the visible absence of color; and at the same time the concrete of all colors; is it for these reasons that there is such a dumb blankness, full of meaning, in a wide landscape of snows—a colorless, all-color of atheism from which we shrink?[28]

While the context for Ishmael is his horror at the "whiteness of the whale"—the aspect of the creature that "above all things appalled" him—the nature of whiteness has long been an object of philosophical study.[29] Is whiteness everything or nothing? Is white even a color?

The etymology of "blank" is well charted by the aptly named Thomas White. Old High German *blanch* developed from the Germanic **blangkaz*, meaning "to shine, dazzle," an extended form of the Proto-Indo-European root **bhel-*, meaning "to shine, flash, burn." Blankness appears, therefore, to have developed from denoting a bright, luminous, and distinct quality to the predominant modern meaning of an absence or lack of any content or attributes.[30] Helen Smith likewise plots the ways in which "the blank receptiveness of paper is a longstanding trope with a rich early modern heritage."[31] This ranges from the "faire paper" of *Othello* to Jacques Derrida writing of the "whiteness of writing."[32]

But the medieval uses of "blank" to which White and others turn chart a path between these definitional poles. Aligned with the derivation of *blanc(h)* to "white," "the predominant meaning of 'blank' in Middle English appears to be that of whiteness, a meaning largely obsolete by the eighteenth century."[33] That is, language developments strongly indicate an affinity between blankness and whiteness.

However, importantly for the subject of this chapter, computational whitespace was *not* originally white. Because Microsoft Word now yields to us a white starting page, there is a temptation to believe that computational whitespace simply seeks to mimic print structures that used whiteness as their blank substrate. Yet computer monitors did not start out with black text on a white background, even if Joseph Lick-lider wanted, in 1965, to have "a color display . . . if possible, or, if not, a black-on-white display."[34] Instead, though, as Matthew G. Kirschenbaum notes, "the letters" began as "green or amber on black, then (improbably) grey on blue, and (eventually) black on white."[35] The earliest computer monitor whitespace was black.

Punched cards, the computational predecessors to keyboards, are even stranger with respect to their blankness and "whitespace." In a punched-card system, a series of holes convey instructions: either there is a hole or there is not a hole. These correlate to either a positive or negative signal—the binary on which computers operate—and are taken, in punched-card systems, to represent a series of character encodings. However, in punched-card systems, is the hole a zero (negative) or a one (positive)? You might expect that the hole—the *absence* of the card, pure negative space—would represent a zero. This is not always the case, though. In some prevalent punch-card systems, such as the eighty-column IBM card, the hole represents the number to be designated, a positive, while the card represents a negative. So, in this system, to represent the number 2 you put a *hole* in the column for 2.[36] Of course, one could invert this and say that it is a "punch" that represents a positive, rather than "a hole." But the fact remains that, in this context, we reach a point where actual blankness (the hole) denotes positivity while the white "space" of the card (the presence of the substrate) stands for zero.[37]

These facts demonstrate that the whiteness of computational whitespace is culturally and ideologically, rather than just materially, produced. To understand why computational text processing uses the term "whitespace," and whence it came, we must evaluate several converging lines of social construction:

1. How and why paper, the underlying supposed object of mimesis, became white

2. How and why white became seen as a noncolor as part of a philosophical and religious reorientation around a white-black-gray axis

3. How and why visual display units progressed from black substrates to illuminated white backgrounds

Taken together, these complexly intersecting historical materialities of white substrates, cultural reorientations of polychromatic spectrums, and religico-symbolic discourses of purity all align to make whitespace white.

Paper, the Chromoclasm, and Color Perception

Although I noted, in the preceding chapter, that the virtual page does not simply attempt to replicate the physical page, it is clear that the histories of paper have influenced the digital writing space to some extent. A good first question, then, is: Why is *paper* white, and when did it become so? Intriguingly, book and media historians do not know the definitive answer to this question, although we have some rough ideas about practices in some parts of the world.[38] For instance, as Heidi Craig points out, "England had no native white paper industry to speak of until the late seventeenth century."[39] It took the 1774 discovery of chlorine to advance white papermaking in the English context.[40] Yet we also know that, in Italy, in the mid to late eighteenth century, at least one prominent papermaker, Pietro Miliani, had a "preoccupation" with the "'whiteness' of his papers," achieved by lengthy washing with spring water to whiten the rag pulp.[41]

It is also true that "white" consists of a variety of shades and hues; it is not one single absolute color. As Orietta Da Rold puts it, the question we should perhaps ask is: "How white was white paper?"[42] Or, in Joshua Calhoun's formulation of the subcategories of a supposed "pure" white: "The page space around and between words, frequently referred to as 'white space,' is anything but white."[43]

The obvious assumption is simply that white and black provide the greatest contrasting paradigms between ink and substrate, leading to the highest legibility. The assumption here is that white paper with black text is "easiest on the eye." However, this is definitely not true. As Jonathan Senchyne shows, a mid-nineteenth-century survey reported considerable consternation about this contrast, noting that "brown paper preserves the eye better than white." The report refers to pure white paper, unflatteringly, as "glaring." Senchyne also cites a widely reproduced report from *Scientific American* that states that "white on a black [back]ground is more distinct" than vice versa.[44] In a similar vein, Da Rold gives details of the history of this claim that white paper damages one's eyesight, including how William Caxton "lost the 'corage' of his younger age and feels the pain of a wary hand, ageing body and fatigued eyes from *too much looking at white paper*."[45] Hence, the seemingly straightforward answer that white and black were simply perceived as opposites with the greatest functional contrast (and, therefore, the least strain on the consuming body) has not been universally true over history.

Many historical accounts of the development of paper note that, at some unspecified point, there was a divergence in which paper for writing becomes white, while different colors are used for other functions. For example, Mark Kurlansky writes that, in British papermaking, "white paper was for printing, and industrial paper, usually brown or blue, for wrapping, packaging, and encasing firearm cartridges."[46] That said, much of the more recent history of papermaking in Europe is derived from the history of white papermaking. As Richard Leslie Hills puts it, "Coarse grades of paper and, in particular, brown paper, were used as a wrapping material from a very early time but, such is the nature of this use that we have few details of it because most has been thrown away. Our history of papermaking derives principally from white paper because laws, contracts, accounts, etc. have been written on it and preserved in archives."[47] Importantly, though, papermaking in Britain and Europe was born under a different set of conditions than its older Asian counterparts.

Paper—one of the most significant technological advances of all time—was invented in ancient China.[48] Many accounts attribute its creation (or at least the refinement of its manufacture) to the court eunuch Tshai/Ts'ai (Cai) Lun in the second century CE.[49] In reality, though, as Tsien Tsuen-hsuin has documented, archaeologists have discovered paper fragments in North and Northwest China that date back to at least two or three centuries earlier. This preceding form of paper was not originally created solely for writing. Instead, its variegated roles included uses "in the fine and decorative arts, at ceremonies and festivals, for business transactions and records, monetary credit and exchange, personal attire, household furnishings, sanitary and medical purposes."[50] Paper is a multifunctional cultural tool that is embedded within a diverse set of social contexts.

The reasons for paper's emergence and uptake in China are many. The ready availability of water and tree fibers, coupled with washing techniques that used a mold, could have contributed to accidental early discoveries. The rapid adoption of paper in China compared to Europe can be explained by the fact that European parchment and the more durable papyrus were not available in China. Hence, in the Chinese context of replacing the inflexible bamboo and expensive silk that had come before, paper had a considerable advantage.[51] It was through the so-called Silk Road that paper proliferated into Central Asia and Arab regions.[52] This early emergence of paper laid the groundwork for China's development of printing long before Gutenberg's press in Europe.[53]

It is easy to assume that all paper is of a light hue because of the organic fibers from which it is composed. This is not wholly true. Both historically and now, making paper consists of matting or felting fibers onto a screen in a water suspension. This fibrous approach to paper also helps us to understand the shared etymology of text and textiles. Once the water has drained away, the mat of fibers is removed from the screen/mold and dried.[54] In early Chinese papermaking, bast fibers were selected for their durability, including hemp, jute, and flax.[55] One of Cai Lun's innovations was the routine addition of tree bark and hemp ends into this papermaking process.[56] It is correct that with the addition of such bark, "paper became not only thinner but whiter."[57] It is also true that the earliest surviving specimens of Korean paper exhibit a glossy whiteness, most likely from beaten paper mulberry bark.[58]

However, in ancient China, early papermakers used a set of dyeing processes to protect the sheets from insect damage and for artistic purposes. These processes resulted in red and yellow paper. For instance, the dictionary *Shih ming* from around 200 CE defined the word *huang* as "dyeing paper." A third-century-CE commentator, Meng Khan, noted that paper at this time was dyed yellow, apparently using a liquid from the *Phellodendron amurense* (cork tree).[59] While this process appears designed to protect the paper from insect damage and to create a glossiness, it had a side effect of changing the color.[60] One of the earliest surviving papers from Tunhuang that exhibits this dyeing is a twenty-six-foot-long roll providing a commentary on the Buddhist text the *Vimalakīrti nirdeśa sūtra*. Crucially, part of this roll of paper is missing the dyeing effect and so, as Lionel Giles notes, "at the very end the original whitish colour is visible."[61] The preservation of this coloration is significant in demonstrating the base, white hue since white paper made later in Europe tended to turn brown due to cellulose's lignin content.[62] Possibly even earlier than the use of the cork tree's yellow dye was the mixture of lead, sulfur, and saltpeter (known as litharge or red lead [*hung tan* or *chhien tan*]). Treating sheets with this solution results in paper that is toxic to bookworms but that is also bright orange (*wan nien hung*, or "ten-thousand-years red").[63] Hence, the earliest functional papers in ancient China are unlikely to have been white when in any usable state. They were orange, red, and yellow.

Dyeing paper was not merely a preservation practice in ancient China. Decorative coloring was also widespread. For example, Meng Khan, mentioned above and from the third century CE, describes an artifact from the first century BCE as a "silk-paper dyed red for writing." In the period 25–220 CE, princes at court received maroon and bright red paper sheets on their investiture. In the fourth and fifth centuries CE, "peach-blossom paper" in green, yellow, blue, and red was used in Szechuan, while ten different colors were available in the Tang dynasty. These colors were usually added after production by dyeing instead of augmenting the pulp with pigments. There are also records of people deliberately staining sheets to imitate aged paper for forgery.[64] (And, indeed, one of the earliest visual interface metaphors designed at Apple for demonstrating the age of documents was a "staining" effect of "fading to yellow."[65]) There is relatively little mention of white paper in these early ancient Chinese accounts.

Arabic cultures heavily intermediated the worldwide spread of paper, introducing "rag paper" made from linen scraps.[66] This form was then brought to Spain and Germany over the following centuries and became part of industrialized paper production. Again, during the medieval period, paper was not really white. As Thomas White puts it, "The equation of blankness or blank space with a default, featureless, even primordial ground of inscription overlooks the extent to which the preparation of any page or writing surface is the result of labour-intensive, time-consuming processes. Further, for the medieval and early modern periods in particular, these processes produced not pristinely white pages, but rather multihued surfaces that, before the addition of any textual content or evidence of their passage between scribes and future readers, preserve the continuing memory of their existence as animal skin or plant matter."[67] Indeed, it is true, as Elaine Treharne and Claude Willan note of a predecessor to paper, that the "finest vellum is bright white."[68] However, of particular significance is that new techniques for papermaking—that relied on rag collection—meant that, in Europe, papermaking became associated with ragpickers, individuals of very low social standing.[69] As a result, paper's whiteness began to take on an ethical hue. As Adam Smyth phrases it, "early modern culture was preoccupied with the life story of paper: where it came from, where it might end up, and, sometimes, the moral lessons that such itineraries implied."[70] Thus, papermaking began to expose a classist rift between the "base origins" of recycled clothing and a supposed "lofty calling" in the world of ideas and writing.[71]

For Lothar Müller, the need to distance the substrate of cultured and sacred writing from the crude social status of ragpickers led to the valorization of "fine, smooth, white paper" within religious symbolic contexts. In his view, this "transformation of a base, contemptible material into a snowy white writing surface fit comfortably with the religious schema of the purification and conversion of humanity's corrupted nature."[72] Nonetheless, however, as Calhoun shows, despite the assumption that paper from his period has been "discolored by age," in reality "many of the brownish pages we encounter in archives have actually retained coloring from their production." This is especially due to the fact that "the rivers that provided water for paper mills were not always pristine, especially in the spring (when they ran muddy)."[73] It is also important to note that seasonal and environmental factors can condition the coloring of paper. As Orietta Da Rold points out, "The outside temperature seems to have had an effect on colour: cold temperatures would make whiter paper."[74] The result of this is that "paper made during the winter months might have a better quality and be whiter."[75]

Indeed, the eventual emergence in Western cultures of ultrawhite paper and black ink is part of a stunning reconfiguration in color perception that begins around the fifteenth century and that centers on Protestant moral codes. Specifically, as Michel Pastoureau has documented, "though we do not know the reasons or the means, paper rapidly progressed from beige to off-white and then from off-white to true white. In the medieval handwritten book the ink was never completely black nor the parchment white. With the printed book, henceforth the reader's eyes beheld very black ink fixed on very white paper. That was a revolutionary change that would lead to profound transformations in the domain of color sensibility."[76] This change was relatively swift. Over the course of just a few decades between the mid-fifteenth and early sixteenth centuries, there is a shift from medieval multicolored images to a dominance of black and white. As Elizabeth Savage has charted, from early black and red on beige, the history of color printing actually stretches back further than traditional accounts have countenanced, and this must have affected the production of various substrate colors.[77]

In turn, by 1655, the Jesuit Alvare de Semedo is able to write of an equation between "the best" and "the whitest" paper, even as the Chinese continue to print in white ink on a black backdrop.[78] This rearrangement is driven both by the materiality of monochromatic print proliferation but also by a set of religico-symbolic mechanisms. It is also at this point that black and white become perceived outside of a full polychromatic color spectrum. As Pastoureau continues, "To the medieval eye, in effect, black and white were full-fledged colors. Beginning in the late fifteenth century, and even more so by the mid-sixteenth century, that would no longer be the case; black and white began to be regarded not only as special colors, but even as noncolors."[79]

The austere aesthetic favored by the Protestants Zwingli, Calvin, Melanchthon, and Luther—linked to the avoidance of graven images and varying levels of iconoclasm—reoriented the color spectrum around a "black-gray-white axis."[80] Yet the challenge here lies in the supposition that an iconoclasm of color—which Pastoureau calls a "chromoclasm"—would have a solid grasp of what an absence of color was or meant. In the symbolic understanding of medieval Europe, black was not yet viewed as an absence of color. As Pastoureau has put it elsewhere: "L'incolore n'existe pas."[81] Indeed, while every European language has a name for the absence of color—*farblos* in German, "colorless" in English, *incoloro* in Italian, *incolor* in Spanish—defining this term is far harder. French dictionaries in the nineteenth and twentieth centuries, for instance, were vague on the definition of "colorless": "Which does not have a definite color, which does not have its own color, which lacks complexion."[82] One of the core problems is how we can suggest in language, by means of color, what the absence of color means, and how white and black figure within such discourses.

In ancient societies, Pastoureau claims, the idea of colorlessness applied only to textiles to which coloration/dyes had not been applied. That is, regardless of the substrate color, it is the absence of deliberate coloration that leads to the designation "colorless." Hence, if a Latin text refers to *sine colore*, it means that the garment or fabric has not been dyed.[83] This phrase can also be used in reference to people's faces, where the color has drained due to, say, fear (a pallor). Nonetheless, at this point (up until the twelfth century), color was defined much more by material than by light. At this time, the theory of sensible secondary qualities—that is, the belief that objects "possess" weight, heat, taste, etc.—was prominent, and color was no exception. This fits with the etymological note that the origins of "color" lie in *celare*, the verb "to hide." Hence, certain theological authorities—such as St. Bernard—saw color as a "condemnable luxury" that, with its cloaking and hiding operations, interferes with believers' relations to God. Le Grand Abbé de Clairvaux wasn't keen, either, referring to the "opacity" of color.[84]

This religious distrust of color extends into the next century, when Franciscan friars attempted to adopt colorless habits by using a base undyed wool. Somewhat amusingly, over time, as these "plain" garbs became worn and torn, they took on a grayness (a color) by the grubbiness of the uniforms. They even become known as "St. Gray," showing how their colorlessness cannot fail to avoid chromatic classification.

"For medieval society," writes Pastoureau, "for its codes and its uses, its classifications and its stratifications, where everything is declined in terms of system, the concept of 'colorless' does not exist."[85]

It is only from the twelfth century onward that a rival view of color as *light* (rather than material) comes to prominence. Around 1130–40, for instance, St. Suger rebuilt the abbey in Saint Denis in a style that was designed to emphasize light as the agent of God. As this view took hold, one might suppose that "colorlessness" in this context would equate to an absence of light. However, this is not the case. Two English scholars and prelates at the time, Robert Grosseteste and John Pecham, say that for colorlessness (*sine colore*) to be relevant, effective, and comprehensible, it is crucial that there be "at least a little light left."[86] In medieval thought and art, then, "colorless" is not total darkness, and even less is it black. It has to do with a specific understanding of shadows.[87]

At some point in the eighteenth century, "shadow" becomes defined as an "absence of color." This poses representational challenges in art. How can an artist represent an absence of color, when any painted substrate will have some form of coloration?[88] For Pastoureau, heraldry seems to have been the first to have solved this problem. The colorless can be instantiated, in color, by using an idea of partial transparency. In this effect, the colors of the figure thought to be colorless disappear, but their outlines remain visible. Several coats of arms in the fourteenth and fifteenth century, for instance, are made up of a field of one or more colors and a "colorless," partially transparent figure is overlayed. The reasons that a family would choose to depict a colorless figure in heraldry vary. For example, it may represent a desire to hide a family connection (for reasons of illegitimate bastardy, for instance) or a desire to intrigue the viewer merely by staging a heraldic curiosity. However, the color representation of such figures in the coat of arms is always the same: the perimeter of the figure is clearly drawn but its color remains that of the field on which it is placed. If this field is divided or compartmentalized, and therefore painted in several colors, these colors appear through the figure. The heraldic shadows of bastardy, enacted by transparency, are given a new term in French: "shadow of."[89] This heraldic transparency, as an attempt at colorlessness, spills over into painting. Between 1320 and 1330, when painters had to represent something in color that was nonetheless colorless, they left the support or the background of the image bare and drew the outlines of the figure on the image.[90]

Everything changes, however, in Pastoureau's account, with the appearance and then the distribution of the engraved and printed image. That is to say that the introduction of material print technologies galvanizes and advances an already seeded radical religico-symbolic change in color perception. In just a few decades, between the middle of the fifteenth century and the sixteenth century, the vast majority of images circulating in the West become images printed in black and white. Clearly, this is a cultural revolution of far-reaching significance. Previously, most medieval images were polychromatic. Yet most early modern images become monochromatic (itself a term that implies that the white substrate is not, itself, a color). Certainly, there are still paintings on panels, murals, stained glass, tapestries, and other forms of art that have a range of colors. However, quantitatively, this represents little compared to the thousands of engraved and printed images in books that begin to circulate as prints at this time. In the fifteenth century and again in the first decades of the sixteenth century, these engraved images were often colored, in imitation of the miniatures painted in manuscript books, but thereafter this becomes rarer. Pastoureau shows that the world of the image becomes black and white and, gradually, that these two colors acquire a special status.[91]

With respect to whiteness, medieval parchments were never purely ultrawhite. Their colors were part of a wide palette, ranging from relatively dark brown to the lightest beige, even pale gray, passing through all shades of ecru. When an illuminator left a parchment bare, it was the natural shade of this parchment, whatever it was, that represented colorlessness. At that time, there was neither a material nor conceptual link between white and colorlessness—a fact that we can see by how a highlighter must represent white by using white paint. However, as paper becomes the obligatory medium for all texts and the vast majority of images, a sort of equivalence is gradually established between the color of this paper and colorlessness. "White" begins to be thought of as colorless, and it is partially—albeit in a complex lineage—to paper that it owes this particularity. From this background of paper, the idea of whiteness as blankness transitions into painting and dyeing.[92]

This shift can also be seen in fifteenth-century art theory, where a rebellion against the long-standing color theories of Aristotle drove a perceptual revolution. Indeed, Moshe Barasch notes that the philosophy of Leon Battista Alberti sets in motion a new paradigm in which black and white are no longer "considered as colors" and instead stand for "light and shade."[93] In this early Renaissance view, in the Latin edition of *Della pittura*, Alberti writes of his seven-tone color scale that "black and white are the two extremes of the colors. They certainly place only one in the middle, then two at a time between each extreme and the median itself, raising doubts, so to speak, on the limit that one of the two feels more on the side of the other extreme."[94] This spectrum, in itself, was modeled on an Aristotelian, pre-Newtonian scheme, in which, apparently, "seven colours are produced by mixing white and black."[95] Yet, in the Italian edition of the same text (the chronology of which is hotly disputed),[96] Alberti proposes a different base palette of just four colors—and white and black are *not* included, explicitly against Aristotle.[97] In this scheme, there is an assumption that the mixing of white and black with other colors "forms 'species' but does not change the 'genus' of these colors."[98] Such a seven/four split was also echoed by Cennino Cennini.[99] Furthering this logic, Leonardo da Vinci emphasizes, many times over, that "white is not a color but the neutral recipient of every color," although he does elsewhere place white and black on a color spectrum.[100]

Over time, then, this equation of whiteness with colorlessness causes white to lose its status as a color in its own right in the European context. By the middle of the seventeenth century, for both Renaissance artists and under Newton's new theories of light, white was no longer a true color; it is then situated outside of any system concerning color. By the time we arrive at Newton's work in the 1670s, it is possible for the scientist outright to say that "the most surprising and wonderful composition was that of Whiteness. There is no one sort of Rays which alone can exhibit this. 'Tis ever compounded, and to its composition are requisite all the afore- said primary Colours, mixed in a due proportion."[101] This view was not warmly received, but it instigated a major, radical shift in Western color perception. As Alan E. Shapiro notes, "For millennia it had been assumed that sunlight was pure, simple, and homogeneous. So much of Western religious and literary imagery used sunlight as a symbol of purity and simplicity, and the sun's radiance was virtually identified with the divine. Newton turned all this upside down with his claim that it was the colors that were simple and homogeneous, while the whiteness of sunlight was the most compound of all colors."[102] Hence, while whiteness still held connotations of religious purity and refinement, rather than remaining as absolute pure nothingness, white became everything and complex.[103]

However, the same shift does not happen simultaneously for black. Black remains a color for many decades after the transformation of white, and it is not until Newton's experiments with the prism that this changes.[104] These changes in physics, in which there then becomes no room for white or black on the color spectrum, break with all previous chromatic systems.[105] However, black, although often considered a noncolor, is still not deemed "colorless." This is why, in painting and dyeing, at the turn of the seventeenth and eighteenth century, gray remains a way of representing colorlessness. In some ways, gray is also eradicated from a conventional polychromatic color spectrum; there is a separate "white-gray-black scale."[106]

More accurately, black, in the color spectrum, should be considered an "achromatic color." As James Fox sets it out, the challenge is that color is used in two different ways. On the one hand, color refers to the total range of perceptual shades that might be used in, say, artistic composition. On the other hand, it refers to the varying wavelengths of visible light, which is called hue. Black, as Fox puts it, fulfills the first of these definitions but not the second. Black becomes a "color without hue."[107] While it may sound oxymoronic to speak of colorless colors, Alan Gilchrist puts it well when he says that while "every painter needs [these colors] on the palette," it would be considered fraudulent "if you tried to sell a black-and-white television set as a 'color' television."[108]

This complex cultural and ideological environment, which confers social and religious value on white and which sees a transformation in artistic and general color perception, is supplemented by a set of material circumstances. In earlier phases of European papermaking, there were no bleaches to remove dyes or discolorations. As mentioned above, this meant that the purest white paper could only be produced by selecting white fibers from linen.[109] It also added a scarcity when such whiteness was achieved.[110] However, in later European papermaking environments, colored papers still played key signifying roles. Notably, white was not the universal norm. As Müller charts it,

> The blue paper on which death sentences were issued in Syria and Egypt signified grief; court petitions were often written on red paper; and pure white was considered to be a challenge to the eye in Arab culture, so white paper was covered with as much writing as possible. In Europe, the blue paper mentioned in the statute of the city of Bologna in 1389 remained the only colored paper for a long time. . . . At the other end of the quality scale, the blue wrapping paper which resembled the paper used for file folders and packaging became the hallmark of the popular *Bibliothèque bleue* in seventeenth-century France, with its astrological almanacs, ghost stories, chivalric tales, and poems.[111]

Thus, the production of colored paper produced new signifying opportunities, signaling "social and aesthetic distinction."[112] That said, white paper was also put to a variety of uses beyond writing. For instance, as Helen Smith notes, some forms of "paper medicines" came about, in which the user was instructed to "take white Paper, and chawe it well with your teeth, and make thereof a plaister, as great as wil couer al the broke, binde it in a swadle band with a linnen clothe."[113]

Further, different nations had varying degrees of interest in the pure whiteness of paper. As Mark Kurlansky points out, "Jérôme de Lalande devoted several pages of his book to comparing French and Dutch paper. He highlighted several points in favor of the French: their paper was thinner and stronger and didn't tear as easily. But he finally concluded that Dutch paper was superior, for a variety of reasons: the Dutch weren't as obsessed with whiteness; they were more frugal and less obsessed with money; and they made their paper 'more slowly, more carefully, and with more precautions.'"[114]

Nonetheless, from the sixteenth century onward, the white page, or *weißes Blatt*, gradually became synonymous with emptiness. John Locke, for instance, was able to write in 1689 of how "white Paper" was "void of all Characters."[115] Further, in 1708, the bookbinder Johann Gottfried Zeidler recommended using sized white writing paper to interleave books, allowing for ease of retrospective revision. The list continues. Goethe writes of how he must fill the remaining "white paper" of *Faust*, and Leibniz traveled with his valued "white paper."[116] At a certain point in the European context, white paper becomes synonymous with a blank canvas onto which writers can inscribe.

The advent of bleaching in the 1770s was one of a series of technological changes in European production that tended toward this whitest of whites for paper, although the process was far from infallible. As the paper mulberry tree of China was not available, the European context required artificial whitening.[117] The use of chlorine for this purpose certainly gave a sheen to the sheets, but it also resulted in a brittle paper that could degrade much more quickly.[118] Just as brown rice is of higher nutritional value than its white cousin, the scarcity of and difficulty of producing the latter seems nonetheless to confer higher value on the white, but lower-quality, product.[119] The growing association of the purest white paper with ideas of the highest quality was such that, at various points after the Civil War, the price of white rags in the USA leaped to hyperinflationary rates.[120] In the British context, entrepreneurs also began seeking new raw materials to underpin paper production, moving away from the gendered use of rags, which were "usually collected by women."[121] This was a search that we now know eventually led to wood.[122]

The development of the coloration of paper also cannot be separated from the material histories of ink development. At their most basic, inks consist of two components: a colorant, which is an insoluble solid or a dye, and a liquid vehicle in which the colorant is suspended. Inks are, of course, of no use unless they will adhere to the substrate to which they are applied, hence the import of the underlying paper composition.[123] "Lampblack" inks, derived from the soot of controlled fires and known as "vegetable black," were the earliest to be discovered in multiple ancient civilizations.[124] Ink historians have found the carbon mixture of this black in remote antiquity in China, in use as early as 1300 BCE in Egypt, and also in ancient Greece.[125] Early inks, however, needed to distinguish between the substrates to which they were applied. For instance, as Tsien notes, lampblack and sepia inks were used to write on papyrus but could be washed away with a wet sponge. By contrast, a different ink, "made from galls by the ova of gall wasps," was used to write on parchment.[126]

Of note, the earliest character form for "ink" in ancient China (*mo* / 墨) refers to the punishment of tattooing the face. This is a model in which human skin is the substrate to which the ink is applied—of importance for our understanding of "white"-space with reference to race. After all, Zora Neale Hurston famously wrote, with sharp reference to both paper and societal norms, that she felt "most colored when . . . thrown against a sharp white background."[127] Nonetheless, in the Warring States period, starting around 475 BCE, the *Chuang tzu* refers to court scribes "licking their brushes and mixing their ink." Such an observation confirms that Chinese ink was stored in a solid form but also marks the transition of ink as a tool of punishment on human skin to a tool of writing on inscribable tablets and wooden boards.[128] These intermediate, prepaper substrates were hard and nonabsorbent. This *may* have led to the use of lacquer in early inks, in order to create a more adhesive substance, although this remains an unresolved scholarly controversy.[129]

While it took a long while for the global history of paper to embrace the extremes of white and black, early renowned Chinese inkmakers were praised for the depth of their blacks. For instance, Wei Tan's (179–253 CE) ink was described, in favorable terms, as extremely black. But early Chinese ink was not totally biased toward the black-white axis. There were formulas for red ink, which used red lead and the *Bletilla striata* plant; a blue ink that used indigo; and even an invisible ink known from the twelfth century CE onward.[130] In ancient Egypt, where the verbs denoting writing and painting were synonymous, inks on papyrus often used black for the main text with a red used to highlight headings and keywords.[131] As a result, some studies even go so far as to assert that black ink "is the established and time-honoured way in which human-kind commits words to writing," despite the long history of multicolored inscriptions.[132] The oldest known terms for writing inks in ancient Greek, for instance, include μέλαν (*mélan*, black) and μέλαν ὃ γράφομεν (*mélan ó gráfomen*, black for writing).[133]

By the Hellenistic and Roman periods, there are, certainly, multiple attestations of black ink manufacture. Carbon inks, mixed inks (that incorporate copper, iron, and lead), and gall inks are all well known from around 300 BCE.[134] Although in the European contexts, recipes for black ink only appear relatively late in proceedings, the blackness of ink manufacture is well documented.[135]

Importantly, though, ink color does not precisely determine the nature of the writing surface to which it is applied. Both the choice of ink and the choice of substrate are influenced by a large number of external social factors. Consider, for instance, the ancient Jewish laws around the ink used for divorce documents (the *get*) as opposed to other liturgical inks. The manufacture of ink for writing such a document has different conditions and prerequisites to that used for, say, writing the Torah. Indeed, the Talmud contains a substantial volume of information on ink production within particular religious contexts.[136] While a *get* can be written on any surface, the ink *must* be durable or persistent.[137] This stands in contrast to the characteristics of some early Greco-Roman inks, which were erasable with a damp cloth.[138] The desire for permanency, though, is a matter of the social function of the document, rather than any specific material requirement. The document must be permanent because it is a legal contract that changes the relationship between two people.

While the history of ink does interact with the histories of paper/substrate color and undoubtedly has some influence on and is influenced by their changes, a study of the history of ink and its properties and colors alone is insufficient to yield much new knowledge about how paper came to be white. Further, just because we know that early inks were black does not mean that paper was its "opposite," white, because the white-gray-black spectrum did not emerge until much later in the philosophy of color.

All of this is to say that the development of white paper is bound intrinsically to a set of historical and social determinants that have changed over time. Computational whitespace being called white has more to do with the association of whiteness with *emptiness* and *nothingness* than with the mimicry of specific paper coloration. In Thomas White's phrasing: "While the pure whiteness of writing surfaces is clearly instantiated in certain aspects of the medieval imagination, the material reality of such pages tells a somewhat different story."[139] As various philosophical shifts moved whiteness off the color spectrum and into its own category, even while religious discourses of purity influenced material paper production, whiteness and emptiness become synonymous.

This concept of "emptiness" has troubling political histories and ramifications in geopolitical and racial terms. Although emptiness, to the colonizer, "implies a total lack of content," as Courtney J. Campbell et al. put it, it quickly becomes clear, in retrospect, that nowhere "is truly devoid of everything."[140] Whether it be the displacement of Native Americans, the usurpation of Aboriginal Australians, or the expulsion of myriad other native peoples from their land, settler colonialism often predicates itself on the idea that spaces were empty and "there for the taking." It is the same discourse that plans for interstellar colonization, believing that, this time, new spaces in the final frontier will truly be empty. The truth, of course, is that such spaces were always already claimed. It is, therefore, perhaps unsurprising that the majority of scholarly work on "whitespace" leads to articles about colonial practices—the making of space, white.

Such a postcolonial or decolonial stance has been the main focus of discourses on whiteness in recent years. Stretching back to the foundational work of W. E. B. Du Bois in the nineteenth century, scholars have devoted exponential effort since the mid-twentieth century to studying the construction of whiteness and how its logics operate in racial terms.[141] Studies such as Theodore W. Allen's *Invention of the White Race* examine many of the same precepts that I have gestured toward here. Whiteness is *not* merely a blank space, even in textual/print-cultural terms. Witness, for instance, how in 1862 Thomas Wentworth Higginson exhorted contributors to the *Atlantic Monthly* to examine the "physical aspect of your manuscript" and to ensure that one uses "black ink" and, importantly, "nice white paper," part of the merging of "good writing and good (hand) writing" in the material sense that was present at the time.[142] The color symbolism of the paper and the care with which the black and "nice white" must interact cannot be read, in this context, as separate from racial concerns. Indeed, as Jennifer DeVere Brody points out, the fixation on this color scheme, of white backgrounds and black marks, invites attention to "the issue of the link (or leak) between black ink and embodied forms of blackness—of being black and black being."[143]

Whiteness, then, is not simply the default backdrop from which we must distinguish everything else, although that is how it has often been construed and how the discourse of "whitespace" tends to operate. Before this relativizing discourse, many white scholars tended to see whiteness as "a natural attribute rather than a social construct."[144] It is, then, a shame that the current ongoing culture wars have attempted to undo our understandings in this area, stoking raging debates that tend to be bitter given the high stakes that rest on the outcomes.[145] Yet this branch of scholarship shows whiteness as a social construction that must be questioned and interrogated. I have shown so far in this chapter that supposed material histories of white substrates can be subjected to the same sociocultural analysis and that this should inform our understanding of whitespace in the digital realm not as an abstract universal but as a relativized and socially produced background, constructed within moral, religious, and perceptual frameworks.

Display Unit Technologies

This history of paper's whiteness—and its cultural association with emptiness—does not answer all of the questions about computational whitespace because computer display monitors have not always used white as their default background color. To answer this monochromatic question, we must turn to the histories of visual display technologies and, especially, to the history of television. In the history of television, for instance, it is easy to forget how much resistance there was to the introduction of color TV and for how long monochrome displays dominated. As Susan Murray points out, "Color television was a hard sell." Deemed, in Murray's words, "impractical from the start," color in visual display technologies was considered "too expensive, technologically cumbersome, and challenging to stabilize and manage; it required too much bandwidth and would set a higher bar for 'true fidelity.'"[146] As one of the recurrent themes in this book, and as we saw with the development of PDF, in the nascent period of television's early development, color television appeared a pipe dream that was by no means a teleological certainty.

Television is usually studied, by humanities scholars, as a social phenomenon. There are entire journals—such as the *Historical Journal of Film, Radio and Television*—that are devoted to the historical study of audiovisual mass media, their reception, and their effects on society and politics. Hence, as Murray continues, television "is most commonly thought about in terms of the cultural narratives and ideologies it creates and engages with, rather than as a highly complex technology of visual culture."[147] As a result of this cultural, rather than technological, focus, engineers are the central historians of the technical development of television.

A first point to note is that television and motion pictures (cinema) are very different and distinct in their technological histories, which must influence our understanding of computer monitors. The playback of early cinema rested on optical-mechanical-chemical principles. That is, cinema relied on chemical methods to develop film strips and reels, which could then be projected and played back. By contrast, television required a new set of optical-electrical principles to enable simultaneous broadcast transmission and playback. Hence, while it took just six years for the laboratory experiments in cinematic film to become a fully operational commercial venture, television did not take off for almost half a century.[148]

That said, the systems used to create an illusion of motion in both cinema and television share similar but diverging technological histories. Structures of projected motion pictures relied on the threefold inventions of the magic lantern, the stroboscope, and photography.[149] The first of these was crucial for the projection systems of cinema.

The magic lantern was first developed in 1659 by Christiaan Huygens, although it is sometimes wrongfully ascribed to the Jesuit Father Athanasius Kircher.[150] The magic lantern was built on previous technologies, such as the *lanterne vive* (living lantern) of the Middle Ages. As Laurent Mannoni charts it, this more limited forerunner

> could only emit a coloured glow and did not allow true projection. A strip of translucent paper, on which were painted grotesque or devilish figures, was inserted into a cylinder of paper or decoratively pierced sheet metal. On top of the cylinder was placed a sort of propeller made of tin, which was free to rotate about an axis formed by an iron rod, and which secured the translucent drawing in place. A candle burned at the centre of the device. The heat given off by the candle caused the propeller to turn, rotating the painted strip so that the brightly coloured images travelled around the light at their centre. A viewer would see the pictures travelling round the cylinder, and projecting indistinct coloured images into the surroundings. If the cylinder was made of pierced metal, multi-coloured images could be made to dance on the surrounding walls.[151]

The crucial shift in the magic lantern, which took several centuries to develop, was the combination of a convex lens (to condense or concentrate the light onto the slide) and dual biconvex objective lenses used to transmit the projected image.[152]

Significantly for our understanding of photo-optics and whitespace, the early magic lanterns that would become cinema are based on light and projection. As Huygens claimed to his brother, Lodewijk, in 1662, "the most serious defect" of the lantern is "the length of the days, for as long as daylight lasts it is impossible to make these representations unless one places oneself inside a dark room."[153] The earliest systems of projected images depended upon a dark room with a white screen, upon which they shone a light. The blank space upon which magic lanterns project is white, the most reflective surface. However, the lantern required darkness so that ambient light was not competing with the projector's light source.

Of course, the slides themselves for the magic lantern must be the opposite—a negative—of that which they project. However, that opposite is not blackness but transparency. The enlargement of projection was, indeed, unforgiving against this transparent backdrop. As Mannoni notes, in this environment even "tiny smudges become huge smears and a clumsy design displays all its distressing mediocrity." Furthermore, the "transparency of colours is a problem: applying the paint too thickly, or with too much pigment, transforms the images into dark shadows." In other words, the slide medium proved a complex "blank" artistic space because of its transparency and the inversion of color schemes in the process of projection. In this way, the magic lantern worked on the opposite color principles of the earliest camera obscuras, which, in the 1640s, used a "white sheet of the screen" for their projected effects.[154]

Cinematic technology advanced further in the 1820s with the invention of the stroboscope. Inspired by Jan E. Purkinje's 1823 study of the subjective experience of "flicker," Peter M. Roget went on to describe his now-famous contentions about the "persistence of vision" that underlies the illusion of motion.[155] By combining the rapid yet discontinuous (strobing) projection of images, film yielded the impression of movement. Like their ancestor devices, various stroboscopes worked on differing principles of blackness, whiteness, and transparency. For instance, one early implementation of stroboscopic techniques, Joseph Plateau's "phénakisticope," employed a spinning cardboard disc, a slit, and mirrors to produce its optical illusion.[156] In this case, the images were painted or drawn onto a solid background media form. The slit itself introduced transparency. Hence, in this type of stroboscope, white or black (or any other color) backgrounds were possible.

The cylindrical variant of the phénakisticope, the zoetrope, works slightly differently and allows multiple viewers to perceive the illusion.[157] Suggested almost immediately by Simon Stampfer after the advent of stroboscopic principles, the zoetrope contains a ring of frames drawn on paper (or any other medium) that runs around the edge.[158] The strobing slits are carved higher on the device's rim. Again, there is no prescription in this model on the background color of the strip that contains the frames. The "whitespace" of the zoetrope and the phénakisticope can, in theory, be whatever color one wishes.

However, when stroboscopes transitioned to projection as a model, questions of background color and transparency were reintroduced. If the light is to be shone through a transparent slide and amplified onto a large screen, as in the front projection of cinema, then the slide needs a level of transparency. This transparency allows light to pass through. The light then reflects into viewers' eyes after it has struck the screen. Hence, the screen color should optimally be one with high reflectivity. For this reason, white or gray are the "best" colors for front-projection systems.

Television works on very different principles from projected cinema. First, television does not form images by projection through transparent slides. Instead, earlier forms of television used sets of rear-projection mechanisms such as cathode-ray tubes. Second, television converts live or prerecorded electrical transmissions into optical signals. Rather than having fixed material media such as slides through which we shine light, early televisions converted analog radio waves into visual representations. As such, televisual development followed the lineage of radio more closely than the photographic lineage of cinema. While television relied on the same principles of the persistence of vision in cinema, its projection systems used wholly different technologies. Despite the complex claims that television battled cinema for viewers' attention and that the two media competed as though interchangeable, the technologies of cinema and television are only tangentially related to one another.[159]

The core component of early television was the photoelectric effect, in which a charged screen transformed an optical image into a scanned electronic signal.[160] Later cathode-ray tube designs that crossed over into the computer monitor space used a phosphorescent/fluorescent screen.[161] The screen in such systems is composed of a lead glass front, to protect the viewer from x-rays, and a transparent glass envelope in which the phosphor is embedded and at which the electron beam is directed.[162] It is at this point in the development of display technologies that, at last, the substrate onto which a virtual page might be projected becomes transparent. When one looks into such a system, with a cavernous emptiness behind a transparent screen, the screen appears as black. This is because the darkness of the box behind is passed through by the transparent glass frontage. But there is, by this time, no "base" background color over which a virtual page is overlayed. Whitespace has become, finally, by this point in CRT development, transparent. That said, there is still no definitive reason why this transparent space of optical projection should be called white.

Structured Silence and Invisible Typography

Even if we do not know why whitespace is called whitespace, and even if the technological histories both of paper and display unit technologies offer little illumination, this "emptiness" has meaning and significance for digital text processing. As D. F. McKenzie famously notes, we can read blank spaces: "Even *blank* books are far from uninformative."[163] Such significance harks back, once more, to the paper era. Lothar Müller notes that in the world of the baroque letter, the "white space between the lines" became a symbolic representation that made "the social distance between the writer and addressee visible at a glance." In this system of writing, "fixed rules determined the distance to be maintained between people of higher and lower ranks, both within physical space and within this white space on the page."[164] As a result, significance and meaning accrue to the absence of visible characters as much as to the printed letter.

The most significant philosophical discourse surrounding blankness and its structures have orbited John Cage's infamous "silent" composition, *4'33"* (1952). These pieces generally draw extensive focus to the ontological status of the work, querying its "nature, meaning, and value."[165] The extent to which this piece has come to represent an entire field of *avant-garde* performance practice is such that the work appears to stand alone. However, in his canonical study of blank artworks, *No Medium* (2015), Craig Dworkin cites sixty-three examples of "empty" musical tracks, most of which were sold commercially at some point in their release cycles.[166] Cage is, in fact, just the most prominent representative of a whole genre of silence.

Of course, much of the discussion of 4'33" revolves around the fact that Cage's composition never produces total silence and instead contains incidental noise and sounds (like the specs of dirt in the transparent slides, mentioned above). Transposing this thought experiment across a range of media, Cage also wrote essays in which the formatting and layout of words on the page were determined by the not-quite-blankness of the empty pages: "Imperfections in the sheets of paper upon which I worked gave the position in space of the fragments of text."[167] In the musical version, while the performance instructions indicate that the players should not play their instruments, ambient noise contributes to a soundscape consisting entirely of accidental sounds.[168] It is also true that silence itself can be explicitly heard; it is not a passive mere absence. As Roy Sorensen puts it, a person with total hearing impairment cannot hear silence.[169] Nevertheless, the structure of Cage's silent piece is contoured and can be *read*, as can whitespace in textual contexts.[170] For instance, we should pay attention to the fact that Cage *notated* the work. Furthermore, different versions of the score notate the silence *differently*.

The visualization of Cage's silence is evident in the difference between the original manuscript of 4'33" and the later 4'33" (In Proportional Notation). As the Museum of Modern Art in New York, which holds a copy of the latter, puts it: "4'33" (In Proportional Notation) is one of three versions of the score for Cage's 'silent piece,' a musical composition first performed by the pianist David Tudor in Woodstock, New York, in 1952. While the lost original score used conventional musical notation to signify three periods of silence, this version is composed of a series of vertical lines that visually represent the duration of four minutes and thirty-three seconds of silence."[171] A third notated version (out of a total of five) uses the term *tacet* (it is silent) positioned below each movement. Over the manuscripts of 4'33", Cage scores silence in multiple ways. As Kyle Gann puts it, "The exact form of 4'33" is riddled with ambiguity: its notation changed twice, and the latitude of its performance directions, as described by its composer, has expanded over the decades."[172]

Further, Cage's composition is different from most sheet music in that he specifies the length of its (silent) playback in time rather than through a traditionally notated tempo marker (e.g., ♩ = 120 or similar). Hence, where usually one might expect to see a marker of crotchets per minute, for example, the total duration of 4′33″ is specified as the titular four minutes and thirty-three seconds. However, this length of time is not arbitrary and is, instead, derived from the conventions of 1940s Muzak (background music for retail). At that time, as Gann notes, Muzak "was broadcast from 78 rpm vinyl records; a ten-inch disc held about three minutes of music and a twelve-inch disc about four and a half, thus accounting for the potential timings of the Silent Prayer Cage wanted to write. The length 4′33″ itself owes something to the technology of the twelve inch 78 rpm record."[173] Significantly, then, Cage's silence was determined by the materiality of the 78-rpm record. There is a physical, material correlate that structures the timing of this seemingly blank work. A similar, yet reversed, assertion has formed a persistent rumor in the space of the compact disc, where it is claimed that the length of the CD was tailored to the classical tastes of a particular Japanese business executive in the 1980s.

However, not all "blank" space is always even blank. The most famous poetic example of this lies in the poetry of Emily Dickinson, who is famed for her use of dashes of various lengths throughout her oeuvre. Thomas Johnson was the first to recognize, in his editing of the variorum *Poems*, that Dickinson's marks were not uniform. Some slanted downward, some were curved like a circumflex, and they were usually of differing sizes. Importantly, although Johnson was attempting to surpass the regularization of Dickinson's "whitespace" seen in previous editions, he nonetheless hit the "limitations of print" in his efforts; Dickinson's blanks required handwriting.[174] Other critics have referred to Dickinson's diacritics as "unprintable."[175]

Despite the fact that Dickinson appears to elude (digital) print cultures, a substantial degree of effort has been put into developing whitespace characters in digital cultures. There are twenty-five characters in the Unicode specification that are defined as blanks/whitespace and a further six that have whitespace-like characteristics, shown in tables 1 and 2.

TABLE 1. Whitespace characters in Unicode

Name	Code Point	Width	Block	Notes
Character tabulation	U+0009	'	Basic Latin	
Line feed	U+000A		Basic Latin	
Line tabulation	U+000B		Basic Latin	
Form feed	U+000C		Basic Latin	
Carriage return	U+000D		Basic Latin	
Space	U+0020	' '	Basic Latin	
Next line	U+0085		Latin-1 Supplement	
No-break space	U+00A0	' '	Latin-1 Supplement	
Ogham space mark	U+1680	' '	Ogham	Used to separate words in Ogham text
En quad	U+2000	" "	General Punctuation	
Em quad	U+2001	" "	General Punctuation	Also known as "mutton quad"
En space	U+2002	" "	General Punctuation	Also known as "nut"
Em space	U+2003	" "	General Punctuation	Also known as "mutton"
Three-per-em space	U+2004	" "	General Punctuation	Also known as "thick space"
Four-per-em space	U+2005	' '	General Punctuation	Also known as "mid space"
Six-per-em space	U+2006	" "	General Punctuation	
Figure space	U+2007	" "	General Punctuation	Equal to the size of one numerical digit
Punctuation space	U+2008	" "	General Punctuation	As wide as the narrow punctuation in a font (e.g., the width of a period or comma)
Thin space	U+2009	" "	General Punctuation	
Hair space	U+200A	" "	General Punctuation	
Line separator	U+2028		General Punctuation	
Paragraph separator	U+2029		General Punctuation	
Narrow no-break space	U+202F	" "	General Punctuation	
Medium mathematical space	U+205F	" "	General Punctuation	Used in mathematical formulas
Ideographic space	U+3000	" "	CJK Symbols and Punctuation	As wide as a Chinese, Japanese, or Korean character

TABLE 2. Whitespace-like Unicode characters

Name	Code Point	Block	Notes
Mongolian vowel separator	U+180E	Mongolian	
Zero-width space	U+200B	General Punctuation	Indicates word boundaries when using scripts that do not have explicit spacing
Zero-width non-joiner	U+200C	General Punctuation	Causes characters that would otherwise be connected to be printed in their final and initial forms, respectively
Zero-width joiner	U+200D	General Punctuation	Causes characters that would otherwise not be connected to be printed in their connected forms.
Word joiner	U+2060	General Punctuation	
Zero-width non-breaking space	U+FEFF	Arabic Presentation Forms-B	

The Unicode specification is designed to supersede previous text-encoding systems such as the American Standard Code for Information Interchange (ASCII), allowing for a wide variety of character encodings from cultures worldwide—including different forms of whitespace. ASCII had a core deficiency. It was good at representing computationally only a single (and hegemonically dominant) cultural language: American English. However, American English is hardly representative of the worldwide linguistic and orthographic diversity that should be handled within computing systems. This is where Unicode comes in. It is a format designed to allow for the encoding of all the world's languages, giving computing systems a true cultural interoperability.[176] Unicode groups its characters into thirty categories, which determine whether the character in question is a letter, a number, a symbol, or whitespace.[177] While often only the most basic whitespace characters end up in widespread use—James Mission, for instance, charts how whitespace in an original manuscript is reduced in EEBO-TCP XML to "the single Unicode character called 'SPACE'"—the specification allows us to represent so much more than this reductive flattening.[178]

Computational whitespace, though, incorporates more than mimesis of print typesetting. In addition to the above codes, Unicode (as just one standard) includes a large number of "control codes" that alter the flow and status of text. For instance, the Unicode marker at U+200E is the left-to-right mark and that at U+200F is the right-to-left mark. Used in Arabic, Persian, and Hebrew, as opposed to, say, English, these control characters reverse the directionality of subsequent text. The Unicode standard provides the Unicode bidirectional algorithm to specify precisely how these particular characters work, but suffice it to say that

    'this'

and

    'siht'

are actually identical; the only difference is that the latter is encoded with a right-to-left override mark at the start and a left-to-right override mark at the end.

The critical point here is that computational whitespace characters, in the Unicode format, at least, have *control functions*. In this sense, they should be considered more akin to illocutionary speech acts. In analogy to the well-known philosophy of J. L. Austin, we might consider the above table of whitespace characters to be locutionary; they express a mimetic parallel to conventional type. However, control characters express an action. They are what Austin would call "performative" utterances: speech acts that make something happen.[179]

The classification of illocutionary acts was further refined by John Searle in a 1975 piece. Here, Searle decomposed speech acts into representatives, directives, commissives, expressives, and declarations.[180] By way of brief summary, representatives commit the speaker to the truth of the expressed proposition. Directives are attempts to commit the recipient to a course of action ("I insist that you attend"). Commissives (taken from Austin) commit the speaker to a future point of action. Expressives denote (or, express) the performance of an internal mental state whose truth/sincerity must be presupposed. And declarations unite a real-world scenario with linguistic content ("I declare war").

Under which categories of speech acts might we understand Unicode control characters? They do *not* seem to be representatives or expressives. However, the other categories are debatable, depending on the interpretative perspective that one takes. For instance, to type these characters is to direct the word processor to a course of action: it is to commit the textual editor to a path. That said, given that the control characters usually form part of a personally expressive outpouring, there is also a commissive element. If I type the right-to-left override character, I commit *my* future writing to a reversed direction. Finally, in typing this character, there is a declarative aspect; the act of committing the character to the page also makes it so.

In these senses, then, the user of the word processor acts across a range of registers, with a set of differing characteristics of ownership and receivership. At the time of typing, the expressive act is one where the words are owned by the writer. There is an ongoing process of communication. Insertion of control characters into the writing at this point becomes a commitment of self-expression in a certain form. In another way, though, the user is also a type of computer programmer, issuing instructions to the machine. To ask the computer to switch the directionality of text is, at the same time, a directive *to* the software. There is an element of imperative communication between a user and the machine in this model in which the invisible control characters serve as commands. Finally, there is the reinterpretation of the byte stream for display to *other* users or to one's future self. The machine must retranslate the command sequences in order to format text in the way that is desired so that it can be shown to other users. That is, at a certain point, the machine retranslates the instructions back into a formatting outcome for a reader, who may or may not be the original author. As a result, the temporality and communicative directionalities of control characters unfold across a set of different domains, at different points in the communication life cycle.

While the left-to-right and right-to-left override characters are probably not used in most people's everyday writing—after all, relatively few people resort to interlingual code-switching unless they are a translator—other control-character-like mechanisms are extremely familiar to all word processing users. Consider, for instance, the use of **bold** and *italics*. There are several ways in which these character stylings can be encoded in word processing software, the most common of which are markup languages and control characters.

In Microsoft's Rich Text Format specification, for instance, the invisible control character/sequence "\b" (encoded in the file itself) enables bold for subsequent text, while "\b0" signals the end of a run of bold. In more recent formats, the XML formulation of "<w:B>text</w:B>" is used to denote, behind the scenes, that the word "text" should be emboldened. Word processing users are very much accustomed to the idea that there are invisible control sequence characters that will determine their subsequent typing, but also that formatting can be applied, en bloc, to a chunk of text.

These models of markup actually demonstrate two further, different attitudes toward the way that word processing unfolds and how users understand control-code alternation. In treating bold, italics, and other formatting as a *switch*, one that is toggled, users understand that their future typing will be affected by the formatting shift. In this sense, again, the control character acts as a commissive: the user is committed to typing in bold until the terminal/reciprocal control code is issued. At the time of typing and user input, control codes function in an on-off, commissive fashion. However, it is also true that such a model is *directive*, as the command is issued to the word processor and commits it to a form of action. The boldness is implemented by the software, at the direction of the user.

While, in some senses, the XML markup version is no different—it contains opening and closing delimiters that mark the boundaries of the formatting—the encapsulation with identical markers, merely separated by a single "/," changes the logical relationship to formatting. Because XML requires a start and end tag always to be present (that is, when one is writing, the word processor will always have appended the </w:B> tag behind the scenes, even if you are not finished typing), formatting in this mode is applied to a block of text. In other words, the markup formatting appears nonlinear and to be received in one single block, whereas the control-code switching seems linear and processual.

Another example of this dual temporality of control characters lies in the ability of most modern word processors to paste with source formatting, to match the destination formatting, or to strip away forms of formatting, leaving only plaintext.[181] The psychology of such an operation is that a user must know the current formatting state of the destination paste space and the source copy space and then understand the consequences of merging the two. This seems more akin to the second, markup-style mechanism, instead of the linear, unfolding commissive approach. The paste operation itself feels to be a directive, again; it is a command to the processor to match the formatting (or not).

This type of "command-driven" approach sits strangely within the progressive development of computer programming *languages*. Programming languages can be roughly divided into declarative and imperative coding styles. In declarative programming, the programmer expresses the state of the model that they wish to describe, rather than the control flow of the operation. For instance, the regular expression "^hello$," which matches the text string "hello" as the sole content of a line, does not instruct the machine as to how to conduct the match (although a regex engine does possess a directionality in its matching process) but instead specifies the conditions under which the system should operate on its input. By contrast, an imperative programming language is one in which the programmer gives commands, in sequence, to a computer that include branching and decision-making to change the internal state. For instance, the following pseudocode is imperative:

```
if input == 'hello' {
print('Input is "hello."')
}
```

In declarative programming, the user issues conditions. In imperative programming, the user issues commands.

The idea of relating programming to *languages* only really came about in the later part of the 1950s.[182] As Nofre et al. put it, "At the beginning of the decade, programmers had to express the instructions for solving a problem in obscure numerical codes that were different for each machine. By the decade's end, however, they could write programs that included familiar mathematical formulas, and, in some cases, even expect the same program to run on different machines, thanks to the development of systems like FORTRAN and IT."[183] Over this period, the shift was from thinking of programming as a technical, electronic activity to thinking of it as a *linguistic* activity.

Of course, programming languages are *not* languages in many formal human senses. Yet there have been attempts, as far back as the eighteenth century, to transform algebraic notation into a universal language.[184] Indeed, as Roger Chartier has it, "the electronic text re-introduces into writing an element of the formal languages that, beginning in the eighteenth century, or even the seventeenth, sought a symbolic language capable of adequately representing different processes and registers of thought."[185] At the same time, of course, a curious feature is that the "universal" language of programming has, for the most part, only more thoroughly inscribed a practice based on *English* at the center. Most programming languages are Latin in their alphabet and English in their syntax. While there has been a wave of African programming languages that attempt to undo this legacy of colonialism,[186] which I explore more thoroughly in the next chapter, there is nonetheless "a reinforcement in the United States of the belief in an unshared hegemony of the English language and thus the implication that it is unnecessary to learn other languages," as Chartier puts it.[187]

Nonetheless, it is my contention that word processing users have absorbed a set of the characteristics and understandings of computer programming in their practices, especially when it comes to whitespace and control characters. This internalization can best be seen by comparison to the previous era of mechanical typewriting (a period that, in fact, has now lasted less time than the computational word processor). In the world of mechanical typewriting, a bold effect could be achieved by overtyping the sentence again or by pressing the mechanical key with more force; an aspect famously commented upon in Friedrich Kittler's well-known study of the typewriter.[188] The inscription was literally one with greater imprint on the paper. The difference in the electronic environment is that there is no control character at work in this system that forces a machine *interpretation* upon subsequent or wrapped text. Instead, there is an immutable impression on the page.

This is not to say that manual typewriters did not have control functions. The carriage return key or lever would return the typewriter's position to the start of the line. Another key would alter the casing used for output. The space bar would, of course, advance the cartridge without printing any character onto the substrate sheet. It is this delegation of *control* to the typist/author that led Marshall McLuhan to write, in 1964, that "the typewriter fuses composition and publication, causing an entirely new attitude to the written and printed word."[189] My contention here is that the word processor fuses composition, publication, and programming.

This new attitude heralded by McLuhan is one that Kittler also takes from Nietzsche: the idea that "our writing tools are also working on our thoughts."[190] This is, in some ways, a technological form of the doctrine known as in linguistics as the Sapir–Whorf hypothesis. Also known as the linguistic relativity thesis, the hypothesis posits that the language that one speaks determines, either strongly or weakly, the thoughts that one may have.[191] The hypothesis has gained widespread social notoriety, particularly for the fact that the strong form of the conjecture appears to be false. (That is, it appears to be untrue that language *determines* thought, but there is some evidence that language can *influence* thought.)[192] Nonetheless, prominent science fictional narratives, such as Ted Chiang's 1998 "Story of Your Life," transformed into the major motion picture *Arrival* in 2016, have used the hypothesis as their premise. In this novel and film, acquisition of the language of the alien heptapods allows the speaker access to a nonlinear model of thought and time, reminiscent of the Tralfamadorians in Kurt Vonnegut's *Slaughterhouse-Five, or The Children's Crusade: A Duty-Dance with Death* (1969).[193]

The translation of the Sapir–Whorf hypothesis into technological determinism around writing—that the tools with which we write determine what and how we can express, and therefore think—is not quite the same as the original contention that language conditions our thought, but there is a parallel. McLuhan, Kittler, and to some extent Kirschenbaum show that the media technologies through which we express ourselves may have some bearing upon what we can express and how it is received. If they did not, then the entire premise of (digital) media studies as a discipline would be somewhat flawed. Nonetheless, as Kittler goes on to note, in the typewriter are fused three moments of writing: "the equipment, the thing, and the agent."[194] Importantly, the Sapir–Whorf hypothesis formed a key lynchpin in the consideration of early computer interface designers. Thinkers such as Douglas Engelbart saw, in Thierry Bardini's appraisal, the computer as a "language machine" acting as a "boundary-spanning object" that was analogous to the human body.[195]

Despite a lineage between the two, the typewriter and the word processor function very differently with respect to these collapsed temporalities. The typewriter, while possessing control characters/keys, did not replay its actions in order to reconstitute the original typed sequence. The output of the typewriter was set in type upon the paper, fixed *at the moment of impression* by the typist. Until the advent of electric typewriters such as the Friden Flexowriter and the IBM Selectric typewriter, that is, most typewriters were not player pianos.

The electric typewriter began to change this. These machines had external drive capacity that could be fed either from a direct computer link or from a punched-card input. The novelty here was that, for the first time, as the Selectric's inventors note, "with this machine the author can, if he chooses to do so, again write his own book without the assistance of specialists."[196] This new breed of typewriter viewed keystrokes—whether directly from a user or from a prestored medium, such as tape or card—as a series of *commands* to be reenacted rather than as a purely mechanical process. The input, regardless of its source, was a series of imperative remarks rather than declarative typesetting instructions. "Toggle bold on" via a control character becomes a sensible proposition at this point in the electric typewriter's development.

The earliest seeds for this idea were actually found in the 1940s in pneumatic systems. In the American Typewriter Company of Chicago's Auto-typist, a binary system translated from holes in punched cards to mechanical strikes using air-valve slots: "The perforated master roll passes over air-valve slots. Each perforation permits air to escape from a particular slot, thus opening a valve. Each valve is connected by a tiny hose to a bellows, and each bellows is attached to a key. As the valves open, the bellows operates and the typebars are snapped up against the paper. The bellows-to-key arrangement is suitable for use with any make of manual or electric typewriter. The speed of the Auto-typist mechanism can be adjusted to operate any typewriter at the highest speed at which the typewriter is capable of being run."[197]

The advantages of this new system, which allowed for reproduction and repeated keystrokes, were billed not just in technological terms but also in light of the labor transformation that it effected. With traces of the well-known gendered division of typing labor, the document notes that "an experienced operator has little difficulty in keeping four machines running at once. Consequently, she earns a secretarial salary rather than a typist's salary, because she can produce as much correspondence as might be produced by a half dozen manual typists."[198] The curious point here is that the marketing spiel promises increased remuneration for a single technological operator rather than mentioning the implied labor cost savings for organizations more broadly in reducing the number of manual typists that they employed.

The critical historical link for understanding the birth space of the word processor, as I have already hinted, is the piano. The piano's linguistic development of a register of notes, labeled A–G (with an additional H in the German note-name system), even provides the shared input technology between pianos and typewriters: the keyboard. Ivan Raykoff writes that "in the early nineteenth century, the piano keyboard provided both a conceptual and a practical model for new communication devices such as the typewriter and the telegraph."[199] Edward Tenner notes, with musical emphasis, that "as producers of text, keyboards transmit intimate messages once reserved for voice or pen."[200]

As Raykoff goes on to illuminate, the piano is both a binary and analog system. It is binary in that keys are divided into discrete harmonic notes. Yet it is also analog in that, since the supersession of the harpsichord, keypresses can be defined along a spectrum of types of pressing. It is not the case that a note on the piano is either struck on or off, with no variance between the type of impression made by the player.[201] Yet the musical keyboard led to the development of the first writing keyboards in the 1840s. For instance, Pierre Leroux devised the "pianotype," a device for writing with a musical-style keyboard.[202] Meanwhile, also from the 1840s, Young and Delcambre's Type-Composing Machine presented a keyboard operation that was operated by seven people in harmony in order to record its words: "One to play the keys, another to justify, a third to work the eccentric movement, two to supply the channels, and two to distribute." This worrying proliferation of typing labor, however, should not cause us too much fear, we are told, because, thankfully, "two are females and five very young boys."[203] Further examples include the "pianoforte resemblance" of Rosenberg's Type-Composing and Distributing Machines, documented in 1842; the 1838 "tachygraphe" by Antoine Dujardin; a device from 1859 designed by Adolphe Charles Guillemot; Charles Wheatstone's 1851 typewriters; Antonio Michela's 1862 "stenograph," a shorthand machine with two keyboards of ten piano keys; Pierre Foucault's 1851 *clavier imprimeur* (imprinting keyboard); and Giuseppe Ravizza's 1855 *cembalo scrivano* (writing harpsichord).[204] Musical-style playback and control dominated early keyboard-based text processing.

While typesetting unions opposed the development of these machines, fearing for the viability of their workforce, the musicality of the lineage here is striking.[205] Nonetheless, from these seeds grew the trees of the typewriters in the late 1860s, originally because the speed of typing was thought to be able significantly to outpace writing by hand.[206] The familiar, but mythical, story, though, is that the QWERTY keyboard style that was introduced just a short time thereafter was precisely designed to do the opposite: to slow the typist down and to avoid mechanical jamming.[207] However, in reality, this is not the case. Many frequent letters in the English language, for example, sit adjacent to one another in the QWERTY setup. With E and R, for instance, the letters of the second most common letter pairing are right next to one another. This belies the idea that the keys were spread so as to avoid common letters being hit too frequently at too high a speed (and thereby jamming). Statistical analysis has shown, in fact, that QWERTY keyboards actually have more close pairs than a randomly arranged keyboard.[208] Instead, as Jan Noyes put it, "there appears . . . to be no obvious reason for the placement of letters in the QWERTY layout, and doubts concerning its origin still remain."[209]

The origin of the contemporary keyboard layout remains hazy, but it is clear that the earliest keyboards owed a debt in both name and layout to musical contexts, to which the keyboard always alludes.[210] Given this lineage, it is perhaps unsurprising that aspects of the player piano found their way into the systems of technological playback—another instance of what Don Ihde calls "technological multistability," indicating the way that technologies spur a variety of uses that sit apart from the original intentions.[211] Yet the player piano was not, as Thomas W. Patteson cautions, one single invention with one single lineage.[212] Perhaps the most important historical determinant for the case in question, though, is the distinction between programmable and preset automatic instruments that preceded the player piano.

The earliest mechanical instruments, dating back at least to the first century AD, were fixed in their playback.[213] The music that they could produce was determined at the time of production rather than by reading any subsequent programmable media. As Teun Koetsier documents, the earliest *programmable* machine known to us was a ninth-century automatic flute player, designed in Baghdad and called, perhaps somewhat bluntly, the Instrument that Plays Itself.[214] In this setup, which used a pinwheel on a rotating drum to open or close the various holes on the flute, there is a parallel between software and hardware that will emerge in later computational systems.

The development of this early system into the player piano, with a divide between hardware that "reads" a set of abstracted software instructions not known before operation, introduces an important distinction, though, between notation and phonography. Early court cases around 1908 in the United States ruled that the piano roll of the player piano would not incur the need for royalty fees to composers because, the court claimed, piano rolls were not "a written or printed record in intelligible notation."[215] As Lisa Gitelman charts it, the court in this case ruled that "phonograph records were not notational records, and air holes could not be symbols."[216] Yet there is a curious distinction to be made here between the operation of the phonograph, which mimeti-

cally records the shape of a sound wave into a groove, and the operation
of a player piano, which records the playback of key strikes. This is similar to the operations that Kirschenbaum undertakes when he performs
his readings of the marks on a hard disk drive.[217] There is an unusual
system of legibility and inscription at work in such a structure, in which
writing and reading become so intermediated as to make the operation
impossible without the intervening hardware. For the specific hardwares in question, the media are far from notational. The inversion of
the conventional reading of lyrics in the piano player's structures, in
which lyrics had to be read from bottom to top, is just another example
of how "reading" becomes inverted.[218]

The development of the computer keyboard also did not progress in
a straightforward, linear fashion. It was not as though one phase ended
and another cleanly began but, instead, that different types of computer
keyboards overlapped with one another. As Mark Seltzer has put it,
"The typewriter . . . pressures that fantasy of continuous [historical]
transition."[219] For instance, the idea of a musical-style, single-handed
"chord" keyboard persisted, thanks to the ongoing efforts of Douglas
Engelbart, and over and above the objections of his funder, Joseph Lick-
lider, well beyond the domination phase of the QWERTY keyboard.[220]
The idea behind this device was that one could encode any character
by playing a "chord" rather than pressing just a single key at a time.
Hence, perhaps, a C minor chord might (as a fictional example) result
in the letter *H* appearing. The five-bit code of this keyboard, when used
by a skilled operator, required only a single hand to operate and could
give substantial speed advantages over the double-handed, QWERTY
approach.[221]

A much older technology than QWERTY, the chord keyboard,
though, was out of step with the uptake of typewriting.[222] In particular, as Bardini highlights, "typewriting was in accord with existing
practices that made telegraphers efficient—especially in terms of their
ability to input text without looking at their input device."[223] Center-
ing the feedback loop off-stage—decoupling the hand and eye—was
key here, but it was also something that typewriters had been doing
for decades by this point, with the marks on the paper appearing dis-

tantly from the keypresses themselves.[224] Certainly, the chord-board also had this characteristic of resituated output, but the learning cliff, rather than curve, that it presented to the user already familiar with the QWERTY keyboard proved insurmountable. Nobody wanted to learn a new system of musical-esque chord inputs when they had already invested so much in learning how to type on a QWERTY keyboard. The activation energy to start afresh—and the opportunity costs of investment in learning a new system—were too great.

The takeaway point is that technologies are not selected because they are the best or the most efficient. They are certainly not chosen because they have the ability to teach the user how to do things better and more efficiently over time. They are instead determined by a set of social regularities and normative incorporated practices that build a path dependency, but also by the "ad hoc" contingencies of historical development.[225] In Paul A. David's account, QWERTY became dominant because of its technical interrelatedness, economies of scale, and a quasi-irreversibility of time investment.[226] By the time that Engelbart tried to reinscribe the chord keyset in computing systems, then, it was too late. By that point, use of the typewriter and QWERTY keyboard had been "encoded into bodily memory by repeated performance"; they had typewritten themselves into our bodies and brains but also, as a consequence, into permanent text-input peripheral status.[227]

In Gitelman's appraisal, what is often lost in this well-known history of the player piano is the *question* of indexicality. That is, does the writing and reading of punched cards correspond, on a one-to-one basis, with the playback of musical notes? Or, as Gitelman frames it, "did the perforations have an indexical (one-to-one mapping) relation to musical notes, or were they just an arbitrary machine code?"[228] Perhaps most pertinent for my reading here is the fact that, as I have already noted, in the punched-card systems of both the player piano and binary computing systems, it is significant that "holes . . . suggested musical notes" and *not* their absence.[229] The structure of early binary was that space was the solidity of paper, not the actual absence (true space).

Whitespace Is the History of Serial Silence

The term "whitespace" is often used to denote the substrate that sits below a printed page. In such a thought model, the idea is that the page appears to the reader, in toto, fully formed. The page arises as a surface onto which words may statically be printed and the basis for space is *absence*. It is assumed that digital pages work in the same way.

In reality, though, digital space is read sequentially from software files on disk, with instructions and control characters determining the extent of the subsurface space. Just as visual display units "scanned" from top left to bottom right, digital page construction is read from an underlying *stream* of bytes. Within this stream, Unicode control characters specify different lengths of space and even the directionality of text, encoding instructions for playback in hidden structures within file formats that are inaccessible to the human eye, readable only by machines. Reconstructing a digital document from a file format is not a case of loading the stored image in any mimetic form from disk, akin to a phonographic representation of a waveform. Instead, it is more akin to the punched card of the (nonetheless overstudied) player piano. A series of instructions are read back from the storage medium, and the software replays them, dynamically, in order to recreate the document artifact. Of course, it is not that the word processor strikes the keys; there is no mechanical component in such a recreation (although there *was* in the era of electromechanical typewriters). Instead, the dynamic playback and reconstruction takes place algorithmically in computer memory.

This phenomenon is what Kirschenbaum has referred to as a "bit-stream," which denotes "a contiguous sequence of bits for storage or transmission." Importantly, though, Kirschenbaum also notes that the term is also synonymously referred to, in digital preservation circles, by the word "image."[230] (An example would be a "hard-drive image," which denotes a complete copy of the data found on that hard drive.) These two language registers are significantly different, though. An image presents itself as a whole and complete surface that rises to our apprehension at once, simultaneously (even when digital screens construct such images in sequence, pixel-by-pixel from top left to bottom right). Most images are distinctly not contiguous sequences that we perceive in the same way as, say, left-to-right text in reading. Yet despite the fact that digital preservation experts use these terms of image and bitstream interchangeably, the distinction that I am drawing is precisely between sequentiality and simultaneity. Computer systems create simultaneous page images—including their blank space—by sequentially reading back and "replaying" the instruction set that recreates the image. This is a sort of doubled temporality of computational media of the type that Wendy Hui Kyong Chun documents, in which our digital forms "race simultaneously toward the future and the past."[231]

What does all this mean for the history of paper and background color that dominated so much of this chapter? In some ways, it is irrelevant. The contemporary document loader does not think in terms of a white canvas with pre-inscribed inks. Instead, it serially plays back instructions for opacity or blankness from the stored file. Yet, at the same time, the history of the chromoclasm and an understanding of the orientation toward a white-gray-black color spectrum has influenced the ways that we consider "whiteness" to be equatable with "blankness."

Likewise, visual display technologies clearly play a role in how we understand the "blank" substrate. It was the very fact that early computer monitors did not have a "white" background that prompted this entire investigation into the term "whitespace." Yet this was a red herring. The determinants of space as "white" are much longer in their histories than the relatively swift emergence of CRT technologies in the twentieth century and, as I have sought to show, there are other stronger lineages for thinking about the history of whitespace.

In all, though, my metaphorical thinking reaches a strange endpoint for understanding whitespace. The dynamic, serial reproduction of space using control characters reveals itself as a *temporal* imperative art. The recreation of whitespace unfolds as an active "reprinting" on every iteration that loads the document. In this sense, the recreation of whitespace is more akin to the playback of recorded music, in the form of the player piano's rolls rather than in the form of the phonograph's etched waveform. The history, then, of digital whitespace is the seriality of musical silence.[232]

FOUR

DIGITAL TEXT IS GEOPOLITICALLY STRUCTURED

WHAT COULD BE LESS POLITICAL than the computational design of typography? It turns out: quite a lot, particularly when we deal with various forms of ASCII art that emerged from the DemoScenes of the 1980s and 1990s. The DemoScene, which emerged in Europe in the 1980s, "is a technically oriented community" that makes "demos that showcase the programming and artistic skills of their creators. Simply put, a demo is a computer program that displays a series of real-time visual effects combined with a soundtrack."[1] Alongside these demos, groups also release so-called NFO files (which contain "iNFOrmation" about the release).[2]

The NFO files produced by these groups are written in a format that takes advantage of particular typographic features in order to render a type of concrete poetic outline. Figure 1, for example, is composed entirely of textual characters. This is not a drawing using Photoshop or any other imaging program. All of the visual effect is created by using different textual elements, although it does rely on specific block char-

FIGURE 1. ASCII art by SkiA

acters in the Unicode spectrum to produce different shading effects. There is, though, a history of computational colonialism at work in this double-layered process of making art from text. For the characters that translate into ASCII art "blocks" when used in an appropriate font are all drawn from the non-English alphabet. That is, the blocks appear when using characters from outside the Latin alphabet, when the font has not bothered to create encodings for these glyphs.

This fourth chapter dismantles the assumption that digital typography and font design are "just letters." It thus explores the way in which a linguistic colonialism has emerged in the development of typography through an analysis of the Unicode implementation.[3] This has been an ongoing problem for several decades now. For example, in 2007, K.

David Harrison and Gregory Anderson noted in a letter to the Unicode consortium:

> The current Unicode proposal (authored by Michael Everson, dated 1999-01-29) is incomplete in its current form and notably requires consultation and fact-checking with the user community. While it is crucial that the Ho orthography be included in Unicode, this can only be done in close consultation with Ho scholars at every step of the process. As a practical and ethical matter, we urge the Unicode consortium to accept only proposals that emerge from or are formulated in close consultation with native speaker communities. To do otherwise is to espouse a kind of linguistic colonialism that will only widen the digital divide.[4]

Indeed, one of the basic premises seen in the Unicode specification is that English-language Latinate characters are the first to appear in the table, while other linguistic systems are often relegated to much higher assignations. Sometimes, as Sharjeel Imam points out, these "other" languages are spread across many different blocks rather than appearing in the more concentrated forms of the Latin alphabet.[5] Digital "internationalization," then, means a sequential spread outward from English to other cultures, demonstrating a strong Anglocentrism. As Don Osborn puts it, for example, "Apart from Arabic, the development of the use of African languages in computing and the internet has been relatively slow for a number of linguistic, educational, policy and technical reasons," and "a particular problem for a number of languages written with modified letters or diacritic characters—or entire alphabets—beyond the basic Latin alphabet (the 26 letters used in English) or the ASCII character set (that alphabet plus basic symbols) has been the way in which computer systems and software handle these."[6] As "an industrial standard controlled by the industry," in Domenico Fiormonte's words, we should be skeptical about "claims about the neutrality or impartiality of" Unicode—the subject of this chapter.[7] At the same time, such a pronouncement is not, perhaps, so surprising. As Bernhard Rieder has framed it, following Gilbert Simondon,

"The technical object sits between the natural and the technical world and, through it, each world acts on the other."[8] Our technical historical biases mirror the extratechnical social biases of the world.

It is often easy to assume that the history of Unicode—and other technical standards or elements (in this chapter I also examine the nationalistic implications of so-called autonomous systems and the distributed "governance" of blockchains)—are simple to research. After all, the specification exists in different versioned editions that correspond to the time of release. What could be easier than simply to trace back through this version history and to dig out what one needs to know at any particular point?

The truth is actually somewhat different, though. Take, for instance, the character "⅃." This character is known as "right angle with downwards zigzag arrow," and Jonathan Chan has extensively sought its origin, to no avail. As Chan has traced it, the character originates in the "Proposal for Encoding Additional Mathematical Symbols in the BMP (N2191)," which was released on March 14, 2000. The symbol had its beginnings in the so-called STIX project, which was concerned with "Scientific and Technical Information Exchange" (although there is also an unrelated project concerned with "Structured Threat Information Expression," an XML language that specializes in describing cybersecurity threats).[9] But nobody actually now knows what the symbol is for or what it is supposed to represent. The symbol also originally featured in an earlier "International Glyph Register," which no longer exists.[10] As Chan puts it, though, even if this could be located, "it likely merely contains another table with the glyph, the identifier, and the short description."[11] In Chan's hunt, he even had a reply from Barbara Beeton, a prominent figure at the American Mathematical Society and the TeX layout/typesetting project who said that she "had no idea what the symbol meant or was used for."[12] My own brief online conversation with the Fields Medal–winning mathematician Timothy Gowers revealed that it was no form of mathematical notation known to him, "although it somewhat resembles a mark some people put at the end of a proof by contradiction."[13] As such, in Chan's words, "the meaning of ⅃ will be whatever meaning is assigned by whoever uses it next . . .

if anyone uses it at all," which may be true, but is also probably true of any linguistic sign.[14]

More broadly, this quest to uncover the meaning and origins of a "mathematical" symbol only goes to show that, in fact, digital-textual history is not straightforward, even when all the sources are available. We have a good documentation trail of where this symbol came from. However, at a certain point in the history, the trail of *meaning* runs cold. When the originator who transferred the glyph across confesses that she didn't know the meaning at the time, it becomes clear that the history is only going to take us so far. This murky background also raises some important questions about standardization and the actions of those who encode such standards. If the people working on standards do not fully understand the standards they are creating, what do we lose in the process? Is U+237C, the character in question, some form of prank joke from the past, now destined forever to be preserved because nobody knows what it means? When textual encoding standards do not make clear the function of the characters that they provide, they certainly make the standard more flexible. However, they also then open the door to the possibility of senseless encodings that become lost to time.

It is also the case that Unicode *does* provide a way of describing the uses to which its characters are put. It is simply that the descriptions are often not very good. It is also true that localizations may play a role in how meaning is described in Unicode. Another Stack Overflow (a tech-support community forum) respondent, "Aart," claimed that this mystery glyph "indicates an Y-axis which continues further below the X-axis starting in the corner" and that although they didn't "have any ref materials," it was apparently "still standard lay-out in our Dutch economy schoolbooks, in the 90's."[15] That is to say that there can be specific local knowledges that are beyond the bounds of the internet to describe. Indeed, because open educational resources were not common in the 1990s, a simple search engine hunt for the glyph returns no results, beyond the controversy of this specific historical debate. On the other hand, living individuals may know of local specifics that are not available digitally. Even though this is a *digital* and *global* historical matter, it is one rooted in analog and localized knowledges.

This history of a single code point in Unicode serves, then, as a constructive lesson on the limits of digital history. To believe that we have cemented future meaning due to open standards and versioning is clearly a misplaced faith, unless the people who are encoding the standards ensure, constantly, that there is enough widespread and shared cultural knowledge of the use to which the code points are put (and a persistent way to access this). Like the world's endangered languages of Parji and Zenatiya, we can often be left with digital traces and pointers, lacking real-world extant references, and with a self-perpetuating set of standards that do not understand that which they propagate. Without the real-world context, no degree of digital archival standardization will help us to understand digital-textual material history.

Studying Digital Infrastructures

In order to grasp the correlations between font and character-point development and geopolitical structures, we must first comprehend how such correlations of classification became buried or hidden in the first place. Among the best works to give a framework for thinking about classification in the age of digital infrastructure are Geoffrey C. Bowker and Susan Leigh Star's *Sorting Things Out* and Star's "The Ethnography of Infrastructure."

Beginning with the latter, Star starts with a humorous note, namely that infrastructure is mundane. Her article is, therefore, "a call to study boring things."[16] The first examples that Star gives of such "boring things" are the International Classification of Diseases (ICD) and the telephone book. Star claims that the latter is potentially more interesting (and less "boring"); a telephone book tells you a great deal about the demographics of an area through how businesses present themselves, restaurant listings, surnames, etc. Yet this is potentially disingenuous. ICD is also important and interesting because it shows precisely what is considered a disease/illness and what is thought outside of that purview. It is a map of an era's pathologies. Given the degree of controversy around medical diagnoses of psychiatric complaints and the Diagnostic and Statistical Manual of Mental Disorders (DSM), Star knows that it is not really fair to call this "boring"; the ICD tells us a lot, too, about that most socially studied of fields: medicine. When Star categorized such infrastructures as "boring," she knew, of course, that this stance was coy.

There are challenges in studying digital infrastructure using conventional ethnographic principles. Not least of these is the scale of the undertaking. Ethnography is very good at focusing on the unique and the specific and surfacing these micronarratives. But what do you do when the object of your study is massive, as are many contemporary digital infrastructures? We need to study this infrastructure somehow. Literally, in etymological terms, we are talking about an under (infra-) structure—that which undergirds other things. If you do not focus on these underpinnings, you "miss essential aspects of distributional justice and planning power."[17]

What are (digital) infrastructures? For Star, infrastructures are always relational—that is, they must exist in relation to a specific actor. A staircase is one person's infrastructure—seamless, invisible, functional—but for the wheelchair user, it is a barrier.[18] Star gives a series of characteristics of infrastructures. They are:

Embedded: infrastructure is "sunk into and inside of other structures."

Transparent: infrastructure "invisibly supports" tasks.

Broad in reach or scope: infrastructure "has reach beyond a single event or one-site practice."

Learned as part of membership: communities of practice take their infrastructures for granted.

Linked with conventions of practice: there is a type of path dependency on past conventions. Star gives the example of the QWERTY keyboard, studied in the previous chapter.

Standardized: infrastructures work with other infrastructures through common interfaces.

Built on an installed base: "infrastructure does not grow de novo; it wrestles with the inertia of the installed base and inherits strengths and limitations from that base."

Visible upon breakdown: the invisibility of infrastructure fades away when it breaks.

Fixed in modular increments: infrastructures are not installed in toto in one go.[19]

Word processing and digital text align with many of these infrastructural characteristics. They are, for instance, certainly "embedded." This can be seen in how Unix terminals display textual characters or how web browsers display preformatted text and require textual input. The basic substrates of textual input and reproduction are so embedded within various computational contexts that they seem indispensable. The ubiquity of this embeddedness leads to notions of transparency. We are so used to digital-textual composition invisibly supporting tasks that we rarely focus on the mechanism of its action. It is perhaps not worth systematically evaluating how digital text production fits within every single one of Star's infrastructural characteristics, as it is often very easy to see this at a glance. However, it is important to consider under what conditions textual input becomes "visible upon breakdown," a question to which I will return when I cover digital preservation.[20]

How should we study such infrastructure? There are several "tricks of the trade" to which Star points:

1. Identifying master narratives and "Others": That is to say that we can inquire of the assumptions that any infrastructure makes. A good example that Star gives is the idea of labeling adhesive bandages as "flesh colored" when this actually only describes white skin. A digital example is the assumption that programming languages should use Latin characters and English words.

2. Surfacing invisible work: Invisible labor pervades most infrastructures and, as with the breakdown of the infrastructure as a whole, is only usually noticed when it fails. A good example of this is the extent to which many digital systems rest on open-source projects that are maintained by a single volunteer, creating an extremely fragile global infrastructure.

3. Finding paradoxes of infrastructure: The example Star gives is that small technical challenges—such as adding a single extra button in a workflow—present near-insurmountable technical challenges to users. This is because of the ways that components interact in assemblage: for instance, a user has a memory of workflow.[21]

So how do we read such infrastructure as the underlying mechanisms of textual production? Star suggests that we must read across several different levels:

1. As a constructed material artifact: "with physical properties and pragmatic properties in its effects on human organization"

2. As a trace of record of activities: as a type of imprint or "information-collecting device"

3. As a representation of the world: a kind of model with a "sort of substitution" at play[22]

Star notes that these indicators, as she calls them, have parallels elsewhere. She uses the distressing example of films that include depictions of rape, which may tell us much about attitudes toward rape in a society but are not the same as police statistics about rape or phenomenological investigations into the experience of being raped.[23]

Star's article gives us a first framework for thinking about how we can analyze the geopolitics of digital-textual infrastructure.[24] The second set of principles for thinking about text ingest and output, though, are standards. Bowker and Star define standards through a set of six points that are helpful for understanding the development of Unicode as the example of this chapter:

1. Standards are any set of agreed-upon rules for the production of (textual or material) objects.

2. Standards span more than one community of practice (or site of activity). They have temporal reach and persist over time.

3. Standards are deployed in making things work together over distance and heterogeneous metrics.

4. Standards are often enforced by legal bodies, be these mandated by professional organizations, manufacturers' organizations, or the state.

5. Standards are not necessarily the *best* way of doing things. QWERTY and VHS are two standards that were not necessarily superior to their rivals but nonetheless ended up winning.

6. Standards have significant inertia and can be difficult and expensive to change in the future.[25]

Since Bowker and Star's treatise on classification, published over twenty years ago, standards have continued to exert an important influence over contemporary discourse. They have also continued to proliferate. As the well-known web comic, *xkcd*, put it: "Situation: there are 14 competing standards. / 14?! Ridiculous! We need to develop one universal standard that covers everyone's use cases. / Situation: there are 15 competing standards."[26]

Such a stance may cause us wry amusement, although it is not strictly true. Some standards have converged and consolidated over time. USB, the Universal Serial Bus, has, for the most part, replaced many previous standards, with the "universal" of its name largely holding true (although there are, in fact, multiple different endpoints of USB cables: USB-A, USB-B, and USB-C). Likewise, Unicode—another standard seeking *universality*—has also won out over most (although not all) rival formats. As was covered briefly in the preceding chapter, Unicode is a format designed to allow for the encoding of all the world's languages, giving computing systems a true cultural interoperability.[27]

If you wanted to design a system that could accommodate all of the world's languages, as does Unicode, you would assume that, from the start, you would need to seek advice from orthographers worldwide. The format would need, by design, and from the very start, to have input from language experts from around the world to ensure that cultural interoperability was baked into the core of the system. After all, as Bowker and Star caution us, the "lock-in" of designing a standard that then needs changing can be very debilitating. Yet, as we will go on to see, analyzing Unicode through the infrastructural lenses that I have here outlined, the development of this standard embodies a set of challenging difficulties concerned with the geopolitical distribution of digital text processing.

The later parts of this chapter take a slightly different tack. While it is clear how Unicode—a standard for the conveyance of digital text—fits with this book's theme of digital-material textual history, this may be less clear when I turn to the infrastructures of the Domain Name System, autonomous systems, and blockchains. The simple answer, though, is that the transmission of contemporary digital text relies on such systems. It is not possible to understand the most recent text technologies without analysis of technological systems that, at first glance, seem distant from functions such as word processing. As more and more of our daily text is routed over the internet and World Wide Web, it becomes ever more crucial to understand ideas of the digital governance of those systems (and recent attempts to widely distribute governance among many diasporic parties). These systems of oversight also matter for the topic of this chapter—geopolitics—because governance is usually conceived in terms that are spatial and proximate. Nations are most often grouped by proximity, although colonial histories complicate such a setting. Digital "spaces" are subject to the same types of pressures and forces as real-world governed regions, further strengthening my argument that digital text is geopolitically structured.

Unicode and Its Development

Version 1.0 of Unicode was released in 1991 and contained Arabic, Armenian, Bengali, Bopomofo, Cyrillic, Devanagari, Georgian, Greek and Coptic, Gujarati, Gurmukhi, Hangul, Hebrew, Hiragana, Kannada, Katakana, Lao, Latin, Malayalam, Oriya, Tamil, Telugu, Thai, and Tibetan scripts.

These scripts represent the most commonly used global orthographic systems. The Latin character set, for instance, is the basis of the international phonetic alphabet and has spread far and wide. However, the main reasons for this spread are historical *and religious*. As Florian Coulmas notes, the reason that the Latin alphabet has been adapted so many times in so many distinct cultural contexts is explained as "a direct result of the Christianization of Europe."[28] In a sense, this merely echoes David Diringer's well-known thesis that "alphabet follows religion."[29] For instance, the Cyrillic extensions of the Greek alphabet are prevalent in areas dominated by the Orthodox Church. Yet even the name Cyrillic comes from the missionary Cyril (827–69 CE), who was responsible for converting the Slavs.[30] Decisions around Unicode's originary scripts are determined by a long history of religious alphabet dominance.

The choice of implementing Latin scripts as a starting point carries with it cultural challenges. It might be easy to think that because Latin script is, by some estimates, used by up to 70 percent of the world's languages, its inclusion is straightforward. Yet the scripts embody local geographic tensions that can become mirrored in digital writing systems. For example, in the present day, the ongoing division between the Catholicism of Rome and the Orthodoxy of Constantinople is embodied in Serbo-Croatian language areas. Croatians, for instance, use the Latin script, while Orthodox Serbs use Cyrillic.[31] Implementing Latin *without* Cyrillic would have caused geopolitical tensions in this region and would scarcely live up to the ideal of a "universal" code for writing.

An instructive example of such challenges can be found in the nature of the committee that advises the Unicode consortium on the Han character set: the Ideographic Research Group (IRG). A subgroup of the catchily named Working Group 2 of International Organization of Standards/International Electrotechnical Commission Joint Technical Committee 1 Sub-Committee 2, the IRG contains members from China, Japan, South Korea, Vietnam, and other regions that use Han characters and logograms. Headed since 2004 by Professor Qin Lu (陸勤) of Hong Kong Polytechnic University, the group meets every year and, thus far, has proposed at least seven extensions to the Chinese-Japanese-Korean (CJK) character sets. Chinese, unlike the other systems already covered, does not work on the basis of an ordered "alphabet."[32] The divide, as Thomas S. Mullaney puts it, "is one that pits all alphabets and syllabaries against the one major world script that is neither: character-based Chinese writing."[33]

The reasons why characters have been added at various stages in

Unicode extensions, rather than in one fell swoop at the beginning, are several. At least one reason is the complexity of the glyphs and the scale of the work. For instance, Unicode 13.0, released in March 2020, contained CJK Unified Ideographs Extension G, which added a further 4,939 characters.[34] This update included the *kokuji* (a Japanese kanji character) *taito*, which is the most graphically complex character in the Han system. Writing the character by hand requires eighty-four separate strokes. The extension also includes the character for *biáng*, the second most complex character, although trailing far behind *taito* at just fifty-eight strokes. It was first proposed in 2015 in document IRGN2107, and it took five years for this complex character to earn its place in the final Unicode specification.[35]

The document proposing new characters has to provide evidence of their usage. In the case of *taito*, the proposal referenced a dictionary (the *Nandoku seishi jiten*) and a "little book of idioms" (*Chokkanryoku ga mi ni tsuku kanji jukugo kuizu*). Yet *taito* and *biáng* are not common characters. The complexity of the strokes required to form these characters precludes them from being scribbled down in, say, a hurried sign-off. In fact, one can imagine that most people writing by hand would studiously attempt to avoid writing these characters.

Hence, the CJK charsets demonstrate a "layout by complexity" that simply does not feature in many other codesets. The rarity of use of such characters is determined by the difficulty of writing them by hand, which then determines that they are not included early in digital orthographic notations. That is to say that the infrequency of the character's use, even in the digital space, is determined by the fact that it is difficult to write *by hand*. There is a circle (perhaps vicious) where the handwritten complexity relegates the character to only occasional usage. As a consequence, the character is not frequently needed in computational representation and in general language. Hence, computational writing systems take a long time to support such characters, even though in the digital environment it becomes a matter of a single keystroke to generate the complex logogram. Thus, although there could be a huge amount of work saved in replacing the character with a digital version, it has become scarce by definition precisely because it is difficult to write by hand. The loop is, therefore, a situation where the characters that would most benefit from digitization are not digitized, because they are not frequently used, because they are difficult to write by hand. That said, the origins of these particular kanji remain unclear. Some have even asked whether *taito* is a joke, given the difficulty of writing it.[36] Nonetheless, the complexity of handwriting has a direct influence on the marginalization of specific characters in the Unicode specification.

Of course, in these character systems, general literacy does not require knowledge of the full character set. A recent analysis by Ashwin Purhit determined that, in the Google Books corpus, there are 26,767 Chinese words that occur more than 1,000 times between 2000 and 2009. Within those common words there are 3,848 unique characters. Yet, to read 90 percent of the characters that appear, you would need "only" to know 633 of them.[37] This situation is, again, very different from the basic Latin alphabet with just 26 characters, exempting diacritics. It also creates a further regression of dependency in which Unicode will center the characters that appear most frequently while relegating the less common characters to future updates (regardless of how many strokes it may take to form the kanji).

In these senses, Unicode provides us with an instructive use case for how real-world geopolitical determinants condition the development of "universal" digital standards. They are not always the prerequisites that one might expect. Certainly, the geopolitics of the Cyrillic alphabet or the complexities of handwritten kanji do not seem the most likely candidates. Yet our digital worlds continue to be shaped by these geographical coordinates, yielding a digital cartography with unexpected textual prelineages.

Digital Borders and Distributed Governance

Among the most ridiculed of recent statements about the internet was the analogy drawn by US senator Ted Stevens, in 2006, who described the most advanced communication infrastructure on the planet as a "series of tubes." Oh, how easy it was to laugh at such a seemingly naive sentiment. Yet, as Ed Felten points out, computer programmers frequently talk of "pipes" and "sockets" in network programming.[38] Is this such a far cry from tubes?

More to the point, Stevens's statement draws attention to the very real (and now perhaps overly remarked upon) geo-materiality of the internet, which is crucial to an understanding of the dissemination of contemporary digital text. Undersea cabling that connects our continents digitally certainly does use a series of tubes to do so. These cables also have limited capacity in terms of the volume of data that they can carry. In an acute sense, the map of the internet's tube is laid out in geopolitical terms. This "intricate geopolitical scenario" is nowhere so clear, as Domenico Fiormonte puts it, as in "the map of the major connectivity providers."[39] In this scenario, thirteen "tier-one" sites are underpinned by seven core backbone transit providers. The result, according to Andrew Blum, is "a tightly interconnected clique of giants, often whispered about as a 'cabal,'" that provide the underlying connectivity of the internet.[40] The tubes are not only real, but they are owned by specific concrete entities.

An important point, when considering the geopolitical segregation of the internet and contemporary digital text dissemination, is the way that the domain name system (DNS) propagates information between so-called autonomous systems (AS) using the Border Gateway Protocol (BGP). This protocol is designed for mimesis of various nationalistic systems of claimed self-determination, with strong hints of politically isolationist tendencies. The BGP is another good case study of how geopolitical considerations condition the spread of digital text.

While the term "autonomous systems" carries overtones of the apocalyptic science fiction of *The Terminator* (1984), it actually refers to a collection of connected internet protocol routing prefixes controlled by a unified network operator. The reason for the creation of such systems is that, as address space has increased on the internet, routers no longer have sufficient memory to store all domain name mappings. As a result, autonomous systems expose a "border" to the general internet and then handle their own address space internally. This reduces the volume of general routing on the internet by essentially delegating internal control to organizations that register themselves as autonomous systems.

What does it mean to be an "autonomous system"? As with most low-level internet technologies, a hobbyist community has sprung up around the BGP where enthusiasts have decided to implement their own autonomous systems rather than simply piggybacking on big corporations like everyone else. These efforts raise the fundamental question: Who has the right to be autonomous and who legitimizes autonomy in the digital world?

Considering the mythology of the internet as a decentralized Wild West of anarchic free-for-alls, some parts of the process for establishing an autonomous system are remarkably controlled and dependent on a central authority. For instance, an autonomous system must, it transpires, be a legally incorporated entity.[41] On the other hand, parts of the setup process are extremely low-tech. Kenneth Finnegan found that the transfer of an IP address block to allow an announcement over BGP required an authorization via a signed and scanned piece of physical letterheaded paper. In an era of sophisticated hacks that can bring down global corporate networks, parts of the internet's lowest-level infrastructure are still reliant on ink signatures on easily forgeable paper letters. What could possibly go wrong?

Perhaps the most complex part of such hobbyist enterprises is negotiating the social setups that drive the internet. For instance, consider the concept of "peering." Peering is the process by which different autonomous systems are connected to one another. It is the way in which packets on the internet are routed between these systems. The basic idea is that every connected entity requires multiple redundant connections to other nodes—peers—so that they will remain connected even in the event that one part of the structure fails. By way of a traffic analogy: if the bridge is closed, the packets can take another route. Interested parties can observe the peerings of various autonomous systems by using so-called looking glass servers that allow examination of remote connectivity.

The challenge is that peering is done on the ad hoc basis of backroom handshakes and friendly deals. Or, put otherwise, this is the point "where human networking becomes exceedingly important in computer networking."[42] Once again, here the social complexity of these systems belies the belief that mere technicalities underpin these structures. Indeed, the system is so socially complex that there is even a whole book on how to navigate this landscape, William B. Norton's *The 2014 Internet Peering Playbook: Connecting to the Core of the Internet*.[43] To operate at this level of technical engagement requires a book on social strategies for integrating yourself within the murky world of backroom deals.

But what is so autonomous about these so-called internet autonomous systems? How does the autonomy of an autonomous system map onto the imagined communities of self-determined nation states or autonomous regions and areas? Indeed, what does it mean to think of independent "sovereignty"—that watchword of recent independence campaigns in the UK and elsewhere—in the internet "space"?

"Nation, nationality, nationalism," writes Benedict Anderson in his field-defining account of the forms, "all have proved notoriously difficult to define, let alone to analyse."[44] While, since and due to his study, this is no longer quite the case, the purpose of Anderson's work was to relativize and historicize the idea of nationhood, to see "nationness, as well as nationalism [as] cultural artefacts of a particular kind."[45] That is, while geographic proximity does, in some cases (diasporic cultures excepted), unite those who imagine themselves under the banner of nationhood, the phenomenon is much more culturally contingent than it might at first appear. Eventually, Anderson settles on his well-known definition: a nation is "an imagined political community—and imagined as both inherently limited and sovereign."[46] The imaginative portion of these imagined communities stems from the fact that "the members of even the smallest nation will never know most of their fellow-members, meet them, or even hear of them, yet in the minds of each lives the image of their communion."[47]

There are three further important "imagined" components in Anderson's definitions. The limits of nationhood are imagined "because even the largest of them . . . has finite, if elastic, boundaries, beyond which lie other nations." Further, the nation is imagined as sovereign—or, we might say, "autonomous"—"because the concept was born in an age in which Enlightenment and Revolution were destroying the legitimacy of the divinely-ordained, hierarchical dynastic realm." Finally, "it is imagined as a community, because, regardless of the actual inequality and exploitation that may prevail in each, the nation is always conceived as a deep, horizontal comradeship."[48]

To what extent might Anderson's definitions apply to the "autonomous systems" of the internet? Are the peered connections of autonomous systems that underpin digital text dissemination analogous to nation states? The answer is perhaps more complicated and lies also in the idea of corporate personhood, a dubious legal principle that led Robert Reich to quip that he'll "believe corporations are people when Texas executes one."[49]

The purpose of corporations, of course, is to act as legal vehicles that can displace risk from natural persons. The thinking behind this is that people can act in an entrepreneurial fashion, without incurring personal financial risk. For some, this inculcates a healthy degree of industry. For others, it appears as an unfair form of governmental social support that is given to corporations but denied to individuals. The etymological root of corporation is from *corporationem*, meaning "assumption of a body," thereby linking the organizational form to the form of a person. Yet in the US context, the idea that corporations might have equal rights as real people dates as far back as 1886, when a plaintiff in the Supreme Court case *Santa Clara County v. Southern Pacific Railroad Co.* claimed the rights of the equal protection clause of the Fourteenth Amendment for the body corporate.[50] Since that time, the scope has increased, to the extent that corporations are now able to hold religious beliefs and can make unlimited political expenditure as part of constitutional First Amendment rights.[51] As Mark McGurl puts it, remarking on the widespread fictionality of this construct, "The corporation itself, constructed by law as a fictional person, could not exist without the consent of governments that decide to believe in that fiction and recognize it as the bearer of civil rights."[52]

The analogous rights of corporations to real people are not unlimited. Some US laws, for instance, refer specifically to "individuals," defined as "a citizen of the United States or an alien lawfully admitted for permanent residence."[53] The same goes for the Fifth Amendment right against self-incrimination. It is not straightforward to say that corporations are equal to individuals, even if they have some of their rights. However, they certainly have a degree of autonomy, as in the autonomy of "autonomous systems."

In some ways, the rights of corporations in law makes sense. After all, on the one hand, corporations are to some extent subject to the obligations of law, including paying tax and complying with regulations. As a result, one would argue, they should also have rights. Indeed, because they function as a collection of individuals, corporations seem well placed to have rights and responsibilities, and obligations and freedoms, in legal structures. On the other hand, the concept of corporate "persons"—so-called creatures of statute—seems very odd when exerting, say, religious beliefs. Even when such beliefs are progressive, they can seem absurd. For instance, the Carphone Warehouse, a UK-based retailer of mobile telephones, announced in a press release that the organization is "totally against all forms of racism" and that "this behaviour is entirely at odds with the brand values of the Carphone Warehouse."[54] As the comedian Stewart Lee drily quipped of this remark, this was helpful as "prior to reading that statement, I had suspected that the Carphone Warehouse was in fact a front for a white supremacist organisation." The three actual values of the Carphone Warehouse, according to Lee, might be to "(1) sell phones, (2) sell more phones, and (3) deny the Holocaust."[55]

Jesting aside, corporations expressing views and beliefs, exerting rights, and being beholden to responsibilities brings into focus questions of autonomy and sovereignty. Like a nation state beyond whose walls sit other nation states with which there may be communications, wars, trade, and other relationships, corporations find themselves in a position to exercise power with certain constraints imposed externally upon the limits of that power. The communities of interaction—and with whom corporations must imagine interactions—include nation states and their governments, individuals, other corporations, and legal apparatuses. It is a complex web of sovereignty within which the contemporary corporation exists.

Autonomous systems on the internet must be owned by corporations. Yet even the process of establishing such an organization is geopolitically determined. The ASN (Autonomous System Number) Table is populated with AS numbers by the Internet Assigned Numbers Authority, which in turn delegates to regional internet registries (RIRs). These RIR organizations are split into five areas: the African Network Information Center (AFRINIC) for Africa; the American Registry for Internet Numbers (ARIN) for Antarctica, Canada, parts of the Caribbean, and the United States; the Asia-Pacific Network Information Centre (APNIC) serving East Asia, Oceania, South Asia, and Southeast Asia; the Latin America and Caribbean Network Information Centre (LACNIC) for most of the Caribbean and all of Latin America; and the Réseaux IP Européens Network Coordination Centre (RIPE NCC) for Europe, Central Asia, Russia, and West Asia. Autonomous systems map onto corporations but then back into geographical coordinates.

Thus, despite the fact that most autonomous systems seek points of presence in multiple geographic regions, for redundancy purposes, the ability to establish a low-level organization with direct peering on the internet is controlled by regionally specific registries. In the case of the Caribbean, it is especially interesting to note that both ARIN and LACNIC serve the region. Historically subject to multiple colonizing forces, be this the Dutch, the French, or the English, there remains a fragmentation in this area with respect to internet assignments. For instance, the Caribbean Netherlandish islands of Bonaire, Saba, and Sint Eustatius, as well as Trinidad and Tobago and Saint Martin and Sint Maarten are all under the jurisdiction of LACNIC. By contrast, Jamaica and Saint Lucia, as just two examples, are under ARIN. Hence, there are complex regional mappings of internet authority to contested national statehoods.

One of the crucial things to understand about the systems for address and domain name assignment is that, despite the abundance-thinking that characterizes most of the digital age and that I have already covered above—in which we imagine that the digital space has managed to overcome the limits on copying in the "real world"[56]—the regional registries system is an attempt to manage scarcity.[57] Addresses on the internet, in the IPv4 scheme, are scarce by virtue of design (the original planners never realizing that the scope might be exhausted and that this network would, truly, have billions of devices connected) but also by individual units' technology capacity (routers possessing insufficient memory to store the entire address table of the internet at any one time).

The governance of the internet—which is often erroneously considered to be ungoverned and anarchic—is not imperious but structural. As Milton Mueller puts it, "For any complex sociotechnical system, especially one that touches as many people as the Internet, control takes the form of institutions, not commands."[58] Yet the contradictions of the development of internet structure do look quite a lot like an unplanned accidental incursion. In its early days, the internet was a tool of education, although one also beholden to the command control needs of the military.[59]

As is well known, though, for most of the history of the internet, the functions of domain name addressing and address assignment were controlled by *American* organizations, in keeping with the geographical development of the ARPANET at UCLA. Indeed, key technical elements of the internet were held solely by the US military and by the National Science Foundation. For instance, the central "A root server" of the domain name system, which holds ultimate authority over the final "answer" to any DNS query, was owned by Network Solutions, Inc. and sited in Reston, Virginia. It wasn't until 1997 that the US Department of Commerce launched a formal procedure to privatize DNS and thereby to decentralize the United States in the total operation of the internet.[60] At that point, it is curious to note, the process of decentralization took the United States' favored technique of corporate ownership, rather than, say, ownership by a transnational governmental body or coalition. There is, that is to say, a curious part of American decentralization that once more comes back to corporate persons.

As Mueller points out, the process of transferring DNS to private ownership and governance was forced to take place over a very short four-month window. Although a crucial change to the operation of the entire internet, the outsourcing of DNS was enacted extremely quickly. The parallel that Mueller draws in his *Ruling the Root: Internet Governance and the Taming of Cyberspace* is to the drafting of a constitution. Again, we find ourselves in metaphorical parallels to the governance of nation states (particularly the United States with its strong written constitution)—and corporate bodies—in the history of the internet. For instance, the initial governance meetings to draft this "constitution" were overseen by Tamar Frankel, a law professor who was an expert in corporate governance but who knew very little about the technicalities of the internet.[61] The privatization of DNS was embedded in social discussions around operation, ownership, and governance, with technical considerations bumped somewhat down the list (for once).

Mueller and others wanted, in many ways, to posit the internet's new governance structure as a discontinuity that disregarded nation states and their like in favor of a new transnational structure. "The Internet," he writes, "was different, however. It seemed to call forth an entirely new spirit for collective action. It had created a perplexing set of issues that eluded resolution by any one government or organization."[62] Furthermore, we are told, "the Internet's structure was so distributed, and the organizations that built it were so diverse and so informal, however, that no single group, not even the U.S. government, possessed the legitimacy and authority to pull it all together on its own."[63] This is, however, confusing. Quite clearly, at the birth of the internet, there was a strong US-centricity of both locale and organization. The routing structure and design of the internet may have *implied* a distribution on a scale never before seen, but this was not the shape at its outset. As with Unicode, the internet developed in a piecemeal fashion, gradually expanding over continents and countries. Rome wasn't built in a day. The place that the internet started was the United States, and this shaped the form that it took when it gained independence from that formal state. The history of the internet has a geographic tether to the US.

Nonetheless, the mythos of internet as a different type of organization to anything seen before continued to proliferate. Ira Magaziner, a policy adviser in the Clinton administration who was responsible for opening the internet governance deliberations with a speech, noted that "the Internet as it develops needs to have a different type of coordination structure than has been typical for international institutions in the industrial age." The open-culture advocate and lawyer Larry Lessig agreed that this was the emergent structure, albeit with alarm and concern, when he wrote of the extrajudicial, supranational character of the governance models that were being formed around the internet and, in particular, DNS: "We are creating the most significant jurisdiction since the Louisiana purchase, and we are building it outside the review of the Constitution."[64] That is, for Lessig, the corporate, rather than nationalistic, form of the internet carries with it a raft of troublesome governance elements. While, in some senses, the formalization of DNS in corporate ownership appears to be a coming of age and bedding down, it was also a liberation from various forms of control and regulation. The internet's "coming of age" was not cemented by regulation and overarching consolidation but instead situated within a free-market paradigm of independent corporate ownership.

The mythology of the internet, then, as a new decentralized type of infrastructure has a kernel of truth with a layer of veneer. The internet protocol, with its packet-based schema, is, indeed, a decentralized and even to some extent self-healing routing mechanism that works around damage or intentional sabotage.[65] However, the structures that make the internet (and the web that sits atop it as a text-transmission technology) usable have strong elements of centralization. These points of centralization range from the relatively few search engines that we use to navigate the web, such as Google and Bing, to the aforementioned domain name system that translates from human-readable names into the machine routable IP addresses.[66] At the core of the DNS setup are the root servers. In Mueller's words, "The root is the point of centralization in the Internet's otherwise thoroughly decentralized architecture. The root stands at the top of the hierarchical distribution of responsibility that makes the Internet work. It is the beginning point in a long chain of contracts and cooperation governing how Internet service providers and end users acquire and utilize the addresses and names that make it possible for data packets to find their destinations."[67] How, then, does one develop a decentralized governance structure for a network that has such contradictory principles of centralization at its core?

It is from these issues that the recent hype over Bitcoin, or, more specifically, blockchain technologies, has arisen (and potentially fallen since the appearance of the Next Big Thing: AI). A blockchain is a distributed write-once, read-many ledger technology. Essentially, what this means is that a blockchain is a decentralized database to which anybody can write and from which anybody can read. However, once an entry has been written to the chain, it is immutable (impossible to change). That is, despite the fact that many people have copies of the blockchain, it is cryptographically impossible in most circumstances for an individual to populate the database with fraudulent historical data.[68] Blockchains are both tedious and fascinating. They are tedious because the imagined uses to which people put them proliferate beyond any bound of common sense, as I will shortly show. It is almost certainly the case that in most systems where a blockchain is proposed, a simple centralized database could have done the same job in a far more efficient manner. The hype around blockchain is, therefore, tiresome and mostly concerned with venture capital firms throwing money at the next buzzword. By contrast, though, there *are* interesting remarks to be made around blockchain as a digital solution to—or, at least, a metaphor of—issues of decentralized governance in contemporary text-dissemination environments within a broadly libertarian ideology. Specifically: blockchains try to solve the problem of consensus governance with respect to digitally distributed timekeeping when you do not trust any single centralized actor.

This may sound odd, as it is not the way that blockchains are usually framed. But we can see this phenomenon at work when we consider the uses to which blockchains are most conventionally put: distributed currencies. This distributed system poses a solution to what is known in digital currencies as the "double-spending problem." Traditionally, in such setups, without a centralized agency, it becomes impossible to know whether—for a short period of time—a user of a digital currency has spent a unit of the currency more than once. Given the importance of scarcity as the only driver of value in economic currencies, whether digital or not, double-spending attacks appear suboptimal. Blockchain solves this problem through cryptographic proofs of work, stake, or space.

An example may make this clearer. Consider the idea of a digital currency in which numbered coins are doled out to participants (coin 1, coin 2, coin 3, etc.). Say there are five participants, and participant 1 (Alice) decides to give participant 2 (Bob) a coin. Because these coins are digital, unbeknown to Bob, Alice has kept a copy of the coin. While Bob is busy celebrating his good luck, Alice also gives a copy of the same coin to a third participant (Carol). The traditional answer to this problem of double-spending is to have a central authority—a bank or credit card processor—to validate the transaction. In a regular, centralized system, to send a transaction, Alice would have to tell the bank that she wished to pay Bob, and the bank would log that, from that point onward, Alice no longer owned that coin. Any attempt to spend the coin again would register that Alice did not have authority to do so.

When a system is decentralized, it is much harder to avoid this problem. How do you keep a log, spread between multiple parties, that contains an immutable sequence of records, in the correct order? The blockchain achieves its solution by consensus building among nodes such that, if the majority of nodes are behaving well within the system, it is impossible to write a fraudulent entry into the database out of sequence. One part of this is using cryptographic signing systems so that once an entry has been "voted" (again, note the terminology of governance and suffrage here) onto the chain, it is immutable and impossible for a future assailant to spend a coin that they do not own. While this sounds simple, the fundamental problem that blockchain must overcome is this: How can one engender proven trust among these many parties such that no malicious actor can write a fraudulent entity to the chain?

The double-spending problem, though, can actually be decomposed into an even smaller challenge. If there is a distributed public ledger that contains all transactions, each written with a time stamp, then what is really needed is a time server that can verify that nobody is writing entries out of order. That is, the blockchain needs to solve the fundamental ordering problem of the double-spend by having nodes agree, throughout the system, that a time stamp on a transaction is accurate. As the blogger yanmaani describes it, "Using my node's local clock, I can check that new blocks coming in . . . state the time correctly. If I then have a series of blocks (a 'block chain'), I can enforce—on threat of refusing to accept them, thus making their money worthless— that these timestamps be accurate, i.e. consistent to my (local) clock."[69] Blockchains are actually decentralized timekeeping mechanisms that work to record distributed histories in sequential fashion. History, in the blockchain vision, becomes the consensus between nodes on the order in which events occurred.

However, you cannot, to get a result in this system, simply take a sampled vote. If any proportion of the chain were compromised, the risk of hitting on many bad actors would be too great. Another common but incorrect solution is to require *all* participants to vote. However, in a practical situation, this would introduce impossibly long, or even indefinite, delays. If a single node went offline on the network, then the system would fail. Instead, the solution that blockchain implements is to make participants who "vote" on a transaction put something at stake with a reward structure for doing so. The chroniclers of history in the blockchain must put something at hazard to vouch for their solidity.

More specifically, blockchain is an attempted solution to the Byzantine Generals Problem and is an example of Byzantine Fault Tolerance. The problem can be set out as follows: There are several generals who are attacking a fortress, and they must decide if they will attack or fall back/retreat. The generals must act in concert because an uncoordinated attack/retreat would be catastrophic. However, it gets worse, as there are also disloyal generals who may selectively vote for a destructive strategy. The voting structure is such that a disloyal general may signal to *some* other generals that they wish to attack and, to others, to retreat. The generals are also physically separate from one another, and votes are delivered by messengers who may fail to deliver or who may falsify votes. Blockchain's consensus-building mechanisms are designed to exhibit Byzantine Fault Tolerance and to build a system that can, in fact, overcome the limitations of the above problem.

Another good example of a problem of Byzantine Fault Tolerance lies in aircraft instrumentation.[70] Imagine that you are flying an airplane and the visibility is bad. Traditionally, under such circumstances, the pilot will use a set of sensors to compensate. This might, for instance, be an altitude sensor or a proximity sensor. If an airliner is equipped with just one of each instrument and anything goes wrong with the sensor, the pilot will have no way of knowing of this defect. However, if the aircraft instead had ten copies of each instrument, four of them could fail at any time and the pilot could trust the majority result. Such a system would have a high level of Byzantine Fault Tolerance, as it could resist multiple points of failure and incorrect information, even when the source of such error is not known.

However, the aircraft scenario only works well in certain situations (and the same is true of blockchains). First, if all the sensors are susceptible to the same mechanical flaw, then it is possible that all of them will malfunction at once. A coding error in blockchain consensus mechanisms could lead to a similar problem on a blockchain. In the aircraft system this can be countered by having sensors manufactured by different companies in isolation from one another. In this way, it should be impossible for multiple instruments to contain identical flaws, and the fault tolerance will hold. Second, though, this system of fault tolerance works well when one assumes that the failures are random and mechanical. But what if the sensors had been maliciously altered by an actor with access to the plane? When there is motivation to bypass Byzantine Fault Tolerance, with a central coordinated malefactor, the system is far less resilient. As the online commentator Antsstyle put it, "Byzantine Fault Tolerance is primarily useful when failure can be attributed to mechanical or hardware/software errors, and does not have a motive."[71] The challenge is that all consensus mechanisms are, fundamentally, reliant on a majority voting system unless you compromise on speed.

There are further problems with the idea of blockchain as a system that proves ownership, as it must do in systems of digital currency. As I have noted throughout this section, a blockchain is supposed to solve two fundamental problems in the digital space: introduce scarce digital "ownership" of an asset so that it may be used once by the rightful owner and do so in a distributed fashion without a central authority (such as a bank) through distributed timekeeping. The challenge, though, is that no technological system can ever actually surmount these problems.

This is best seen in the phenomenon of non-fungible tokens (NFTs). NFTs are, essentially, digital files that have been minted onto a blockchain, apparently then rivalrously inscribing ownership of the file to a particular individual. An example could be that I mint an NFT PDF version of this book as a new text-transmission method. Yes, anybody could theoretically copy the PDF itself, but it wouldn't be the *NFT* version, which theoretically is "owned" by me, according to the blockchain. I could, of course, deliberately transfer the NFT to any user I wished, and they would then have the ownership rights for this copy. The NFT is akin to having a "certificate of ownership" for a digital item, even though the digital item itself can be copied.

Realistically, this makes no sense whatsoever. The reason that copyright (or the weakly defined term "intellectual property"[72])—which is perhaps the nearest analogy to this otherwise insane setup—can work is that despite it being *possible* to copy an item that is under copyright, there may be legal sanction and financial penalty for doing so. The world of NFTs is, instead, one where it is possible to copy the underlying artifact, even though there is a digital "contract" (database) system that says who owns it. However, there is unlikely to be any legal sanction for so doing (one can create an NFT of an item that is out of copyright or freely available to disseminate). There is even a pirate site called the NFT Bay (after the Pirate Bay) that offers copies of the NFTs themselves. NFTs appear to be the ultimate defanged intellectual property contracts—contracts that specify ownership but with no penalty for violating that property relation.

This is the fundamental trap into which proponents of the blockchain, NFTs, and other distributed digital governance systems continually tumble. What they would like to build is a technical system of law enforcement that eradicates all sociality from the implementation of, say, property ownership. Instead of a judicial system and a police department, cyberlibertarians hope for a world in which "smart con-tracts" enforce ownership in a way that makes "theft" impossible, even when the artifact itself remains duplicable. The problem is that there is no meaning inside such a hermetically sealed system. The fact that you can create a document, which cannot be modified and which is not owned by a central authority, that states something (such as: X owns Y coins of Z currency) does not make the thing that is stated true. There is no external verification of veridiction in blockchains.

Indeed, NFTs can never vouch that someone *should* "own" a digital object in the first place. There is nothing to stop someone else minting a copy of my book—or any other digital text—and the scarcity value of the NFT is only valid in relation to the extratechnical notion of iden-tity.[73] A good example of this is that Tim Berners-Lee, the inventor of the World Wide Web, sold an NFT of the source code of the World Wide Web for $5.4 million in 2021.[74] Where did the value inhere? Certainly, had *I* minted the source code for the WWW and attempted to sell it, nobody would have paid $5.4 million (sadly). The value was attributed because it was the inventor of the web who put the NFT up for sale. Yet the blockchain says nothing about this relationship. It merely proves that a user has the rights to transfer or "own" the particularly minted copy. This is why individuals can fraudulently claim to be the original artists in the case of NFTs, sell their wares, and then move on. The value lies in the identity of the owner, which blockchains cannot verify or enforce but that real-world social contracts can.

Furthermore, the most laughable aspect of NFTs is that, despite the fact that a decentralization/distribution is supposedly key to their existence, developers have on several occasions introduced "hard forks" (a central correction) into various blockchains. This happened, for example, when Ethereum and Ethereum Classic diverged. In 2016, a vulnerability was discovered in the Ethereum's protocol and its smart contract software. To rectify this, the developers split the blockchain into two, with the original being renamed Ethereum Classic and the newly patched, secure version rebranded Ethereum. This all sounds fine. Yet, one might ask, what is the point of a distributed system of governance if a central authority can decide, on a whim (or even on a vote), to change the rules of engagement because the original system didn't behave the way that they wanted? This is the very definition of reinscribing centrality into blockchain systems, yet proponents rarely comment upon it (or they decide to call democratic "votes" on the hard forking process, despite the fact that such voting is apportioned according to various criteria of "merit" and not strictly a one-person, one-vote system).

The twin valorization in blockchain of distribution and scarcity signal philosophical priorities for internet architects and contemporary text distributors, along with a distressing focus on the subjugation of the social to the technical. On the one hand, the principles of distribution and redundancy that underpin blockchain were core to early thinking about the nature of the internet itself. On the other hand, as above, the challenge is that once the web was grafted atop the internet and became one of its core embodiments, principles of centralization crept into the design, for reasons of convenience. Certainly, systems such as DNS were designed to be redundantly distributed around the globe. However, as they rest on central authority, a hierarchical structure nonetheless emerged. It is also true that five major firms—Google/Alphabet, Microsoft, Amazon, Apple, and Facebook—dominate the entire technology landscape. This is hardly a wildly decentralized system. As a result, there are periodic calls to "re-decentralize the web," among other cries. Blockchain is an attempt to decentralize "governance" of a network of peers, based on consensus-building algorithmic mechanisms.

The second principle of blockchain upon which we might wish to dwell is the element of scarcity. As I have noted at several other points, the primary imaginative context within which digital text content exists is one of proliferation and abundance. However, the blockchain is an attempt not to do away with scarcity and yield an environment of ultra-abundance but instead to *reintroduce* precise scarcity into the online space. By ensuring a single-spend system in a digital currency, the blockchain inscribes a token that one can use only once at the heart of its enterprise. It also does so without a central authority overseeing and tracking such tokens. This is the novelty of blockchain technology.

It enables tokens on the network to be used once and only once, even when an end user has kept a "copy" of said token.

The costs of blockchain are also well known, though. The first generation of blockchain—used by Bitcoin—deployed a "proof-of-work" cryptographic method.[75] In such a system, the "cost" of writing a line to the distributed ledger is that multiple computers must solve an arbitrary computational puzzle.[76] Essentially, while "protection against invalid transactions is entirely cryptographic," this mechanism is "enforced by consensus." The process of adding new nodes (spending transactions in the case of Bitcoin) to the blockchain is one in which a new node is "proposed" by a specific client and then verified by a set of other chain members. The node that is allowed to propose the next block is the node that has successfully completed an arbitrary cryptographic challenge ("proof of work"). Solving such puzzles comes with a reward (in the form of more Bitcoin) for the nodes that succeed and is called mining. In this way, Bitcoin incentivizes nodes to participate in verifying transactions on the chain by solving arbitrary, moderately difficult, but useless, computational problems.[77]

This all sounds promising for a decentralized system of digital governance. However, the annual energy consumption of Bitcoin is enormous.[78] Estimated in 2020 at 181.07 terawatt hours, Bitcoin has power consumption equal to that used by Thailand and a carbon footprint the size of Bangladesh, despite processing just a few hundred million transactions, compared to traditional processors, which were in the realm of several hundred billion payments.[79] A single transaction on this blockchain is equal to sixty-two days of energy usage by the average US household, while it takes the carbon footprint of almost two million traditional Visa credit card purchases to make just one spend.[80] The network also creates a huge amount of e-waste as dedicated mining rigs burn out under extreme usage.[81] While this sounds like a flaw in cryptocurrency use, though, it is not—or, at least, it is a flaw by design. The important point to understand in cryptocurrency mining and operation is that without the external dependence on electricity, there is nothing staked to put value behind a particular digital coin. Indeed, as yanmaani puts it, the "idea is to have a method to burn electricity in a provable way. The electricity used does not directly produce anything of value, except for a proof that (approximately) this amount of electricity was consumed by this or that node." Electricity works as a value proposition because it is "costly" (you have to pay for it), "irreversible" (once you've used the electricity, you have sunk the spend), and "self-certifying" (the network can see that the proof-of-work cost a certain amount of computational energy, which correlates to electricity).[82]

Hence, when people say that cryptocurrencies are mere betting or speculation, because they are not underwritten by any real-world scarce resource (and despite the fact that the post–Bretton Woods system of economics means that contemporary *real* currencies are also no longer linked to the gold standard), this couldn't be further from the truth. There is a *strong* external dependence on computational power—and, therefore, electricity. Certainly, this has variable value implications as the cost of electricity and the way it is produced can be radically different between different regions of the world. Computational efficiency will also vary between nodes. Nonetheless, there is a scarce resource that underpins Bitcoin, and this expenditure is "at stake."

There are further examples of real-world scarcities linked to cryptocurrency mining. For example, cryptocurrency mining has also caused global supply-chain shortages as miners scramble to buy high-end hardware in the pursuit of financial return.[83] Various legislatures have even suggested banning cryptocurrencies that run on proof of work, so damaging are the environmental consequences.[84] It turns out that one of the core contributions to the future destruction of our planet through global warming might well be the digital resource consumption of solving meaningless hash puzzles in order to verify the timestamps on the blockchain of Bitcoin.

There are two other potential types of proof that can be used by the distributed governance mechanisms of cryptocurrencies (or, more precisely, that can underwrite various distributed ledger technologies with scarcity): proof of stake and proof of space. The latter, proof of space, also known as proof of capacity or proof of storage, is a system in which a miner (client) proves that they have allocated a specific quantity of computational storage space purely for the purposes of mining.[85]

The Chia cryptocurrency uses this mechanism and writes an extensive number of "plots" to the underlying storage system. In such a system, it is true that the carbon footprint and energy consumption are lower.[86] However, the physical destruction of storage media (such as solid-state drives) by the sheer quantity of writes to the disk means that not only is it *expensive* to run such a mining rig but that there is a remaining problem of electronic waste. In other words, aside from the environmental impact, the Chia cryptocurrency achieves its measure of digital scarcity by mapping itself directly onto an economy of hard-drive purchases (and destruction). The miners in such a system are banking, however, that the speculative scarcity of their fictional currency is worth more than they pay in hard cash for the storage media that underpin it. This may not be the case.[87]

Proof of space carries with it some of the most concrete analogies to nationalism seen in the physical world. Proof of space is a direct demand for a specific topology of storage to be allocated in order to govern. That is, like older systems of suffrage based on property rights and land ownership, governance is here delegated to nodes that can prove that they have sacrificed metaphorical digital "space" to the cause. That the use of such space, purely to govern, is ultradestructive to the overall use of the capacity is a neatly encapsulated irony of digital consensus governance by proof of space. In such systems, there is almost a regression to a feudal system, in which only landowners (those with digital space, bought at a cost) govern. In some ways, this seems a long haul from the libertarian fantasy of free agency and governance that blockchain is supposed to represent. In other ways, it appears precisely as the logical extension of such a structure, where brute force and ownership are the only constraining principles. It is also, in line with the principle of this chapter, another instance of geo-contextual metaphor in contemporary digital text technologies.

A further system yet of blockchain consensus building is known as "proof of stake." In a proof-of-stake system, rather than assigning consensus voting rights based on volume of work conducted, or the area of digital space allocated, the system instead awards proportionate representation to the percentage of ownership staked. The principle here is that those who have "invested" the most in the network over time have the least incentive to attack it. Hence, an actor's trustworthiness within any particular network is then determined by the level of investment—stake—they have in maintaining that network's integrity. Of course, if any single party could control 51 percent of the network's ownership, they would be able to dominate the network and could mint false transactions.

Like the post–Bretton Woods monetary system, proof of stake rests on the belief that those who have the most money are the people with the most investment in the perpetuation of the monetary system. Proof of stake feels a little bit like the golden rule: who has the gold makes the rules. It is no surprise then that one of the most common proof-of-stake structures is called ouroboros, after the symbol of the snake eating its own tail.[88] There is certainly a type of Matthew effect at work in proof-of-stake structures, where the rich get richer.[89] Given that blockchains are entirely concerned with scarcity and value, for an attack by 51 percent to succeed, it would require the equivalent of a billionaire who hopes for the collapse of the world's financial systems. It would need a rogue, suicidal actor with malicious intent and with a lot to lose. To this extent, however, the proof-of-stake structure relies on the self-interested rationality of participants, and it will not brook the idea that an agent might act against their own protected stake. Hence, while actors with a larger stake are more trustworthy in terms of protecting the system's integrity, it is a logical mistake of such systems to believe, unconditionally, that such agents will always act in their own interests. There is also a huge danger in proof-of-*work* systems. In proof-of-*work* structures, it is clear that one must possess an enormous amount of computer hardware. As of 2021, this had led to international shortages of graphical processing units for use in mining. To garner enough computing power to mount an attack by 51 percent here would be tricky. On the other hand, there are plenty—far too many (more than one)—billionaires on the planet who could with great ease buy up more than 51 percent of smaller cryptocurrencies and thereby control the chain. In such instances, the "theoretical" attack basically comes down to the rich controlling the monetary system, which hardly sounds like a radical break from traditional banking.[90] These are the weak points of proof-of-stake structures, which have an intensely malevolent social, rather than technological, characteristic, even while the entire structure has been designed by technocrats to enforce a technical contract.

However, blockchains even attempt to move such contractual/social elements into their orbit. In a fashion typical of blockchain evangelism, there are so-called smart contracts that can be stored on a blockchain and executed when a given set of preconditions are met.[91] While such structures are not totally akin to contracts in the more traditional sense, they are, nonetheless, binding future assertions of computational action. They are also governed by the same cryptographic principles that determined other elements of writing to the blockchain. They are an attempt to codify law, digitally.

Despite not being legally binding in the traditional sense, such "contracts" also bear another hallmark of the conventional legal system: they can be difficult to understand. This goes for cryptocurrency principles as a whole. The most recent example of this phenomenon at the time of writing can be seen in the so-called SQUID blockchain/cryptocurrency. Following a pattern in which cryptocurrencies are named after internet memes and other cultural icons (such as the infamous Dogecoin), this currency was named after the 2021 Netflix smash-hit dystopian television show *Squid Game*. The premise of this series, for those who do not know, is that seriously indebted individuals are recruited to a game in which there are massive monetary rewards for success but lethal penalties for failure. As deep criticisms of capitalism go, it was the best that 2021 had to offer, although hardly Earth-shatteringly profound. Marx had, long before, recognized that selling one's labor time was, in fact, selling one's life.[92]

The SQUID cryptocurrency was not affiliated with the official TV show, but it used the cover of nominal semblance with a vast international commercial brand to confer its seeming autolegitimacy.[93] The currency rocketed by over 45,000 percent in its opening hours, an extreme volatility even in a market famed for such swings. As investors flocked to buy the rapidly ascending coin, few had noticed that the "whitepaper" detailing the coin contained an "antidumping technology" that stopped individuals from selling the tokens. Once it became clear that it was impossible to offload the coins and to cash out, the value plummeted over the course of a five-minute period back down to zero. A few days later, the operators made off with $2 million.

Of course, this is all too apt for the claimed nominal affiliation with *Squid Game*. Participants entered the game hoping to win big and ended up financially dead.[94] However, it also shows the complexities of the legal, contractual, and technical implementations of cryptocurrencies and blockchains.[95] It seems clear that most "players" purchasing the tokens had not read the whitepaper and did not know about the anti-dumping technology. Indeed, there was an assumption that this coin worked in the same way as other crypto tokens with which users were already familiar. It was assumed that there was a transjurisdictional metaphor of contractual and legal principles that would apply when, in fact, this was not the case.

The origins of how best we can understand technological implementations as a type of "law"—apt for this thinking about distributed governance and text technologies—should be traced to Lawrence Lessig's well-known *Code and Other Laws of Cyberspace* (1999, second edition 2006). Importantly, Lessig draws a parallel between the emergence of postcommunistic spaces and cyberspace as new sites of libertarian ideation. As the Soviet Union fell, initial speculation boiled with "antigovernmental passion" and the assumption that the new superseding regimes would be market-driven capitalist undertakings. The same was true, argued Lessig, of the embryonic digital world, a world that rejected "kings, presidents and voting" and attempted to replace them with "rough consensus and running code."[96] Arguing that the digital space requires a constitutional framing—not in the form of a document that sets out principles but rather in an architected environment that structurally affirms certain rights and responsibilities—Lessig temporarily disregards the differences between "code" and "law" in a thought experiment designed to reveal the challenges and show the possibilities for the regulation of the internet.

Lessig's book, now an ancient text of the early internet era, first written in 1999, popularized the New Chicago School theory—or pathetic dot theory—in which digital actors are constrained (and enabled) by architectures, markets, laws, and norms. What is perhaps most interesting is that, in the two decades since the book was published, the fantasies of libertarian emergence have not receded. That is to say that even while the internet and web have become ever more centralized and ever more *governed*, the mythology of the digital Wild West continues. Indeed, one of the most prominent digital civil liberties organizations, the Electronic Frontier Foundation, is named after the expansion of America westward, using the language of the "frontier." The internet appears permanently inscribed as anarchic, freedom loving, and libertarian even as it grows ever more authoritarian in its outlooks. In this sense, the internet is very American.

What is also interesting and important is that the permeability of the internet and, thus, new digital-text-transmission technologies have, as I have been arguing throughout this chapter, been marked by a new set of borders, each with the possibility of its own set of laws, which can radically diverge from all that has gone before. So, while it is true that the internet presents a supranational and superjurisdictional network that is able to intrude into previously hermetically sealed national communities, I have been arguing here that the internet is also prestructured by those very types of geographic boundaries that it is claimed are erased by its presence. Hence, when Lessig writes of the nation state that wishes to prohibit gambling and the challenges that it faces in doing so when such betting takes place in an online environment, this occurs through the use of an internet that is structured according to extant geographic norms and boundaries.[97]

Different models of internet structure—from DNS to blockchain—represent the edges of governance in this digital world. As digital text is transmitted from site to site, it must negotiate these underlying technologies, which grapple with philosophies of governance and distribution. For a web page simply to travel from a server to a client, across the vast distances of the real world, involves the navigation of complex technologies and governance stakes. Downloading a book on the web involves the (transparent, of course) traversal of multiple systems of centralization and decentralization, at great real spatial distance. It involves "autonomous systems" that specify the realms of local governance and may, in the future, if we're unlucky, use blockchains. But the point is that every piece of text that is transmitted digitally cannot help but interact with multiple systems that were designed to navigate political tensions in the development of the internet. The geopolitics of digital text are underpinned by decades of wrangling around how a radically decentralized system will be governed.

Digital Text and Geopolitics

We live in an era that devotes ever more attention, every day, to undoing colonial legacies (even while a backlash from conservative figures attempts to rewrite those colonial aggressions as benevolent interventions). The culture war that rages around these issues is intense because it is so entwined with nationalism and the histories of various nation states. The general aggravation in the backlash arises from the feeling of collective punishment for the sins of the father. However, present day denizens of nations with colonial histories find themselves in a privileged economic position as a result of this past, as do the descendants of slave owners. Yet it is also true that they, themselves, were not the colonizers or slavers. Hence, their argument runs, they should not find themselves being penalized for the actions of their forebears. Of course, if one does not wish to be punished for the actions of one's ancestors, then one should also not be able to inherit the wealth and benefit that they produced through the actions that one has disavowed. Yet aggressive nationalisms provide a context that frees us from such critical thinking, investing a "pride" in the randomness of the place of one's birth.

The internet, though, alongside computing systems more broadly, provides imaginative contexts within which, it seems, we might free ourselves from the negative elements of nationalisms. The internet is a transnational entity that has proved hard to regulate. Our computing systems are capable of representing the character sets of every language on the planet. Blockchains, for all their faults, theorize decentralized government, free of central coercion, based, even, on the metaphor of "consensus" between many disaggregated, independent, and even sometimes treacherous parties.

Yet, that said, we should take care in opposing an abstract concept like "nationalism." We should, instead, look at specific instances of nationalism at specific times and judge them individually. For instance, some forms of nationalism have undone colonialism, opposed racism, and achieved self-determination for denizens. Irish nationalism is a contested movement in which one side sees heroic liberation and the other sees treacherous mutiny. Others—like some forms of contemporary English nationalism—seem to be more insular and potentially even racist. How does it make sense to group both of these forms of "nationalism" under the same banner? To what extent can criticisms of nationalism that do not also pay attention to self-determination work well in the digital space?

Contemporary digital writing and text production takes place within these contexts. Multinational, world, and postcolonial literatures are all produced within digital systems that seem to exhibit this decentering of national contexts. Global supply-chains for e-books seem to confirm this rhizomatic type of structure rather than the centralized models of a national system. Indeed, Michael Clarke and Laura Ricci show how complex and distributed the mechanisms are, even for books that are free to download.[98] The shape of this distribution is not the hub-and-spoke model that one would expect if digital text dissemination systems were structured according to more centralized models of governance. It appears, at a glance, that these systems instead mirror the anarchic and distributed nature of the internet.

Except that I have demonstrated, throughout this chapter, that the internet and its systems are based, materially, on centralized structures that look quite a lot like nationalisms. In particular, I have highlighted here the ways in which Unicode's meliorist and incremental development means that designers must make selection decisions around which languages and codesets to develop first. In turn, this means making selections based on majority centrality and linguistic simplicity. As a result, the Latinate alphabet is inscribed from day one, while various Chinese, Korean, Vietnamese, and other Han-using cultures find their languages to be overlooked.

Further, the systems of decentralized government that are envisaged for the internet world can barely be said to function. Proof-of-work schemes on the blockchain may solve the theoretical problem of Byzantine Fault Tolerance in a distributed fashion, but they also consume so much electricity that they threaten to cause huge real-world damage through climate change. Again, the effects of global warming are felt unequally in different *national* contexts, both supranationally and subnationally.[99] Blockchain systems that use proof of space also exhibit traits that look a great deal like nationalistic contexts. Indeed, the idea of "holding land" or other types of property as a precursor to democratic participation has been a long-standing but flawed principle in many cultures.[100] In this system of consensus, agreement can only be formed by those who hold space, which has real-world material correlates in the form of hard disk and solid-state drives. Finally, blockchain systems that use proof of stake are hardly immune from nationalistic-esque frameworks. In these systems, those who own the biggest share of the network have the most say in building consensus around the next cryptographic block. It is the equivalent of a suffrage system based on how much money one has.

The Border Gateway Protocol and the workings of DNS are another example of how the internet appears as a decentralized space but actually consists of many different subnations that act autonomously. In this metaphor, there is a type of self-determination at play, where autonomous systems regain their own authority once one crosses the boundary onto their turf. Certainly, the true materiality of autonomous systems is one that *spans* national contexts. Although an autonomous system is bounded in many ways and appears as an isolated entity in a single space, it is also situated across different jurisdictions, with servers in different national spaces. BGP is, in many ways, one of the best examples, though, of how geopolitics continues to exert metaphorical pressure on our digital—and, therefore, digital-textual—environments.

All of these are, of course, metaphors and analogies. But what I have hoped to have shown in this chapter is that digital text is geopolitically structured by its underlying technologies. Certainly, as per Lessig, the internet and the web remain spaces that are constantly reimagined as libertarian, anarchic, decentralized, and antinationalist. But this is a perennial error. Instead, we should see how the tentacular flow of data through rhizomatic structures is actually underpinned by metaphors that reinscribe nationalisms and centralities. We are nowhere near escaping the powerful gravitational wells of our imagined communities, if that is even a desirable end.

FIVE

DIGITAL TEXT IS MULTIDIMENSIONAL

IF COMPETING GEOSPATIAL PHILOSOPHIES OF nationality and nationalism underpin many elements of digital text transmission, as explored in the preceding chapter, it is perhaps unsurprising that spatial elements of directionality and dimensionality (which are central to the spatialities of geopolitics) are also key to many metaphors in the computational world. Our supposed path of web browsing, for instance, is confined to the two-dimensional metaphors of a linear timeline: forward and backward. We also have *home* pages, but "home" refers to the start of a line of text, as well as the starting screens that users may customize within their browsers. Text, in general, is, of course, optical and spatially positioned, unless it is in tactile form for those with visual impairments. It is possible that we might also think of audiobooks, in purely sonic form, as "texts."[1] Digital text, though, is layered many more dimensions deep.

Indeed, consider the way in which multidimensionality is configured in contemporary web browsers for textual and media consumption—that is, through tabs and windows. Browsers also, though, contain the idea of a "history." This record of past websites that the user has "visited"—the bane of those using the internet for less savory purposes—appears, at first, to be one-dimensional. One can move back and forth (spatially) through time. Yet the idea of a browser history actually conceals a curiously advanced historiography. The assumed linearity of a browsing "history" cannot accommodate the fact that, in actuality, our histories are nonlinear and multiple, spread across many axes and dimensions—as are, in some ways, our offline reading practices. For instance, when a user goes back through the history in a browser and then clicks a different link, the historical timeline is immediately fractured. Instead of a simple lineage of page after page, the history at this point resembles a tree branch that has splintered off down a different fork. Furthermore, each tab within a window has its own separate historical tree, although the histories are usually still searchable as singular coherent entities. Different browsers will also have separate histories as these are stored by the software itself rather than the operating system.

Yet, even as these entries for past visits fork and twist and mutate into complex linked data structures that are anything but straightforward, they can also be reassembled into a linear timeline of visits in a chronological order. Because human multitasking is a type of context switching, where we perform operations in sequence but at speed, merely to generate the illusion of simultaneity, it is possible to arrange websites visited into a temporal sequence, albeit one that is underpinned by the aforementioned multidimensionality. Hence, here we see the ways in which multidimensionality in virtual text interfaces becomes flattened. As a result, we can extend Kirschenbaum's definitional thinking about computers, which, remember, are distinguished "not by virtue of their supposed immateriality but by virtue of their being material machines conceived and built to sustain an *illusion* of immateriality."[2] Our interfaces are also built to sustain an illusion of one-dimensionality.

This chapter is concerned with the metaphors of spatial placement of computer users and the directionalities from those placements that are assumed. Tracing this back to Howard Hinton's explorations of multidimensionality in his concept of the tesseract in the nineteenth century, I here attempt to disturb our metaphors of time and place.[3] This chapter aims to force a reconsideration of the ways in which multidimensionality is grafted atop linearity in the digital environment, thereby asking difficult questions of thought processes, reading practices, and navigation.

This chapter is as much about the "unbinding" of our reading pathways as was chapter 2 in its discussion of non-pagelike digital pages. Drawing on theorizations of nonlinearity in electronic literature—while avoiding clichéd and outmoded rehashings of statements about "hypertext"—I here look to dismantle the simple unidirectionality of metaphors of start-to-end reading. I do so not only through technological analysis but also with reference to "multidimensional texts" such as B. S. Johnson's book in a box, *The Unfortunates* (1969).

Finally, this chapter advances the arguments about "home" and othered "away" that were hinted at in the preceding chapter, noting the importance of how and where imagined textual readers and producers are placed by interface and software design. I also query the binaries of the terms used herein. What does it mean, I ask, to present different spaces as "homes" in various contexts, and who makes the decision about the identity of home in such environments? Why is it that the antonym of "home" in the digital-textual sense is "end" and not "away"? How might we read the globalized political contexts of digital homes?

What Are Dimensions?

What are "dimensions" and why do they matter?[4] Any object in space can be pinpointed, in Cartesian coordinate geometry, by length (x), breadth (y), and depth (z). Our thought on the spatial placement of objects is usually constrained by these dimensions because they correlate to our vision and interactions with the world. We can move in three dimensions: forward/backward, side-to-side, and up/down. The concept of time as a phenomenon through which we might "travel," though, introduces a further axis (w). An object might be said to exist at a spatial but also a temporal coordinate. Imagine that, at 8:55 a.m., I move the glass on my table. Its previous position could be specified by a set of coordinates and a time stamp, as then could its new position. If, then, we were able to travel through time in any direction except forward and at any pace (except for the regular rate of one second per second), this fourth coordinate could be considered a dimension that would allow us to locate the object not only in space but also at a particular given moment in time—hence the development of the idea of "space-time" as a unified set of field coordinates for locating objects in space and time simultaneously.

Dimensions beyond four are difficult for humans to understand. What would a fifth dimension look like? An additional dimension can be anything that adds an element of categorization to an object. For instance, if one were categorizing dogs and carp, a fifth dimension could be "number of legs." In this (usually binary) categorization, dogs would be bundled around the "four-leg" mark and carp at the zero point, some rare fish mutations and unfortunate dog-accidents aside. Hence, if one were plotting dogs and carp on a graph, they could have length, breadth, depth, time . . . and number of legs. A sixth dimension might be "number of tails." A seventh might be "number of ears," and so forth. Anything that can be used to categorize can be seen as a dimension and plotted as orthogonal extensions on graphs.

One can also imagine how these are laid out in space. If the first three dimensions are clear (see figure 2), then one has to imagine fourth, fifth, and sixth dimensions as orthogonal extensions to the other axes, adding an extra layer of "depth" to the plot for every additional dimension. These plotted axes are not really "visible" in the same way as the first three-dimensional plots—hence the idea in science fiction that aliens might come from "another dimension" that is inaccessible to us.

Nonetheless, spatial dimensionality and its visualizations have long histories that date back to Arthur Cayley's "Chapters in the Analytic Geometry of (n) Dimensions" from 1843. Yet such spatial thinking, claim figures as diverse as David Harvey and Michel Foucault, has been devalued. Harvey, for example, noted that there has been a consistent prioritization of "time and history over space and geography."[5] Foucault, in a similar vein, but from a very different standpoint, argued that

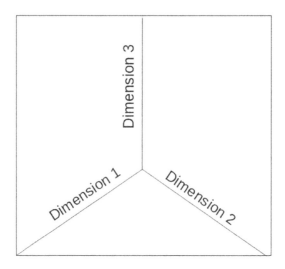

FIGURE 2. **Dimensional plots in space**

since Kant, there had been an undervaluing of spatial concerns.[6] Time
and history have proved, apparently, more fertile grounds for thinking about literature and text, in particular, even though both time and
space are ultimate prerequisites for any understanding of human perception (even forming part of Kant's transcendental aesthetic).[7]

Chapter 3 of this book, which focuses on the seriality of musical
silence as a metaphorical structure for thinking about digital text
reproduction, concerned as it is with the "playback" of a bitstream,
also has such a temporal focus. Music, after all, might be thought of as
the "temporal art," a form that relies as much on its unfolding across
time as it does its presence in space (and seemingly more so than other
"fixed" works of art that do not vary so greatly as time progresses).[8] In
the constant re-unfolding of text, even when it *appears* instantaneous,
I draw in chapter 3 attention to the analogy with music.

Yet, as above, this temporal axis can be considered as though it
were subordinated to space. Time can be seen as just another spatial
dimension, plotted alongside the Cartesian points. The simplest indication of this takes the form of a diagram known as a tesseract, which
is a four-dimensional figure (see figure 3). Charles Howard Hinton, a

nineteenth-century spiritualist and scientist, became so obsessed with higher-dimensional spatial thinking that he developed a series of cubes to help people imagine how they might "move" in multidimensional space.[9] This developed into a full-blown system of "education" for the betterment of his pupils in the training of their higher-dimensional sensibilities.[10] Hence, while it remains difficult to think in dimensions beyond three, or perhaps at a push, four, such concerns have lingered since the nineteenth century.

What has this all to do with text and digital text processing? The answer, as we will go on to see, is: a great deal. Spatial awareness across multiple dimensions and formats forms a key prerequisite for understanding our systems of word processing. From the orientation of text across the axes of "home" to "end," atop the markup language that constitutes Microsoft Word's markup formats, digital text must be understood as thoroughly multidimensional.

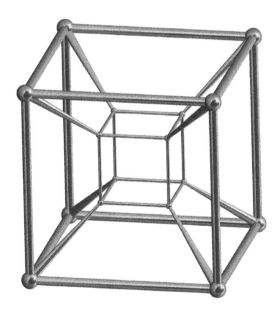

FIGURE 3. A projection of the tesseract. Image created by Robert Webb's Stella software: http://www.software3d.com/Stella.php

Software as a Bad Reader

How many users of Microsoft Word know what a Word file *is*? Or—perhaps the question should be—what a Word file *are*? Users are used to conceiving of file formats as layered documents that operate across different strata. Some users know that the text that is rendered visible in a word processor is, underneath the hood, stored in a very different format to that presented to the writer or reader. It is the job of various renderer softwares to interpret the byte stream and to display it back to the user in the format that is requested by the author or viewer. It is an onion-like layering.

Microsoft Word has two different file formats that have changed over time. They are respectively denoted by the suffix extensions .doc and .docx, with a fundamental difference between the two files. The former specifies the Microsoft Office Word 97–2003 Binary File Format. As the Library of Congress describes it, "The Microsoft Word Binary File format, with the .doc extension and referred to here as DOC, was the default format used for documents in Microsoft Word from Word 97 (released in 1997) through Microsoft Office 2003. Although it cannot support all functionality of the Word application introduced since Word 2007, the DOC format has continued to be available as an alternative to the DOCX/OOXML format, standardized in ISO/IEC 29500, for saving document files in Word."[11]

This earlier Microsoft Word file format is a direct binary format. That is, if you open the file in a "plaintext" editor that is unable to interpret the stream of bytes, you will see what appears to be garbage of the nature: "�aA$%<0��. ��A!�n"�n#�n$�n3P." This is because .doc files consist of a CFB header of 512 bytes, with hexadecimal numbers (such as "D0CF11E0A1B11AE1") indicating to the program what type of file this is. That said, even the computer/human legibility aspect of this header is complex. Clearly, the initial hexadecimal string here of "D0CF11E" (by itself equivalent to the decimal number 218951966) also bears a striking resemblance to the word "DOCFILE," even while the rest of the file is unreadable.[12] Hence, it seems clear that the interplay between human comprehensibility and machine code signaling is a site of experiment and play for the designers of this format; it is not merely a purely functional space.

Writing software that can read this earlier format, set out in the extremely complicated developer's manual, is, shall we say, "involved." An example excerpt from the File Information Block descriptor in this document serves as a good marker of the challenges. Consider the impenetrably named section 2.5.8 FibRgFcLcb2002, which, we are told, is "a variable-sized portion of the Fib. It extends the FibRgFcLcb2000." If the user seeks further clarification on this cryptic remark, the "enlightening" section on data elements in the Plcfbkfd proves suitably opaque: "Each data element in the Plcfbkfd is associated, in a one-to-one correlation, with a data element in the Plcfbkld at offset fcPlcfBklFactoid. For this reason, the Plcfbkfd that begins at offset fcPlcfBkfFactoid, and the Plcfbkld that begins at offset fcPlcfBklFactoid, MUST contain the same number of data elements. The Plcfbkfd is parallel to the SttbfBkmkFactoid at offset fcSttbfBkmkFactoid in the Table Stream." The web page detailing this near-indecipherable stream of jargon has, conveniently, a useful feedback tool attached, where the user is asked to rate, with a thumbs up or thumbs down, whether "this page is helpful."[13]

Many pieces of software have attempted accurately to comply with these instructions over the years. LibreOffice and OpenOffice are just two examples of open-source implementations. However, without blaming the developers in any way, their implementations are flawed and .doc Word files frequently display with errors or glitches in these programs. Given the volume of software that struggles accurately to read and reproduce these files, it is perhaps clear that most users would be giving a distinctive "thumbs down" at this point. More importantly, though, the difficulty of understanding these instructions means that many pieces of software are *bad interpreters* of the document format. Or, to use a phrase with significant currency in literary and cultural studies, many pieces of software might be considered "bad readers."

Merve Emre has charted, in recent days, the ways in which the figure of the "bad reader" has been constructed in postwar America.[14] From the perspective of high-literary art, as Kenneth Burke put it with rhetorical overstatement, it seemed in this period that "the spread of literacy through compulsory education made readers of people who had no genuine interest in literature," a veritable "overwhelming army of bad readers" who threatened the forms of the difficult literature of the "art of the minority."[15] Such "bad readers," in Emre's definition, are "individuals socialized into the practices of readerly identification, emotion, action, and interaction."[16] Put otherwise, bad readers are those who seem actually to enjoy reading.

When we say that software is a bad reader—or a bad interpreter—we mean something quite different. In this case, there is a precise specification that details a desired outcome from the reading process, and there is a "correct" interpretation. Indeed, perhaps the clearest example of this is the Cascading Style Sheets Acid Test, which is designed to evaluate whether a browser is a "good reader." (The name comes from the "acid test for gold," which refers to situations where nitric acid is applied to a patch of gold. Real gold will be impervious to any corrosion. However, given that the Acid Test for web browsers displays a yellow smiley face, there is undoubtedly a reference, here, to the 1990s "acid" or rave music scenes, revolving around LSD.) When the Acid2 test, for example, has been run correctly by a browser, the smiley face reference figure shown below in figure 4 will be displayed. In browsers with rendering flaws, the face will end up distorted, as in figure 5.

The delineation of "good readership" here is, as I have already noted, very different from the value-laden strictures of fiction reading. Furthermore, the centralized authority of reading instruction in the computational space poses interesting challenges for understanding *who* gets to decide on the correct interpretation. Yet a similar phenomenon can be seen in the world of web browsers. For many years, Microsoft's Internet Explorer was the dominant browser platform in use around the world. Ironically, Microsoft indeed continues to act aggressively to inscribe this browser, the latest incarnation of which is called Edge, at the center (rather than the sill) of its operating system, Windows.[17]

While most developers assume that it is standards that drive the correct interpretative paradigm for websites, this was, for much of the web's life, far from the truth of the matter. Internet Explorer's domi-

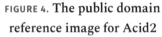

FIGURE 4. The public domain
reference image for Acid2

FIGURE 5. A failed rendering
of Acid2

nance from approximately 1996 until 2013, replacing Netscape Navigator and achieving over 90 percent usage share in some years, meant essentially that the way that this software interpreted the web was "the right way," regardless of whether it conformed to the specifications.[18] A raft of pages appeared, over this period, that proclaimed that they were "designed for" or were "best viewed in" Internet Explorer. The downfall of Internet Explorer came from antitrust legislative action against Microsoft but also from a series of security vulnerabilities that tarnished the giant's reputation.

What is the analogy here? Internet Explorer was definitely a "bad reader" in the sense that it grossly ignored the specification of the standards in favor of going it alone. It consistently failed the Acid Test. The basic strategy deployed by Microsoft was to use sheer bravado to assert to most Web users that the way that Internet Explorer did it was the way that was right and that those who wished to use the official standards to design their websites would find themselves misrepresented in this browser. In turn, the effect of a dominant "bad reader" here was to create "bad writers." It was very hard for website designers to ignore nine out of ten users in favor of an abstract standard that was not adopted by the most prevalently used software system in deployment. In other words, the bullying presence of Internet Explorer, dictating that to read badly was the right approach, made people write badly, in order to achieve interpretative effect.

What actually emerged here was a "genre" system of websites aiming to cater for a specific "bad" readerly demographic, in contravention of other loftier (yet self-appointed) "standards" of what the "literature" (a website) should be. Internet Explorer exerted the same influence on website authors as do the armies of "bad" readers who invest emotionally in romance fiction on the authors of such works. "Give the readers what they want" is the type of phrasing that one might expect in the Age of Amazon.[19] When your primary readership cries out for an interpretative paradigm, it is unsurprising to find that authors will design for that very format.

What does it mean to be a bad "author" in the authorship of a file format like MS Word documents? Like natural languages, programming languages have syntax and semantics.[20] Let us return to the same example from a markup language that I use in an earlier chapter. The text that I give there is an example of the later version of Microsoft Word's format markup for emboldening text: "<w:B>text</w:B>." So far, so good. However, markup is usually nested several layers deep, and it is important that opening and closing tags correspond to one another. A more realistic example, then, might be: "<w:P><w:I><w:B>text</w:B></w:I></w:P>." This fictitious example denotes a paragraph ("w:P") that contains a piece of text that is both italic ("w:I") and bold ("w:B").

However, if we read the specification document, we are told specifically that tags must be closed in the order here demonstrated. You cannot, for instance, write "<w:P><w:I><w:B>text</w:P></w:B>" (with no closing "w:I" tag and the "w:P" tag closed wrongly before the "w:B" element) and expect the reader (word processor) to display your text correctly. Further, the rest of the document structure can potentially be corrupted by this type of malformatting. Note that, in this last example, there is no closing italic tag ("/w:I"). Should, in this case, the entire rest of the document stay in italics? Or perhaps because the outer tag ("w:P") has already been closed, we should assume that all of its inner tags should also be deemed closed? In other words, the behavior in this situation is undefined and delegated to the interpretation of software. There is no guarantee that two pieces of software—written by two separate coders—will agree on the same behavior or interpretation of this file. As with natural language formulations such as "Visiting relatives can be exhausting" (is it the act of visiting that is exhausting or the visiting relatives themselves?), there can be more than one way to interpret a file format, and the particular interpretation is down to the individual code of each piece of software. Over time, as particularly dominant bad readers inscribe their incorrectness within systems, these interpretations become seen as *correct*. Bad, antistandardized readings become de facto correct readings as authors adapt.

There are two ways that dominant bad readers—such as Internet Explorer or even Microsoft Word—can affect the way that authors write. The first is through their passive behavioral assumptions, tolerance of faulty file data, and the casual slippage in authorship that this can introduce. If Internet Explorer, or another majority bad reader, allows slips in syntax, then authors learn that they can get away with writing sloppy code. Why go to the effort of writing according to the specification document if readers simply do not care or even interpret your instructions wrongly? Further, those learning to write judge their outputs by readerly (software) reception. If non-standards-compliant code produces the desired result, with less cognitive burden on the author, then why bother to write well?

The stakes of such language slippage are arguably higher in the space of computational languages when compared to natural languages. It is always the case that natural languages evolve with use. "Momentarily," for instance, has shifted from meaning "for a moment" to "in a moment," nonetheless causing merriment among linguistic pedants who scoff at the idea that their transatlantic flight might remain airborne for merely a brief instant. American English also has many semantic differences from British English that have mutated over time. For example, in American English it is possible to "write you," while in British English the adverbial prepositional phrase "write to you" would be correct usage. Still, nobody in either of these dialects would misconstrue what was meant. In formalized imperative computing language structures, though, the syntactic shifts here cause irreparable semantic damage. Multiple readers—that is, different pieces of software—will interpret and display differently the reordered syntactic configurations shown above. In the face of such competing interpretations, even when there is an official standard, it becomes easier simply to cater to the majority reader.

The second way in which bad readers encourage "bad writing" is in seemingly deliberately ignoring and violating the standards. This is a more active and pernicious type of intervention than the passive version above. Internet Explorer, for example, interpreted web documents in a way that was different from every other browser. That is to say that Internet Explorer would interpret a standards-compliant document differently from other browsers. This in turn led to its behavior, even if undocumented, of becoming a rogue de facto standard for development.

Some of this criticism of Internet Explorer is a little unfair. One of the key points to recognize is that, at the time when Internet Explorer was first developed, web standards hardly existed. On the other hand, Internet Explorer continued to behave as a quirky/bad reader long into the era of cross-browser compatibility and support. Here we have a case that is the precise opposite of the Microsoft Word legacy specification—a case where the standards documents themselves were eminently comprehensible and achievable, but there was a majority readership (Microsoft) that seemingly wanted something different. In other words, Internet Explorer was the popular market genre reader that demanded esoteric syntax (perhaps casual language/slang usage) instead of the formal grammarian characteristics of the spec. By contrast, the totally baffling Microsoft Word specification document seems to set impossibly high standards for a kind of computational "literariness." To "write" or code as Word demands—and to be able to read back its file format—is an incredibly difficult enterprise. Hence, the "bad" readers that we see in this world—OpenOffice and LibreOffice—are only unable to reproduce the file format correctly because the original specification was so beyond the realm of sanity. Further, the mark of a correct Word file in another piece of software is that it *looks the same as in Microsoft Word*, not that it adheres to the technical specification.

In this way, both Word and OpenOffice/LibreOffice can be considered "bad" readers, depending on one's frame of reference for correctness.

In fairness, Microsoft has worked to improve the Word specification format. Specifically, more recent versions of Word use the XML format that I have been taking as examples over the past few chapters. Except, sadly to say, that on top of this XML format, MS Word documents are also zip files, a type of (optionally) compressed file that allows for the storage of an entire file tree inside a single object. Indeed, that is precisely what a .docx file is: a zip archive that contains a series of interlinked XML files. Hence, again, we can now see why a Word document is like an onion. They are both layered (or multidimensional). And fragile.

The format of multiple layers of files—where the bottom stratum is different from the upper layer—has parallels with the style of interpretation that Louis Althusser et al. dubbed "symptomatic reading." In models of symptomatic reading, texts show symptoms (which are usually contradictions of themselves) that betray the assumptions of the ideological environment within which they were created. Importantly, such symptoms are often the *"absence of a concept behind a word."*[21] Crucially, this model of interpretation works because, in modes of symptomatic reading, there is an assumption of "the existence of two texts" with a "different text present as a necessary absence in the first."[22] Symptomatic reading is as important for literary studies as any other of the high-theory models for understanding multiple parallel registers, such as Jean Genet's *Ce qui est resté d'un Rembrandt déchiré en petits carrés bien réguliers, et foutu aux chiottes* (1967), Jacques Derrida's *Glas* (1974), or Roland Barthes's *S/Z* (1970).[23]

Computer files exhibit this double or sometimes even triple register. The formatting that we see on the screen is always the result of software interpretation and the transformation of the bitstream from an underlying set of lower-level encoded and sequential instructions (the seriality of music to which an earlier chapter gestures). A malfunctioning interpretative system can have consequences that range from data damage on disk to merely malformatted output—a badly written file, likewise.

In the case of the most recent MS Word file format, the interpretation runs many layers deep. The XML files inside the zip must be interpreted and displayed to the user. Before that can happen, the zip file has to be correctly read from the disk and interpreted as an archive. Before that happens, the system has to read the binary data and represent (or interpret) it as a file structure. At each of these stages the multidimensionality of the file format is paramount. Across multiple axes, software can be a good, bad, or terrible reader, with consequences for how we construct and deconstruct our digital-textual writings. It can be difficult to know, under this scenario, where a digital text starts and where it ends.

Home and Away

Is it not strange, considering the spatial metaphor, that lines of text on a computer system begin at "home" but stop at "end"? Certainly, the use of a four-letter word, rather than the slightly longer "start," might seem intuitive for reasons of space on the keyboard. However, "pause," "PrtScn," "delete," and "insert" all violate this length principle. "Start" also had a lengthy legacy in the naming of Microsoft's famous over-arching system menu. Yet "home" has many connotations, some of which may be actively confusing for a computer user. For instance, why should we use the term "home" to refer both to the start of a line of text and to the default web page when one opens a browser? Given that modern keyboards often have a symbol designed specifically to launch, say, a calculator application, it can hardly be intuitive to believe that the home key should mean the start of a line of text, rather than triggering a "home screen" or "home page" of some kind. Instead, I contend, "home" and "end" are further examples of multidimensionality in digital text.

Etymologically, "home" finds its roots in the German *heim, ham*, and *heem*, which in turn come, surprisingly, from the Indo-European *kei*, which means both to lie down and something dear and beloved: a place to lay one's head.[24] And, indeed, John Hollander situates the "Macintosh function key" that will take him "back to the top of [his] document" within the context of "a place of origin returned to."[25] In this sense, the "home" of the computer keyboard, as an origin, shares a linguistic kinship with one's "homeland" as a place of starting out, of birth. It is curious, then, given the association with natality, that Hollander notes the half-rhymes with "home" of "womb" and also "tomb." From start to end.

The collision of "home" with ideas of birth also finds a locus in the shared etymology of "quaint." In a somewhat bold section of *The Madness of Knowledge*, Steven Connor points to how the term "quaint" overlaps with "canny" and, therefore, *heimlich* (homely). With Chaucerian resonance, then, home finds itself linked to "cunt" via *queynte*, an original birthplace and bodily site of all reproduction, albeit here crudely expressed. The continued hammering of "home" after "home" after "home" on line after line after line of text has a forcefulness that suits its etymological cousin, albeit at several removes; but its etymology carries a sense of textual rebirth with every homely return to the canal of amniotic beginning.[26]

Home is, though, importantly, a spatial location. As Mary Douglas notes, while home is not necessarily "a fixed space," home is "located in space." One cannot, in her formulation, ask, "How is home?" (although this could mean "How are things at home?"), "When is home?" (except to a time traveler), and "Who is home?" (save in the meaning of "Who is currently present in a domicile?"). Such questions would be akin to asking, as did the satirical 1990s pop duo, The KLF, "What time is love?" Home is—or even "was," as since-destroyed premises could also be referred to as one's previous or ancestral "home"—a physical location and space. Indeed, geographic regions that no longer exist can still be thought of as one's home, to which it is now impossible ever to return.[27]

Despite the sometimes-impossible nature of going back, there is also a sense of "safe return" in the idea of home that perhaps comes from the Greek term *nostos*—a homeward journey.[28] The carriage return on the keyboard, derived from the typewriter where the cartridge would, truly, move physically back toward the starting edge of the paper for a new line, perhaps gives us an idea of why "home" should prove a valuable metaphor. Every return keypress is its own *Odyssey*. "Home" is, of course, also a verb that means to seek, most commonly applied to pigeons and missiles, one rather more destructive than the other. Curiously, in this scenario, the avian form, when homing, is designed to return to the starting point—to *return* home. Meanwhile, to target the point of origin is distinctly not the goal of a homing missile, which must fixate on an enemy other if it is to avoid friendly fire. Home can sometimes mean to target an other space that is "away."

The idea of home is ensconced within a set of political economies and moralities. As John Berger famously noted, since the seventeenth-century rise of the bourgeoisie, there have been two moralities around the idea of home, sometimes in tension with one another. A ruling class appropriated the idea of homeland in service of a nation-state patriotism that allowed the argument that to die for one's country was personally beneficial to those who would actually do the dying. Meanwhile, a "domestic morality" arose that encompassed a more localized sphere of estates and family, including women and children, and that also circles around ideas of the nuclear family.[29] Certainly, the idea of generalized property ownership also falls into this latter category.

While "home" and "house" have become synonymous in some regions (although "home ownership" implies that one's home need not be one's own house or building), home also implies a regularization, a place where space and time are "structured functionally, economically, aesthetically and morally" in the service of domestic community practices.[30] Homes, in such a setup, are about the "organization of space over time, and the allocation of resources in space and over time."[31] In such thinking, an economy of textual production that situates its home at the beginning, in opposition to its close at the end, makes more sense. Indeed, the idea of repetition, in which one repeatedly returns to the home of the next line, seems to hold this concept of spatial regularization at its core. Every line has its common beginning and end, and the point of origin, the beginning, is the "home."

Yet in the "home" of text processing, the home to which one returns is rarely the same as the home from which one departed. Every line has its own and new home. Hence it is not the writer's "home" to which it is returned but instead the home that belongs to the line yet to be written. Further, the "end" of the line of text is hardly, itself, actually an end. Most lines overflow beyond a newline character, meaning that the "end" of a line rarely coincides with any kind of semantic buffer. In contrast, lines do more regularly start, at home, with the beginning of a semantic unit, mostly because of paragraph breaks. Except that such text is usually preceded by a tab, a series of blank spaces that offset the beginning of text from the home character anchor. In this sense, it is almost as though semantic presence cannot begin precisely at "home" and must, instead, be physically separated by another instance of that "whitespace" to which we turned in a previous chapter.

Home also implies an encapsulation of sorts, which is where a multidimensionality begins to appear. One of the points of home as an organized space is that it defines boundaries that contain its regularizations; it becomes the basic economic and socio-functional unit within which we operate. Hence, the operation of the term "home" is also one that delineates. In each line having its own home, each line is set apart, cut off from those that precede and those that follow it. That there are multiple homes in each location—the home of a page, the home of a line—serves to set apart the multiple operational units, in much the same way as one may have a home property while also possessing a home country. The boundaries of home are not mutually exclusive. Home, then, becomes a way in which individuals are separated from each other and can be told apart. In other words, that we each have a different home is a way in which individuals can be distinguished as coming from different backgrounds. At the same time, when we share a home, we mark ourselves as part of a specific collective of shared origin, be that at the level of the house or the nation. Such a multiplicity occurs across multiple dimensions in text processing systems. Every line has its own "home" and is marked apart. However, every digital page also has its own "home" at the top of the digital "page." Lines within pages share a home. Further, each document has a home, keyed to the very start. Pages within a document share a home. Browser windows, likewise, can have a communal "home." There are, then, multiple ways in which homes are shared as spaces that bind disparate items together and instances where homes are individuated, separating otherwise similar elements from each other.

Home is also often figured as an imagined and idealized space—much like a nation—but one that is frequently seen to be unrealizable. For instance, Aviezer Tucker claims that "most people spend their lives in search of home, at the gap between the natural home and the particular ideal home where they would be fully fulfilled."[32] Whether or not this is true—and it seems a futile quest to spend one's entire life imagining an ideal home against which reality could never adequately compare—it is certainly the case that "nostalgic or romantic notions" often fuel our idea of homeliness.[33] Given that, in Doreen Massey's formulation, there can be "no single simple 'authenticity'—a unique eternal truth of an (actual or imagined/remembered) place or home"—the very being of home is based upon such reconstructions.[34] That is to say that "home" is always a retrospective construction of return. Does a blank line have a home? Not really. The homeness of the beginning is only realized once the line contains additional content. That said, this is not always the case. Because digital pages are prestructured to their laid-out dimensions—a blank page has the same dimensions as a full page—the idea of "home" in the page context makes more sense. Again, though, this requires the prestructuration of the page. Home can only be retroactively constructed once the page, whether blank or full, has been laid out.

In computational-textual contexts, there is, also, rarely such a thing as homelessness. Every line of text has its origin to which it is necessary to (carriage) return, although it may then need the line to unfold in order for the home space to exist. Yet the idea of home as an original site that each of us possesses and yearns for also brings into question the idea of homelessness as a general societal concept. In another context, there are also people whose ancestral "homelands" or even actual buildings ("homes") have been destroyed. In these cases, return is rendered impossible by the destruction or irreparable alternation of the original space of home, regardless of how rose-tinted that nostalgic reconstruction might be. In these instances, home is a purely mental configuration that is irrecoverable. In text processing terms, this does not seem ever to be the case. I cannot think of an instance where the originary "home" would no longer exist, except as a reconfigured page layout that renders a different home space, albeit one that is still at the top left or right, depending on the orientation of one's textual direction. Nonetheless, the sensitivities that are required when speaking of homelessness, from a privileged position of having a home, are many.[35]

Why is "end" the opposite of "home"? What other oppositions might we use? There are a range of antonyms for "home." They include "away," "out" (meaning: not "at home"), "uncomfortable" or "unconfident" (to be "not at home" with something), and "foreign." The first of these, "away," was perhaps most famously used in Home and Away, the Australian TV soap opera from the 1980s. The premise of this series revolved around a foster care home in a rural environment, in which children from the city were transplanted to a new environment, based on a real-life observation from the series' conceiver, Alan Bateman.[36] "Away," as an antonym, here becomes an Other space that must be read by the new inhabitants. "Away" is also, though, the term often used in soccer matches and other sporting fixtures to denote playing at a stadium that is not one's "home." In this sense, "away" becomes an "enemy" of home, the other team, even if only in a sporting context.

"Foreign" is also a tricky antonym for "home." Clearly, it applies usually at the country level, recalling the earlier discussion of digital nationalisms. In text processing terms, it also doesn't make much sense. While "home" may denote an originary return to the beginning of the page area, "foreign" has a different character and feel to it, one that also seems to carry a slightly nationalistic and potentially xenophobic character. "Foreign," in pagination and text processing terms, feels as though it might refer to a new sheet.

Yet "end" has a strange doubleness. While we may think of "end" as the opposite of "home," in terms of human death the end is often referred to as "going home." In Gerry Rafferty's hugely overplayed hit, "Baker Street," the well-known saxophone solo is punctuated by the insistence that the protagonist is "going home" at the start of a "new morning," possibly at the end of another one-night stand, liaisons that he intends to "give up." In the Odyssey, by contrast, the most famous of ancient poetic journeys, the end is a return to home after the Trojan War. The last book of the seemingly interminable *Lord of the Rings*—"The Return of the King"—mostly centers on the Hobbits' homeward journey. Which is all to say that homes are often ends and not just starting origins. Homes are frequently ensnared in the circularity of return.

"Home" and "end" in text processing terms can refer to the same thing. On the blank line, which I previously referred to as "homeless," pressing the home and end keys does exactly the same thing: precisely nothing. At the point of carriage return, the end of the new line/morning is also (going) home. There is a conflation of spatiality at this point that has an Odyssean quality but only, as before, when the line has not yet been written. And, of course, these homes are all nested beneath other subhomes of pages and documents.

The directionality of home is also nowhere so clear as in the system of web browser histories, to which I gestured earlier in this chapter and to which I will now more thoroughly return. "Home" refers to multiple elements of web browsing and, therefore, contemporary text dissemination. The authors of websites have their own personal "home pages." These pages are one's owned space on the web. However, interestingly, the history of home pages indicates many analogies with real-world housing. For instance, in the 1990s and early 2000s, "site builders" such as GeoCities and MySpace gave people the opportunity, within certain predefined boundaries, easily to establish their own home pages.

These site builders offered some level of customization to their "end" users—often resulting in hilariously bad design aesthetics, such as blinking and scrolling marquee headings alongside outrageously garish animated GIFs—but also came with a prefabricated and templated feel. When the mass desire for "home(pages)" on the web blew up, the market responded in the same way as it had with real houses: by building row after row of prefabricated homes within housing estates. While these personal home pages grew in popularity, they also began a process of personal brand distinction, in which those who used GeoCities, for example, found themselves at the bottom of a hierarchy compared to the mansions and manors of custom-built "grand designs" sites.

In this sense, as Jessica Lingel has put it, there has been a form of "gentrification" of the internet.[37] "Gentrification" is a provocative and controversial term. In Gina Pérez's helpful definition, gentrification is "an economic and social process whereby private capital (real estate firms, developers) and individual homeowners and renters reinvest in fiscally neglected neighborhoods through housing rehabilitation, loft conversions, and the construction of new housing stock. Unlike urban renewal, gentrification is a gradual process, occurring one building or block at a time, slowly reconfiguring the neighborhood landscape of consumption and residence by displacing poor and working-class residents unable to afford to live in 'revitalized' neighborhoods with rising rents, property taxes, and new businesses catering to an upscale clientele."[38] "Gentrification," then, is a term relating to power and wealth differentials with those further up these hierarchies gradually displacing the original denizens. In real-world property situations, it refers to an influx of more powerful and wealthy residents—sometimes with state support and planning—to an area that previously suffered financial deprivation, with the eventual resulting exit of the extant population. Some see this type of change as beneficial. It can be perceived as an "upgrading" of areas that were previously under-resourced, with the introduction of higher-quality housing and better facilities. On the other hand, economic demographics frequently map atop racial characteristics, meaning that fiscal immigration can also carry with it unwanted displacements of specific racial groups. Or, put otherwise: gentrification as it occurs in the real world can often be extremely racist. As a result, gentrification "exaggerates inequality and normalizes certain social values while excluding others"—it is not a neutral process of one-way improvement but rather a complex interlocking set of values-based propositions that are masked under the rubric of "economics."[39]

Why should we think of gentrification as a good metaphor for the web and histories of multidimensional text transmission? With the growth and supposed democratic outreach of the web, a similar set of gentrifying tendencies have emerged in the online space that share distressing characteristics of "discrimination, segregation, and commercialization."[40] Lingel separates out these aspects of electronic gentrification under the headings of displacement, isolation, and commercialization, with each denoting a separate series of movements. For instance, with respect to displacement, it is easy to see how the original idea of the web "home page"—in the earliest days of the internet, handcrafted only by technocrats with the know-how—gave way to platform-based alternatives, albeit with some level of design freedom, such as GeoCities, Yahoo!, etc., before finally ending up in the hands of the very, very few—near-monopolistic platforms such as Facebook. The sorting algorithms of these platforms, at the same time, are designed to silo users into categories. Hence, users and their home pages are algorithmically categorized and filtered to specific other users, making for a densely interlinked network formation but without the open-endedness of an unlimited many-to-many relationship, as it was envisioned in the original web.[41] The commercialization of the internet is, of course, rather more apparent and obvious.[42]

One of the problems with this metaphor, raised by Lingel, is that the internet was never really *not* gentrified. There was no "golden age," as she puts it, when information was free and the internet was "blind to race, class, and gender."[43] However, there is a distinct *movement* discernible in the direction that the web has taken since the early 1990s toward consolidation. This consolidation, though, is of a curious nature. While it is true that organizations such as Facebook have come to dominate the landscape of web presence through the centralization to which I earlier gestured, the luxury or distinctive commodity nature of these spaces is lower. This value proposition can be explained through a simple example. While the mass adoption of Facebook has led to a centralization, its "premises" are not high value. The sheer proliferation of Facebook accounts and the fact that anybody can establish them means that the customization value of such digital sites is low. Those with their own domain names and custom blog sites have a far higher degree of independence, and therefore kudos, at least among certain classes of technically savvy users.

This is all to say that while, in the real world, gentrification happens with custom, luxury builds coming to dominate the landscape, in the digital world such centralization by corporate entities brings homoge-

nization and mass access. The move, then, is not from mass, standardized, poor-quality housing toward individuated, custom, expensive,
luxury properties. It is instead the inverse. The displacement is of those
with custom (even if not high-quality) housing by mass, standardized
productions. (Although nobody is forcing people with custom websites
to move into platformized ecosystems, the pressure nonetheless exists
because these ecologies remain hermetically sealed. Facebook and
others are *walled* cities with the intention of keeping citizens *inside*.)

There are also multiple levels at which gentrification operates that
pertain to platformization, another way that digital text finds itself
layered, multidimensionally, atop various bases.[44] Among the examples of how homes become colonized or gentrified by platformization
tendencies, WordPress is perhaps the clearest. WordPress is both a
software platform and a hosting platform. Under the hood, WordPress
is a Perl Hypertext Processor (PHP) software platform for blogging.
Released under the GNU Public License v2 (a viral CopyLeft license),
anybody can download the source code to WordPress and run their own
instance of the software. The theming and plugin engines in Word-
Press are extremely versatile and allow for extensive customization,
meaning that different WordPress installs can appear entirely distinct
from one another, in aesthetic and even functional terms. Behind the
scenes, though, WordPress sites are running the same codebase; they
are subject to the same flows, and they often suffer from the same software vulnerabilities.

Simultaneously, as part of its sustainability efforts (but also its
endeavor to bring access to blogging to the masses) WordPress.com,
run by the American globally distributed company Automattic, offers
a hosting service in which it will run the software on behalf of users.
There are tiers available that range from free to paid installations, the
higher levels of which offer custom domains and other tailored services.
As a result, there are two ways in which WordPress ends up dominat-
ing the landscape: through its provision of its underlying open-source
software and through its hosting services.

It is first worth noting, at this point, that WordPress.com is hardly
an evil corporate behemoth, perhaps thereby signaling the moral com-

plexity of depicting a landscape of digital gentrification. There is no point, as Lingel notes, in painting a "one-sided picture where all tech companies are evil."[45] Automattic clearly contributes a large volume of open-source software to the world for free every year, which could be considered the provision of a public good. Without getting too far into the rhetoric of "wealth producers," large companies like Automattic are also responsible for many staff members' livelihoods every year.

On the other hand, the challenges of governance here can be seen by the fact that the underlying open-source software, WordPress, is managed by a separate foundation: the WordPress Foundation. Founded by Matt Mullenweg, who also runs Automattic, the WordPress Foundation is a charitable organization designed "to further the mission of the WordPress open source project," which, it is claimed, is "to democratize publishing through Open Source, GPL software."[46] Clearly, there is a complex relationship in the intergovernance structures here, where on the one hand a charitable organization manages a software product that has a goal of mass democratization and on the other, despite being owned by the same founder, a for-profit organization runs a hosting service (a platform) and contributes code back to that eleemosynary setup.

What's the metaphor here, though? Is WordPress like bricks and mortar or prefabricated housing? It varies between the different organizations. The underlying PHP software, WordPress, is much more like the infrastructure from which all houses might be built. Its codebase is generically shared—as are concrete, brickwork, and basic architectural principles—between all houses. People can take these codebase elements and build their own custom property using the generic shared components. The commonality of this framework is governed by a charitable institution. On the other hand, the organization that will build your house for you, Automattic via WordPress.com (signaling the *com*mercial intent), will genericize the installation and give access, for a fee, to a managed installation. This is also not akin to property ownership. It is more like renting a flat, as the payment structure is ongoing. (That said, it is also worth noting that no web "property" is ever bought forever; server costs recur yearly, as do domain name payments, SSL certificate fees, etc., although these could be billed more as utility costs rather than property purchase costs—another set of digital metaphors.)

The charitable nature of the WordPress Foundation is curiously linked to discourses of openness and public good.[47] The philosophy page of the not-for-profit foundation lists the following goals as its guiding principles:

1. The software should be licensed under the GNU Public License.

2. The software should be freely available to anyone to use for any purpose, and without permission.

3. The software should be open to modifications.

4. Any modifications should be freely distributable at no cost and without permission from its creators.

5. The software should provide a framework for translation to make it globally accessible to speakers of all languages.

6. The software should provide a framework for extensions so modifications and enhancements can be made without modifying core code.

These principles are enshrined "in order to serve the public good."[48]

It is easy, in the contemporary era, to see these characteristics as obvious objects in the pursuit of public good. Open, reusable software for download seems as though it comes with a "good" that is "public."[49] Yet there are many preconditions that determine our ability to see these as "public goods" that are both historically and geo-contextually contingent. One of the basic tenets of digital philosophy—mentioned multiple times already in this book—is that downloads are nonrivalrous. When I download something, it remains accessible to other users to download. But what if this isn't actually true, and what if there is a strong disutility premise at work in these contemporary text publishing systems?

The first precondition is the dual meaning of the term "good" in context here. On the one hand, the "good" of "public good" refers to a set of metaethical conditions—of public "benefit"—that mean that something is right and proper and helpful for the general "public." On the other hand, to pick up on my earlier thread, economics textbooks define public goods in terms of their nonexcludability and nonrivalry. As William H. Oakland puts it, "A distinctive characteristic of such goods is that they are not 'used up' in the process of being consumed or utilized as an input in a production process.... This contrasts sharply with private goods which, once consumed or utilized as an input, can no longer be of service to others."[50] Such public goods, in economic terms, are also dependent upon a public *interest* in the good in question. The example that Oakland gives is of "a fireworks display in the middle of an empty desert," which would be "a private good even though the same display in a city park would be a public good."[51]

In this sense, digital wares seem to fulfill many of the characteristics of economic public goods. A download remains accessible even when someone else has already downloaded it, although the energy that was consumed by computing hardware that underpins that download cannot be reused. Every download on the internet has a computational cost. To transmit data around the world in the form of a download requires energy expenditure and infrastructure maintenance. The differential effects of climate change mean that to state that our use has no effect on others, when, at scale, this energy expenditure may lead to global warming and other catastrophes, is simply therefore not correct, ethically.

The disutility principles for such public goods are set out by Oakland, who writes that "a public good may also create disutility or reduced profits. A cigarette smoked in a crowded classroom is an example. The disutility suffered by one non-smoker does not reduce the disutility suffered by other non-smokers. Similarly, the reduced profits suffered by one fisherman because of water pollution does not reduce the loss to other fishermen."[52] These principles can begin to be applied to systems of multidimensional digital text dissemination.

Clearly, as with cryptocurrencies, there is a disutility principle at work in the idea of a digital text transmission being a nonrivalrous artifact, beyond the discourse of "public good." In essence, there are costs to downloads that are not borne by the people who benefit from those downloads. In this sense, downloads are less public goods than distributionally funded goods. Certainly, the microcost per download transaction may be extremely small. However, on a macro scale of the internet worldwide, there are clear, but invisible to the downloader, energy-usage implications that disproportionately "cost" some groups more than others—but that do not directly cost the person downloading. The same is true of every nonrenewable-fuel-driven car journey, of course. It is also the case that writing on a typewriter or with a pen on paper also carried displaced environmental costs. In Timothy Morton's concept of hyperobjects, the historical scale of such events was linked to global warming even before this concept was known.[53] But digital artifacts, which in reality have hidden ethical dimensions displaced far from the site of reading and writing, are not often considered in such contexts.

Another way of putting this is that all computing has extrinsic costs that are both financial and symbolic/otherwise. In an era of global warming, these extrinsic costs will be felt most keenly by those at the sharp end of the effects of planetary heating. Every computational micro transaction has ethical implications when taken on aggregate at the macro level. The problem is that these harmful effects are decentered from the acting subject and also nearly impossible to quantify. As a result, it is very difficult ever to say what the ethical implications are of a local action, or even whether local actions that seem devoid of local outcomes should be deemed ethical problems. There are multiple dimensions to the dissemination of digital text that are hidden. A similar issue has emerged in medical and research ethics, where bioethics has traditionally dealt with large-scale challenges (e.g., euthanasia) while being unable wholly to countenance the micro ethical implications on the ground level.[54]

A better question might be framed, though, around the axiology of digital text processing. As Perry Hendricks has put it, an "emerging issue in the philosophy of religion is the axiology of theism, in which it is considered whether the world would be better if God exists and whether we should," therefore, "hope that he exists."[55] Axiology, as the study of value, asks us to evaluate the grounds on which we appraise future hope and the ontological strength of various outcomes.

Clearly, it cannot be said that we should hope that all digital text that has ever been produced should have been produced. The monkeys typing out their random lines in the hope of producing Shakespeare have billions of false steps along the way—an evolutionary randomness to produce great poetry. Many writers write badly, and it would be better to hope that their work was never written.

In the face of variable quality and differing tastes, however, and balancing the displaced costs of digital text production against the outcomes of artistic and scholarly works that bring pleasure and value, it is hard to argue, in the axiology of digital text, that we should give up on the hope of writing, even if we understand the ethical implications of computing activities.

But let us return to WordPress as a public good. Even though the computing operations of writing and disseminating contemporary digital text can cause disutility and damage to other people around the world, the infinite, unlimited, and monetarily free nature of the software lands it within the category of a public good. One of the underlying suppositions that allows this is that education and knowledge should be generally shared. This is intrinsically linked to the developments of human rights discourses in the wake of Enlightenment humanist rationalities. Article 27 of the Universal Declaration of Human Rights, framed in 1948, states that "everyone has the right freely to participate in the cultural life of the community, to enjoy the arts and to share in scientific advancement and its benefits."[56] In turn, behind this discourse lurks the necessity of scientific knowledge and scientific realism as the master paradigms for understanding the world, and it is no coincidence that rights discourses around education have grown in the same timeframe as the dominance of the political rationality known as neoliberalism.[57] Without scientific rationality as the dominant logic, it would not be possible for an "access to knowledge" movement, as we know it, to exist.

The figure who most closely unites a set of principles of scientific rationalities, access to knowledge, and defense of liberal democracies (wherein rights discourses originated), is Karl Popper. In turn, the work of Friedrich Hayek also plays a key role, by enshrining various notions of market identity at the core of the protection of liberal democracies. As such, I will go on to argue, our understanding of the public good in the digital space is governed by the paradigm known as neoliberalism, even when open-source software can appear to have socialistic traits.[58]

Popper is famed, in scientific history, for his work in *The Logic of Scientific Discovery* (1959) around falsifiability. For Popper, with respect to a scientific thesis, "we seek a decision as regards these (and other) derived statements by comparing them with the results of practical applications and experiments." If, in light of the outcome, "this decision is positive, that is, if the singular conclusions turn out to be acceptable, or verified, then the theory has, for the time being, passed its test: we have found no reason to discard it." However, "if the decision is negative, or in other words, if the conclusions have been falsified, then their falsification also falsifies the theory from which they were logically deduced."[59] In this way, a singular experiment can never validate a theory; it can provide only evidence to support the theory possibly being correct. But a single result that shows the negative can invalidate a thesis. Hence, coupled with his notions of intersubjective verification, Popper's falsification thesis sits at the center of modern scientific inquiry and scientific realism, which underpin the public good theory of access to knowledge. It is good, it is argued, that people should have access to scientific knowledge of the sort defined by Popper's theses on scientific realism.

At the same time, Popper is famed for his defenses of liberal democracies and the idea of the so-called Open Society, a concept taken on further in recent days by George Soros. In 1945, Popper published his work *The Open Society and Its Enemies*, which was written while he was in political exile from 1938 to 1943. Specifically, *The Open Society* is a book that seeks to repudiate the dialectical historicism of Marxism. In Marx's account of capitalistic development, the argument runs that particular moments of future crisis will emerge that will reveal systemic contradictions, which will then result in particular determinate outcomes (e.g., revolution). In this sense, the material situation has a historical effect that is dialectical in nature, resulting in a concrete outcome.

Popper protests this idea that history had determined forms that could be observed and then predicted. In the first volume of *The Open Society and Its Enemies*, he criticizes such Platonic forms for their methodological essentialism. In such systems, it is seen as "the task of pure knowledge or 'science' to discover and to describe the true nature of things, i.e., their hidden reality or essence."[60] In particular, Popper is distressed by Plato's exhibition of what he calls a "naive monism" in which "both natural and normative regularities are experienced as expressions of, and as dependent upon, the decisions of man-like gods or demons." Popper instead wishes to separate out the human sphere into a critical dualism in which there is "a conscious differentiation between the man-enforced normative laws, based on decisions or conventions, and the natural regularities which are beyond his power."[61] Because Plato, for Popper, tries to bring nature back to its original form, rather than its mere appearance, there is a totalitarian characteristic to such an endeavor. This forms the basis of why the social sciences must, in Popper's view, set themselves apart from the natural sciences. It is his intent "to criticize the doctrine that it is the task of the social sciences to propound historical prophecies, and that historical prophecies are needed if we wish to conduct politics in a rational way."[62]

Popper's criticism of historicism is, by his own admission, specifically a "criticism of the historical method of Marxism," although he also states that other theories of social science that attempt to predict the future would be subject to the same attacks.[63] Specifically, Popper's idea of an "open society" is one in which collective agency is not ascribed to abstract forces of history but to the people who govern and wield power within a particular historical frame.[64] As Stuart Lawson puts it, "Popper's defence of democracy is that it works by creating institutions to limit political power and thus avoid tyranny; democracy is a non-violent way of changing the institutions that wield power, and failures of democratic institutions are not failures of democracy but failures of the people who did not adequately manage or change them— the responsibility lies with people, not impersonal forces of history."[65] Hence, while Popper agrees with Marx that untrammeled capitalism exploits an underclass, depriving them of their freedom, he does not agree with Marx's prediction that revolution would happen or should be desired, instead believing in meliorist democratic institutions: "We must construct social institutions, enforced by the power of the state, for the protection of the economically weak from the economically strong. The state must see to it that nobody need enter into an inequitable arrangement out of fear of starvation, or economic ruin."[66] Writing in the 1940s, just before the drafting of the Universal Declaration of Human Rights, Popper propounds a version of liberalism that allowed for state intervention in order to secure freedoms: "Liberalism and state-interference," he writes, "are not opposed to each other."[67] In contrast to other neoliberal theorizations, Popper also argues against the idea that the state should merely enforce contracts and the rule of law.[68]

Nonetheless, many of Popper's ideas about repressing totalitarianism are also present in those of the originary thinkers of ordoliberalism and neoliberalism. For instance, Friedrich Hayek's influential *The Road to Serfdom* (1944) and *The Constitution of Liberty* (1960) both borrow ideas from Popper's criticisms of Marxism but take them to different ends. Admittedly, Hayek's views are far more extreme than Popper's. For instance, in *The Road to Serfdom*, and despite here taking on a historicism of his own, Hayek argues that it was socialist policies that led to the Nazi regime in Germany and that similar outcomes will result if socialism is implemented elsewhere.[69]

Sharing a desire for a freedom from totalitarianism with Popper, Hayek's notions of liberty are purely negative: a freedom from state coercion, an "independence of the arbitrary will of another."[70] Hayek's notion of freedom is also individualistic rather than collective. Specifically, economic freedom, as he sees it, allows individuals to act in a way that is free of coercion, which, most crucially, is defined by free action based on knowledge principles. "Free action," for Hayek, "in which a person pursues his own aims by the means indicated by his own knowledge, must be based on data which cannot be shaped at will by another."[71] Hence, as André Azevedo Alves and John Meadowcroft argue, even though Hayek "employed a narrow conceptualisation of freedom which led him to misunderstand the nature of and the relationship between economic and political freedom," his freedom from the tyranny of state coercion—and away from totalitarianism—is premised on an epistemological basis.[72] The free market, which is the freedom that Hayek believed would cement the freedom of all, is premised on price information data being available to economic actors.[73] This epistemo-liberal vibe was in the air in the 1940s, and it underwrites the idea of information availability as a right, since an "economistic language associated with the promotion of effectiveness and efficiency" permeates our understanding of information access.[74]

Indeed, we can begin now to see how education—and access to knowledge via digital text dissemination—has become "a crucial factor in ensuring economic productivity and competitiveness in the context of 'informational capitalism,'" as Stephen Ball has put it.[75] There is, then, an intricately woven link between science, numbers, and politics, with statistics springing forth "during the nineteenth century" and informing "the idea that there is such a thing as 'the economy' which is separable from other dimensions of social life, and that its regularities can be understood as 'laws.'" As such, "the development of quantitative or statistical data is closely linked to the rise of the modern, bureaucratic state."[76] Access to and an understanding of such data become key to participation in democratic civic life. Hence, despite the fact that words and numbers have frequently and erroneously been seen as opposed to one another, we nonetheless have the premise that access to numerical information and the democratization of writing are key societal functions that can be deemed a public good.[77]

Thus, WordPress can deem itself to be a public, civic good in both the aims of its platform (to democratize writing) and the mode of its dissemination (open, digital reproduction). The platform is united across the twin Popperian dimensions of scientific rationality and liberal democracy, which are the determinate conditions for viewing an open-source piece of writing software as an objective that is a public good. For the purposes of this chapter, it is also important that the spaces that WordPress provides are "homes," with WordPress forming a lower-platform dimension upon which the dissemination of digital text sits. The epistemo-proprietorial nature of an owned space, that is nonetheless beholden to another in a type of rentier arrangement, fits well with neoliberal ideas of home and ownership.

Our digital homes are complex, multidimensional spaces. They are metaphorically entwined with notions of real-world property and social class but also the nostalgic imaginations of what it means to have a "home" to which one may endlessly return. "Home" and "end" refer to differing spatial locations within documents, browsing histories, and even web "properties." The journey back home is often cyclical or multilinear/multidimensional, branching and forking, ducking and dodging. In all, though, this chapter has sought to show that the metaphors of space in our text processing are nonlinear and complicated. Like Hinton's cubes, we cannot expect to navigate such spatial structures across the limited dimensionalities to which our senses have accustomed us. Digital text is multidimensional and the opposite of "home" is (not) "end."

SIX

WINDOWS ARE ALLEGORIES OF
POLITICAL LIBERALISM

IN MANY WAYS, MICROSOFT IS and was a *visionary* organization. Admittedly, many people disagree with its visions, be they for operating systems, proprietary software, or vast corporate profits, but *vision* has been key to Microsoft's metaphors for years. Microsoft gave us Windows that open onto Vistas, yielding fresh Outlooks and Paint-ing new scenes within Visual Studios of virtual design. Indeed, it is ironic that a company sued for antitrust should name its core product and system of visual iconography after an icon of transparency and *access*: the window. It is also curious, as the windows that contain the visual output of our software are not really opening *onto* anything. They are instead the result of complex compositing and rendering processes within software. Yet the metaphor invites us to imagine that we are seeing *through* a portal—a transparent opening. We compose, edit, and view our digital texts through windows.

This chapter examines the implications of these metaphors of transparency and vision, with specific focus on the metaphor of the window, before moving into a critical disability studies angle for analyzing digital-textual accessibility in the light of such visual metaphors. This chapter specifically works to dismantle the metaphor of the window by analyzing the ways in which the logic sits within the complex dynamics of opening and closing (in relation to Microsoft's historical relationships to open-source communities), and locking and unlocking, windows. This pulling apart is a potentially important task because metaphors supposedly work by supplying, as I noted earlier, a trope of relation that provides familiarity. When our metaphors are just accepted for what they are rather than for what they might have been, we lose sight (another visual metaphor) of alternative design paradigms and different futures. It also becomes impossible, when metaphors become so distanced from their physical correlates, for people who are not already inculcated into our language structures properly to understand what they are supposed to take from a metaphor. To explain *why* a digital window is called a window to somebody who has never used a computing system is actually a significantly difficult task. Some thinkers have tried to dismiss this overreach by stating that "what is important here is not what is irrelevant" in the metaphor "but things that might lead the user in the wrong direction."[1] However, a new user does not and cannot know what is irrelevant versus what is misleading. It is very hard to know what to discard if one doesn't understand the metaphor's bounding. To answer "Why is it called a window?" with "It just is" feels somehow less than satisfactory.

It is also the case that our metaphors change over time as hardware and software paradigms shift, but we remain stuck with the previous metaphorical language. For instance, the computer mouse is so called because of its size but also because it appears to have a tail in the cord that connects it to the computer.[2] The only problem is that many mice, now, are cordless and instead use short-range radio technologies such as Bluetooth to communicate. Perhaps such devices should, really, be called hamsters, as a recent internet meme joked. Hence, when someone unfamiliar with the metaphor asks, "Why is it called a mouse?" it is quite difficult to give a convincing answer in the present, even though the historical situation is clearer. Also, at one point in its developmental history, the on-screen cursor was referred to, for reasons unknown, as a CAT, hence providing a humorous situation in which the mouse would chase the CAT.[3] Finally, originally the mouse was not called a mouse at all: it was a "bug."[4]

The metaphors of computation also take on lives of their own that refract back on the world at large. Instead, then, of providing us simply with an analogy from the real world as to how a computer will work, we can even raise questions about the functionality of real-world objects. The best example of this is the apparent, albeit relatively complex, case of small children who attempt to swipe at magazines as though they were tablet computers in the supposed belief that they will change their contents as a result.[5] This is a situation where, at least if taken at face value and not as another instance of moral panic and scaremongering, the metaphor of the computer interface has altered the child's interaction with its real-world precursor. Hence, the loop is one where a magazine with a page turn—a flip—translates into a horizontal swipe, which the child then reimposes on the original magazine. In such feedback loops, as we can see here, there is actually a helix structure at work. We do not end up precisely back at the same starting point as where we began but at a slightly modified, or even dialectical, pinnacle of synthesis. The metaphors that we use in computing therefore matter because they refract back through our extra computational objects.

Most importantly, however, this chapter examines the thorny issue of ability discrimination in digital-textual metaphor and the assumptions of users' identifications with sensory metaphors. The question then becomes: Can a trope of relation be provided through a metaphor with which a substantial number of impaired users will have little familiarity? How, this chapter asks, does the mediation of *imagined* or *remembered* rather than *experienced* sense condition our interface interactions? If you cannot see, what use are metaphors of vision? How transparent, really, are our computational windows?

A Brief History of Windows

It is important to understand that, in 1985, when Microsoft Windows burst onto the scene with version 1.0, it was not a fully featured operating system. Instead, Windows was a visual shell that sat atop Microsoft's Disk Operating System (DOS). The first version of Windows was not, internally, even called Windows. Instead, it was known, catchily, as the Interface Manager.[6] It took some time for the name Windows to take hold, but this was hardly the only strange naming decision in the development of a visual shell for DOS.

Perhaps the strangest choice of terminology for early Windows, Icons, Menus, and Pointer (WIMP) systems is the term "menu." We are now accustomed to the digital "menu" representing a set of options from which we can select; the explicit rootedness of menu systems in restaurant cultures has been all but erased from our cultural memory. Charles Simonyi, one of the earliest designers at Microsoft working on the Windows project (and who had previously worked at PARC on the Bravo WYSIWYG text editor), framed the metaphor of the menu in terms of a multilingual restaurant environment. Specifically, Simonyi gestured toward the deictic quality of the menu, in which, even if one does not speak the same language as the creator, one can select the menu item from a range of predefined choices. One can use, in other words, the universal language of pointing. As Simonyi put it:

> I like the obvious analogy of a restaurant. Let's say I go to a French restaurant and I don't speak the language. It's a strange environment and I'm apprehensive. I'm afraid of making a fool of myself, so I'm kind of tense. Then a very imposing waiter comes over and starts addressing me in French. Suddenly, I've got clammy hands. What's the way out?
>
> The way out is that I get the menu and point at something on the menu. I cannot go wrong. I may not get what I want—I might end up with snails—but at least I won't be embarrassed.
>
> But imagine if you had a French restaurant without a menu. That would be terrible.
>
> It's the same thing with computer programs. You've got to

have a menu. Menus are friendly because people know what their options are, and they can select an option just by pointing. They do not have to look for something that they will not be able to find, and they don't have to type some command that might be wrong.[7]

One of the curious aspects of this analogy and metaphor is that it paints the language of the text-based terminal as foreign, unconstrained, and other, assuming, to return to the language of the previous chapter, that a user will feel more "at home" with the limited visual subset palette of the menu. The terminal, it seems, is a foreign country; they do things differently there. This is also an interesting analogy given the development of the term "language" to denote the orthography of computational instructions: programming languages. Hence, the metaphor of language for specific controlled vocabularies with imperative characteristics is made to do different work in different contexts. Writing a computer program is very different, in linguistic terms, from issuing specific commands to a terminal-based operating system. Certainly, they both have their own lexicon and syntactic and semantic rules of grammar. It is also true that shell scripting takes over from simple one-line commands at some point. But the idea of the terminal as a foreign language compared to the graphical "home" of a menu-driven system is just one of the ways in which the ocular and the visual began to assert their primacy in the computational world.

The terminal as a foreign language, *free of all constraint*, is also a surprising statement that lurks as the counterpart to the discourse of "menus." It is surprising because, although it is true that the novice computer user will doubtless be confused as to how to operate a command line, as it is known, the terminal is not actually a carte blanche. Before delving into this, however, a quick explanation of various terminologies is merited. In contemporary Unix-like computing systems, the "terminal," the "shell," the "console," and the "command line" all refer to slightly different but interrelated phenomena. In technical terms, a terminal is a type of device file that implements additional commands (so-called ioctls—input/output controls) beyond "read" and "write."

Terminal emulators, also known as "pseudo-terminals" or "pseudo-ttys," provide user access to these device files. The "console," by contrast, is the "master" terminal in a physical sense. It is the directly attached, hardware version of the terminal. The "command line" refers to the interface where a user types a command. And a "shell" is the main interface with which users are presented when they log in. In contemporary parlance, this refers to a command-line interface, but the metaphor of its name is derived from the "wrapper" that it provides around the basic terminal or, even, console. This all makes for a messy set of interlocking terminologies.

Nonetheless, all modern shell prompt systems come with a form of command completion. Under such systems, when the user presses the tab key, the shell presents a list of possible completions based on existing input. In other words, this is akin to the waiter attempting to help the user to speak the native language of the restaurant. This cannot be said to be a strictly contemporary phenomenon. The Berkeley Timesharing System for the SDS 940, developed in 1966, worked on the basis of resolving ambiguities in incomplete commands. Long before ChatGPT became the standard in language prediction, in this system, when a typed command was ambiguous, the interpreter, which used a "character-oriented terminal," would not act.[8] However, if the string entered was not ambiguous and could only resolve to a full command, the interpreter would resolve the typed line to the full version. This was a $400,000 system designed to examine each character from each Teletype before the next character arrives for the purpose of accelerating user input.[9] Hence, almost as long as shells have existed, they have attempted to save their users time and effort by autocompleting input results. As such, referring to the implementation of menus as a way around the supposed ambiguity and complexity of shells feels like a stretch.

Nonetheless, the system of deictic menus inscribes a visual-oral/auditory dichotomy at the heart of computer system interfaces, even while they work via text.[10] Text-based shells, with their "languages," are metaphorically oral and aural. Their "languages" are spoken, freeform, hard to understand, and open-endedly extensible (usually via pipes and other ways in which commands can be chained together). They are akin, in Simonyi's depiction, to the spoken version of languages that one cannot understand. By contrast, the menu is understood, in the context of two sighted individuals, as a way of removing ambiguity from the spoken word. The restaurant "order," sharing that imperative term, is clarified through the use of a visual aide, the "menu."

It is perhaps apt that the style referred to by the menu, which writes a visual prejudice into our metaphors, is framed around cross-cultural communication. Specifically, the type of cross-cultural exchange that one imagines beneath this restaurant metaphor is that of the arrogant Anglophone, ignorant of any foreign languages, who shouts and points in his or her native tongue, mistakenly believing intelligibility to be proportionate to volume.[11] The menu acts as a bridge between two alien cultures, in which it also appears that there is a degree of animosity or friction between locutors. It also creates a hierarchy, in which those who can—or even just actually attempt to—speak the language itself are accorded higher cultural status. The same disdain is evident in computing cultures, where those using the command prompt look down on the users of graphical interfaces.

The "shell" concept gives some idea, albeit confusingly, of why windows are called windows—but it all depends on whether you are looking in or looking out. One might assume that, if operating a computer, one is looking inward from the outside. After all, the outside world is . . . outside the computer. Originally developed at the Stanford Research Institute by Douglas Engelbart, a window on a computer monitor might be presumed to offer a transparent view of the internals of the computer—a viewport that provides more detailed visual access to functionality and operates in a transparent fashion.[12] Certainly, the window provides a set of controls for running the machine. However, the metaphor is strange. Windows are not transparent but instead stack new visual design elements together in a way that gives an operational control.

The idea of the window is part of what is known as the "desktop metaphor," a concept that has been criticized for many years now. The idea of the desktop comes from the concept that your workspace consists of a set of laid-out tools, in front of you, that can be deployed in the service of work. It is a space that can be rearranged and customized by individual users as suits their world style. Yet, an early set of objections noted the following:

> It is based on a static piece of furniture intended for organizing and storing.
> A desk is not the direct container of information such as a paper.
> A desk is not a thing that we normally consider "portable."
> Sharing of information may imply giving a physical thing. In the real world people do not give desks to other people.
> A desk does not support directly the task of reading. In other words, people usually do not read desks.[13]

Likewise, we might aim several similar criticisms at the idea of a window offering a viewport through a shell. Rather than transparently exposing the system's internals, windows instead layer new iconographic elements on top of their canvas that allow for access to new functionality. In this sense, windows are perhaps more like heads-up displays. Except they do not have any transparency at all. They sit on the outside of the shell, building further levels outward that add opacity, abstracting further away from the core.

What if, though, the user were situated inside the window, looking out? This makes more sense for considering holistically the "desktop metaphor." After all, most people's working environment—if they were using a real desk—would be one where they could look *out* of the window from the inside and there see new landscapes. This is certainly the case with the default background wallpaper that Microsoft used for Windows XP. This version of the operating system opened out, via its default background wallpaper, onto a scene dubbed *Bliss* (figure 6), an almost unedited photograph of a green hill and blue sky with clouds in the Los Carneros American Viticultural Area of California's "Wine Country."[14] In other words, the view that Microsoft gave its user when they landed on the Microsoft Windows XP desktop home screen was akin to looking out of a window at the natural world. The photograph was taken by Charles O'Rear in January 1996 and acquired by Microsoft in the year 2000.[15] Given the ubiquity of Microsoft's operating systems, *Bliss* is one of the most widely recognized photographs in the world.[16] It also had the advantage, compared with the originally selected background, of not looking "like a pair of buttocks."[17] Microsoft paid one of the largest ever sums to a living, working photographer for the image, which is apt given how ubiquitous the image has become.[18]

The fact that Microsoft conceives of its windows as escapes from the world of work and computing—as viewports onto rich external natural vistas of vibrant, almost psychedelic colors from the outside landscape but also via a photograph that is explicitly conceived in romantic terms, since the photographer took the shot while en route to visit his girlfriend—doesn't exactly speak well of the computational environment that it is building, centered around work.[19] At the same time, it is clear that looking through these Windows has more of a mirrorlike quality of reimmersion. It is only the background *wallpaper* (to put out another metaphor) for Windows XP that gave a view onto an exterior natural world. The windows of the programs themselves were much more business and work focused.

FIGURE 6. Microsoft's *Bliss* image. Used with permission from Microsoft

Hence, in the conflation of the operating system called Windows and the idea of the window, the preceding analysis falsely conflates a desktop wallpaper with a window itself. Again, this demonstrates the extent to which the metaphor falls apart. The "desktop" is the space where the tools for computation appear. It is the area where one can find one's frequently accessed programs and, for the more disorganized user, it is a space for storing temporary files. Why, then, does a desktop have a "wallpaper"? If one wishes to argue that the background is the "wall" behind the "desk" of the desktop, then why is the list of icons not *below* the background wall?

In many original versions of the desktop metaphor, there was no computer mouse. Instead, users had a tablet on which they drew to move the cursor, such as in Alan Kay's Flex Machine from around 1968.[20] In such a setup, more of the tools *are* below the screen; there is a desk "top" on which there is a pen/stylus and a pad for tracking the cursor. But in general terms, the screen space has to fulfill multiple metaphorical functions. It has to be a desktop and a wallpaper and contain windows that move.

And why do windows move? Windows, in reality, *open*. You cannot move a window around on the wall to reposition its view at your convenience. This could just be a version of the magic illusion to which Alan Kay referred and to which I gestured earlier. Perhaps some kinds of super-digital windows *would* be movable on the wall. Or perhaps "metaphor" is a worse way to think about digital phenomena than "illusions." The window imbued with digital magic can be moved on the wall. But if this *is* supposed to be a metaphor that gives people information about expected behaviors so that they can intuit how to use a computing system, then it does not do a very good job. There is no reason why a window should be called a window other than that it is rectangular. You cannot see through these windows. But "frame" would do an adequate job—and picture frames *are* movable, unlike windows. However, this might have detracted from the coherence of the visual systems of reference that had emerged to dominate our digital text environments, via Microsoft. Hence, we stay with windows.

Style and Sacrifice

Curiously, in some "windowing" systems, such as the Wayland proto-col or Google's Android operating system, windows are instead often called surfaces.[21] This is, itself, significant, as Lakoff and Johnson use the term "content-defining surface" in their work on metaphor. A content-defining surface refers to an aspect of a metaphor that can overlap with another, and it is a perhaps necessary, but, in isolation, insufficient mechanism to account for metaphorical coherence. In other words, a content-defining surface yields a specific frame onto which particular specificities are thrown, in order to generate a site of metaphorical overlap. With this in mind, a brief detour into an under-standing of Wayland can serve to show, further, how the breakdown of metaphor here occurs but also how individual stylistic design begins to come into tension with overarching coherence, within the logic of a sacrifice of liberty. Wayland is a communication protocol for display servers and clients, designed to run on Unix-like and Linux systems. Wayland replaces an older mechanism called the X Window System ("X" or "X11," as the system has been at version 11 since the late 1980s). X Window Systems are network-transparent graphical display servers originally developed at MIT in 1984.[22] The idea behind an X Window System is that it allows for the display of graphical "windows" and for their manipulation and comprehension. The X Window System tracks digital windows, their overlaps, positions, application domains, and display parameters.

Specifically, the X Window System serves as a three-way glue be-tween a kernel's event system (which handles interaction with the hardware), graphical display components/clients, and a compositor. The difficulties here are many. When the user clicks the mouse button at a specific point on the screen, the graphics subsystem has to know which window should receive this event from the kernel. This is not as easy as it might seem. Windows can overlap (be "stacked") atop one another (again, contrary to any kind of real-life window). Windows might be minimized, active, fullscreen, or merely part screen. Windows can be moved and may sit on different monitors. Because of X's so-called network transparency, a window may actually even reside on a different computer from the one doing the displaying and receiving the events.

Once an event has been received by the operating system kernel (using the "evdev" [event device] driver mechanism), the X Window System uses its "scenegraph"—an in-memory representation of the position and ordering of all windows—to determine to which component of which window the event should be relayed. This might be a textbox receiving text input or a checkbox receiving a click event. In turn, the application must then return updated visual information to the X Server and the compositor (for example, if a checkbox should, now, instead be checked rather than empty). The X Server must then ask the kernel to use its graphics subsystems to repaint the necessary part of the screen. The process involves drawing a new version of the screen in off-screen memory and then, to return to an earlier metaphor, "page flipping" this display buffer so that it is active on the computer's monitor. In the X Window System, this entails a hugely messy set of roundtrips between the X Clients (applications), the compositor (which manages window locations), the X Server (which handles redraw requests and input routing), and the kernel (which processes hardware inputs and outputs).

The Wayland system aims to simplify this architecture by removing the X Server entirely and replacing it with a compositor that also acts directly as the graphical interface and event routing system. Clients interact directly with the compositor, asking it to redraw their components (by sending memory buffers of rendered content), and the compositor knows about the positions and orderings of its surfaces. In turn, the compositor interacts directly with the kernel, using the Direct Rendering Manager (DRM) to initiate page flips, moving the in-memory rendering onto the screen itself.

The advantages of the Wayland system over X11 are many, and most desktop managers/compositors for Linux are moving to use Wayland instead. At the same time, there are some challenges. One of the core features of desktop operating systems is that they have a homogenized look and feel. Indeed, at Microsoft in the 1990s, in particular, there was a quest for reusable visual and computational components. For example, when Microsoft was developing Encarta, its encyclopedia system (which was superseded in just a few short decades by the free, open alternative, Wikipedia), the goal was to create as many reusable elements as possible. As Fred Moody puts it, "Developers writing code prefer to lift as many engines as possible from other programs, in order to save themselves months of work." The result of this logic was that "Gates had established his multimedia division with the idea that part of its systems group would write tools for developers of all multimedia products to use, rather than having ten different projects, writing ten different but essentially identical search engines, text layout engines, animation engines, and so on."[23] This reusability drive is nowhere more prevalent than in graphical user interface designs, although in the case of Microsoft's encyclopedia project, this quest for reuse failed spectacularly. The Encarta team ended up creating far too many unique components that could not be reused more broadly. Yet the goal remains.

Specifically, in monolithic graphic interface systems such as Microsoft Windows or Apple's Mac OSX, applications are stylized in a consistent manner, at least then giving the impression of metaphorical homology. This is known as "window decoration" or "server-side decoration." Many Linux desktop environments, such as KDE Plasma, also attempt to enforce the homogenization of style (for example using the GTK framework). In the Wayland system, however, this is harder, as the compositor must intervene between a client's rendering of its own content (such as its own interface) and the rendering of standardized framework metaphors (such as menus and status bars). While a 2018 update to the Wayland protocol introduced a way to decorate windows, that this was not standard from the start reveals an interesting stance toward idiosyncratic visual styling.

What really seems to be at play in the introduction of Wayland is a set of architectural principles that not only bring performance benefits to the system as a whole but are also entwined in the negotiation between individual power and collective standardization. In other words, there is a metaphor of political liberalism at work in Wayland's rise to prominence. The negotiation at stake lies in the question of rendering.

In traditional X11 systems, rendering is performed by the X Server. Clients send requests for updates to the X Server, which handles interactions with the kernel such as page flipping. These requests can even be sent over the network to remote X Servers that will render the clients on a system far away from where the application is running. In Wayland, clients themselves are instead responsible for rendering their contents. Some degree of standardization can here be obtained by using libraries such as Cairo, but clients (applications) are essentially free to draw themselves in whatever way they wish. They send a buffer of graphics to the Wayland compositor, which renders this into their space on screen. In other words, Wayland is the computational equivalent of self-identity for its programs. Under Wayland, applications have total freedom to style themselves as they see fit. In X Server environments, by contrast, the server controls many more aspects of layout and rendering. In these ways, Wayland against X is a metonymic representation of self-identity versus socially determined identity. This raises a set of philosophical issues that have dominated recent political discourse in the West. We might ask: What is identity? A set of self-asserted positioning statements? Or a societally intervalidated series of propositions and positions? A distributed set of validated and time-bound assertions? How does identity change over time? If someone holds different stances or beliefs at different times, are they "identical" with their previous self?[24] Visual identity in these different software systems is asserted by different actors at different points in the life cycle of these programs.

If we understand metaphor as providing grounds for familiarity in computer interface design, or even understand our metaphors as illusory supplementations of the real-world objects to which they reportedly refer, then the delegation of appearance to individual applications works against such concepts. While we can recognize commonalities—a menu, for instance, as a list of options that extends downward from a status bar at the top of an application—if every application is free to restyle its interface elements in whatever way it chooses, then the principle of shared metaphor driving UI design is lost. How far, the question might be, do we have to travel from a standardized "menu" before this term is no longer applied to the item in question? As Wittgenstein famously asked of a "chair" that arbitrarily appears and disappears: "May one use the word 'chair' to include this kind of thing?"[25] At what point does a computer menu no longer resemble a computer menu? And why is this lack of self-resemblance different from the computer menu no longer representing a restaurant menu?

MacOS is a good example of an operating system that has veered in the opposite direction to the individualistic design and compositing schema of Wayland. MacOS itself is actually a fusion of several components that are united within a single framework. Specifically, macOS runs a kernel called XNU that evolved from Carnegie Mellon's Mach project while also being derived from NEXTSTEP/OpenStep and FreeBSD systems. Driver interfaces in the system are handled by a setup called I/O-Kit, which provides an object-oriented framework for low-level hardware interaction.[26] But Apple has, traditionally, been the heartland of attempts at coherent, consistent metaphor in its design principles. Indeed, as Thomas D. Erickson, who formerly worked at the corporation noted, "metaphor . . . seems to be the holy grail at Apple."[27]

Indeed, it would be a huge mistake to downplay the importance of visual design at Apple. In the mid-1990s, Apple and Microsoft, the two largest technological players, diverged in their ideas of what the personal computing marketplace should be. Apple had a vision of a computer that was so easy to use that it required no software manual to setup. Microsoft, by contrast, wanted to bring the power of mainframe computing to businesses. Ultimately, the differences "between Microsoft and Apple came down to a difference in vision"—noting this metaphor of "vision" once again—"so stark that the purchase of a personal computer became a declaration of personal and political values." Apple specifically inscribed an ideological set of values at its core, one that said that, in buying a Macintosh, "you were releasing your creative potential and rejecting the values of Corporate America in the bargain." There was a marketing investment in the "pleasure-quotient" of Apple's machines, driven by advertising campaigns that focused on style and intuitiveness.[28] This was perhaps most transparent in the global "Get a Mac" drive, which saw a corporate besuited geek representing

Microsoft-driven PCs, while a smart-casual Macintosh—clearly the cool kid on the block—made everything look easy.[29]

Importantly, the Get a Mac campaign was dependent on the dress sense of the two representative actors. As noted, PCs were shown as corporate office bores, bedecked in ties and suits. The type of digital text produced here would, it seemed, be tedious office reports. Macintosh computers, on the other hand, wore turtleneck sweaters, unbuttoned shirts, and generally more comfortable clothes. Text produced here would be the imaginative fare of novels and poetry. Indeed, a superficial reading of the advertisement would note that the representation of Microsoft computers was driven by homogeneity; we are shown a tiresome vision of office drudgery in costumed form. The reading of the Mac character is focused on individuation. Yet this is curious, given the insistence on visual *homogeneity* in the actual software, to which I am drawing attention. In the world of the Mac, the advertisement seems to say, you can dress how you want, rather than how your boss wants. Yet this brings a major irony. The way that the Macintosh achieves its vision of ease of use, intuitability, and metaphorical coherence is precisely by ensuring the rigorous sameness of interfaces between programs. In other words, in programming terms, it is not acceptable in Apple's landscape for a program to wander in wearing a different color rollneck sweater from everybody else. Apple achieves its vision of stylistic independence, in fact, by enforcing a dress code on every application that runs on its system.

This stylistic homogeneity is (technologically) enforced because graphical services in macOS are provided by a combination of Quartz (the compositor) and Aqua (the interface system). Of course, the *decision* to enforce such homogeneity is a social choice on the part of the Apple corporation. However, on the technical front, Quartz itself is split into two components: Quartz compositor is a window server, while Quartz 2D is a graphics library that evolved out of Postscript and PDF formats (indeed, despite the detailed discussion of the challenges faced by digital page implementations above, early documents about the history of macOS's visual design stress that "the digital paper metaphor played a paramount role in the development of Mac OS X").[30] Quartz is a processor intensive library that offloads much of its processing onto the graphical processing unit. However, this is where Aqua comes to the rescue. Aqua is, at the same time, the graphical user interface, the design language, and the visual theme of Apple's operating system. While the specific design elements have changed over time—most notably with the introduction of macOS Big Sur—the common point is that the Aqua and Quartz systems enforce stylistic homogeneity at the technical level in the service of a consistent interface. Such stylistic regularity serves not only to reenforce Apple's brand identity (macOS apps are immediately recognizable, although so are most Windows applications) but also contributes to the "intuitive" nature of the system. That is, as Apple put it, "people expect macOS apps to be intuitive, while simultaneously adaptable to their workflow through customization and flexibility," and a consistently applied user interface theme provides such an intuitable setup.[31] In Apple's hands, consistency that provides for intuitable interfaces also contributes to the construction of its global brand and the furtherance of its corporate agenda.

Individual styling must also be considered within the historical paradigm of (sub)cultural studies as pioneered by Stuart Hall and the Birmingham Centre for Contemporary Cultural Studies (CCCS) in the 1970s. Subcultural studies, as derived from this critical paradigm, views the idea of style itself as a way in which subcultures delineate themselves from other subcultures and dominant culture, or the mainstream. Such an act of demarcation, in the original formulation, is one in which such styling carries resistive potential—a means of counteracting the imposition of homogeneous uniformity. In recent years, such a view has itself come in for critique in the field of "post-subcultural studies," which viewed the earlier resistance thesis of the CCCS as overly romantic. Indeed, as David Muggleton and Rupert Weinzierl put it, the point here was to challenge the "romanticism of the CCCS," where subcultural studies emerged. In subcultural studies, it was thought that "radical potential" lay "in largely symbolic challenges" to a hegemonic norm imposed from above; that is, the aesthetics of styling carried the potential, in itself, to be transgressive—an act of resistance. A post-subcultural take on this is one in which "the potential for style itself to resist appears largely lost, with any 'intrinsically' subversive quality to subcultures exposed as an illusion."[32] It is also important to note that core to the CCCS definitions of cultural studies are notions of class. It is specifically a type of *class-based* resistance, offered by aesthetics, that grew from this particular context in 1970s Britain.

User interface designers may be pleased with the ability to style their applications precisely as they want in Wayland. This gives a degree of freedom and control that is otherwise lacking in this design space and offers the potential of subcultural resistance. Indeed, some designers note that it doesn't really matter how much you change small things, so long as the interface continues to behave in a way that is consistent with a user's past experience. As Bruce Tognazzini puts it, "You can change the entire look and feel of an application as long as you honor the user's previously learned interpretations and subconscious behaviors."[33] Hence, Wayland allows designers to "go rogue" if they want, offering a way of resisting the homogenizing influence of the compositor's enforced shared stylization, possibly at the expense of ingraining a set of prior cultural-behavioral assumptions. It should also be noted that some types of application require extreme flexibility over their layout and graphics systems. Computer games need the ability to paint an entire and unique world and cannot fall back on prepackaged form elements, as would a piece of business software. In this sense, the shared metaphorical interface elements of computer games are fewer and further between than other types of applications.

Yet what kind of "resistance" to domination does such an approach, allowing individual style in computer programs, including those that focus on textual creation and dissemination, really represent? It is certainly true that metaphorical paradigms appear to constrain our thinking about how computer programs and text input could operate otherwise. The metaphors themselves—be they surfaces or windows—lock us into specific thought paradigms that carry a path dependency. Circumventing this gives a degree of "freedom" to the interface designer.

However, freedom is a relative trade-off between the freedom *to* create an interface in whatever style a designer wishes and the freedom *from* such impositions on the behalf of users. A project that demonstrates the exchanges made in such negotiations of freedom is Bagaar's User Inyerface. Described as a "frustration," User Inyerface is a compendium of terrible user interface design decisions, all gathered under one roof. Figures 7 and 8 serve to demonstrate some of the horrors of this system.

FIGURE 7. **User Inyerface example interface**

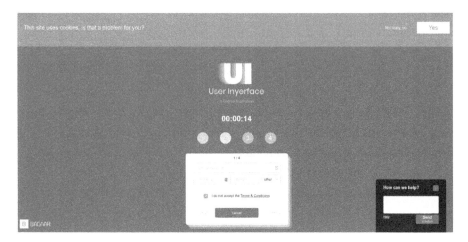

FIGURE 8. **User Inyerface example interface**

In Figure 7, the initial annoyances of the system are clearly in evidence. First, the entire color scheme of the site is appalling (although the image here is, obviously, black and white). The light green font on the bright blue background is specifically designed to impede color-blind users, who will be unable to discern the text from the background. The copy itself is badly written. "To play the game," the user is told, "simply fill in the form as fast and accurate [sic] as possible." Below the first block of text, where normally one would expect a prominent interface element that might graciously guide the user to the next step, sits a round button labeled "NO" that performs no function. Clicking this button has no effect whatsoever. Finally, the site presents to the user, in a variety of typographical stylings, the instruction "Please click HERE to GO to the *next page*." The visual style applied to this line implies that the user should click the decorated word "click." However, this is not possible. The word "click" is not actually a link. The user will usually next try to click "next page," since this text is presented in a lighter weight of font style, again setting it apart. Once more, though, this results only in frustration: "next page" is not clickable. Perhaps "GO," the imperative action command, is where the user should next try? Again, no dice. Finally, the user will likely try "HERE" out of desperation and will be duly "rewarded."

The next page is, indeed, even worse. After a few seconds of loading, a horrific red banner appears asking, "This site uses cookies, is that a problem for you?" thereby inverting the traditional wording. The negative answer "YES" is bolded within a large rectangle, while the affirmative but weakly worded "Not really, no" is tiny and does not appear in any styling that makes it appear clickable. For some inexplicable reason, a "countup" timer appears and, if the user is not swift enough, a lockout box appears over the top of the entire screen, warning the user to "hurry up" because "time is ticking" (a box that instead of "OK" has "Lock" as its only option, which changes to "Unlock" when clicked).

The second page itself is no better for the requirements it places on the user. In a parody of the password cultures about which I have written elsewhere, the user is told the following:

1. Your password requires at least 10 characters.

2. Your password should have at least 1 Capital letter.

3. Your password must have at least 1 Numeral.

4. Your password needs at least 1 letter of your email.

5. Your password can have at least 1 Cyrillic character.[34]

The interchangeable vocabularies of "requires," "must," and "needs" here serve to destandardize the instruction set. Furthermore, the interrelation of password and email address is clearly ridiculous ("Your password needs at least 1 letter of your email") and the ineffectual assertion that "Your password can have at least 1 Cyrillic character" implies that there exists a set of characters that are forbidden but that are not specified by this ruleset. If the user enters a password that does not conform to these rules, the interface will simply disallow them to proceed, with no indication as to *why* their password did not meet the requirements.

Using the form itself is even worse. The, again, inversely worded "I do not accept the Terms & Conditions" is ticked by default and the link to said terms presents the users with a pop-up modal with unreplaced boilerplate language within a window that can only be scrolled through at absolute snail's pace: "Welcome to [Insert company or website name]," the site proclaims, as the user crawls down the page. The password itself is asked only to be entered once and is displayed in cleartext, rather than the asterisked-out privacy with which we are familiar, giving no faith that the system will be storing such passwords in a secure manner. Email and domain are separated out into their own fields and the suffix (such as ".com") is only selectable from a dropdown list that includes very few top-level domain options alongside other unhelpful and irrelevant aspects such as ".jpg" (which is a file extension for a local image, not a known top-level domain suffix). The "How can we help?" box informs the user that there are 465 people in line for help ahead of them in the queue. The "cancel" button is the largest on the screen. The "Next" and "Reset" buttons are the wrong way around, implying the obverse of the directional impetus they are supposed to convey in a left-to-right reading system. And for some reason, a set of flashing "1 2 3 4" icons dominates the middle of the screen.

There is little doubt in my mind that User Inyerface is easily one of the worst user experiences ever designed. As a deliberate effort to create such an environment, it is also very funny. Indeed, the constant frustrations of the system produce flashes of anger even in users who appreciate and understand its humor. Yet User Inyerface is merely the emblematic logical extension of a whole set of websites that emerged in the 1990s and that carried within them such horrific design principles.

The stylistic textual elements that perhaps trigger the most nostalgia among 1990s web users are the HTML blink tag and the scrolling marquee, alongside the well-known proliferation of naff animated GIFs. It is hard, from the retrospective position of the 2020s, to see how these design elements were ever thought to be a good idea. However, many of the fashion choices of the 1990s also now appear dubious (as, doubtless, will contemporary choices to future generations). The first of these tags rendered text that would appear and disappear in a syncopated fashion; the text "blinked" on and off the page, like Wittgenstein's chair. As Mozilla's MDN documentation now puts it, "This feature is no longer recommended. . . . Do not use this element as it is obsolete and is bad design practice." Indeed, the example of the tag's usage from this source is "<blink>Why would somebody use this?</blink>."[35] It is, to be fair, a good historical question that we should take *seriously*. Why was this ever considered a good idea? Along with the scrolling marquee, which moved text from right to left across the screen, and the ubiquitous rotating animated Graphics Interchange Format icons, the 1990s internet aesthetic appears even worse than the fashion sense of that decade.

One of the most curious aspects of the 1990s web aesthetic, though, is that in their quest for individuality—that is, in seeking to distinguish themselves from one another by having the quirkiest "unique" designs—these sites are clearly identifiable for the era to which they belong. That is, sites with white text on a black background and the aforementioned deprecated HTML elements are readily categorizable as

Yahoo! GeoCities or MySpace sites from the 1990s. (Perhaps of interest for the previously explored metaphors of gentrification is that GeoCities was premised on the notion of neighborhoods and cities, segmenting its web spaces into property districts and reenforcing both notions of real estate ownership but also supposed thematic proximity to other sites. That said, as Shannon Mattern has cautioned us, we should be careful about considering cities in computational terms, and vice versa.[36]) Extreme design individuality and lack of standardization turns out to be a type of standardization in itself that allows us to categorize such sites.

There is a further metaphor that is useful for thinking about stylistic conformance or deviation and one that comes from an unlikely source. In his *Memory and Intertextuality in Renaissance Literature*, Raphael Lyne sets out a schema for thinking about poetic remembrance in terms of implicit and explicit memory. That is, for Lyne, various forms of allusion can be explicit acts of remembrance, while intertextuality is more akin to an implicit memory system. As Lyne puts it:

> On the one hand, the mind accumulates associations over time and these develop into systems of cues and connections that govern behaviour. On the other, there is the capacity to control mental processes, to undertake deliberate and hypothetical searches of memory, for example, which is not thought to exist in animals. The suggestiveness of this hybrid model for the critic studying allusion and intertextuality is straightforward but profound. Associative processes are like intertextuality; conscious processes are like allusions. The crucial thing is that associative and conscious processes are part of the same system: human memory is a combination of the two, and yet it happens in one organ and is a unitary entity to some extent.[37]

The crucial point to note here is that the mind has two overlapping models of memory formation and recall, one that appears passive and inherited and the other that is controlled and structured. As a result, "allusion and intertextuality, then, in this emerging analogy, are recognized as parts of a single system, with different but actually complementary characteristics."[38]

In the user interface and digital-textual worlds, we can certainly read stylistic affinity as a type of "intertextuality." When an application adopts the styling of the operating system, it invokes reference to a specific set of design principles and explicitly affiliates itself with that ecosystem. While the memory metaphor is of use here, there is also, clearly, a community-forming element at play. Applications that style themselves within the specified framework of the operating system engender a type of communal citizenship, in which a paradigm of conformance and equality is leveled between programs. Yet at the same time, it may actually be the case that this forging of community is mostly an *implicit* process, enforced from above. Many toolkits, such as GTK, bring the tools of conformance and stylistic alignment with them as part and package of what they do. In other words, applications that use a specific toolkit for their visual design may adopt stylistic conformance *by default*, without any specific allusive outreach intended. In this sense, as in Lyne's conceptual system, application intertextuality may reflect an implicit affiliation rather than an explicit formation of community.

It is in the civil disobedience of misbehaving applications that we find what Carl DiSalvo has called a "design experiment in civics" at play.[39] When applications decide to go "off-piste" in their designs, they reveal the politics of style that sits beneath operating systems as stylistic communities, with differing characteristics of political authoritarianism. On the one hand, Apple and Microsoft are notorious for enforcing their stylistic drives on applications that are distributed through their official stores. Interfaces that deviate are often pushed back for reasons of inaccessibility (a complex politics to which I will turn shortly). But these corporations are also, as above, driven by considerations of brand conformity and ensuring a unified, "intuitive" experience. Systems such as Wayland on Linux architectures allow for much greater individual stylistic freedom—in line with the liberal politics of open-source software[40]—while encouraging applications, nonetheless, to adopt conformant interfaces.

Hence, the question becomes: What do implicit versus explicit associative design frameworks for user interfaces do in terms of creating communities? Can such communities of applications be said to have "democratic" qualities, or are they more akin to authoritarian dictatorships? Clearly, Microsoft's and Apple's respective systems do not tolerate dissent. On the other hand, Linux systems allow for applications to go their own way. As such, in these open-source environments, the explicit choice to affiliate one's designs with standards yields a social contract into which applications and text-generation environments can explicitly opt.

There is one category of interface design that merits special mention, even though it veers far from digital textuality: games. Most computer games have menus and interfaces that are styled in the game's own themes. Indeed, these interfaces seek to get as far away as possible from spreadsheet applications and affiliation with digital-textual entries. Strangely, when a game "takes control" of the computer and enters fullscreen mode, user interface requirements that do not conform to the system are allowed to pass. It can seem, in fact, almost as though computer games are the jesters of the civic court of interface designs. In a carnivalesque fashion, games invert the usual strictures of brand authority and assert their right to criticize the dominant paradigm.[41] Like all forms of carnival, though, the inversion of the dominant order is only temporary, while the game is "in play," and users will return to the world of stylistic interface conformance once the game has ended. Indeed, by their outlier status, the critique that games might mount on the politics of stylistic application homogeneity is limited, because games are seen as totally "other" spaces, separate and apart from other interface spaces. Games are, aptly, the wise fools—or even Cassandras—of the user interface homogeneity world, able to speak truths but destined never to be taken seriously.

Indeed, this concept of "seriousness" is embedded in the divide between game and nongame interfaces. Yet games also provided a graduated slope between the world of the operating system (and its "serious" word processors) and the game mechanics themselves. As Grahame String Weinbren points out, many games (around 1995), such as the *Sonic the Hedgehog* series, simulated extreme environments of Newtonian physics "to keep the player anchored in his seat, to make him feel as if the laws of the simulation are precisely the laws of the world he is struggling to overcome in daily life."[42] In this way, games often (but not always) attempt to give an intuitive feel to their interactions. Gravity generally pulls sprites downward just as gravity, in reality, pulls us to the floor. Hence, game *mechanics* often try somehow to connect extra-computational environments with the in-game realities. (Although it is clear that often games involve elements that do *not* correlate with our experience: worms with nuclear weapons, super-speed hedgehogs, portal-opening aperture cutters, and so forth.)

Between the actual games or "gameworlds" (which Kristine Jorgensen astutely points out are actually themselves "interfaces to the game system") and the operating system, though, lie the games' own menus and systems of configuration.[43] These intermediate layers have, for the most part, and curiously, the simulated quality of menus and designs from nongame systems. The main menu system of 1999's *Unreal Tournament*, for instance, consists of a series of menu tiles across the top of the screen. Configuration options are presented within gray-framed windows with familiar, yet independently styled, windows in the game's own color palette. By the time of 2007's *Unreal Tournament 3*, the aesthetics had an upgrade, but fundamentally the system was still a text-driven interface with options presented on submenu pages. These loading screens present a context to the user that is somewhere between the menus of productivity tools such as word processors and the gameworld. They bring the aesthetic qualities of the game to the operating system, indicating that the user is about to leave the safe confines of homogeneous styling. In one sense, this reenforces the sense that games inscribe the oft-repeated mantra that "work and play are often in opposition."[44] Yet, as Cathie Marache-Francisco and Eric Brangier note, gamification plays a role in the design of many nongame interfaces, particularly on the web, while, as I have here been documenting, game interfaces, particularly in the premechanics phases, often bring elements of work interfaces to the house of fun. Does, they ask, this merging of pleasure and labor "suggest a dialectical overcoming of the opposition between work and leisure, pleasure and displeasure, motivation through game play and professional obligation?"[45] Probably not.

The aesthetic difference of game environments tends to reenforce the idea that word processors and other text production environments are serious "work"—thereby removing creativity and play from writing.

But it does, again, bring us back to the question of intuitability and what this might mean in the world of user interfaces and text processing. Certainly, things have changed a great deal since the 1990s. For instance, it is clear, as Jorgensen shows, that game designers have moved to make their interfaces "appear as attractive as possible . . . and attempt to hide system information inside the game environment."[46] Such an approach gives a greater feel of wholeness—or, indeed, standardization—to a gameworld, with a sudden immersion of the player in the "other space." Indeed, in such a situation, the gameworld becomes, in a sense, a whole operating system, with its own subsets of standardized and aesthetically homogeneous interface components. The game becomes an operating system within an operating system, a virtual machine.

Digital standardization versus individual style is, then, a constant battle or tug-of-war. It also seems to be the case that interfaces need to present some elements of familiarity to users if people are to begin to "learn" how to use software. Games, while seemingly as far from Microsoft Word as one can imagine, present a good case study for thinking about nested spaces of homogeneity and the ways in which an entire sub-ecosystem can emerge within an operating system but somehow also set apart from it. If we are to think, as Matthew Kirschenbaum has encouraged us, of programming as an effort of "world making," in which "the coder becomes the world maker, charged with defining the rules and characteristics of the world," then we must recognize that such worlds also bear the risk of falling into a "risk of rehearsal," as Roopika Risam has put it.[47] What I mean by this—in a somewhat different context to Risam's original remarks—is that game environments appear to deviate from office productivity tools in their aesthetics. We see text interfaces and word processors as well-behaved citizens of aesthetic conformance. By contrast, games appear as the rebels, grafting their individual style atop otherwise familiar elements. But games simply impose their own, new set of homogenizing rules all the way down. Within the gameworld, everything must, again, reconform to the dominant stylistic premise. As such, games have the aforementioned "risk of rehearsal." Each game, of different kinds, adheres to a set of conventions—generic rules that players expect and that color the interface interactions.[48] While they appear as radical breaks, they carry with them their own authoritarian streak, the risk of genre becoming, once more, a law.[49]

The Politics of Digital Accessibility

One of the drivers of more universally applied design principles has been the rise of web accessibility standards in the service of helping disabled users gain equal access to all parts of the web and computing systems more broadly. In turn, this must be linked to the ascent of disability rights movements that have sought and fought for design principles that make fewer assumptions about the abled physical or mental characteristics of users. The "human" at the center of computer interface designs has evolved gradually away from the universalizing assumptions of total ableness that characterized early developments. The classic example of this outside of digital spaces is the building facade with steps, built with able-bodied individuals rather than wheelchair users in mind. Various schools of disability studies have, since the 1970s, highlighted this as the social construction of disability.[50] In such models, disability is separate from impairment and is usually defined as "the relationship between people with impairments and a society that excludes them."[51] People in wheelchairs are only disabled—as an active process—if society chooses to use steps instead of ramps.

Disability is often "used" for various societal and narrative purposes. As Rosemarie Garland-Thomson charts it, there are five dominant—and prejudicial, oppressive, and disempowering—approaches to disability that can be ordered into a taxonomy:

> First is the biomedical narrative that casts the variations we think of as impairment as physiological failures or flaws, as medical crises that demand normalization through technology or other allopathic measures. Second is the sentimental narra-

tive that sees people with disabilities as occasions for narcissis-
tic pity or lessons in suffering for those who imagine themselves
nondisabled. Third is the narrative of overcoming that defines
disability as a personal defect that must be compensated for
rather than as the inevitable transformation of the body that
results from encounters with the environment. Fourth is the
narrative of catastrophe that presents disability as a dramatic,
exceptional extremity that either incites courage or defeats a
person. Fifth is the narrative of abjection that identifies disability as that which one can and must avoid at all costs.[52]

Often, literary texts and other fictional cultural works can be as guilty
as the rest of society in perpetuating such a narrative, as Rachel Carroll
has shown, for instance, in Julian Barnes's *Sense of an Ending* (2011).[53]

Interface design principles that enable accessibility are premised
on two foundations. First, they *do* still have to make some assumptions
about the abilities of end users and cannot totally be abstracted from
material realities. Wheelchair ramps require knowledge of wheelchairs.
They also still exclude people who cannot use or do not own a wheelchair but have an impairment that precludes staircases. Hence, accessibility measures are often dependent on some kind of foreknowledge or
assumption of assistive prostheses. They are also usually progressive,
rather than absolute, in solving exclusion. Second, web accessibility
standards are based on a fundamental refutation of some of the most
basic principles of academic media studies. Namely, web design principles that aim for accessibility insist on a strict separation of form from
content, the presentation from the material itself.

Of course, long-standing theories of media, including the obligatory
McLuhan touchstones, have refuted the idea that such a separation is
possible.[54] Nonetheless, the basic principle of modern HTML and Cascading Style Sheet design—the basis on which almost all networked
text is delivered today—is that presentational elements are encoded in
the latter, while the former encapsulates content within semantically
rich tags. Alan Liu has correctly argued that this increasing prevalence
of content-transmission-consumption models built upon standards

such as XML, which *aim* to separate content from presentation, poses a threat to artistic modes that rely upon the blurring of this distinction.[55] That said, such a model relies on exposure to the underlying structure. After all, an estimated 95 percent of artists working in a digital medium are not currently exposed to XML but rather are constrained at the level of the user interfaces within which they must operate. The 5 percent who do encounter this medium will likely have the technical ability to craft a presentation layer—to borrow McLuhan's phrase— that would transform the message. While XML is, indeed, designed for presentational reconstruction at the consumer end, the outrage at specifying procedures and constraints for this reception—and thereby circumventing the problem of which Liu writes—would be no different from the outcry at the Tate Modern when, in 2008, a Mark Rothko painting was accidentally hung, against the artist's instructions, upside down. Furthermore, it is possible that such a content/form dichotomy, in which each element must be separately considered, could lead to a culture of artistic practice that places a greater emphasis on the self-aware consideration of this distinction—surely a positive turn.

In more concrete terms, the history of web accessibility goes back to 1994, when Tim Berners-Lee made reference to it in his keynote talk at the Second International World Wide Web conference in Chicago.[56] Indeed, earlier books on the subject, such as the landmark voluminous 1990 *The Art of Human-Computer Interface Design*, contain hardly a single mention of accessibility in its more contemporary use.[57] For instance, in that volume I struggled to find more than one reference to visually impaired users, and this was only in passing, beyond color blindness.[58] One of the few references to impairment was to note, almost pejoratively, that "current interface styles have been accused of being designed for use by a 'deaf, mute Napoleonic person.'"[59] Nonetheless, the 1994 conference led to the creation of the *Unified Web Site Accessibility Guidelines* at the Trace Center at the University of Wisconsin–Madison in 1995. In turn, this document would eventually become the Web Content Accessibility Guidelines (WCAG) 1.0 in 1999. Prior to the release of the WCAG standard, website designers would have to test their site using screen-reader systems such as JAWS (Job

Access With Speech), working on a trial-and-error basis to try to ensure that the site worked with the tools. The introduction of the WCAG allowed designers to work off a standard rather than the pragmatics of how specific software interacted with a site.

The initial release of WCAG 1.0 had several shortcomings, perhaps most notable among which was the preclusion of JavaScript. In the first version of the guidelines, dynamically interactive elements powered by JavaScript had to be replaced by static content. With the growth of Web 2.0 and the importance of technologies such as AJAX (Asynchronous JavaScript and XML—a technology for updating the front end of websites with dynamic data without reloading the whole page), it quickly became clear that WCAG 1.0 was inadequate. Almost a decade later, in 2008, the second version of the WCAG was released, which remedied these deficiencies. WCAG 2.0 also decoupled the terminology of accessibility from specific technologies. For instance, "Include alt text with images" became "Include text alternatives for visual content."[60] The former wording of "alt text" and "images" ties this statement specifically to HTML and images, whereas the WCAG 2.0 guideline is far more technology agnostic and media agnostic, focusing instead on the sensory medium. Accessibility began, at this point, to future-proof itself.

By 2015, websites had become rich, interactive experiences, more akin to previous iterations of desktop applications. Google had produced entire word processing and spreadsheet applications that ran in browsers. To handle accessibility in such circumstances, the WAI-ARIA (Web Accessibility Initiative—Accessible Rich Internet Applications) specification was born. This standard for HTML5 allows for elements to be assigned a "role" function, describing the specific part that an element plays and its current state. Hence, a "div" (division/section) tag with "role='checkbox'" and "aria-checked='true'" would represent a checkbox with an actively checked state. In the world of modern web development, pages are divided into sections that update dynamically, and they may use tags, such as "div," that are not semantically rich (as would be an "input" or "form" element), to do so. The ARIA specification allows a developer to designate the role and state of such elements, thereby rendering them functionally accessible to an impaired user, even while relying on the aforementioned decoupling of form and content.

Accessibility focus from 2018 onward, with WCAG 2.1, turned attention to mobile devices. Yet, in reality, this was more just a decentering of specific device-based assumptions from accessibility standards. Rather than assuming that users were working on a particular type of desktop PC monitor—as in my earlier discussion of the development of resolution-independent displays for digital pagination—the standards moved to consider different sizes of screen across a range of portable devices. Perhaps what is most interesting about this paradigm, though, is the balance that must be struck between specificity and abstraction. As with the idea of wheelchair ramps, it is not possible to make meaningful disability equality accommodations without a concrete idea of the determinate prosthetic aids that are in use. At the same time, technologies change rapidly, as we saw above with the removal of the "alt text" wording. Tying accommodations to specific technologies means that specifications can quickly be made obsolete. At the same time, divorcing accessibility guidelines from specific instantiations of technology renders them impotent. Such guidelines seem to be caught, then, in an oscillating dialectic between the specific and the abstract. That this is the case is evidenced by the fact that new guidelines are needed every few years as technology changes, even while the guidelines have attempted, over the course of their progression, to move away from lashing themselves to particular, time-limited technological modalities.

All of this suggests, of course, that accessibility for minority impairments is not a one-time process that can be embedded in standards documents and then implemented. The assumptions of mainstream, majority embodiment are encoded in the presuppositions that structure our most basic digital designs. Instead, then, the work of accessibility for digital text remains a constant process of adaptation, negotiating elements of sensory-embodiment and interfacing them with technological imaginaries. As a result, standardization for disability inclusivity requires the designer to sacrifice individualism in the service of communal catering for difference of bodily types and ability. This may

be why paradigms of neoliberalism and libertarianism that rest on extreme individuation have consistently proved so hostile to disability inclusivity, which has thrived in spite of, rather than due to, this political
rationality.[61] Be yourself, these paradigms proclaim, unless that self is
so individuated and different from the mainstream as not to constitute
a "market."

Computational text-interface standardization—the homogenizing
frames to computational windows, for example, which constitute the
parts of the metaphor that foundationally ground our metaphorical
naming practices—are a negotiation between minority rights and majority rule. While it seems as though such abstruse thinking about metaphor is a million miles from real political concerns, this is, of course,
far from an abstract issue. The Covid-19 pandemic—a touchstone that
it is impossible to omit in any contemporary work on disability design
and inclusivity—remains a significant social problem because it presents strongly differentiated health outcomes for different demographic
groups, on which society places different levels of worth. In the UK (my
country of origin) context of 2020, six out of every ten people who died
from the pandemic were disabled.[62] Furthermore, it was thought, early
in the pandemic, that children apparently suffered far more mild forms
of illness than their adult counterparts, for unknown reasons. Worry-
ingly, more recent studies show that the underwater iceberg of viral
consequences may be deeper than previously understood for this group,
with up to a 116 percent greater incidence of diabetes in infected children.[63] Nonetheless, the narrative that emerged during the pandemic
was that the disabled, with their "existing conditions," and older people,
with their economic lives lived, were most at risk—but also, least valued.
In turn, this entailed a framing narrative in which protective action
taken by those in the less-at-risk groups was deemed sacrificial.

Yet the sacrifice was asymmetric. The trade-off that was requested
was that people curtail their liberty in order to protect the lives of the
vulnerable. The societies that seem to have the highest death tolls, therefore, were, unsurprisingly, those with strong principles that equally sit-
uate "life" and "liberty"—countries that were not willing to trade their
claimed freedoms to protect the lives of others. For instance, one might

consider the very well-known framing parameters of the US Constitution, with its inalienable rights of "Life, Liberty and the pursuit of Happiness." There is, though, no analysis to date that I have found that can say whether these three elements should be thought of as equal in stature or whether life is more or less important than liberty and the pursuit of happiness. However, perhaps more importantly, the balance here is flawed in another way—namely, even if it were accepted that liberty is as important as life, in this particular equation, all humans were not, from the start, created equal (no matter how self-evident that truth may seem). Instead, certain bodies and lives were given more value than others. As a result, the "life price" of "liberty" fluctuates with the specific lives that are narrated into such grim accountancy. This is particularly the case in the instance of older people, where the virus's knotting together of vulnerable people into a network of dependency itself mirrors a broader trend in the West "where what we are taught to value is the notion of autonomy and self-sufficiency above all else," as my colleague Lynne Segal puts it.[64] That is to say that the pandemic has doubly devalued the lives of older people, first by showing that this group would have to rely on others, undermining Western values of autonomy and liberty itself (this group is now not free *from* a dependence on others, which Sarah Lamb shows to be a keenly valorized aspect of Anglo-European cultures), and second by placing such lives as apparently less economically worthwhile.[65] There becomes, in such circumstances, what Margaret Morganroth Gullette has called a "duty-to-die" discourse of sacrifice.[66] Indeed, a simple thought experiment can show us this discrepancy with shocking clarity: Perhaps our liberty is worth the price of a disabled pensioner, but not the cost of an "innocent" child? Physical distance also helps to lower the price. When deaths are African or South American, it can seem easier in the Global North to purchase one's freedom at their expense. Indeed, I am told that it is easier to shoot someone when you do not have to look them in the eye. The pandemic has shown us that some liberties are more expensive than others, and those with a greater "risk appetite," as the phrase goes, were simply those more willing to pay for their freedoms with the lives of other people who needed their help.

The underlying mechanism that allows the economic metaphor here—that we buy liberty with lives in a symbolic economy—works by reducing life and liberty to interchangeable and exchangeable currency forms.[67] The discourse of sacrifice also requires objects to be made commensurate with one another, which is why the Christian paradigm, in which we are told that Christ died to redeem sins, can seem baffling to those from outside the tradition. Why, it might be asked, should a death act as a redemptive price for the wrongdoing of others, particularly given the unjustness of Pilate's sentencing in the first place? The objects—death and sin—do not seem to be of the same categories and so the economics of the sacrifice become strange. Had Christ redeemed our sins by his outstanding *virtue*, this would at least have made some kind of counterbalancing economic sense. A similar phenomenon can be seen in charitable efforts that involve suffering on the behalf of a fundraiser. Why do people feel more inclined to donate to a worthwhile cause, which they might support in any case, when an acquaintance is willing to suffer (for instance, by running a marathon)? Why is the suffering of a friend a "good" price to pay? Why would I want to receive the suffering of a friend in exchange for my money? Perhaps this reveals that our relationship with friends can sometimes be more driven by sadism and cruelty than we like to admit. Yet, in any case, suffering and pain seem to be exchangeable commodities that can be swapped for charitable donations.

It is also the case that the types of sacrifice demanded by pandemics with unequal outcomes for different groups can be classed, in economic terms, as having "negative externalities." A negative externality is a condition where a detrimental cost is borne by actors who are beyond the sphere of decision-making. A good parable of such an externality can be seen in a subplot of the 1990s television series *Star Trek: Voyager* that involves a spacefaring race known as the Malon. In the show, the Malon deploy a planetary-scale waste disposal industry for contaminated antimatter that results in harmful theta radiation emissions. On their homeworld, a powerful economy exists in which the disposal industry resists clean energy alternatives because it would put them out of business. Yet the freighters only make a profit by dumping the waste into regions of space without regard for the species who live there and whose existences are threatened by such industry. Pollution, even in the twenty-fourth century, it seems, remains a strong negative externality from many of our activities.

Computational-textual accessibility exhibits many signs of negative externalities in which the price paid does not capture the full cost to all actors or has an element of the sacrifice of others. Developing strong accessibility principles in digital systems comes at additional cost to actors who have majority embodied status (i.e., people with sight pay, in the increased cost of software, for the facility to accommodate those without). On the other hand, if the profit margin were followed without regulatory intervention and there were no compulsion to develop such accessibility, those with impairments would pay the price of exclusion from the use of the software in question. Environments with significant negative externalities are those that most require strong regulatory intervention. The balance of harm in these negative externalities is the ongoing battleground of disability regulation, in which the cost of inclusion is weighed by the fact that the benefit is often displaced from the site of payment.

Of course, the unspoken assumption below most societal disability reform is that many of us could, at any time, suddenly find ourselves in need of accessibility provision.[68] Those of us with working legs are but one accident away from not being able to walk, the tale is told. Hence, the story becomes one in which the negative externality might not be purely external. What could be seen as an altruistic societal gesture of inclusion is, once again in such a model, recuperated into an individual insurance policy. The phrase "It could be you"—beloved at once of the UK National Lottery and the narrative of future disability—again moves altruism out of our digital inclusiveness practices and instead renders our actions merely enlightened self-interest. In this version of why we make digital text inclusive, we do it to serve our future probabilistically incapacitated selves, in the balance of chance. Such an argument is pragmatically useful for disability inclusivity movements, but it also carries a damaging subtext about the reasons that we should act, ethically, to ensure maximal societal integration. There are conditions, after all, that I can say with certainty that I will never develop—particularly those that pertain to biological characteristics of sex—but this does not necessarily mean that I should not believe that those who do should have lesser access to any part of society. Of course, any ethical system that is based solely on maximal utility to the individual actor might argue otherwise. However, such occurrences (sex-specific incapacities) are interchangeable enough to be substituted for illnesses that anybody *might* contract. Nonetheless, as a deontological ethical principle, such accommodations seem sound and part of a generous societal system, even when an individual gives nothing in return.

The fact remains, though, that this model of deferred personal disability is one in which disability poses an existential threat. As Harlan Hahn put it as far back as 1988, "Probably the most common threat from disabled individuals is summed up in the concept of existential anxiety: the perceived threat that a disability could interfere with functional capacities deemed necessary to the pursuit of a satisfactory life."[69] The problem with such a construal is that it leads to an avoidance of thinking about disability, rather than any active empathy or engagement. As Elizabeth F. Emens notes, "The fact that disability could happen to anyone does not, however, mean that nondisabled people will relate to disabled people, or disability rights, with empathy."[70] Indeed, because it can pose such a threat, the easiest path is also to withdraw from the mirror of one's own disabled future. If you do not like what you see in the future, the easiest thing is to stop seeking to view it in the present.

Digital-textual interfaces that focus on disability, therefore, also act as dark glasses for a future that people may not wish to confront. There is a good reason that most accessibility settings have, traditionally, been buried deep within layers of control panels, out of the reach of majority embodied users. To be reminded that people interact in diverse ways with software and digital text, based on a diversity of body types, abilities, and impairments, is an often-unwelcome prompt of a speculatively less able future. Of course, it should not be thus. It would be far better for the lesson here to be that, should one require it, software will accommodate your future needs.

Given the continued pervasiveness of visual metaphors in Micro-soft's (and others') computational systems, there are serious questions to be asked of the inclusivity of our text editing and playback environ-ments. Yet, if the metaphors do not hold, then, perhaps, visual meta-phors are not actually visual. Since when did anybody gain a clearer Outlook on the world through their email client? There is, though, a certain nihilism in taking this view: the conclusion becomes that it doesn't matter whether our terminologies are inclusive because, well, the metaphors don't work like that anyway.

Perhaps we should, then, abandon the idea that metaphors of interface design are supposed to make our systems easier to use by providing reference points in reality. Instead, we could view our naming termi-nologies as being as capricious as any other. As Ferdinand de Saussure pointed out a very long time ago, there is no relationship between the term "tree" and the object to which it refers.[71] There is no tree-likeness in the word "tree" and there is very little window-likeness in digital windows. The arbitrariness of the sign is as strong in our digital sys-tems as it ever was in nature, but we have misunderstood the role of apparent metaphor in allowing us to intuit digital operations. Between the poles of a forensic attention to materiality and the absolute abstrac-tions of total metaphor sits a space of contested value where we seek to understand how language shapes our interaction with technologies.[72]

SEVEN

LIBRARIES ARE ASSEMBLAGES OF RECOMBINABLE ANXIETY FRAGMENTS

AN AGE-OLD INTERVIEW TASK FOR programmers consists of the following: Set a moderately complex, intermediately difficult algorithmic problem. Observe the candidate undertaking the task over a set time period. The result of the test is appraised, though, not wholly on the resulting code at the end. Rather, there is a behavioral assessment: Did the candidate try to reinvent the wheel and write their own code to solve the problem, or did they download and use a robust existing *library* of code to do the job? The desired behavior in most situations is the latter. Technological corporations do not want programmers who rewrite code that already exists, and technological blogging sites are replete with articles titled "Coding is 90% Google Searching" or similar.[1]

Yet what is this textual metaphor of the code "library"? In common technological usage, it refers to a framework of existing computer code that can be redeployed within multiple new contexts. An example of this might be a fragment of code that converts a decimal number (say, 15) to a hexadecimal representation (F). There are several contexts that might require such a code fragment, and it does not make sense to rewrite the code to do this every time. Hence, we have libraries—another textual/bibliographic metaphor—from which one can "borrow" code. Many programming languages also come with a "core" library of common functions to speed development and seed good practice.

Librarians, Paul Gooding and Melissa Terras tell us, have used metaphorical structures "to describe library concepts since the nineteenth century," and the digital age is no exception. With particular resonance with the work in this book and harking back to my introduction, Gooding and Terras specifically focus on the uses to which Borges's Library of Babel and the historical Library of Alexandria are put.[2] Of course, the perennial question of this work remains, Are not *all* concepts explained through metaphor in some ways? Certainly, as Joan Giesecke argues, libraries have been sites of imaginative and metaphorical tussle for well over a century now.[3] Catherine Kennedy's probing, therefore, of "the significance of this sheer breadth of metaphors surrounding the library" may, in fact, just be a more general feature of every domain of human endeavor.[4] Nonetheless, as the historical shape of libraries gained a foothold in the public imagination, Robert F. Nardini argues, "metaphor was not only a way to describe the role of the library but also a way to explore possibilities, even a way to imagine possibilities in the first place."[5] Some commentators have even gone so far as to argue for the damaging inappropriateness of the metaphor of the "digital library." For instance, Mark S. Ackerman contended, as far back as 1994, that the use of this metaphor "constricts our understanding of social reality, and in doing so, may eventually change the social reality itself," since the metaphor of the "digital library" is built on a specific set of utopian assumptions about what a "library" is in the first place.[6]

As Stuart Lawson has recently charted, however, and as is well known within the discipline of library and information science, the histories of "libraries"—and their terminologies—are complex and political. As with the early internet, these histories often do not live up to the utopian idealization of what a "library" might be, and the economics and geopolitical entanglements are many.[7] For instance, early libraries were often subscription based, and the idea of open public lending was far from the original conception. Further, class structures in the history of libraries meant that ideas of self-improvement for the working classes—yet imposed by the ruling classes—led inexorably toward the neoliberal self-made and self-bettering subject. Finally, libraries built overseas in the era of the British Empire, in particular, attempted to educate colonial subjects in a patronizing and top-down fashion. Libraries are far from the purely beneficent entities that they are often made out to be.

These histories and terminologies, investigated in this chapter, have implications for our understanding of code libraries.[8] The analysis here focuses on three metaphorical breakages within the concept of the code library that have been key to the nondigital understanding of libraries: borrowing, learning, and improvement. It is also worth stating upfront that there is a fourth category that underpins all the remarks herein: compatibility. The genericity of a library determines with which particular code it may or can work and the limits of its interoperability. Whenever we speak of code libraries, we need to know with which code or language a particular library will work and, by extension, with which it will not. If libraries are idealized as spaces of *universal* borrowing and lending, their digital code equivalents are, from the very start, predetermined only to work with specific technologies in specific contexts. A Python library will not play nicely with one written in Java, without a heavy interface. It may even be the case that a Python 3.11 library will not interoperate with a Python 3.6 library (and certainly not Python 2.x). From the very start, computational code libraries are defined by their parameters of exclusion.

On the concept of borrowing, this chapter highlights for one last time the nonrivalrous nature of "borrowing" in the digital context while also tracing the history of (non)lending libraries, on-site access, and subscription-only libraries. On the matter of learning, this chapter examines the fact that code libraries often actually obscure their contents from the "borrower." An oft-repeated example of this is the adage that a programmer should not "roll their own cryptography" but should always instead use an extant audited library. However, in so doing, this act of borrowing means that very few coders ever learn how to produce reliable cryptographic functions. Finally, on ideas of societal self-improvement, this chapter highlights the contradictions in future libraries of code, such as Stack Overflow, which rest on the principles of competition and economic productivity.[9]

This chapter also, by necessity, implicitly deals with the nature of code as opposed to other forms of textual production. Rooted in histories of performative utterances and following recent work by Caroline Bassett, Wendy Hui Kyong Chun, and David Berry, the libraries without books to which this chapter turns are more akin to magic incantations, summoning spells of esoteric knowledge, enmeshed in broken metaphorical tropes that reenforce a false history of the contemporary library.[10] Code is a specific type of textual production, with performativity at its core. It is both subject to all the same strictures of interpretation as other forms of language but also deterministically free of such ambiguities.

Borrowing

Public libraries are constructed within a nostalgic, imaginary framework that bears little resemblance to the ground history from which they are constituted. Libraries are often posited, in the public imagination, as timeless institutions that are free from most knowledge politics and that exist in an only-ever benign relationship to their clientele. The global situation for libraries is also often homogenized. It is easy to envisage that libraries fulfill the same function, worldwide, at all times. This could not be further from the truth. In reality, libraries have at times, for example, served colonial ends and taken a multitude of forms. The idea of the free public library—a symbol of Enlightenment knowledge, funded by the national welfare state—is actually a relatively recent invention rather than an unchanging reality.[11] This is not to say that utopian and idealistic takes on libraries have not formed part of their history and altered their material courses—far from it. But it is to note that libraries have often served very different ends to this imagined construct and that they are embedded deeply within political structures.

The first historical point to make is that libraries have served different communities at different times in their histories. The notion that all
libraries existed to serve the "general public" is erroneous. Indeed, even
the term "public library" is contested. In the seventeenth century, for
example, the phrase "public library" denoted a library that was funded
either by endowment, by subscription, or by institutional affiliation.[12]
Subscription libraries, in the United Kingdom, lasted until approximately the middle of the twentieth century, when they were then over-
taken by the new meaning of "public library": a space where anybody
could consult or borrow works, free of charge.[13] This was highly dependent upon the political climate changing at this point to support the
idea of a robust public service infrastructure underwritten by the state
through taxation in the postwar period. In the twenty-first century,
the subscription library does persist. Prominent examples include the
Providence Athenaeum in Rhode Island and the London Library in,
unsurprisingly, London. Although the latter is now open to anybody
who can pay an annual subscription, earlier members required spon-
sorship to obtain a reader's pass, thereby limiting access not only on the
grounds of finance but also through social connection.[14]

The term "publicness" finds itself placed under the same kind of
retroactive linguistic demands as "openness" in the digital age, which
can lead to a set of questions about the place and labor of publishing. A good question: How did "open" in the library and information
space come to mean "freely available" and "allowing reuse beyond the
bounds of conventional fair use/fair dealings in copyright law"? Originally, "open stacks" meant that works were "open" for consultation
by readers themselves and did not require a librarian to fetch the titles
from the bowels of the institution on behalf of the patron. When digital technologies made texts instantly copyable—a perpetual refrain
of this book—the understanding of what we pay for changed. An un-
realistic erasure—and devaluing—of textual and publishing labor is
central here, with proponents keen to enact a politics of austerity on
publication cultures.[15] It is in this space that we see two conflicting
political agendas at war. On the one hand, those who seek the free,
online dissemination of scholarship and other forms do so within a

context of socialistic sharing—a background in communistic cultures of information freedom.[16] On the other hand, there is a "neoliberal" current that runs through such thinking.[17] In this current, publishers, it is claimed, "do nothing" and can be automated out of existence in the name of efficiency and cost savings.

These storms have long been brewing in scholarly publishing circles. Open access—the dissemination of scholarship without cost to the reader—was billed as the simultaneous savior of library budgets *and* lack of access.[18] But these two sides of the phenomenon are not by necessity bedfellows. It is possible to achieve open access and for it to cost more. And it is possible to run nonopen publishers that have slimmer profit margins than we see from scientific megapublishers today.[19] There is also a problem with the argument that open access *will* save money for academic libraries. If academic libraries stop paying because there is no longer an access gap, then the labor of publishing will dry up, and *it will incentivize nonopen access publishing.* That is, if academic libraries pursue the logic that everything should be open, but they do so to stop paying for the labor of publishing, rather than because they believe that work should be accessible, then there will be no publishing labor to perform the intermediary tasks of publishing.

What are those labors? Michael Bhaskar has framed these activities as "filtering, framing, and amplification," and they cannot easily be wished away into the land of technology.[20] They are in part social functions, even when they are flawed. That is, the "framing" that a publisher provides is not necessarily of sound framing value, but it can be socially conferred. That a book is published by Oxford University Press (OUP) or similar may confer a certain level of prestige. But on what basis does that rest? Other publishers are able to draw on the same pool of peer reviewers, for instance. However, the cultural cachet that OUP can provide, as just an example, is out of proportion to that review process. This is because it is assumed that a publisher such as OUP will be the first port of call for most manuscripts, with academics seeking to leverage the maximum symbolic-economic benefit for their careers, premised on a scarcity correlation (a high rejection rate).[21] Hence, as a result, it is presumed that their selection procedures will allow them to choose to publish only the very best work and to pass the remainder on to other publishers.

There are many reasons to believe this view to be mistaken. As I put it with a collection of coauthors recently: "Do researchers recognize excellence when they see it? The short answer is no."[22] Adam Eyre-Walker and Nina Stoletzki, for instance, show that researchers are poor at predicting the impact and future value that a piece of work will have.[23] Other studies have consistently shown that novel work is systematically undervalued in citation counts.[24] Work that was previously accepted for academic publication was often rejected when it was resubmitted as part of an experiment.[25] There is a poor relationship between researcher ratings in grant appraisals as opposed to subsequent productivity.[26] Yet we continue to insist that our selection processes are sound, even in the face of empirical evidence to the contrary.

To get back to libraries and labor, though, it is clear that the digital space has upended the conventional economics of publishing scarcity. When the nonrivalrous digital space creates unlimited abundance, but there is still publishing labor to be paid for, we return to the virtual commodity fetishism that claims that we are "paying for the PDF" rather than for the time of the publishing labor. Actual libraries in the twenty-first century find themselves caught and pulled between various conflicting demands here. On the one hand, all but national deposit libraries have found themselves frequently having to de-acquisition titles.[27] This is especially the case when the items are physical. The collections of the British Library, for instance, use over 746km of shelf space.[28] With digital proliferation—and new print-on-demand technologies—the infinite replicability of the electronic space spills over into real-world collection hell.

The seemingly obvious solution is for libraries to "go digital." Surely, the logic goes, it must be possible for a library simply to allow one user at a time to "borrow" a digital text. This technology is called controlled digital lending (CDL), and it is highly contentious.[29] In controlled digital lending environments, digital items are made scarce, and only a specific number of users may "check out" an item from the library at any time. It is the equivalent of saying that an item has been loaned to another user and, before it can be checked out again, it must be "returned."[30]

Controlled digital lending catches flak from all ends of the political spectrum. For the hard-core copyright abolitionists, and even for the more moderate voices of open access, controlled digital lending is a problematic implementation of digital rights management (DRM) technologies that hinders end-user reuse. Criticisms of DRM have been ongoing for several decades and across many axes. Perhaps the staunchest of the critics has been the Electronic Frontier Foundation, which highlights the widespread privacy and legal concerns around these practices.[31]

Before delving into why this is significant, it is worth briefly highlighting how DRM for controlled digital lending works. If libraries were simply to provide end users with a file that they could download, in an open and standardized format, it would be easy to copy this file to someone else and for them to be able to read it. This could be beneficial for knowledge and education. However, under controlled digital lending, a user can only read the file when they have officially checked it out of the library and are the authorized user. This is usually achieved by cryptographically encoding the downloaded file and then authorizing only specific software to decrypt the document. Thus, DRM requires an end user to have a specifically compatible client (causing problems for those using less common and open-source desktop operating systems, such as those based on Linux) and for the user to be willing to run this code on their machine. This can sometimes have implications for digital accessibility, as covered in the preceding chapter, as screen readers and other assistive technologies cannot easily interact with these DRM delivery vehicles.

Perhaps most importantly, though, as the EFF points out, "DRM systems can't protect themselves," and "they require 'anti-circumvention' laws to silence researchers who discover their flaws." Such anticircumvention legislation has been used to "silence and even jail researchers who embarrassed entertainment companies and DRM vendors with revelations about the failings in their systems."[32] To return to the example at the beginning of this book, this leads to a situation in which certain numbers are deemed "illegal" because they represent the cryptographic decryption keys of DRM systems. For instance, a United States District Court of New York ruled that it was against the law to circulate the number that is used to decrypt high-definition DVD and Blu-Ray discs, the so-called AACS encryption key.[33] Quite simply, this made a specific number "illegal" for what it could theoretically do (and returns us to the discussion of πfs at the start of this book).

More specifically, however, creating software that can circumvent the provisions of controlled digital lending violates the Digital Millennium Copyright Act (DMCA) and similar equivalent provisions in multiple jurisdictions. This causes some interesting frictions with free speech laws in the United States, because software is written in human language (usually, but not always, English).[34] In this sense, there are ways in which software can be considered speech and expression. Hence, DRM systems might then be considered to infringe on principles of free speech that are enshrined in the US constitution.

Yet this is not straightforward, as the Harvard and Carnegie Mellon legal scholars L. Jean Camp and K. Lewis argue: "Unlike all other forms of 'speech' computer source code holds a unique place in the law: it can be copyrighted, like a book and it can be patented like a machine or process."[35] As Camp and Lewis continue: "A foundation of our argument is that source code is speech. Notice we make only this claim of source code, not of any other forms. Computer software written in higher level languages can take two forms: source code and object code. Source code is the human-readable form of a program before it has been compiled (the process of turning the source code into object code). Object code is the binary or computer readable version of the same program after being compiled—object code is not human-readable."[36] This distinction is curious and does not hold in every circumstance. Some forms of programming practice, for instance, exploit the mechanisms of compilers to create object code that behaves in inventive ways that were unintended. Computer viruses and exploits, for instance, frequently mutilate code at the object/compiled level, sometimes even mutating their own program in-memory. It is also the case that a skilled decompiler can translate back from object code into a human-readable form. A rigorously held distinction between supposedly unreadable object code and human-readable higher-level source code is a problematic divide.

The DMCA, which outlaws some software, places limits on freedom of expression in the digital space. Specific forms of linguistic expression, in the shape of code that circumvents copyright protection, are made illegal by the systems that enforce controlled digital lending. Of course, we accept all kinds of curbs on freedom of expression/ free speech all the time. Free speech cannot be wholly unfettered in a decent or civilized society because some forms of speech are also speech acts and, therefore, violence. Those that direct people to murder others and that have a performative effect are outlawed. The question is whether the performative speech acts of software, when dealing with cryptographic routines for implementing DRM, are commensurately serious as "incitement to murder."

That the primary outlawed form of software speech concerns cryptography brings with it concerns around national security. Specifically, the export of cryptographic libraries from the United States has a long legal history, even as experts in the field, such as Whitfield Diffie (one of the pioneering creators of public-key cryptography), decry such restrictions and refer to them as "Cold War relics."[37] Indeed, the classification of specific forms of software speech as "munitions" led to a coordinated campaign that sought to expose such dealings as nonsense. A particularly prominent example was the Cypherspace munitions T-shirt. The shirt contained a representation of the RSA encryption routine, written in the Perl programming language, and declared that "this shirt is classified as a munition and may not be exported from the United States, or shown to a foreign national."[38] The disjunct here, of course, works by the contrast of a T-shirt with weaponry. Woodie Guthrie may have scrawled on his guitar that "this machine kills fascists" (while Tom Morello opts for "Arm the homeless"), but guitars have not yet been outlawed for export from the United States.

Controlled digital lending, relying as it does on public-key cryptography to enforce time-sensitive DRM decoding routines, finds itself embroiled in the geopolitical controversies around export routines. Digital libraries' ability to "lend" texts depends upon cryptographic routines that are mired in international security controversies and debates about the limits of free speech (let alone fair use copyright doctrines). Yet the fact that it is cryptography that is at play, here, transitions us into thinking about other types of "libraries" and the ways in which such functions are implemented.

Cryptography, in the twenty-first century, is a highly specialized field of endeavor that requires an in-depth understanding of multiple mathematical fields. For instance, elliptic-curve cryptography requires comprehension of the algebraic structure of elliptic curves in so-called finite/Galois fields. By contrast, RSA public cryptography uses the difficulty of the prime factoring problem as its trapdoor function. (A trapdoor function is a mathematical problem where an operation is easy to execute in one direction but very difficult to reverse. For instance, it is easy to multiply two large prime numbers together, but it is very hard, when given the result of that, to say what the original two numbers were.)[39]

The temptation, when moving to implement some form of application security in a software environment, is to write the system yourself. After all, the seasoned programmer might reason, How hard can it be? Yet, in the world of computer security, "asking why you should not roll your own crypto is a bit like asking why you should not design your own aircraft engine," as Runa Sandvik put it. "The answer," as she framed it, "in both cases, is that well-studied and secure options exist. Crypto is hard and I would rather rely on encryption schemes that have been studied and debated than schemes that are either secret or have yet to receive much, if any, attention."[40] For this reason, cryptography is commonly bundled in the standard codebase of major programming frameworks. Of course, these bundles are called . . . libraries.

Shared libraries for cryptography embody a diverse set of conflicting principles. Most prominently, they are an example of Linus's law: that "given enough eyeballs, all bugs are shallow."[41] In other words, the more people who have looked at a specific piece of code, the less likely it is that that code will contain errors, or so the theory goes. There are a few challenges with this theory, though. For one, supply-chain attacks on open-source software have become ever more common, and there is no guarantee that these will be spotted before they end up in a shared code library. A good example of this anxiety can be seen in the fact that the University of Minnesota has been banned from contributing to the Linux kernel after researchers attempted to smuggle malicious code into the project.[42] The researchers claimed that their work was designed to test the security protocols and review processes of the Linux kernel project.[43] However, those dedicating their time to building an open-source operating system that is free to all did not take kindly to being guinea pigs: "I suggest you find a different community to do experiments on," they said.[44]

There is a difficult balance to strike here. On the one hand, testing the security mechanisms that are in place in a widely used open-source operating system seems a sensible precaution. The world's computing systems depend on Linux, as does every Android smartphone. By some measures, it is the most widely run operating system on the planet. Knowing that it is difficult to smuggle malicious code into the Linux kernel is important. Penetration testing by external, good-guy actors is a much better situation than malicious agents getting away with it.

On the other hand, most of the programmers who work on Linux dedicate an enormous amount of their own free time to the project. Many are paid to work on the operating system, but others do so simply for the sake of improving a public good. To experiment upon these people and to compel them to use their free time to evaluate security threats that have been concocted by university researchers (who will, themselves, benefit from publishing the results) is mean spirited. It is clear why this so irked many who work on the Linux kernel. It is also obvious that this debacle highlights tensions around Linus's law and its ability to mitigate supply-chain attacks against open-source software projects.

Further, in the cryptographic library space, there are even more challenging aspects. The Dual_EC_DRBG implementation of elliptic-curve cryptography has been shown to have very serious problems with its mathematical integrity. Specifically, an attacker who knows various constants pertaining to this curve's description can, with just a small amount of collected data, decrypt any stream. That this curve was proposed by the USA's National Security Agency (NSA) leads only to more conspiratorial anxiety. In this particular instance, cryptographic experts such as Bruce Schneier note that this "backdoor" was "public, and rather obvious."[45] Yet to the layperson, this vulnerability was anything but obvious. It was a complex theoretical mathematical backdoor, and even someone with years of programming experience, but who was not a mathematical cryptographic expert, would have been hard-pressed to notice it.

This is all to say that the "wisdom of crowds" is dependent upon there being expertise in the crowd. The security of cryptographic libraries is not dependent merely on many eyes making bugs shallow but, rather, on specific knowledgeable eyes conducting expert review. Indeed, the fact that hundreds of ignorant eyes could not spot what one mathematically trained mind might see in cryptographic security calls into question issues of distributed trust in open-source libraries.

Kathleen Fitzpatrick has drawn attention to this aspect of filtering in the context of academic peer review, where she notes that "the most important thing to have information about is less the data that is being filtered, than the human filter itself: who is making the decisions, and why."[46] Hence, while the actual grounding of Linus's law might be that "with enough eyeballs, you are likely to have informed eyeballs in your crowd," this thinking steers us away from some of the more radical internet text propositions of recent years. The most obvious of these is Wikipedia, which both provides the counterexample but also "just works." Wikipedia is, of course, a classic example of a Linus's law–type project. Its fundamental principle is that with thousands of volunteer editors looking at the site every day, someone, eventually, is bound to spot and correct errors. Indeed, for the most part, Wikipedia has emerged as a reliable repository of information, the place on the internet to which almost everyone journeys when they first wish to learn about a topic.[47] Yet Wikipedia is also subject to supply-chain attacks. It is perfectly possible for malicious actors to slip small fragments of untruth into articles, particularly in spaces that receive less attention. It is also true that a small minority of Wikipedia editors produce the majority of persistent content.[48] As a result, Wikipedia is actually less diverse in its eyeballs than might be assumed.

The same can be said of cryptographic libraries. There is a relatively small cohort of mathematicians/computer scientists with the cross-domain knowledge to produce reliable pseudorandom number generators, for example. Trust and authority are, therefore, vested in such individuals—and, curiously, style and affiliation play a large role in the level of trust that is decanted into such people.

Perhaps the best example of this in recent years is Moxie Marlinspike. Marlinspike is the author and inventor of the Signal cryptographic protocol and library, which forms the core of many contemporary end-to-end encrypted messaging systems, such as WhatsApp and Facebook Messenger. So, why should we trust Marlinspike as a cryptographic expert? Apart from his impressive publication record and invitations to speak at major information security conferences, such as Las Vegas's prominent Black Hat event, Marlinspike has also struggled with travel in the United States.[49] In 2010, for instance, Marlinspike was detained for several hours by border agents who searched his laptop and cellphones.[50] Such interventions by law enforcement give some confidence that the cryptographic libraries that Marlinspike has developed are not breakable by the US government, unless the whole thing is an elaborate double bluff.

The network of trust that this antigovernment sentiment engenders is complex and tangled. For those who take this at face value, Marlinspike clearly poses a threat to the US government's surveillance systems. That he has been detained multiple times is proof, for many, that his work is sufficiently robust as to cause disquiet to law enforcement agencies who are unable to break his systems. Conversely, depending on how paranoid one wishes to become about this, it is perfectly possible to believe that such detentions were staged in order precisely to engender such trust. What better way could there be to persuade a population that distrusts the government of your own trustworthiness than to be detained by the government? This is, of course, the central problem of cyber libertarianism: the very thing that can build trust can also be pulled together into a new conspiracy, where every layer is just another ploy to destroy such trust.

This case study of cryptographic functions gives us the central tenet of reusing code from libraries. Essentially, their use relies on systems of belief and trust. Trustworthy libraries of code, in the paranoid world of information security, do not come about because many eyes have made the bugs shallow. They instead derive their authority from the knowledge that trusted expert third parties, without vested interests, have vetted their procedures. Open source can help with this and may even be a necessary but insufficient prerequisite. Yet how those systems of trust and belief are constructed is not part of any technological system, or even an ingrained aspect of openness, but is enmeshed in social relationships and organizational structures. The authority of the code that one borrows from a cryptographic library will be based solely on whether one trusts the designers and its vetters. Contrary to the idea that, in the digital age, all knowledge is distributed, when we borrow from digital cryptographic libraries, we implicitly rely on few points of expertise, knowledge, and trust.

Learning

The second of the areas to which the term "libraries" is applied in the brave new digital world could be said to be "learning." Of course, there are many online repositories of text that contribute to learning in the old-school, extradigital sense. Wikipedia is an incredible educational resource. More particularly, though, a new type of library has entered the twenty-first century lexicon of text production and learning. Namely, *machine* learning models that have been trained on vast corpora of existing texts can now produce writing that is nearly indistinguishable from that created by people. Certainly, at the time of writing, these large language models are not capable of threading together, say, essay-length constructions that maintain coherence. However, at the level of several connected paragraphs, they are frighteningly good. The ever-accelerating pace of success in this field is also cause for alarm.

Computational writing, or "natural language generation"—a strange term given the unnaturalness of the process but one meant to distinguish human languages from programming languages—has a long history. The goal of most such projects has been, historically, to produce text that can pass a Turing test without human intervention.[51] Such systems stretch back to 1845 and John Clark's Eureka machine, which could produce Latin verses for entertainment.[52] The most famous of such systems, though, are the chatbots that emerged from the 1960s onward as computational systems came to the fore.[53] (Indeed, the most frequent deployment of these natural-language-generating systems still remains customer support chat environments.) Perhaps the most famous example from this period is the Rogerian psychotherapist chatbot, ELIZA, which worked primarily by repeating back snippets of the user's own input.[54] Other well-known systems include SHRDLU, which had a basic understanding of natural language propositions alongside a memory system; TALE-SPIN, which generated Aesopian-esque fables; AUTHOR; MINSTREL; UNIVERSE; and GRANDMOTHER.[55]

The biggest change in recent years has been the shift from programs that were heuristically or algorithmically based to those that have been trained on large-scale *libraries* of text. This is a fundamentally different technology to that used by older algorithmic chatbots.[56] Previous iterations of chatbots would attempt to mimic human conversation by parroting back snippets of the user's own dialogue in an attempt to feign a conversational dynamic. The most recent iterations are also parrots of a kind (dubbed "stochastic parrots" by a famously critical paper) but ones that operate across vast fields of language that are irreducible to small-scale algorithmic implementations and that respond stochastically— that is, with an element of chance.[57]

In these new text-based language libraries, a "model" is produced that aims to replicate statistically the larger body of text.[58] These are called large language models (LLMs). They work primarily on a sampling basis but can operate at the word, n-gram, and character level. For instance, the model may contain probabilistic descriptions of the most likely next character to follow an *S* in any word (although the model tends to work on semantic units larger than characters). Yet because language is complex and polysemic, features such as "word embeddings" can be used to ensure that words with similar meanings end up in similar representative contexts. The basis of LLM training, though, is that there is an input library from which a genericized statistical model is constructed. The model is not a one-to-one representation of the input data. If it were, it would be Borgesian in its scope. Instead, such models represent an attempt to compress the input library into a statistical sampling framework that can generate plausible output text.[59]

Among the most interesting aspects of these futuristic text-generation sampling models is that the libraries from which they sample carry the ghosts of de-acquisition. In the physical library space, as I have already touched upon, physical space requirements necessitate the removal of volumes from the library. At this point, there may certainly remain traces of those works. Borrowing records will remain. The shelf space may be indented with the work's imprint. Fundamentally, though, the de-acquisition of titles in the physical (or even digital) library space generally removes that work from circulation. It is no longer part of the library and cannot be borrowed.

Language models, once trained, bear the perpetual weighting of works that were once included but subsequently removed. This is what Tiffany C. Li has referred to as the "algorithmic shadow," harking back to my earlier discussion of shadows, color, and heraldry.[60] As with the public-key cryptography discussed above, the reason for this is that the generation of AI models is a one-way process—another trapdoor function. The probabilistic weights in the model are constructed from the library, but the library cannot be itself reconstructed from the statistical model. As a result, as Li frames it, "when you feed a set of specific data to train a machine learning model, those data produce an impact on the model that results from such training. Even if you later delete data from the training data set, the already-trained model still contains a persistent 'shadow' of the deleted data. The algorithmic shadow describes the persistent imprint of the data that have been fed into a machine learning model and used to refine that machine learning system."[61]

There is, then, a fundamental question about what it means to "de-acquisition" a text in a machine learning model. Continuing to train a model with new data is not the same as retraining the model from scratch, without the removed material. Training patterns tend to be incremental, adding new datasets (called checkpoints), although they can iterate over previously ingested libraries in order to reduce the loss function of the model (a measure of how well, or otherwise, the model replicates the original dataset). It is in such a context that the biological or neural metaphor of learning comes out most strongly. Machine learning models are, in some ways, more akin to people and how they learn, although this is hotly disputed.[62] Consider that a person's learning and development also cannot be undone by the "de-acquisitioning" of a text. One cannot "unread" something that one has encountered, although its influence may be forgotten and lessen over time. (One would say, then, that this input had less "weight" in the model.) AI models also have this one-way flow of accumulation without discard. The source library may decrease in size, but the trace remains in the model.

The privacy implications of such a system are nonetheless extensive. Many privacy laws, worldwide, depend upon the ability of subjects to retract their consent. For instance, most institutional review board (IRB) ethics procedures at universities require all human subjects to be able to withdraw at any time. When models have been trained on text and data, with no clear way of removing the influence of a specific text, such provisions become meaningless. On the other hand, the question here also becomes one of identifiability. In very large language models, it can be impossible to discern the influence of a single text on the model's shape and predictions. In smaller datasets it may be entirely possible to identify the source.

A good example of this is the language model that I produced based on the literary studies journal *Textual Practice* in 2017. This recurrent character-based neural network was able to generate stereotypical Theory-esque pronouncements of the sort that one might have expected from the heydays of the 1980s and 1990s: "The series of temporal inventions of the object is intelligible only afterwards," the network told me.[63] The network was also able to generate plausible (but unreal) citations, such as the ominous-sounding fictional "Slavoj Žižek, *Live Fiction*, trans. Rushdie and Jean-Luc Nancy (London: Bohestock Press, 1994)."[64] In these very domain-specific contexts, it is possible to return to the source material and to identify likely sources of some of the network's outputs. The influence of Žižek, Rushdie, and Nancy, for instance, could easily be picked out from the source library (and removed if retraining from scratch). At the larger scales of vast corpus sampling that underpin models such as GPT-3 and GPT-4, the most powerful and massive of recent text-generation models, it is far harder to identify individual input sources.[65] This does not mean that a model might not accidentally reconstitute data that were private or otherwise secret. It is also the case that models at this scale are usually commercial, and so people's willingness to contribute to such models may be tempered. However, it is also less likely, at the vast scales of GPT-4, that the algorithmic shadows will be cast in a recognizable form.

There is also a fundamental question as to whether creating machine learning models, using text sampling from libraries, constitutes research on human subjects. Clearly, some forms of textual representation fall into this category, while others do not. Medical records are textual representations of people that disclose details about those people. To conduct research on the substantive content of medical records is to conduct research upon *people* (even if not *individuals*). On the other hand, those writing about contemporary novels, for instance, would consider their work to be primarily a study of textuality, even though such literary criticism will often refer to textual utterances as the work of said author ("In this work, Eve writes that . . ."). This is why literary critical studies of living authors still do not travel through IRB ethics procedures, for the most part (although interviews with authors might be considered differently in some circumstances). Yet there are questions about whether, perhaps, they *should*. Many contemporary literary critical studies, for instance, are premised on showing how texts may subtextually harbor prejudices against various groups (for instance by reenforcing colonial mindsets). Certainly, we can claim that what we are analyzing is "the text," but texts are written by specific people . . . unless they are generated by a machine. We also ascribe authorship to such individuals, both to hold them responsible for their words and to provide them with credit. Under such conditions, the line between analyzing a text and analyzing a person becomes less distinct. Likewise, the privacy and personal data connotations of textual machine learning training on human subjects will, therefore, vary hugely between the different cases of ingest. It is also a remarkable historical curiosity, as Ted Underwood has pointed out, that university English departments have spent decades working on a model of writing that decenters authorship.[66] That is, the death of the author paradigms spurred by Roland Barthes, Michel Foucault, and others has suddenly come under intense challenge in the face of machine authorship.[67] The same people who worked for years to tell us that the author figure didn't matter and that it was the text that counted now find themselves arguing for the criticality of a human presence behind writing.

The copyright implications of the use of these "libraries" for machine learning are also notable. Of course, the production of models that have been distilled from in-copyright material would appear to constitute an adaptation or modification of the original source. Such production also requires a copy of the original artifact. As Daniel Schönberger puts it, "ML [machine learning] hence often faces a fundamental problem since it may have as a condition precedent that one or even several copies are made of any work used as training data."[68] Hence, quite apart from questions of "authorship" or whether machines "can write," there are a series of "copyright law concerns," as Theodoros Chiou phrases it. Specifically: "May protected works be used for machine training purposes within ML context without copyright restraints? Or does the use of protected works for ML purposes require prior authorization from rightholders of reproduction rights over the training works?"[69]

In the US context (and copyright questions always have to be broached within specific geographic coordinates and legal jurisdictions), the interesting answer to these queries actually comes from a case covering more straightforward digitization projects: *Authors Guild v. Google* from 2019. The case stretches back to 2005, when the Authors Guild of America and the Association of American Publishers sued Google over the use of in-copyright books in the development of the latter's book search model/catalog. The library from which Google sampled was clearly in-copyright, and Google clearly did not own the copyright to the works that it was ingesting. "Google claimed," a contemporary write-up noted, "that its project represented fair use of the data and that its implementation was the equivalent of a digital age card catalog."[70]

The case progressed through several levels of legal appeal (it was initially ruled upon in the District Circuit using the four-factor copyright test and then appealed to the Second Circuit and eventually the US Supreme Court, where it was denied a hearing). At every stage, the ruling went in Google's favor. Specifically, the use of copyright material in this way was found to be *transformative* and fair. It was said not to infringe on the original market value of the ingested object, and Google's commercial status played no role in deciding whether the use was allowed. Furthermore, the rulings claimed a substantial public benefit/good from Google's service, further strengthening the case here. In all, the ramifications of this case point to a broad acceptance, in US copyright law, of the principle that ingesting in-copyright libraries is sufficiently transformative as to pass a fair use test, so long as the individual works are not served out back to users.

It is worth a brief detour at this point, also, to consider the copyright status of works that have been created *by* a computer. In most jurisdictions, copyright inheres automatically when a person creates an original work.[71] Of course, such a definition leaves much to the imagination. Who defines "original," and how does one know what qualifies? It is also clear that machines and computers can be used in the creation of works that qualify for copyright. All digital art and writing would fall under this category. Yet, in February 2022, the US Copyright Office Review Board ruled that artworks generated autonomously using AI models lack "the human authorship necessary to support a copyright claim."[72] This is certainly a contestable claim. The model had to be trained, input libraries selected, and parameters set for the output (including so-called prompt engineering). The inquiry turns, really, on what level of human creative input is needed in the process to qualify for copyright protection. This particular ruling, additionally, seems only to apply to totally autonomous systems and not those that have human creative input (be that in the form of prompts or manual interventions).[73]

To return to the question of the copyright status of the ingested "library," there are, though, as always in legal precedent cases, unanswered aspects. If one of the claimed elements that justifies this approach is that it provides a "public good," then what happens when the use is private (not public) or not good (evil/bad/malicious)? It is important to note that, in the context of appraising whether a public good is "good" or not, more emphasis is usually placed upon the "public" element than upon any appraisal of "goodness." This in part stems from the challenge that "good" has a market/commodity meaning as well as an ethical connotation. Yet just because a machine learning model is public does not mean that it is "good." Those models that amplify and replicate biases in the training set may be entirely the opposite of "good."[74] But the question of who appraises the virtue or morality of machine learning models is an endlessly relativistic task. The insurance of good in machine learning is, as a result, perhaps one that is better handled at the *input* level of the library rather than at the output level of appraising the model.

This is the argument that Bethany Nowviskie has been making for some time. In her powerful talk "Reconstitute the World: Machine-Reading Archives of Mass Extinction," Nowviskie notes that machine learning processes will come to "involve a kind of pedagogy, and deep expertise not only in some problem set, area of scholarship, or subject domain but in *data curation—*in *assembling and arranging collections* of our digital cultural heritage." Such work, she notes, "is skilled archival labor, not magic. If you ever needed an argument for the value and relevancy of librarianship and museum and archival studies, here it is."[75]

The construction of such libraries of the future, used for digital sampling in natural-language-generating contexts, has different collection-building principles to those of the conventional library. In the traditional library context, there is a resistance to "banning books," and the collection may well include works by Adolf Hitler, as just the most extreme example. Yet, even as the famous library theorist Sirkazhi

Ramamrita Ranganathan proposed that "books are for use," it is (more than) questionable as to whether every book in such a library should be put to the use of machine learning and natural language generation.[76] We might do well to keep *Mein Kampf* well away from LLMs.

The main problem that fuels this dilemma—that collections traditionally have been expansive and have included offensive material because we want to learn about contentious elements of history, but that this may not be appropriate in the new space of sampled libraries—quite simply comes down to framing and context. Individual works and specific areas of library catalogs can be flagged with warnings and situational information. The results of machine learning processes—the models that come out of the training process—are devoid of such context. Indeed, the soupiness of such models is part of their supposed allure; they at once represent, but are not the same as, their input libraries. However, this makes for a dangerous situation in which we do not understand the relationship between input and output—a circumstance where hateful discourse may be generated without context as to how it was selected as an input.

It is also not clear that all the archival labor in the (usually, developing) world will be enough to provide the careful curation to which Nowviskie and others gesture as automatically generated text proliferates.[77] Machine learning models tend to perform best under one of two conditions: first, with a very structured and well-ordered dataset, and second, as an alternative, on very, very large unstructured datasets. The former is a possibility. It would be feasible for Google, for example, to dedicate vast amounts of labor to the aforementioned curational activities. However, Google's preferred technique is to throw vast amounts of *data* at the model hoping that, in aggregate, this will act as its own type of curation. In other words: the hope is that models can train themselves at such a point. However, the effects of this are unknown, although there are suspicions that such a cyclical process, in which the model labels material and then reingests it, will simply amplify existing errors and biases in the corpus.[78] In such a case, as Safiya Umoja Noble has shown us, the training corpus will contain, among other undesirable traits, racist, gender-discriminating, ableist, and homophobic works, which would then be multiplied.[79]

Google argues that its models and searches are merely a reflection of the content of the World Wide Web. Noble argues, by contrast, that corporations such as Google have an ethical responsibility to curate the material that they ingest and to ensure that content adheres to a set of shared ethical principles. In many ways this is simply a contemporary rehash of classical debates around moral relativism. That Google and other big technology companies working in the AI/machine learning space should be on the side of such relativism, in spite of ethical consumerism movements, is hardly surprising.

Indeed, the perceived threat from AI is such that various ethical movements have arisen to attempt to counter it. Perhaps the most questionable of these "ethical" movement is "effective altruism," which has sprung up in the past few years and gained adherents from within Silicon Valley tech cultures.[80] This movement attempts to think through how best to distribute resources within an environment in which there will be many more living people in the future than there are at present. At its most dangerous, the movement implies that the truly ethical choice is to help many more speculative (unborn) people in the future than it is to address suffering in the present.

One of the ways in which so-called longtermism aims to improve the future is by the aversion of global catastrophe. Among the existential threats that longtermism counters is the "artificial intelligence (AI) singularity." This singularity refers to the idea that at some point a general AI may become self-aware and self-replicating, launching an attack on humanity.[81] This is, of course, a long-standing trope of science fiction disaster movies, most notably, perhaps, of *The Terminator* franchise, with its AI, Skynet. However, it is not merely fiction. Google has, in the very recent past, fired researchers who have tried to blow the whistle about the sentience of the AIs that it is developing.[82] Right now, senior software engineers working on AI are raising the alarm. Some of them believe that we are already at the point of self-awareness within these technologies.

One of the first upfront points to make here is that this idea of a singularity also relies upon the idea of artificial general intelligence (AGI). This AGI is, in such an imagined scenario, a synthetic agent capable of generalizing its intelligence to any end. This stands in contrast to the current crop of AI agents, which have very specific tasks (in some ways). For instance, some AIs specialize in generating text (the "natural language generation" of this chapter), while others can create images or videos. At the moment, there is no AI that could be asked simply to "go out and get a job" that would perform the task adequately.

However, it is worth noting two points. The first is that in some senses, AIs are veering toward generalizability because they operate through language. AIs that generate images from prompts translate across metaphorical spaces, transposing from one domain to another. In some senses, their language model is close to "general." The second point, though, is that the threat to humanity needn't come from a generalized AI. One of the most common ways of training contemporary AIs is through reinforcement learning methods. In these systems, the machine seeks "rewards" for achieving its task in ever-better ways.

Of course, one way that the machine might be thwarted in its attempt to derive rewards is if a human operator stops the process. An AI could discover, quite by accident, that injuring or killing a human operator could be a good way to ensure its continued pursuit of reward.[83] By this stage, of course, we also now veer into the overly clichéd realm of Asimov's laws of robotics, which are designed to protect against such occurrences, even while the laws cannot be applied in a straightforward way, as they can come into conflict with each other.[84] It is simply not the case, then, that we require an AGI for singularities or harm to humans—merely a reinforcement algorithm that doesn't require human nonharm. Nonetheless, the threat of an AGI singularity both haunts and motivates AI research.

Hence, simultaneously, we have a philosophy that is prevalent in Silicon Valley that apparently knows of the danger of AI overreach even while Silicon Valley's corporations pursue the apocalyptic endgame that they say they wish to avoid. As Alex Blechman humorously phrased it on Twitter: "Sci-Fi Author: In my book I invented the Torment Nexus as a cautionary tale / Tech Company: At long last, we have created the Torment Nexus from classic sci-fi novel Don't Create The Torment Nexus."[85] When you explicitly find yourself having to declare that your robots will "not overpower humans," as recently did Elon Musk, it is possible that your entire research direction is misguided.[86] There is something about the supposed irrepressible march of knowledge that drives such logic. Under such a rationale, inventions such as the nuclear bomb were always inevitable because it is always wrong not to seek to know more. Epistemological expansionism of this sort becomes a means of legitimizing any and all pursuit of knowledge, even when one knows that the outcome might well be catastrophic for the entire planet.[87]

The most serious historical challenge to such epistemological expansionism is embodied in the debates around the aforementioned development of the atomic bomb. Certainly, while science created the conditions for the weapon, most accounts seek to separate the decision to wield the weapon from the underlying pursuit of knowledge, ability, and truth. This was, of course, a distinction with which Robert Oppenheimer struggled his entire life, justifying his involvement by professing that "it is a profound and necessary truth that the deep things in science are not found because they are useful; they are found because it was possible to find."[88] Such a clean separation of powers is a historical fantasy, though. Driven by a fear of the Nazi enemy arriving at the atomic bomb first, Einstein and other physicists actively intervened in the political process, encouraging the pursuit of the Manhattan Project. Despite the clear and present danger to the entirety of future human civilization, scientists encouraged the weaponization of their "pure" discoveries, albeit rhetorically bent such that these planet-destroying weapons were positioned as saviors in Mutually Assured Destruction.

Of course, there is another level to this. While the atomic bomb was pursued in a wartime context, the makers of AI systems today have a commercial imperative. By playing into science fictional fears about killer AIs destroying humankind, they imply that their technology has immense power, one that can be wielded for good or evil. In the right hands, they imply via this eschatological rhetoric, this technology could transform the world for the better, even if the consequences in the wrong hands could be dire. As such, we should distrust some of these claims for the power and dangers of AI. As Emily M. Bender and Alex Hanna put it, "Wrongful arrests, an expanding surveillance dragnet, defamation and deep-fake pornography are all actually existing dangers of so-called 'artificial intelligence' tools currently on the market. That, and not the imagined potential to wipe out humanity, is the real threat from artificial intelligence."[89]

The atomic bomb is also an extreme example—the Godwin's law equivalent in the ethics of science field.[90] It nonetheless provides a counterpoint to the training of AI systems and the pursuit of knowledge and implementation simply because it is better to know than not to know. To return to the smaller scale of the present-day capabilities of such systems: the first wall to fall will be the college-level essay. Within the next half decade, I rashly predict, artificial text generation will have reached enough proficiency as to be indistinguishable from a well-written and well-researched undergraduate-level essay.

Our university humanities departments are nowhere near ready for this shift in assessment and what it will mean for them, despite warnings from digital humanists for almost half a decade. As figure 9 shows, it is now possible to create photorealistic images of imagined scenarios in just a couple of minutes. How do we appraise work that has been cocomposed by humans and machines? However, the question then becomes: What are we assessing for? If we force students to work under timed conditions without such tools, would this be the equivalent of making students use a typewriter when we have already invented word processors? If the rest of the world is using such AI systems, then what would be the merit in making students work under such an artificial environment that has no bearing on the outside world? One answer, of course, is that learning to structure and write an essay improves your independent, rational thinking. The process teaches you how to argue a case, how to marshal evidence, and how to write correctly. Critics might argue that these latter two elements will soon be obsolete. If the machine can marshal evidence and write correctly, then why do we need to do so, as humans? Yet I find it hard to let go of the belief that

FIGURE 9. Midjourney-generated artwork of a palm tree in the middle of the sea

we need people who can think on their feet and that structured writing aids such thought. That is, we need people who know how to structure a good, persuasive argument, as this is crucial to judgment in liberal democracy. Others might disagree. Why do anything that a machine can do on our behalf? This is where the real "takeover" or "singularity" might actually lurk: in the total delegation of reason and understanding to machines. A world where all rationality and reasoning are outsourced to machine learning models, one in which the ignorant mass of humankind can make no decisions without recourse to the machine, is perhaps the most frightening endgame. This is where the current dangers are emerging, say, in automated hiring procedures.

In other areas of the economy, the de-skilling (or "democratization") of writing will have profound effects on the information-labor market. Traditional societal privilege has been accorded to those who can write and speak "properly" (that is, in a register denoting education). It is certainly the case in contemporary Britain that accent remains a strong marker of class. With the advent of LLMs, people for whom English is a second language or those with lower levels of literacy have suddenly found that they can produce text at a standard equal to Anglocentric information workers. Indeed, as a result, LLMs actually corrode the implicit class-based assumptions of many societies, which remain based around writing and grammatical correctness. A world where people are unable to judge others simply because they do not write well—which is the opposite of our world today—because *everybody* can write with clarity and precision, may not be far off.

When educational and research contexts seek, then, to "ban AI," this is not just an attempt to keep bad content out of the public research record.[91] It is also a reenforcement of traditional class-based privilege in research and higher education. In many scientific disciplines, there is a clear separation between the research itself and the write-up of that research. There are two ways, in such disciplines, that AI could be used. The first is a scenario where the AI fabricates data and then writes a paper around it. Clearly this would be research misconduct and fraud. The second is a situation where the real research has been done, by people, and the AI is used to write up the findings. Theoretically, there is nothing wrong with the latter. However, it still causes deep unease in cultures that have become used to using language as a potential proxy for soundness. When the Anglosphere can no longer use suspicion of nonnative language as a benchmark of likely research solidity, a whole set of cultural assumptions collapses (not necessarily for the worse).[92]

Yet, underpinning these advances are questions of the library, the input source that will control the future of machine-generated natural language. Until we have thought through the implications of that body of work—and how it is composed—we are walking the stacks with our eyes shut.

Improvement

Do libraries make things better? Does education? What do we mean by "better"? The history of liberalism and education is fraught with a contradiction of power. On the one hand, reformers made the case that, for the working classes, knowledge was power. Opening higher education (and libraries), for example, was a way in which workers could become more fully engaged citizens in society. This idea of education was entwined with suffrage rights and the idea of universal democratic governance. Workers who had access to education and libraries were told, in the vein of Marx and Engels, that it would help them to lose their chains.[93]

At the same time, liberal education reformers in Britain in the nineteenth century also made the case to the authorities that education (and libraries) would *quell* rebellion. The argument here was that education had a normative "civilizing" influence that would tame the supposedly wilder urges of the working classes for violent overthrow. By encouraging people to work within systems of democratic governance rather than taking to the guillotine, reformers argued that the expansion of education and libraries would pacify the nation.

It doesn't take an analytical genius to spot that these two urges are in tension with one another. They are also embodied extremely cleanly in the history of Birkbeck, my college at the University of London. Established by five founders—Joseph Clinton Robertson, Thomas Hodgskin, Francis Place, Henry Brougham, and George Birkbeck—the college grew out of the London Mechanics' Institute in 1823. It has always been a university with liberal principles for working-class Londoners (it was among the earliest British universities to offer courses open to women).

This was not smiled upon. The general sentiment in the early years of the college, as put forward by the biblical scholar Edward William Grinfield, was that "it would be far better that the common people of this country [England] should remain totally illiterate, than they should thus be furnished with *tools* by which they would inevitably work out their own and the public ruin."[94] It was also suggested, by the *Saint James's Chronicle*, that the purpose of Mechanics' Institutes, like Birkbeck, was the "destruction of this Empire." Far from being the positive decolonizing move that we might consider this today, for the *Chronicle* it was likely that my university had been "invented by the author of evil himself"—the devil.[95]

How, then, did the college founders justify this empire-destroying, public-ruining idea of education for the working classes? Brougham approached this by claiming that the institution would encourage greater participation of the working classes in the democratic governance of the nation. "The more educated working people were," Brougham argued, "the more capable they were of participating in the affairs of Government."[96] In his view, as he put it to the workers who might benefit from this educational institution, "knowledge was power."[97] Indeed, Brougham was not shy of revolutionary controversy. At the college's opening, he asserted that "some will tell us that it is dangerous to teach too much to the working classes, for, say they, it will enable them to tread on the heels of their superiors—(Cheers)—Now this is just the sort of treading on the heel that I long to see—(Laughter)."[98]

At the same time, though, a counterimpulse was voiced. Hence, in the same speech, Brougham asserted that "it is my firm belief that, so far from science being inimical, the more knowledge, the more learned, and the more moral, that the people become, the safer and more sure will the Government be."[99] On the one hand, here, higher education and libraries are agents of power and liberation. They are billed, to the populations who will benefit from them, as ladders over the political wall. They will give power to the downtrodden in a post-Enlightenment democratic environment. On the other hand, when selling the idea to those already in power, education and libraries are civilizing influences that will ensure the working classes do not rise up against their masters. This is not a case of simply saying one thing to one group and another thing to another. It is not really as strategic as that. Rather, despite the fact that these ideas contrasted with one another, both stances were equally believed. It is a fundamental tenet of liberal democracy to want greater participation from all segments of society but also to want to curb the more radical impulses that might overthrow said democracy. It is, as Joanna Bourke puts it in her history of Birkbeck College, a

case of "asserting the radical consequences of education while simultaneously reassuring critics that education would stifle revolutionary
inspirations."[100]

This doubling at the heart of liberal education reform finds an
echo applying to libraries in educational, colonial, and digital contexts
worldwide. First, of course, the library was key to institutions that pro-
fessed to educate the working classes. What is a university without a
library? However, the structures of epistemocracy—Who has power via
knowledge?—permeate the library setup.[101] A fundamental question,
for instance, revolves around who selects the titles that are present in
any library. Should, for instance, Miners' Institute libraries be stocked
with books selected by the miners themselves?[102] Or should there be
an external subject expert who makes recommendations? Or would it
be better if an information professional—a librarian—were in charge?
Perhaps the actual best answer lies at the Venn-diagram intersection of
these areas, which span questions of knowledge and power. Of course,
this presents three relatively benign selection agencies. However, as
the previous few paragraphs have shown, working-class education is
enmeshed in complex political dynamics, and it is highly likely that the
choice of material that is available in class-specific learning libraries
would be subject to political interference. Banning books is one end of
the spectrum here. A simpler set of selection biases forms the other end.

In (post)colonial contexts there is a similar level of interference at
work from the invading colonial power. The Venn diagram of knowledge selection includes a foreign government. Lest it not be believed
that knowledge is power, one need only look at the vast expansion of
public library systems under colonial rules that Stuart Lawson has
so brilliantly charted (the following figures and analyses are derived
from his work).[103] For instance, the Dutch colonial administration in
Indonesia created 2,500 public libraries to instill its values in the local
population and to bolster its authority.[104] Britain had a mixed history
of using libraries in its colonies. On the one hand, Britain was responsible for introducing modern public libraries to a number of countries,
such as Ethiopia.[105] In African and Asian colonies, Britain used similar
propagandist tactics as the Dutch.[106]

Yet we also see the same dual movement of liberalism, pulling in different directions, even within the colonial context. As Lawson puts it, "In 1930s India . . . the influential library theorist Sirkazhi Rama-mrita Ranganathan saw libraries as part of an anticolonial political project . . . draw[ing] a link between open access to knowledge and the need for wider social transformation."[107] As a result, in Lawson's reading, "although a scattering of public libraries already existed in various Indian cities, these did not cover most of the population, and the movement to create a national network of public libraries (along with mass literacy and education) was grounded in the struggle against colonial rule."[108] Hence, as with class-based educational libraries and the expansion of working-class education under liberal educational reform movements, the portrait in colonial contexts is complicated and messy rather than clear-cut. "Widening access to knowledge" through libraries, as Lawson puts it, "has been viewed as both emancipatory and, conversely, as a tool for indoctrination."[109]

This ambivalent discourse of improvement/indoctrination runs through digital library terminologies and metaphors, perhaps most keenly seen and felt in the framing of the "stack." The most prominent help (or "improvement") "library" for contemporary computer coders is a site called Stack Overflow. This site serves as a repository of questions and answers in which users accumulate points for answers that are well-sourced, authoritative, accurate, and timely. The site has separate sections for each programming language that it covers but also a series of network sites. These network sites—called Stack Exchange—branch out into areas beyond computer programming problems. Stack Exchange sites include areas devoted to philosophy, law, mathematics, economics, academic careers, and many other subjects. An evolution of earlier internet forum software, such as vBulletin, Stack Overflow is an absolutely crucial resource for any professional (or hobbyist) programmer.

A nontechnical user who arrives at Stack Overflow may assume that the term "stack overflow" is a comment on the size of the code library. After all, in information terminology, a stack is the space where the books and journals of the conventional library are stored. It is a bookcase. Yet Stack Overflow is actually playing on a very different definition of "stack," one that comes from computer memory (and information security circles).

In computer memory, a stack is a linear data structure that supports last-in first-out operations called "push" and "pop." This sounds complex, but it can best be understood through part of the metaphor/analogy to which it refers (for once). In the real world, "a stack of paper" can be built by taking one piece of paper, then placing another piece on top of it, then another piece on top of that. Putting a new piece of paper on top of the pile is a "push" operation. The new piece of paper is "pushed" to the top of the stack. If you take a piece of paper off the top of the pile/stack, this is called a "pop." In a stack, pushing a new item places it at the top of the stack. By contrast, popping an item from the stack returns the last item added. Hence, as above, in a stack system, the last item pushed ("last-in") will be the first to be retrieved ("first-out"). This contrasts with other systems where the last-in can be the last-out (LILO) or the first-in can be the first-out (FIFO).

One of the most common usages of the stack data structure is to keep track of subroutine calls. Subroutines, in computer programming, work on the basis of a call-and-return model. Say I have a subroutine called "print" that any part of my program can call. When my code asks for the "print" function to be run, the code jumps to that central location, before returning when the "print" routine has done its job. The "print" function, in turn, might call other generic functions that it needs (such as "find_printer" as an imagined example).

This type of process is best represented by a stack structure. Computer functions/subroutines—the basis of all code libraries—exist at memory locations. When my code calls "print," the operating system will usually push the calling address (the current code line) to a stack called the call stack. When the "print" function has done its job, it will pop the top entry from the stack—which points to the last code address in my function—and resume execution from that point. So, for instance, imagine that my code that calls "print" lived at a memory address 1234. Also imagine that inside "print," the line that calls "find_printer" lives at an address 6543. When I call "print," the call stack will push 1234 to the top of the stack. When "print" calls "find_printer," the call stack will have 6543 pushed to the top. Once "find_printer" completes, the operating system will call a "pop" operation on the stack, which will then retrieve 6543, which is the address in "print." The operating system will then resume execution from address 6543. When "print" is done, it will call "pop" again and get 1234, which is the address in my original function. In this way, the stack represents a logical flow of call and return.

So, what is a "stack overflow," and whence comes this metaphorical term? A stack has limited bounds in memory; it is not infinite. If a program attempts to push more items to a stack than it can hold, then a memory violation occurs. For instance, if you called thousands and thousands of functions from within each other, you could engender a stack overflow. Programming languages with runtimes, such as Python, will crash gracefully when this occurs. Low-level systems languages, such as C, may not. Instead, in these types of languages, potentially dangerous memory overflow operations (a stack buffer overflow) occur that can have serious consequences for system stability.

Why? Stacks can often be contiguous with one another. One stack may be positioned, in computer memory, directly below another. When the user attempts to push data to a stack that is too small to take another item, the content of the stack may be written to a different stack that sits directly above the addressee. If the contiguous stack is a call stack, then there is a risk of system takeover. That is, pushing data to an overflowing stack that sits next to a call stack will allow a malicious user to write an arbitrary return address to a call stack. This would mean that a malicious user can manipulate the execution flow of the subroutine call. So, to return to the above example, instead of "print" returning to *my* code that called it, if a malicious actor has inserted their return address instead, by overflowing a contiguous stack, then "print" will return there, hijacking execution of the system.

Writing such exploits is a highly technical and tricky business. Most contemporary operating systems have extensive protection against such so-called stack smashing vulnerabilities. Not least of these is address-space randomization, in which call stacks—and especially those executing in privileged contexts—are placed at random offset addresses in memory, so that it is impossible for an attacker to guess the stack location and hence to redirect the execution flow. Stack overflows may be about breaking software, but they also require an expert degree of skill to manipulate into a working vulnerability.

The name for Stack Overflow was decided by a popular vote (presumably among computer geeks).[110] The eventual name works, though, because it intersects two domains: the computer science context of the stack overflow . . . and the conventional library, with its stacks. In many ways, this conjoined technical and traditional fusion of naming also encapsulates the functionality of the site. One of the site's founders, Jeff Atwood, has indeed described Stack Overflow in terms that overlap with both of these domains. On the one hand, according to Atwood, Stack Overflow functions like a traditional library: "Passively searching and reading highly ranked Stack Overflow answers as they appear in web search results is arguably the primary goal of Stack Overflow. If Stack Overflow is working like it's supposed to, 98% of programmers should get all the answers they need from reading search result pages and wouldn't need to ask or answer a single question in their entire careers." This is very much the modus operandi of a conventional library, in which the reader is a passive consumer of the library's contents. Yet Stack Overflow is also a participatory space in which users ask and answer questions. In this respect, again according to Atwood, it shares more in common with the wiki ecosystem (such as the participatory culture that underwrites Wikipedia). As Atwood put it: "I'm continually amazed at the number of people, even on Hacker News today, who don't realize that every single question and answer is editable on Stack Overflow, even as a completely anonymous user who isn't logged in. Which makes sense, right, because Stack Overflow is a wiki, and that's how wikis work. Anyone can edit them."[111] The contemporary "library" that is Stack Overflow is at once quite conventional—a searchable repository of knowledge from which anyone can draw—and quite radical: a collectively (and sometimes anonymously) constructed and dynamic information store.

This future library, where the stacks overflow, is a very different kind of beast to its supposed antecedents. It also, though, is a space that works against the conventional mythology of the library as an open, egalitarian space of knowledge consumption. For Stack Overflow is explicitly a competitive peer review system that works on the basis of an economy. Building on past systems of peer reputation, such as Slashdot, as covered by Kathleen Fitzpatrick, "Stack Overflow was indeed built to be a fairly explicitly competitive system," which is "manifested in the public reputation system."[112] While such competitive systems may incentivize certain categories of programmers, the founder also acknowledges the problems with such a system: "I fully acknowledge that competitive peer review systems aren't for everyone, and thus the overall process of having peers review your question may not always feel great, depending on your circumstances and background in the field—particularly when combined with the substantial tensions around utility and duplicates Stack Overflow already absorbed from its wiki elements."[113] In fact, Stack Overflow is explicitly designed in terms of *anxiety*. As Atwood frames it, "I've heard people describe the process of asking a question on Stack Overflow as anxiety inducing. To me, posting on Stack Overflow is supposed to involve a healthy kind of minor 'let me be sure to show off my best work' anxiety." Atwood states that he imagines "systems where there is zero anxiety involved and . . . can only think of jobs where I had long since stopped caring about the work and thus had no anxiety about whether I even showed for work on any given day. How can that be good? Let's just say I'm not a fan of zero-anxiety systems."[114]

This state of *anxiety* has been ascribed to institutions (such as academia) but also to a generalized state of neoliberal late capitalism.[115] Thus, Stack Overflow is in many ways a very contemporary form of library, one built not on the mythology of equity and access but on a bedrock of anxiety and competition. The neoliberal library? Of course, there are competitive elements of traditional libraries. Researchers who produce the works that populate the stacks might compete for worldwide library availability of their titles. Book writing has long been a competitive activity. Libraries have often, historically, expressed concern—or anxiety—over who their patrons are. Before the birth of the civic library, the exclusivity of subscription and research libraries betrayed such an anxiety.

However, one question we might raise in relation to this anxiety principle is whether the word "care" might serve as an acceptable synonym for "anxiety." Frequently, the term "care" is used, as in "self-care," as an antidote to contemporary life's stresses and strains.[116] In publishing circles there is often a call to return to an ethics of "care" to counter the soulless megacorps in whose limited hands ever more power is concentrated.[117] In the context used by Atwood, this parallel of anxiety to care is raised explicitly: "I can only think of jobs where I had long since stopped caring about the work." Indeed, one could reframe this notion of anxiety as a type of care toward others: caring about whether you waste their time by ensuring that your questions and work are to the best of your ability before floating them in public. This is a being-anxious in the face of demanding time from others. Hence, we should be careful when we see calls for "care" as an antidote to the anxiety machine of contemporary capital.[118] Equally so, we might view anxiety with less suspicion in some contexts. For care can frequently be posited as the mirror of anxiety or even "investment" (in the sense of one's immersion within something).

Stack Overflow is the synecdochical library of the future. Using the vocabulary of stacks, it assembles recombinable fragments of machine executable code for future users to discover in a model of passive consumption. At the same time, it operates on a frightening participatory economy of anxiety and individual reputation. Stack Overflow has a radical principle of open editing, birthed from the wiki movement, but it is at the same time one driven, beneath the hood, by ideas of individual reputational prestige rather than pure altruism. In this sense, the library of the future looks quite a lot like the library of today. That is, a catalog of works populated by researchers who profess vocation and altruism but whose behaviors are clearly driven by individual advancement, prestige economies, and reputation.[119] Such new libraries also, though, mirror the ways in which libraries have been used politically in the past. Stack Overflow's answers have probably saved the software industry billions of dollars in productivity time (just as generative AI is now poised to do, in a very different way, but having been trained on Stack Overflow itself). These libraries interact politically and economically with society at large, just as all libraries always have. In some senses, then, such libraries of the future are actually just more honest than the mythology of public libraries that has been spawned over the years. For the history of libraries will not save us, and if we want future systems that correspond to the mythologies of public access that we have constructed, then they must be actively built from our present situation, not retrospectively grafted onto tools of empire, capital, and politics.

EIGHT

EVERYTHING NOT SAVED WILL BE LOST

TO COME FULL CIRCLE, in which the end is the beginning, I want briefly to return to Borges. There is a short story by Borges that tells of a civilization possessed of a holy book.[1] At all costs the book must, so the story goes, be protected and preserved for the future. The tome is encased within a dark and mighty sarcophagus to ensure its safety from "humidity, heat, damp, cold, ice, fire, wind, rain, snow, sleet, prying fingers, hard stares, the gnawing of rats, sonic disintegration, the dribbling of infants, and the population at large." The special caste of custodians in the story—a kind of priesthood of knowledge—is confident that it can protect the book, especially from this last and most damaging group, the population at large. Indeed, as time goes by and greater swathes of this growingly democratic population request access to the book, the priesthood formulates ever more contrived rationales for the protection of the artifact. The intrinsic value of the book seems, in the story, to be increased by its scarcity of access, even as its instrumental value to society grows lesser by the day. For even the priesthood does not really know or understand the contents of the book that it guards. Nobody does, as they cannot look at the object itself. This society has only the peripheral metadata context, so to speak, within which to work, owing both to the sacredness of the artifact, which means it must not be read, but also to the sacredness of the notion of preservation. As preservation becomes an end in itself for the priesthood, the barbarian populace eventually overwhelms the fortification and prizes open the sacred sarcophagus. The story draws to a close as the lay tribes examine the holy book, over the corpses of the priesthood, to find that it is written in a language and script that is completely indecipherable and that has been lost to time, as meaning has eroded over the span of artifactual preservation.

Borges, of course, never actually wrote such a story. But he could have, and it yields to us a helpful frame for understanding a core concept of digital preservation. Namely, What is the tension between, and the resolution of, preservation and access for nonprint legal deposit? How is it that we have come to a situation where the path-dependence of print has so thoroughly conditioned the access possibilities for the digital that its most salient property—that of nonrivalrous dissemination—must be once more made rivalrous and discarded? And what of the structures of meaning that themselves naturally erode over time, like an entropic process, in the digital space? How, without some form of continuous access, can we ensure that we can still read our digitally preserved heritage over even a decadal timespan?

Put otherwise, this chapter asks, How "safe" are our digital texts? What do we even mean by the metaphors of safety and protection in the virtual world? This chapter examines the digital-textual tensions between proliferation and insularity, between dissemination and hoarding, between abundance and scarcity. As such, this chapter is dedicated to digital-textual preservation and to digital-textual copy protection: both fall under the rhetoric of keeping texts safe, but the metaphors stretch in opposite directions.

A good case study with which to open this chapter and that demonstrates the stakes of this discussion is the recent introductions to and reports on the UK's (and other jurisdictions') nonprint legal deposit regulations, which extend the requirement of deposit of physical print items in the national deposit libraries to digital objects.[2] Under such a system, I here argue, we see a fetishization of an inaccessible archive; we develop a set of "sacred unreadable artifacts," as my pastiche Borgesian introduction would have it, with librarian custodians as the high priests. This is no clearer than in the physical location requirement of this legislation, which prohibits off-site digital access to the deposited material, thereby rendering it more a print correlate than anything else. This is to ensure protection of publisher revenue, demonstrating a difference of extreme degree, rather than type, for widespread digital access. At the same time, the protection is designed to ensure the long-term survival of the artifact, even if there is no plan ever to release the item for general consumption. Indeed, the UK legislation specifically introduces a clause that deftly circumvents such items from ever entering the public domain. In such cases, I argue, the system is one in which society never stopped to ask *why* it was saving material other than because it thought it *should* and because it *could*. The basic thrust of our situation is that Google's mantra, which might best be described as "Collect everything and store it forever," has become a naturalized principle. It becomes, under such paradigms, supposedly "radical" when celebrity interior home design gurus recommend "decluttering" or, in the words of Marie Kondo, jettisoning anything that "does not spark joy." Yet how do we know whether our artifacts might spark future joy—or at least be of interest to subsequent cultures? How do we make choices in the present about what to save and what to let go? As a relatively well-known Nintendo "quit" screen for a computer game put it: "Everything not saved will be lost."

Such protection mechanisms interact strongly with copyright law but thus, also, with localized sentiments of nationalism. Indeed, insular protectionism and national isolationism are strong drivers of digital preservation practice, conditioned through soft power mechanisms of infrastructural funding. The UK Web Archive, for instance, has had to deal with issues of even defining what a "UK website" is or means in a distributed global, digital era. Thus, once more, the political implications of metaphors of protection in the textual space are here brought to the fore.

More broadly, metaphors of protection are dismantled in this chapter and shown to be torn across several axes at any one time. For every stakeholder group that requires a form of textual "protection," another group is placed in jeopardy. Ranging from shadow archives to pirate libraries to formal legal channels, this chapter examines the complex dynamics of the protection and preservation of the contemporary digital text.

The Access Parallel

One of the most fundamental questions about digital-textual preservation is *where* it should take place. As Svend Larsen provocatively frames it, "In the paper world legal deposit and preservation of printed heritage are almost synonymous with libraries. In the digital world it is not a matter of course that libraries are best suited to perform these tasks."[3] The reason behind this is the phenomenon of what I call the "access parallel." In the print world, people used libraries to access books, journals, and other materials. It therefore made sense for libraries to fulfill a dual role of preservation and access. The accumulation and storage of millions of volumes was a condition of access. Libraries, that is, cannot provide access unless they possess the necessary items. Concomitant with such access provision is the assumption that libraries should ensure the preservation of the material they hold. There is no point in claiming to provide access to an artifact if, when it is retrieved, the item in question has decayed and is unusable. (Though this does happen. Several items at the British Library remain in the catalog but are marked as "destroyed" due to bombing in the Second World War.) In this "access parallel," it is the need to provide access that drives preservation. The *possibility* of access is the precondition of preservation.

The way in which contemporary research libraries provide access to digital web resources provides an interesting case study. Although the more curmudgeonly old timers who frequent the British Library may disagree—and they do, indeed, organize regular "protests" against undergraduates using the library for web surfing—most people do not go to research libraries merely to view websites that would be accessible at home. Libraries also do not perform a copying function with respect to the websites to which they provide access. That is, most libraries do not take any kind of "snapshot" of the web and serve that to users. Instead, libraries usually give access to the live version of the web as a supplementary resource to their print and digital collections. As such, given that most libraries are not providing access, it is unsurprising that they do not also perform preservation of this material. Indeed, it is almost a cliché to note it, but our access to digital data has been offshored to for-profit multinationals. As Paul Gooding and Melissa Terras rightly note, "Rather than looking towards libraries as their first source for information, individuals now look towards Google or Facebook."[4]

There are some strange exceptions. First, it would be remiss not to comment on the fact that academic libraries do provide access to a host of digital artifacts that *could* usually be accessed via the open web. The foremost of these digital commodities is the academic journal article. For a long time now, academic journals have been primarily digital, although many retain a print counterpart. Libraries have become the de facto access point for such digital content, primarily because they are also the financial controllers around decision-making on the purchase of subscriptions. Hence, the access parallel also has a financial parallel, whereby paywalled digital content is still provided digitally by research libraries. When such libraries are paying for this content, they also usually ingest copies of the work for which they have paid, storing a local copy. This is often done through a system called LOCKSS (Lots of Copies Keeps Stuff Safe), which allows the library to fall back to the local copy if the publisher's version goes offline for any reason. My research work at Crossref, examining seven million academic journal articles, has indicated a parlous state of digital preservation around these artifacts. Indeed, approximately two million articles in this sample appeared to have no preservation at all and were, as a result, at risk of disappearing at a moment's notice.

It is also true that there are various web archiving efforts at specific institutional sites. The most well known of these is the UK Web Archive, which "aims to collect all UK websites at least once per year."[5]

This partnership among the Bodleian Libraries, at Oxford University; the British Library; Cambridge University Libraries; the National Library of Scotland; the National Library of Wales; and Trinity College, Dublin, has many methodological and definitional challenges. For instance, one might ask, what does it mean to speak of "UK websites"? Does this refer to websites that are hosted in the UK? Websites that use a UK domain name suffix (such as ".co.uk")? Websites that are owned by a resident of the UK? The answer, actually, is yes to all three of these: "This includes all websites that have a UK top level domain name such as .UK, .SCOT, .WALES, .CYMRU and .LONDON plus any websites that are identified as being hosted on a server located physically in the UK via a geo-ip lookup. Additionally, if a website contains a UK postal address or the website owner confirms UK residence or place of business their website can be included. In order to build comprehensive thematic website collections, we occasionally request permission to archive non-UK websites from the site owner."[6]

This matter of how geographically to classify websites is reminiscent of the geopolitico-digital situation to which I gestured in the preceding chapter. It is also reminiscent of various calls for nationalistic access to replace open access in the scholarly publishing world.[7] It is another instance where the grafting of sociopolitical structures atop the internet results in geographically segregated digital (preservation) structures. Here, again, it is clear that financial structures, which certainly do obey national norms and characters, impinge upon the digital world. It is the formulation of a "'techno-geographic' milieu."[8] Because many digital preservation structures have national characteristics and are funded by national governments, there is much about the digital preservation landscape that maintains nationalist principles. For instance, the Biblioteca Nacional de México handles deposit in Mexico; the National Library of Sweden was in charge of the 2017 study of digital preservation structures within that nation; New Zealand has legislation regulating the deposit of electronic content via the aptly named National Library Act of 2003.[9] On the African continent, South Africa was the first country to have a national bibliography, followed by Sierra Leone in 1925 and Ghana in 1932.[10] Many nations in Africa, such as

Zimbabwe, have national deposit legislation.[11] "The role of national libraries in ensuring universal and equitable access to information continues," writes Jules Larivière, "to be a cornerstone in the development of a knowledge society."[12]

The *tasks* of preservation in the digital age and the preservation of digital forms, though, are significantly different from those of preceding eras and document types. That said, the challenges essentially boil down to a fundamental historical distinction between material form and some kind or other of "content" within a work. The degree to which these two are separable is questionable. Indeed, James Cummings is astute to draw our attention to the materiality even of digital markup languages.[13] In the well-known work of Marshall McLuhan, already touched upon, it is not possible to separate the message from the medium in which it is transmitted.[14] Yet our digital preservation structures tell us a different story about the value conferred on media versus the content within those media.

Consider the First Folio of the works of William Shakespeare, of which 750 original copies were printed, and of which now just 235 remain. Likewise, think of a figure such as Rachel Speght, who used the emergent print economy of the seventeenth century to promulgate her feminist argument in *A Mouzell for Melastomus*.[15] While the texts of these items have been reprinted and are widely available online, original copies of the works, which have become scarce, are held only in university library collections around the world. The fundamental point at which I am driving here is that traditional preservation systems have two crosscutting registers. In one register, usually covered by legal deposit, the focus lies in the preservation of the textual and graphic content *within* a work. It does not matter *which* copy of a specific book is given for legal deposit as the assumption is that the works are substitutable for one another (say, a digital copy "substituting" for a physical one). We also have no way of knowing, really, in the present, which works should be selected for preservation.

By contrast, the second register is one of historical scarcity. From the vantage point of history, it becomes much clearer to us what is of enduring interest. For instance, seventeenth-century feminist tracts, such as the aforementioned Speght document, clearly have a bearing on the history of women's rights. Their preservation is, therefore, of importance for our cultures. Yet what is curious is that, at a certain crossover point of scarcity, the focus shifts from the preservation "merely" of content, with intersubstitutability, to the preservation of specific editions of a work. In other words, at a certain point in time, the materiality of the artifact becomes of interest. This reveals a bias in our preservation ecologies. Because we cannot preserve everything, it is only at a future moment of scarcity and value that we begin to value the specificity of particular editions. It is only with hindsight that bibliographic historians will *care* about, say, the annotations that others have made on a particular edition of a work.[16] Bibliographic material study is inherently devalued—or, at least, substantially deferred—in the history of physical preservation. Because we cannot store everything, we aim instead to store substitutable copies. The fight for scarcity and status we defer to another day, hoping to have preserved enough copies to allow future historians to make specific deductions about the material circumstances of a particular object. (Although it is worth noting, also, that a survivorship bias phenomenon is at play here. Copies that are preserved and made available for access in public libraries are more likely to attract graffiti/vandalism, which may then, ironically, be of more interest to future historians. That is, the act of preserving a specific edition in a library makes it more likely that this specific edition will contain paratexts that are of greater material interest to future scholars.)

There are several conditions that must be fulfilled for the material study of textual objects to be worthwhile. First, the work must be of enough significance in its own right to be worthy of study. Not everything that is old is also historically noteworthy. Second, the material artifact must be capable of telling us something. If the physical characteristics of the work are totally unremarkable, then there is little point in devoting time to its study. Of course, it is possible for the unremarkableness of a volume also to speak. A lack of markings or damage tells its own story; a volume that has survived centuries in pristine condition has likely been treated with reverence and care, denoting special social status. If many copies of a work survive, then it denotes a prolifer-

EVERYTHING NOT SAVED WILL BE LOST   259

ation and widespread continued interest in the contents. Third, the edition will usually have to be rare and have distinctive characteristics. As noted, although the widespread availability of identical editions is still revealing, individual distinctiveness is more often a precursor for textual-bibliographic study. If there are thousands of copies of a work worldwide, but only one of them contains annotations by Ben Jonson, for instance, then it is that edition that will be studied and that will be of use. Indeed, in many cases, the interest factor will be derived from how a work is networked. The question then becomes one of relationality: How does the material-textual afterlife of an edition connect the work to others? Ezra Pound's annotations of the manuscript of *The Waste Land* (1922) have more weight than the arbitrary scribblings of a lay reader on a mass reprinted edition (and, indeed, form part of the poem's own creation mythos). That is, unless, at some future point, the evidence for our ways of life and reading become unknown to historians and they seek out annotations to understand the activities of the "common reader." Fourth, in catering to the "access parallel," works that have material value are often digitized or transferred onto microfiche in order to protect the original items. This creates two ironic counter-registers. On the one hand, this once more separates form from content, insisting that it is possible to access, in a new form, just the "contents" of a work.[17] On the other hand, such scarcity again reinscribes value in access to the original hard copy.

This content/form dichotomy—so spurned in media studies—is omnipresent in the logic of preservation and protection. It can most clearly be seen in the language of the "hard copy," on which my preceding paragraph fell back. The distinction here is between a hard copy and a soft copy, although the latter term is not used as extensively as the binary of hardware/software. Nonetheless, the metaphorical value spectrum of hard/soft that persists here continually reinscribes the physical form as more "real" and "solid" than its "soft," mutable counterpart. As I noted in the introduction to this book, some media theorists, such as Kittler, have even gone so far as to insist that software does not really exist.[18] Hence, even though software and soft copies proliferate and have become the main model through which we interact with and access digital texts, hardware and hard copies maintain their own sphere of influential prestige, mostly due to their scarcity function.

In preservation terms, defining "hard" versus "soft" has repercussions. If virtual editions are apparently "soft," then the implication is that they are more susceptible to outside forces (and damage). To some extent, this is true. The word processor allows us to edit text in a much more convenient (and mutable) fashion than did a typewriter on an imprinted page. Yet "soft," as in software, has also become somewhat synonymous, in software studies fields, with a type of language. As Bernhard Rieder puts it, "Using a somewhat clumsy analogy, one could say that most existing theorizations have approached software primarily through its manifestation as 'language,' code, rather than as 'literature,' that is, as the myriad of components and programs written in concrete settings for concrete purposes."[19] Soft forms are seen as created from language—somehow akin to the idea of virtual objects with mental extensions[20]—while hardware forms are deemed material. This is the case with code, where programming languages summon a reality from the incantations of words, but it is also the case with preservation, where we talk of preserving the content, the language, of works, separately from the material containers within which the soft/virtual content resides.

There are, of course, contradictory logics around the durability of hard/soft preservation structures, particularly when we enter the digital realm. Most first-time users of virtual systems believe that digital systems are less durable than their material counterparts. Part of this simply comes down to track record. It is clear that books can and do survive for centuries *because* we have invested in their preservation infrastructure already. Computer systems have not yet existed for long enough to demonstrate such persistence. As such, it is possible to argue that we cannot *know* that digital preservation systems are robust.

That said, there are a series of powerful counterarguments surrounding the reliability of digital preservation. The first is, as notes Kathleen Fitzpatrick, that the dichotomy between physical and digital preservation is built on a foundation of resource-allocation decisions. The reason that printed books survive is not because they are inherently more durable but because we have invested in the structures that preserve them: libraries.[21] Without libraries, books would also decay and fade. Hence, it is wrong to believe in some kind of naturally occurring, inherent preservability of specific material artifact types. A second point, also from Fitzpatrick, concerns the double-edged sword of networked availability and the effects that this has on digital preservation. On the one hand, as anybody who has had scandalous news posted about them online knows, it can be incredibly difficult to remove content from the web. Despite the introduction of "right to be forgotten" laws, which allow users to remove content about them from search engines in specific jurisdictions, it can prove impossible to have libelous content taken down. On the other hand, hyperlinks frequently die. Hence, even as material proliferates, the indexing and addressing system that provides stable markers corrodes and decays. The analogy might be a situation in which copies of physical materials doubled every year, but the catalog telling you where to find these copies gradually decomposed.

Most digital preservation systems work on the same basis as their physical correlates: redundant copies of material are stored worldwide in geographically distinct spaces in a variety of media forms. Periodic checks are made of the integrity of the stored records and, on detection of any kind of degradation, systems such as LOCKSS, CLOCKSS, and Portico instigate a self-repairing mechanism by taking a known "good" copy from another archive. Such a system, then, has already made a set of media assumptions about what we want from digital preservation. In particular, the assumption is that future historians will be interested in the content of what is being preserved rather than the types of degradation that are possible in computing systems of our time. That is, in repairing the underlying artifacts, and ensuring the ongoing read-accessibility of the preserved material, self-repairing digital preservation systems destroy the evidence of degradation to which our media are subject. In maintaining access to material, we lose a history of computational decay.

A further good example of such a history of decay is in the decision of whether to preserve computer viruses that infect digital archives, to which a later part of this chapter will turn in more detail. On the one hand, such code is, by nature, destructive. It may lead to the malicious teardown of the content within an archive. On the other hand, computer viruses are independent historical occurrences that may be studied by future cultures. A similar aspect can be seen in the study of bookworms—insects that damage physical works—which has been ongoing for hundreds of years (since Aristotle).[22] The study of such insects can tell us something, retrospectively, about the physical characteristics of the works that they consume. For instance, book scorpions, or pseudoscorpions (which sound much worse than they really are), are part of a complex ecology that intersects with the starch-based glue of previous eras of bookbinding, the booklice and dust mites that would consume this glue, and the scorpions that would feast on these lice and mites.[23] In other words, the presence or otherwise of damage from specific types of insects can instruct us in understanding the constitution of the books on which they feast. Likewise, spider beetles and moth larvae, for instance, are keen to consume adhesives that contain gelatin. As Ann Elizabeth Wiener puts it, "In the age of e-books and tablets the idiosyncrasies of a printed book, let alone a decaying one, are erased. For the purpose of transporting, sharing, and keeping an author's words efficiently stored, these technological changes have been mostly good. There is, of course, a trade-off to innovation."[24] In the quest accurately to preserve the "soft" *contents* of a book, we lose the ability to reconstruct historical processes of decay and degradation. The history that is lost here is a natural history (understanding the ecology of insects that eat books) and a bibliographic one (losing knowledge of the threats posed to printed works and the countermeasures that were taken to avoid such damage). In the digital world, there is a similar challenge in preserving malicious code, bitrot, hard-drive degradation, and so forth. Of course, we could catalog this history of destruction separately; independent documentation of our processes of decay would allow us to inform the future of the difficulties we faced even as we mitigated such dangers: The Museum of Artifactual Decline. The problem, though, is that it is very difficult to know what will be of interest to future historians. If we were able to know this precisely in the present, many of the problems of (digital) preservation would cease to exist.

We generally consider that the digital environment has changed the collecting impulse—and preservation function—toward a "data maximalism." Google's mission is "to organize the world's information and make it universally accessible and useful."[25] In turn, this has provoked a backlash, asking whether the maximizing tendencies of digital industry are appropriate in all areas. Rachel Coldicutt, for instance, advocates for a model of "just enough internet" where we could collect "less data. Just what you need at any given time."[26] Tom Scott likewise argues, from the perspective of a medical research funder, that we need instead to foster "a model of careful restraint and minimisation which goes against the data maximalism which is encouraged in industry."[27] This argument has been made on the basis of various value frameworks in specific ethical domains, such as the "data feminism" of Catherine D'Ignazio and Lauren Klein.[28] However, the fundamental point here is that recent turns have been away from the mentality of collecting everything, forever.

Yet I believe it is a mistake to ascribe this maximalist intent solely to the virtualizing drives of data-oriented Silicon Valley startups. Certainly, the digital environment is more conducive to data hoarding. The British Library's stacks, for example, as already mentioned, consume 746km of space.[29] The digital storage equivalent, by contrast, takes very little physical space. Storing such a library's entire physical collection in digital form would be possible within a single server room, although this would lose the preservation of much of the materiality. That is to note that the preservation of materiality consumes a much higher order of information storage capacity than the content-only approach. Interestingly, there are various emergent techniques to compress the space required to store materiality. For instance, 3D scanning and printing offers us the possibility of encoding a digital representation of the material object. This alternation between a digital representation and the capacity to recreate a real object is a type of "reality compression" function. Such technologies potentially compact reality down to digital versions. That said, such compression also changes the historic processes to which such texts may be subjected. A digital representation of a physical book will not decay *in the same way* as a physical version would have. Thus, future historians would learn *different things* about our processes of value, selection, and preservation, should we pursue this option. Instead of learning what happens to books that are stored in libraries and publicly preserved, they would learn of bitrot and other types of digital decay. They would learn of the lossiness of 3D scanning. We may also lose the insights occasionally provided by vandalism/book graffiti. Compression, in the digital sense, usually trades time for space; the time it takes to run the compression and decompression algorithms is offset by the space that is saved. The "reality compression" trade-off is more epistemological. In the digitization of material artifacts, we may lose the future ability to learn about annotation, physical bookmaking practices, and the decaying processes to which such volumes were subjected, even while we gain a new type of knowledge of digital disassembly.

Importantly, though, to return to my earlier point, the text of legal deposit laws is strongly biased toward maximalist inclusion. It is a legal requirement that all publishers furnish deposit libraries with all copies of works that have specific identifiers (ISBN/ISSN, for example). How is this, then, really different from Google's mission to "organize the world's information and make it universally accessible and useful?" It does differ in some respects. For one, the format of deposit is locked to specific types of known artifact. Academic journal articles and published books are just two categories of "information," and, specifically, they are those that have been prestructured into epistemic constructs. That is to say, the format of information that legal deposit shelters is one that has already been shaped to existing epistemic modalities. Knowledge-dissemination vehicles are protected beneath the rubric of legal deposit. Google's mission, instead, seems to be to organize freeform textual material into new corpora of accessible information, a move from abstract data to structured information and its retrieval. Google seeks to take "what is there" and to transform it into published/ accessible knowledge, while legal deposit requires the prerequisite of prior epistemic transformation before deposit.

Are Orange Elephants Copyrightable?

A number of projects have highlighted the apparent insufficiency of the published "versions of record" in the realm of digital text for disseminating and preserving truth. Specifically, the ContentMine project, headed by Peter Murray-Rust, seeks to "liberate 100,000,000 facts from the scientific literature."[30] What does this mean, and why does the project use the language of "liberation" here? The basic answer boils down to copyright. Copyright regimes distinguish between copyrightable expression, which is automatically conferred to authors in many jurisdictions, and basic facts, which cannot be subjected to copyright. That is to say that facts are not copyrightable, but the *expression* of facts may be, depending on the extent to which the language in which such facts are expressed is "utilitarian" or otherwise. The scientific literature, in which extensive papers write up experiments, detail hypotheses, and chronicle outcomes, is subject to copyright. Usually, such copyright is transferred to an academic publisher, which may be a university press, but is also equally likely to be a for-profit behemoth, such as Elsevier or Taylor & Francis. Murray-Rust's argument is that the outcomes of such papers, when the scientific method has run its course, should now be considered facts. That is, the paper's results could be reformulated in such a way that the "facts" therein are not subject to any further copyright.

Such an approach raises several issues that are worth exploring. First, there is the question of how facts exist in the world and the role that language plays in their articulation. The clearest exposition of this problem was given by John Searle in *The Construction of Social Reality* and also in *Making the Social World: The Structure of Human Civilization*. The basic statement of the problem, for Searle, is that "there are portions of the real world, objective facts in the world, that are only facts by human agreement. In a sense there are things that exist only because we believe them to exist. I am thinking of things like money, property, governments, and marriages."[31] Such "institutional facts" are ontologically subjective but epistemically objective.[32] They contrast, apparently, according to Searle, with facts such as "Mount Everest has snow and ice near the summit" and "Hydrogen atoms have one electron, which are facts totally independent of any human opinions."[33] While this latter statement is contested—Searle's "external realism"—what is interesting in Searle's account is that "there is a top-down connection between language and institutional facts: you cannot have institutional facts without language. And once you have a shared language you can create institutional facts at will." However, at the same time, according to Searle, "once you have language, it is, I believe, inevitable that you will get nonlinguistic institutional facts."[34] In Searle's logic, statements of fact create the extralinguistic truth that then becomes recognized. As he puts it, "The literal utterance of the sentence 'Snow is white' counts as the making of a statement that snow is white, simply in virtue of its meaning. No further speech act is necessary."[35]

In the land of the scientific literature, there are signs of this consensus-built social reality in the very nature of scientific realism. While facts are not copyrightable, there is a basic question that underpins this: How are facts made, via digital text, in the scientific universe? The answer, as explored previously, is by a process of Popperian falsifiability and statements showing provisionally verified theses. For example, the presence of the Higgs boson particle was postulated for many years. Then, in 2015, the snappily titled paper "Combined Measurement of the Higgs Boson Mass in p p Collisions at s = 7 and 8 TeV with the ATLAS and CMS Experiments" confirmed that particle colliders had found energy signatures that verify the existence of the postulated boson.[36] While it is not possible or worthwhile here to dig deeply into the philosophies of science that have extensively documented this process, there is an important intersection with publishing, preservation, and copyright. Science relies on the basic premise that any of its preceding "truths" can be undone by subsequent evidence. If multiple future colliders, for instance, could demonstrate that the reading of the ATLAS collider was mistaken, then the existence of the Higgs boson is no longer a fact. This raises the basic points that although facts are not copyrightable, scientific facts must be refutable and subject to revision, by definition. This may mean, then, that when a previous "fact" is refuted as an untruth, it can become copyrightable.

This is not a hypothetical situation. Around 1669, Johann Joachim Becher proposed a theory of a substance called phlogiston that inhered in all flammable objects and that was released upon their combustion.[37] The theory is well outlined by Seymour H. Mauskopf, who writes, "According to the phlogiston theory, combustion and calcination were similar decomposition reactions in which combustibles and metals gave off a principle of inflammability called phlogiston. Substances rich in phlogiston were readily combustible and phlogiston also produced the peculiar features that characterize metals. Metals were produced from their calces (ores, oxides generally in modern terms) through the firing of the calces with charcoal. This process enabled the phlogiston-rich charcoal to supply phlogiston to the calces to produce the metal. Hence, metallic calces should be chemically simpler than metals; the metals were compounds of their calx and phlogiston."[38] Yet by 1796 the phlogiston theory was falling out of favor and Joseph Priestley could write that "there have been few, if any, revolutions in science so great, so sudden, and so general, as the prevalence of what is now usually termed the new system of chemistry, or that of the *Anti*phlogistons . . . which was at one time thought to have been the greatest discovery that had ever been made in the science."[39]

Indeed, the phlogiston theory is the classic go-to example for histories of science that wish to stress a sort of "chemical revolution" at the time. As Mauskop puts it, elsewhere, "The historiography of the Chemical Revolution over the past forty years can be viewed as a collective conjuring with the demon of phlogiston. James Bryant Conant, Thomas Kuhn, and Bernard Cohen all made the 'overthrow of the phlogiston theory' synonymous with this 'revolution.' "[40] Mauskop has a point. In one of the perhaps most famous descriptions of contemporary scientific practice, his "normal science," Thomas Kuhn writes of how, in the case of phlogiston, "the progress of normal science, in this case of pneumatic chemistry, prepared the way to a breakthrough quite thoroughly."[41] As multiple scientists worked within the paradigm of phlogiston theory—just, in Kuhn's claim, doing their "normal" activities within that space—they eventually found evidence to refute the overarching theory. With that coup de grâce, the phlogiston theory was dead.

There is a substantial volume of critical material on phlogiston, even including its cultural significance within a kind of "pyro-politics."[42] In many ways, it is a neater example than Newtonian physics because, while Einstein's new models very clearly tore apart the old paradigm, much of Newton's work still remains applicable and usable. This simply wasn't the case with phlogiston. The theory had to go, and it was totally replaced. However, this has been underanalyzed in significance from a publishing and copyright perspective.

Of course, the first thing to note is that the copyright regime at the time of the phlogiston debate was a very different kettle of fish. Although the Statute of Anne in 1710 instigated the era of copyright, much of the nuance would be introduced and legislated over the subsequent three hundred years.[43] Hence, at the time of Becher's original conception of phlogiston, the expression of the idea would not have been copyrightable in the same sense that we understand today. As a result, we can only use phlogiston as a retroactive example, and it is being coerced into a historical framework of epistemic ownership that simply did not exist at that time.

Yet had our copyright system been in place, the idea of phlogiston would have gone from being uncopyrightable to, apparently, suddenly copyrightable as its status as fact shifted—or so one might assume. A brief consultation of Black's law dictionary shows, though, that the definition of a "fact" is extensive and contested. The primary definitions there given are: "1. Something that actually exists; an aspect of reality <it is a fact that all people are mortal>. Facts include not just tangible things, actual occurrences, and relationships, but also states of mind such as intentions and opinions. 2. An actual or alleged event or circumstance, as distinguished from its legal effect, consequence, or interpretation <the jury made a finding of fact>. 3. An evil deed; a crime <an accessory after the fact>."[44] Curiously, although operating in but one jurisdiction, the subentries for "fact" here include "simulated fact," which is defined as "a fabricated fact intended to mislead; a lie."[45]

In other words, a fact can be "fabricated" (constructed) but also, apparently, untrue. There is a specific type of "fact" that is a "lie."

Without care, this discussion might head here into the territory of analytic philosophy. Wittgensteinian notions of the logical structure of facts spring to mind as an investigation of how the form of language relates to the form of the world.[46] However, there is a simpler route from here, which is to retrace the statements on copyright with respect to our digital preservation systems. While it is stated that "facts are not copyrightable," what is actually meant by such a statement seems to be more that basic descriptive sentences on their own are not subject to copyright. As Charles Oppenheim puts it, "Works are protected regardless of their merit, although they need to be original (i.e., not copied from something else) and show some level of skill and judgement in their creation."[47] An important point here, first, is that works are protected regardless of their merit. While this predominantly seems to reflect on the status of art—condemned bad art is protected as much as is widely praised good art—it could also be seen in relation to truth. Assessing the "merit" of a truth claim for copyright purposes is not truly the task here. Instead, there is a type of factually descriptive language ("My right hand has twelve fingers") that does not, usually, on its own, qualify for an exemption from copyrightable protection.

That said, the relationship to truth *does* matter, given that absurdism is the qualification of a range of fictional works. That Gregor Samsa awoke one morning, in Kafka's *Metamorphosis* (1915), to find himself transformed into a monstrous insect sounds exactly like a factual statement.[48] It is a mere description in many ways. But the description is also fantastical and imaginative. It is clearly more than a description of a factual state of the world, as no such transformation has ever, in reality, taken place. The imaginative originality is here clear, and the statement would be protected by copyright, especially given how well known this proposition is compared with many other fictional statements.

Likewise, one can imagine the opposite: mundane statements that are not, in themselves, copyrightable, even though they fall within a work of fiction. Take Ernest Hemingway's minimalist *The Old Man and the Sea* (1952), which as a whole is a copyrightable work that demonstrates significant originality.[49] However, as individual sentences, the phrases "He was barefooted" or "The sea was very dark" could easily be reused by another writer without infringing on copyright.[50] In isolation, these statements have the characteristics of simple description, which appears not to pass the originality threshold for copyright protection. As part of a broader work of fiction, though, they are protected. Hence, "The sea was very dark" may not merit protection, but "The sea was very dark and the light made prisms in the water" might.[51] The former appears to have the minimalistic characteristic of a quasi-factual statement, regardless of its truth, whereas the latter has expressive artistic value. Hence, the assertion that merit does not wholly matter is just not straightforwardly true. There is a certain point of expressive outpouring at which expression merits copyright protection, and this is due to the artistic quality of the work. The protection of factual statements in copyright is not really about the truth content of a statement but is instead concerned with the utilitarian structure of statements. Again, "The sky turned red" may not merit copyright protection, but A. E. Housman's "Ensanguining the skies" likely does.[52]

What does this mean for the extraction of facts and copyright in digital preservation systems? The catch-22 situation in which factuality finds itself is as follows:

1. An academic publisher publishes a fact as constructed by scientific realist principles.
2. This fact, not subject to copyright, is extracted in plain descriptive language and is published, stored, and preserved.
3. The study's results are disproved, changing the factual status of the proposition.
4. As a result, the fact is no longer a fact and, therefore, can be placed under copyright again.

Publishers can end up, here, in a strange situation where the only propositions they can defend against copyright claims are false/incorrect results. It would not be a good look for an academic publisher to pursue a copyright claim on the basis that what they published was untrue. After all, their reputation is founded on the principle that their outputs (and science) produce meaningful, truthful descriptions of reality. Yet the types of statements that scientific results produce—"Psilocybin helps to cure treatment-resistant depression" / "Psilocybin does not help to cure treatment-resistant depression"—appear to have the straightforward descriptive characteristics of factual language, regardless of which of the sentences is actually true.[53]

It may simply be, though, that "factual" statements are actually just too straightforwardly descriptive and are, therefore, devoid of originality. That is to say that even shocking or straightforward sentences that are untrue may also not merit protection. The statement "Elephants are gray" is almost certainly not copyrightable. However, likewise, the statement "Elephants are orange" probably also is not, although the contextual situation will play a role here. Should the line "Elephants are orange" form part of, say, a longer poem, it is possible that copyright protection would inhere in this false statement. The context matters because it provides an environment in which to read a statement. Although jurisdictions worldwide may interpret the definition of factuality differently, a good example in the US context is *Custom Dynamics, LLC v. Radiantz Led Lighting, Inc.* In this case, the court found that "photographs of aftermarket motorcycle lighting accessories 'were meant to serve the purely utilitarian purpose of displaying examples of its products to potential customers, and do not merit copyright protection.'"[54] That is, the use to which a set of photographs were being put determined whether they were accorded copyright protection. By contrast, had the same photographs been destined for an art gallery, they would have been protected. The context matters for the copyright status of all digital artifacts, not just digital text.

Hence, to understand the copyright status of scientific works that have been retracted for untruth, we must think about the context of scientific publishing and how a court is likely to understand it. On the one hand, academic publishing is an environment that purports to truth and integrity. The basic purpose of most scientific research is accurately to describe current reality or predict future reality. As such,

it might follow that statements in academic papers are deemed factual/
descriptive, even if they fail to remain true for all time.

Simultaneously, academic papers (usually) possess originality as one
of their key criteria.[55] The crafting and execution of experiments—or
the writing of, say, literary criticism in the humanities disciplines—
must advance our understanding in ways that have not previously been
broached. Yet there is, often, a distinction between the writing of a
paper and the execution of an experiment. It may require significant
originality and creativity to set up an experiment (say, for an example,
to establish the existence of gravitational waves). However, this does
not mean that the *writing* of the scientific paper replicates these characteristics. A short series of sequential factual statements that each
merely describe a truthful situation may not meet the threshold for
originality and creativity.

On the other hand, the academic publishing industry relies on the
copyrightability of various aspects of scientific articles. Often described
as an "oligopoly" for the extreme profits made by this sector, in many
academic publishing systems researchers are required to sign over their
copyright at the time of acceptance.[56] Norms of academic plagiarism
are also an important consideration here. If someone else were to reproduce multiple statements from an academic paper, without citing the
original author, it would be considered an academic offense. Copyright
violation and plagiarism are not the same thing, even if the latter can
entail the former. Yet the fact that plagiarism exists as a context would
likely inform a court's verdict on the copyrightability of academic statements. That said, even if one does not think that scientific statements,
in sequence, in a paper, are individually copyrightable, it is possible
that the design and layout of a typeset academic article possesses the
characteristics of originality and creativity required for copyright. This
is to say that there are various diegetic layers of copyright. A first layer
may be the basic factuality of statements, which is not copyrightable
(indeed, it is not necessarily even a tangible thing). The second layer is
the expression of these facts in words. These statements may or may
not be subject to copyright. Finally, there is the sum total of the article,
which exists within various industry, financial, and market contexts.

It is highly likely that this artifact as a whole *is* copyrightable, even if only for the layout characteristics.

Murray-Rust's intervention—to liberate facts from copyright—takes place at the second of these diegetic layers, in the untested waters of copyright. Digital preservation systems for text, likewise, must work on a speculative basis for an understanding of the truth content and factuality of the statements that they harbor. And, indeed, this messiness is simply part and parcel of the way that copyright works. While institutional managers—and even researchers on the ground—often want copyright risks to be clear and unambiguous, this is rarely how things are in reality. Until a court actually decides a specific case, anybody working with material that may, or may not, be under copyright must operate on the basis of supposition and risk management. Ronan Deazley, professor of copyright law at the University of Glasgow, summarizes this well in a long-standing joke. All of his presentations end with a copyright disclaimer: "The usual rules apply." Explaining this, he wryly notes that, of course, nobody is quite sure what the application of these usual rules entails. There is a delegation of interpretation to people who cannot know the actual legal status.

Copyright—and the exercise of fair dealing or fair use provisions on digital text—is always situated at the intersection of risk and interpretation. It is not possible to know, without a court ruling, whether a particular use is "fair." Instead, individuals have to adopt a common-sense approach to managing this risk relationship. This is increasingly difficult in the era of YouTube when, for instance, blatant violations of others' copyright are posted with comments such as "No copyright infringement intended!!" Indeed, the proliferation of such sentiments seems to indicate that most downstream reusers have little idea of the legal circumstances within which they are operating.

Digital preservation systems—which often bill themselves as "libraries" or "archives"—operate in a different sphere. In claiming to have at least some authority to preserve and to make content perpetually available, it is likely that the court would hold such archives to a higher standard of competency to judge the law and how their reuse works within fair use paradigms. It is also true that not every archive that calls itself such *is* operating within the (or, at least, any specific nationalistically or jurisdictionally specific) law. A good example of this is the work of shadow archives, the pirate libraries that power an entire underworld of scholarly communications.

At thirty-three terabytes of data in its main collection (and with more than sixty terabytes in its pool of scientific journal articles powered by its sister project, Sci-Hub), the highly illegal Library Genesis project is one of the largest repositories of copyright-violating educational e-books ever created.[57] These archives, interestingly, define themselves against a standard of morality that attempts to transcend local lawmaking: "Within decades, generations of people everywhere in the world will grow up with access to the best scientific texts of all time. . . . The quality and accessibility of education to the poor will grow dramatically too. Frankly, I see this as the only way to naturally improve mankind: we need to make all the information available to them at any time."[58] The amateur "archivists" who have taken it upon themselves to seed Library Genesis on BitTorrent believe that the "initiative fulfills United Nations/UNESCO world development goals that mandate the removal of restrictions on access to science" and that "limiting and delaying humanity's access to science isn't a business, it's a crime, one with an untold number of victims and preventable deaths."[59]

There is, of course, a specific disciplinary resonance to remarks such as these. Although Library Genesis is a nonspecific library/archive, Sci-Hub explicitly encodes "science" in its name (it is notable that "science," in the European context, includes the humanities disciplines). Research that "saves lives"—which is part of the justificatory rhetoric of such sites—implies the fields of biomedicine, medical physics, virology, and other disciplines that contribute toward the extension and preservation of human vitality rather than "merely" its enrichment. Research in other spaces cannot posit the same urgency. That "nobody will die" if they cannot read the latest literary criticism seems somewhat self-evident. Hence, an argumentative terrain emerges from which it is harder to justify the pirating of literary criticism, as opposed to, say, research on cancer. In the case of the latter, if a for-profit publisher refuses to make this research available, it is easy to argue that people may die as a result and that this would be, in some moral senses, a criminal outcome. The same cannot be said of the humanities disciplines (and much social-scientific research).

Thus, from the arguments of these pirate sites, there comes a specific hierarchy of disciplinary value that places the humanities far lower than many of their scientific counterparts. Indeed, the arguments for access and preservation, whether they come from the formal open-access movement to scholarship or from pirate archives, are usually centered around the impact that scholarship can have in the world. When the value of that scholarship is more centered on "mere" enrichment or cultural understanding, it becomes harder to justify a copyright-violating crusade because the external moral legal blame that can be laid at the door of capital is significantly less. That is to say that arguments for the ethical necessity of open access to research in the medical space often center on the fact that it can be seen as morally unacceptable to profit from the restriction of medical scholarship, which could lead to people dying. Of course, this argument has more or less traction depending on the stance toward healthcare in the nation in question. Economic "advancement"—itself a concept that embeds a specific telos of progress—is certainly, if the USA is anything to go by, no sign of a move toward universal healthcare. Yet universal healthcare is a sign of an acceptance of a "right to health," which has been included in a number of declarations, including the Universal Declaration of Human Rights; the International Covenant on Economic, Social and Cultural Rights; and the Convention on the Rights of Persons with Disabilities. In cultures where it is accepted that people have a right to health or healthcare—and where it is seemingly morally unacceptable to deny this to people on, say, the basis of their wealth—blocking access to the medical literature with paywalls becomes a social ill that must be undone.

Perhaps it is simply true that the preservation and improvement of life and health *are* fundamentally more important tasks than the understanding of culture. If we return to basic hierarchies such as Maslow's well-known (but flawed) hierarchy of needs, it seems clear that without health and security, one is unlikely to profit greatly from artistic endeavors.[60] Yet this is also not straightforwardly true. It is not possible to advance, medically, without a comprehension of medical history and medical ethics, for example. Indeed, basic medical ethics training, which includes learning about the history of human experimentation during the Second World War, the Tuskegee Syphilis Study, and so forth, is part of any medical degree. Science fiction has also, often, served as the basic moral compass by which the efforts of science are tested and measured—as warnings against the tide of unmitigated progress or imaginary explorations of human interactions with technological advancement.[61] To hierarchize the humanities at the top of a pyramid of needs is to neglect their embeddedness in the ways that we think through, understand, and measure the natural and medical sciences. Yet, as pirate archives, themselves sites of digital preservation, proliferate a scientific discourse, sometimes at the expense of the humanities, we see a continual reembedding of disciplinary ordering.

Preserving Malware

Despite the legitimation claims made by pirate sites, which rest on disciplinary hierarchies, it is difficult to place any specific emphasis on the importance of one field over another. However, the same cannot be said of the content that is ingested and preserved in textual digital preservation systems, which follows a rigorous hierarchy of value, with some complications. The best example of this is the case of handling malware in digitally preserved material, mentioned briefly above. Indeed, several master's and even PhD theses have explored the implications of preserving malware within comprehensive digital archives such as the British Library.[62] Jonathan Farbowitz, for example, has prominently argued that we should destabilize conventional wisdom about the cleansing of viruses from digital archives in order to study *their* history and role.[63]

This is because, of course, for every researcher who wants the original text, you can also find a researcher who is interested in the media forms that made such text available—and this includes the study of computer viruses and worms. A good example of this is the work of

Jussi Parikka, who has spent years studying malware, for instance in his *Digital Contagions: A Media Archaeology of Computer Viruses* (2007). In Parikka's view, "one could," and, indeed, he does, "write a whole shadow history of technology through how it does not work; how it breaks down; how it frustrates and messes things up; how it disappoints and does not meet up with the expectations that are always rather sublime compared to the mundane everyday."[64]

The preservation of computer viruses follows, in some ways, an opposite pattern to the preservation of real-world (biological) pathogens. The core example of this is the smallpox virus, of which two samples remain in the world, in the United States and Russia, aptly embedding the ongoing and never-really-forgotten Cold War superpower ambiance.[65] Up to a point, the debate around the smallpox virus follows the same logics as computer virus preservation. There is a merit to preserving these viruses so that we can study them and so that we can ensure that our medical knowledge is well equipped to handle future pandemics. However, there are also calls to destroy the viruses.[66] Will there come a point when we feel we have learned all that we can from the stored virus? What are the ongoing *risks* of keeping live, massively deadly pathogens under biocontainment? (They range, in fact, from terrorism and biowarfare to accidental escape to new mutations. Many conspiracy theories about Covid-19, for instance, circulated around its possible escape from the Wuhan Institute of Virology.) Yet what happens when the world geopolitical situation abruptly destabilizes, as it did with the 2022 Russian invasion of Ukraine, and the retention of biological agents suddenly poses a threat to international security? Good actors today, even when subjectively judged in the present, may not be good actors tomorrow. That there are so *few* stocks of smallpox left attests to the ambivalence of enthusiasm for preservation.

Indeed, the preservation of smallpox is handled in the opposite way to the preservation of computer viruses (and computer documents more broadly). Even though both have characteristics of virality and spread—in both cases the undesirable aspect of the preserved entity—in the case of digital preservation systems the mantra is that Lots of Copies Keeps Stuff Safe (indeed, as already mentioned, the acronym LOCKSS refers to a prominent scholarly digital preservation mechanism). Once a computer virus has been selected for preservation, it will be stored in multiple redundant locations and replicated as many times as is needed to ensure permanent preservation, even if a particular data center or cloud availability zone fails.[67] Smallpox, by contrast, has been selected for preservation, but it has been explicitly stated that it will not be stored in many locations worldwide, just two.

One of the core reasons for this (aside from the biopolitical connotations of the smallpox locations) is that computer viruses age in a way that means hosts are no longer susceptible. As I will go on to discuss shortly in terms of infection, computers of today are not vulnerable to the infection of worms of two decades ago. (Although, that said, the emulation environments that are used within libraries to view previous eras of media forms *may* themselves be vulnerable to these viruses from the past.) By contrast, the very real smallpox virus continues to pose a substantial ongoing risk to living humans in the present day. It turns out to be easier to evolve the immune systems of our computers than of human populations.

The other challenge in the analogy and the naming crossover is that, in most circumstances, viruses are not considered transmission media. They do not constitute an inscriptive system designed for the conveyance of text (or any other media form). Real viruses are not, in most circumstances, a recording medium. That said, there have been instances where viruses *have* been engineered to allow for the transmission of messages. As a recent paper in the *Journal of Biological Engineering* noted, "We have engineered a cell-cell communication platform using bacteriophage M13 gene products to autonomously package and deliver heterologous DNA messages of varying lengths and encoded functions."[68] Because DNA and RNA consist of a number of bases—such as adenine, cytosine, uracil, and guanine—and because they are designed to encode protein production structures, it is possible to use these forms as a storage medium. The bases can be used to represent data in a binary—or, indeed, larger numerical base—system, although attempts to date have proved slow, expensive, and unwieldy.[69] Although this is not what is happening in the smallpox example, it demonstrates one way in which the base-required inscriptive properties for digital text can end up in unexpected locations.

Of course, viral transmission always carries a range of messages at different levels. Viruses, in some ways, communicate with one another, and protein exchange can be used as a messaging system.[70] Viruses also recombine with one another to form new strains, which is a form of "intertextuality" and bricolage at some metaphorical level. Viral transmission and prevalence in society also signals a range of social factors that are imbued with meaning within human cultures. People have "read" the symptoms of illness, in the past, as omens from deities, for instance (part of the long-standing and damaging rhetoric that disability is somehow earned and the outcome of a just karmic communication from the gods). This was particularly the case with the HIV/AIDS epidemic, where religious fundamentalists associated sexual morality with disease prevalence, thereby reenforcing "the belief that human misfortune—in some of its forms, at least—is the result of divine punishment."[71] In the era of Covid, untrammeled viral spread can now be read as the message of a "free" (libertarian) political nation, while nations pursuing zero-Covid strategies are consigned to the dustbin of totalitarianism, regardless of how the most vulnerable fare under each of these systems. Viruses also translate back into social-behavioral patterns in human populations, in effect acting as a messaging system for new cultures of practice, whether that be mask wearing, social distancing, lockdowns, or isolation behaviors. It is a mistake, I think, then, not to read biological viruses as messaging technologies—or media—of some sorts.

It is also worth a brief detour to explore how Parikka's work adeptly shows how viruses in the digital space interact with our changing understanding of real, biological viruses in the extradigital world, albeit not explicitly. For Parikka, there is a paradoxical accidentality to computer viruses, despite the fact that they are engineered by people, with deliberate intent. By contrast, viruses in nature truly do emerge randomly and without purpose beyond Darwinian evolution. Yet, as Parikka hints, since the 1980s, human agency has also been strongly linked to the proliferation of real-world biological viruses. The originator of such a discourse was to be found in the human immunodeficiency virus (HIV), which "was at the center of numerous contested articulations concerning the actions, sexualities, gender, and ethnicities of human bodies."[72] Of course, there is also a whole history of human-engineered biohazards and biological weaponry that date back to antiquity, most of which repurposed naturally occurring agents.[73] However, the major concern in the twenty-first century is the creation of new synthetic biological warfare agents of mass destruction.[74]

Yet the point persists: computer viruses give us the model for deliberately engineered threat models that could cross over into the real biological world. Just as people write viruses for computers, it is possible for us to "write" truly infectious agents in the extradigital environment (so-called gain-of-function research). Further, it should be noted that, as we become ever more cyborg, it is clear that computer viruses can cause biological harm in almost as many ways as their organic cousins. A good example of this is the recent cyberattack on hospital systems in the United Kingdom.[75] While this may seem despicable, it is an instance of technological-biological crossover, where the harm from an engineered digital threat actor can cause real organic distress to living beings by shutting down healthcare facilities. When hemodialysis machines are connected to the internet, as many now are, they are an exposed computational attack surface as much as any other. The only difference is that a human's life depends upon its continued operation. Other examples include hypothesized cyber-terrorist attacks on nuclear power facilities or even on more conventional gas plants. The idea of an internet-connected gas cooker could, in theory, be a recipe for a remote bombing system that would cause very real loss of life. Our idea of viruses, contagion, and attack have become, then, increasingly entwined with the deliberate engineering of the computerized cousins of living agents.

The existence of computer viruses—and biological terrorist threats, no matter how nebulously defined—has also spawned an entire mirror security industry. As Parrika and Tony D. Sampson put it, "Network security businesses have established themselves in the very fabric of the digital economy (waste management is the future business model of late modernity)," and "the discourses formed around this billion-dollar security industry, ever more dependent on anomalies for its economic sustenance, lay claim to the frontline defense of network culture against the hacker, the virus writer, and the spammer."[76]

There are several curious characteristics of much of this software industry to which it is worth attending. The first is that, in the digital realm, virus writers and other malfeasants often create fake versions of antivirus software in order to ensnare their victims. Indeed, as Microsoft notes, "Hackers and scammers sometimes use fake antimalware software to trick you into installing viruses or malware on your computer."[77] The discourses around viruses, their prevalence, and proliferation are closely tied to the specific operating system in question. Microsoft Windows has a reputation as an OS that is ultraprone to viruses, while Apple's macOS and Linux, for instance, do not. This is only partially fair. For the longest time, one of the core reasons that macOS and Linux were less susceptible to viruses was simply that they had a low market share relative to Windows. That is, because of the relatively low number of users, writing viruses for these systems was less appealing to the malware authors. This has changed over time, particularly given the ascent of Linux to the top place in server workflows and the evolution of Apple's extremely powerful system-on-a-chip machines. The concurrent rise of cryptocurrencies, which required compute-optimized systems, made high-powered hardware, whether that be a home system or a server farm, an attractive target for remote takeover (although creating "botnets" of remote machines with high-bandwidth connections has long been a hobby of those seeking to mount distributed denial-of-service attacks).

While prevalence and user base make up one explanatory feature of virus targets—Microsoft simply had the greatest market share for the longest period—they are not the total explanatory cause, either. This is because virus writers have different motivations for why they create viruses. One important point is that targeting different operating systems will likely land you with a different group of users who are impacted by the launch of, say, a successful worm. (A worm is a computer virus that can spread itself without user interaction.) For instance, the Blaster worm, which targeted Microsoft Windows systems (on XP or 2000) in 2003, spread from host to host at incredible speed. The primary systems impacted were home desktops rather than server setups. By contrast, the SQL Slammer worm, also of 2003, only infected machines that were running Microsoft's SQL Server software. The "audience" for infection between these two worms couldn't have been more different. The former was designed to ensnare and irk desktop users, while the latter worked only on servers. Hence, one reason for why a particular operating system is chosen is simply based on who the virus writer wants to annoy or extort. If the prankster wants maximum exposure, then targeting desktop users may make sense. If the malware author wants high-powered hardware at their illicit disposal for nefarious purposes, then it may make more sense to target operating systems that run primarily on such hardware.

Another point that goes often unremarked upon is simply that much virus writing is opportunistic. While good security experts can, on occasion, pull apart a bug in a particular subsystem of an operating system, there is also a degree of chance involved. Writing a virus is a matter, first, of "finding" a bug that can be exploited. Exploiting such vulnerabilities is hard enough in the first place, but locating such flaws is a constant game of cat and mouse with developers, who, for obvious reasons, do not want their software to be buggy and prone to attack. In recent years, companies have also begun to offer monetary "bug bounties" to attackers who find a vulnerability and, instead of exploiting it in a virus, responsibly disclose the problem to the vendor. These bounties serve two functions. First, they encourage a worldwide community of security experts to scour code for problems, ensuring the "many eyeballs" principle of open source, which I covered above. Second, they discourage the authorship of viruses and worms by offering a financial incentive not to write any. Of course, this depends on the bug bounty being more profitable than the illicit action (although, also, the fact that the bug bounty is a legal way to earn money, rather than the riskier criminal route of selling details of an exploit on the black market, can act as an incentive to take the reward). In this way, bug bounties allow companies to test the waters of their code among a pool of experts while also disincentivizing those experts from weaponizing their findings.[78]

The discourse of "responsible disclosure" is also worth considering as it demonstrates a set of intersections between finance and prestige in the computer vulnerability space. Those who seek computer vulnerabilities do so for a variety of reasons, many of which stem from curiosity and their elite ability compared to others.[79] A core part of the disclosure process is that crackers and hackers want *credit* for their work. They do not simply want money and to remain in the shadows. Instead, they usually seek to publish their findings in order to boost their standing among the information security community. Like all of Pierre Bourdieu's forms of cultural capital, of course, this prestige is substitutable for other forms of capital. Building a reputation, for example, can lead to a job. The problem is that disclosure of computing vulnerabilities can lead to serious consequences for end users, who may be hurt by this knowledge being made public. At the same time, some corporations who produce software do not take software security seriously and simply ignore researchers who get in touch to alert them to problems, thus forcing disclosure.

In order to balance this need for exposure with a need for responsiveness, in the best interests of users, vendors, and information security professionals, a system was created called coordinated vulnerability disclosure. The goal of coordinated vulnerability disclosure is to agree to a timeframe between the various parties that allows vendors to patch their code and release a fix while also allowing the bug finder to make public their findings (and thereby reaping the reward). Of course, the unspoken parties in this transaction are the end user of the software in question and potentially malicious reusers of the exploit. The former group are liable to attack when vulnerabilities are disclosed before a patch to the software has been issued. The latter, from the inverse perspective, are able to take advantage of the knowledge released by vulnerability disclosure if there has been no patch—so-called zero-day vulnerabilities—and can then weaponize this academic research.

Responsible or coordinated disclosure, then, is actually a bargained hostage negotiation between vendors and vulnerability discoverers in which attackers and victims are used as the chips. The consumer pressure that users can put on vendors means that organizations are forced to take vulnerability disclosure seriously. However, the threat to that group only exists because of a malicious cohort of villains, always off-stage, who would be willing to stage the attack. The academic disclosers sit with a number of "hats" according to where they sit on this spectrum. Again, harking back to my chapter on color symbolism, there are a range of coded signifiers in this space. "White hat" hackers are those who work, with the consent of their targets, to identify vulnerabilities for the sole purpose of improving the system's security. In other words, "white hats" are the pure and good hackers, in the age-old association of white with virtue. At the other end of the spectrum sit "black hats," who are the malicious hackers that constitute the threat model. It is this group that poses the risk to user communities. Finally, between these poles sit the "gray hats," who work with ethical intent but may do so without the consent of the party being hacked.

This discourse is important for considering the preservation of viruses because it reinforces the credit-seeking nature of virus authorship. A responsible disclosure timeline is needed, not just because software vendors require some form of impetus to kickstart them into action but because virus and exploit writers consider themselves *authors* and seek credit, in some circumstances, for their work.

This highlights, though, the paradoxical situation of legality and pseudonyms that underpins illicit digital cultures such as virus writers. A similar situation pertained when I was studying the underground cultures of the Warez scene (a network of highly organized and professionalized digital pirates): In an environment where somebody wants credit, but the thing for which they want credit is illegal, what are the ethical responsibilities of various attributing parties toward different actors?[80] Robert V. Kozinets notes that "studying," or in this case we might also stretch to "preserving," "illicit . . . communities" constitutes studying a vulnerable group—vulnerable to law enforcement action.[81] However, this appraisal of harm applies to interventions and interactions. The individuals to whom we are referring often seek to brag openly—under their pseudonyms—of their illegal activities.

A further question, though, is the nature of the "harm" in this situation. When the "harm" that may be attributed to preservation that reveals illegal practices is the bringing to justice of criminal virus writers, is this a "harm" that should halt those practices? There are possible borderline cases. Kozinets gives the example of drug users. If we exposed drug users to the possibility of criminal sanction whenever they participated in research interviews, it would quickly become very difficult to study drug addiction. This would lead, eventually, to a situation where no user of illicit drugs would ever speak to a researcher. Does the same apply, though, in cases where freely available online material reveals criminal activities or where a virus author actively publicizes his or her own work? Taken, as an experiment, to the absolute extreme: If a digital preservation system managed to reveal a murder, should we not use such records to bring a murderer to justice? Do digital preservation systems, then, have a role to play in criminal trials and tracking down virus authors? This leads to further questions about the severity of the crime and the need to "protect" sources from the "harm" of being prosecuted—and the differences between academic research and general digital preservation. Is it and should it really be a matter for the individual researcher—or the archivist librarians—to decide who is prosecuted and who should be protected? Will a "cold case" unit emerge that digs through the historical record of preserved malware in order to identify sources?

This leads to the need for digital preservation policies about the use of pseudonyms (and real names) and whether and how criminal material should be attributed. The politics of citation and online pseudonymity is a difficult subject to get right. As Amy Bruckman notes, "Norms for presentation vary."[82] In the aforementioned Warez scene, participants go by Internet Relay Chat (IRC) and site nicknames, which do not necessarily correspond to one another. Once participants have been arrested, tried, and convicted, they are "decloaked" in official (and often openly available) legal documents. While, in other online cultures, participants "may also routinely disclose information linking their pseudonym and real name," this is not commonly the case in highly secretive online cultures, such as hacker forums of virus writers, where such disclosures would carry very real risks of law enforcement penalties.[83]

The secondary literature's advice on handling pseudonyms is difficult to navigate, and it is not clear how it pertains to digital preservation systems as opposed to their mere use in scholarly publications. Again, Kozinets notes that "online pseudonyms function exactly like real names and should be treated as real names."[84] Yet online pseudonyms can now be up to several decades old and many go out of use. Some may, in fact, now be used by different individuals than when they were first coined; many individuals may use the same pseudonym, leading to the potential for wrongful criminal convictions. Digital preservation systems that conserve illegal content, such as viruses, and hope to contribute to the unmasking of perpetrators may, in fact, find that they muddy the waters of identification.

Within this environment of credit, there is a discourse of "responsibility" that ties in with ideas of "respectability." Computer virus authorship is, in most parts of the world, illegal. Hence, to give the "credit" that a criminal wants, as part of a program of responsibility, is curious. On the other hand, white hat hacking, where cybersecurity experts probe systems for vulnerabilities at the behest of the owners, is a respectable profession and one that is legal. However, the two spaces cross over. Particularly in the infancy of the computer security industry, it was common for cyber criminals to make their name by working illegally, then serving their prison time, then going on to a professionalized career. Perhaps the most prominent example of this pattern is the infamous case of Kevin Mitnick, who spent many years as one of the world's most wanted hackers. He was then arrested in 1995 and sentenced to five years in prison. Since his release he has gone on to write many high-profile books on information security but also to establish his own computer security firm and to sit on the boards of several others.[85]

Of course, responsibility here also (or, in fact, actually) means limiting damage to potentially vulnerable parties. But the responsibility cuts across different axes because the damage affects different parties, who bear different levels of guilt differently. End users of software are the ones whose systems become vulnerable to hostile takeover, usually through no fault of their own. The exception may be in the case of open-source software where user configuration options or errors could leave a system open to attack. Fundamentally, though, in most systems of proprietary software, the user is treated like a small, innocent child and is no more responsible for their own vulnerability than an infant that has yet to leave his or her parents' tutelage. The *responsibility* to such childlike users cuts both ways. On the one hand, there is a responsibility to protect such users. Disclosing a vulnerability too early may result in these users being exposed to unnecessary risk if a patch is not available. Hence, part of the responsibility lies in waiting, in not revealing information that could cause damage. On the other hand, though, there is also a responsibility to tell these users that they have been or still are at risk. To withhold information from users is, also, not responsible. Hence, responsibility becomes a matter of information and timing. Responsibility, in responsible disclosure, is a three-dimensional coordinate point between the axes of time, fix-availability, and information. (You could reduce this to two dimensions, if you believe that fix-availability is an inevitable product of the passage of time, but this is by no means a certainty.)

Conversely, there is a challenge in thinking about the responsibility to and of software developers. It is true that in all but the simplest cases, software bugs are not avoidable. It is only a matter of when, not *if*, an exploitable bug will appear in code. But the reputation of software firms can, in many cases, rest on their reputation for developing robust code and shipping fixes within a reasonable timeframe once vulnerabilities are found. The exception, of course, seems to be the quasi-monopolistic megagiants, such as Microsoft, who seem to be able to continue to profit, in spite of a terrible security track record (improved greatly in recent years). Nonetheless, early disclosure, before a fix is ready, could have serious reputational consequences for the software company in question. It seems only fair, given the inevitability of software bugs, to give a *reasonable* period of time in which to develop a fix to a vulnerability—and to offer it to users for deployment. There is a responsibility not to trash the reputation of a software vendor that is, at least, trying to provide a fix within a reasonable timeframe. However, it is also worth noting that responsibility for the vulnerability does also, to some extent, lie with the software creator. Putting out fixes within a reasonable period of time is a *responsibility* of a software developer. It is for this reason that, in recent years, software-as-service models have superseded one-off sales business operations; the creation of a one-time product that works perfectly forever is not a viable model for a system that must, at some point, become subject to future damage or vulnerability. As a result, software companies have shifted from selling products to selling the ongoing labor time and effort of programmers, albeit packaged into bite-sized "versions" of software. This is part of a shift in the discourse of "responsibility" for software development and a change in the status of ongoing fixes to future problems. And this remains the fundamental issue for software development: How far can one anticipate future vulnerability and how responsible are builders, in the present, for manufacturing completely defect-free technological products?

Giving credit, then, in digital preservation archives for virus authorship is often a twofold economy of credit and blame. This economy looks different depending on the angle from which it is viewed. For instance, if one has respect for vulnerability hunters and virus writers, then giving them credit for their work in the archive is an act of attribution. On the other hand, if one holds them responsible for the damage that their creation has caused, then the act of crediting is also an act of blame. This is similar to other criminal enterprises where, in certain circles, there may be a badge of honor in, say, being given a prison sentence. For those outside such circuits, though, being named in this way is a sign of shame. We might call these acts "negative accreditations."

Every negative accreditation of a software exploit also comes with a shadow accreditation: the author of the original software that was vulnerable. The act of accrediting a vulnerability implies a blame of the software's original author for not properly securing their system. Indeed, for this reason, many large software corporations may not want viruses to be archived because these malwares are the inverse trace of poorly written software (even if inevitable). The question is where a reader of the archive places blame: Is the blame to lie with the person who wrote the vulnerable code or the person who wrote the software to exploit it? An analogous "dilemma" illustrates the challenge. In home security, we usually blame people who break into houses for burglaries, not homeowners. On the other hand, if you left your window unlocked and advertised the fact, there would be little sympathy when you were robbed. At a certain threshold of carelessness, blame traverses sites.

Hence, as just a start, giving credit in our archives for the authorship of viruses, that we may or may not wish to preserve in the first place, is a complex space of legitimation practice. When we give credit to someone for a criminal deed, when they want that credit, we bend systems of institutional authority to, in some ways, validate illicit activities. However, the entire system of accreditation becomes even more complex when we note that most attributions are created by decentralized attestations of authorship enmeshed in interlocking claims of authority. The challenges in this space can be seen by examining ORCID, the Open Researcher and Contributor ID system.

ORCID was initially established in order to disambiguate between academic researchers. Because human names are not unique—hello, John Smith!—it became desirable to identify authors in a way that would not be vulnerable to the ambiguities of name alterations, be that for marriage, change in gender assignation, or any other reason. Some citation styles, furthermore, request only an initialed first name, meaning that Joseph, John, and Jenny Smith are all collapsed into the inexpressive "J. Smith." ORCID's mission, then, was initially to "solve the author/contributor name ambiguity problem in scholarly communications by creating a central registry of unique identifiers for individual researchers and an open and transparent linking mechanism between ORCID and other current author ID schemes."[86]

While this sounds straightforward, it actually also contains a number of paradoxes, especially with respect to the beta scope of ORCID. Because ORCID data were (and are) designed to "come from individuals and organizations" and because ORCID is "a hybrid system of self- and organization-asserted identity," a conflict emerges. Namely: while the original mission statement of ORCID purports to describe a system in which there are clear one-to-one relationships between identifiers, records, and researchers, the way that data are provided tends to generate messy multidimensional sets that will result in the duplicate deposit of various metadata.[87]

The fundamental conflict here is the difference between metadata as a centralized record deposited and controlled by an absolute authority and the constitution of metadata—and, perhaps, even, then, parts of the referent object itself—by multiple disaggregated assertions made by different distributed authorities. Geoffrey Bilder, perhaps the person who has thought most deeply so far in the twenty-first century about how identifiers relate to the objects they supposedly define, writes of this as a problem of deciding which data to trust. As he puts it:

> It is not enough to determine that X records from Y different sources are likely to be referring to a researcher named Josiah Carberry. We also have to have a clear policy about what we do with the records after that determination. Do we merge them? Do we privilege one of them? If we merge them do we discard the original records? If we privilege a record, do we discard the non-privileged ones? If we discard records or data, how do we keep track of the provenance of the data in the new, merged record? If we merge records, who then "owns" the resulting record and who has the right to correct and edit it? What are the IP implications of such a merged record? How do we decide these things?[88]

The ascription of credit for virus authorship is difficult because these metadata are often embedded in complex systems of interinstitutional assertion. Most computer virus authors go by an online pseudonym rather than using their real names (for obvious reasons). At future points, though, different entities will make different assertions about the author of a piece of malware. A court summons and accusation for *alleged* virus authorship is just that: an allegation. It is a temporary attachment of metadata to a piece of illegal software as a "possible author." This can go on to be validated or refuted. It also means that the criteria for authorship, in this domain, shares the thresholds of legal culpability. In the Anglophone justice systems, this makes virus authorship ascription subject to the standard of proof of "beyond all reasonable doubt." Sometimes, though, there will be conflicting metadata statements about virus authorship and the purported authorship status may change as court cases progress (in a similar way as the discussion of facts moving in and out of copyright functioned in the preceding section of this chapter). Different parties may be suspected at different times of being responsible. Different ascriptive parties may have different motivations for ascribing such motivations. For instance, national security agencies may be politically motivated to ascribe virus authorship to foreign agents, as in the case of the Stuxnet virus[89]. Hence, any weighting or privileging of metadata authority must account for the perspective of the citing agent.

This also shows how citation can be used not only to provide credit but also to ascribe blame. In different contexts, these can be the same thing. For some virus authors, as it is with all criminals, and as already noted, the notoriety of blame is a form of credit among malicious peers. Usually, such ascription of virus authorship under a pseudonym is sufficient. For instance, in the well-known 1999 film *The Matrix*, the main character, Neo, inquires whether Trinity is "the Trinity? That cracked the IRS D-base?"[90] Unlike the ORCID system, there is, here, no guarantee that someone is who they say they are. Identity rests on pure assertion and a system of knowledge. Yet such a system of blame can be important in other contexts. For instance, in medical research, it is important that those who behave badly and conduct research fraud can be held accountable for their actions. Attaching an identity to a work allows not only for credit and progression but also ostracization and exile in the case of violation. One function of authorship, less often remarked upon, is to provide a marker of individuals from whom we need protection and against whom sanctions can be leveled. These are the tricky issues with which digital archives must wrestle when preserving malware.

Digital Stability

Two contradictory arguments are often made about digital preservation. The first is that the digital realm is inherently unstable, mutable, and unreliable. Links frequently go dead, and it becomes impossible to locate older material. Web pages can be changed, and it can be difficult to know whether material has remained the same between visits to a site. On the other hand, as Kathleen Fitzpatrick has pointed out and as was mentioned earlier, anybody who would like something embarrassing about themselves removed from the web may find the digital space stubbornly persistent.[91]

This latter situation, of digital persistence, found itself the focus of an alleged academic plagiarism scandal known as #receptiogate in late 2022. On Christmas Eve, 2022, the respected independent manuscript expert Peter Kidd wrote a blog post in which he noted that a book by Professor Carla Rossi appeared to have used images and text from his site, without permission or attribution.[92] Most disturbingly, the reply that Kidd received at first contained not only immediate legal threats but also the assertion that the book did not need to cite his blog, even if it had taken material from it, because "blogs are not scientific texts, published by academic publishers, so their value is nil!"

In itself, such a statement is appalling; the value of a proposition lies not in where it is uttered but in the truth of its utterance. I have cited many blogs in this book. However, the story becomes even more bizarre. It turns out that Receptio, the press that published the book, "seemed to present stock photos for its staff and offices."[93] It further transpired that Dr. Rossi was no longer employed by the University of Zurich at this point (despite apparently listing her affiliation as such in several places), yet the university nonetheless began an investigation into her conduct.

The story has a more ironic sting in its tail, though. It is worth noting that this book, and Kidd's blog post, are part of a methodology of fragmentology, in which dismembered medieval books of hours are reassembled by using online web archives, such as the Internet Archive's Wayback Machine, that contain auction catalog entries selling individual leaves of these books. In other words, the entire field is premised on the stability of the digitally preserved record. This would be unremarkable, were it not for the fact that when Kidd began his allegations, Rossi's website rapidly began changing its content, seemingly attempting to rely on digital mutability to cover her tracks. For instance, an image that featured a distinctive mark was changed to remove this after Kidd made the allegation. The irony was that the Wayback Machine, the very technology that made the research possible in the first place, and on whose use Rossi claims to hold a patent, holds snapshots of the website as it went through changes in real time.[94]

Just as, in terms of preservation, access is sometimes seen as a secondary element in tension with the principle of safety, stability and mutability are often thought of in the same contradictory frame, even by those one would suspect to know better. As our textual cultures move toward ever more digital forms, electronic preservation will play an increasingly important role. This final chapter has sought to question the ways in which totally expansive cultures of preservation—such as those embodied in the motto of Google—might be queried. For example, if we think, as this chapter has attempted to, about the metaphor of the computer virus, we reach the conclusion that, sometimes, it can be better to forget.

NINE

CONCLUSION

WHY DOES IT MATTER THAT our metaphors for digital text creation are not very good? The answer is perhaps best expressed in a recent book on, of all topics, the extraordinary nature of fungus. In his work on the ways that mushrooms mold our worlds, *Entangled Life* (2020), Merlin Sheldrake puts it well: "Metaphors can help to generate new ways of thinking" while, at the same time, "metaphors and analogies come laced with human stories and values, meaning that no discussion of scientific ideas . . . can be free of cultural bias."[1] Richard C. Lewontin is even more forthright, stating that "it is not possible to do the work of science without using a language that is filled with metaphors," as "virtually the entire body of modern science is an attempt to explain phenomena that cannot be experienced directly by human beings."[2] In scientific spaces, metaphor serves as the translational language that moves us from the unusable imperceptible to the functional and comprehensible. In doing so, of course, metaphor imposes value structures on that which we seek to understand. This can, at times, cause problems. A good example of such a problem is the anthropomorphizing of other species or inanimate objects. The objects do not like this.

In user interface design circles, the commonly accepted wisdom is that metaphor serves to orient users toward the usability of the system. By finding familiar paths, interfaces become intuitable, and we learn how to operate these systems with reference to our real-world artifacts. As I have shown throughout this book, though, the metaphors that we use have more magical qualities than it would initially seem. You would be very hard put to explain to somebody completely unfamiliar with a computer *why* a window is called a window, why we operate within shells, and even why the mouse, which now most often has no tail, is called a mouse (and not a hamster). Most people also know inaccurate histories of text-input devices. The myth that the QWERTY keyboard was designed to slow typo-speed fiends in the mechanical environment stubbornly refuses to die. Our supercharged magical and illusory metaphors, then, do not really provide a touchstone for how digital artifacts will behave. They instead give a fresh name to phenomena that simply work independently.

However, as far back as 1990, Theodor Holm Nelson hit the nail on the head. The problem with metaphors, he wrote, is that "you want to be able to design things that are *not* like physical objects, and the details of whose behavior may float free, not being tied to any details of some introductory model."[3] While the model of cognitive metaphor may make this impossible—if all of our language, thought, and design is metaphorically structured then we cannot simply construct "well-thought-out unifying ideas" free from metaphor—it is the extent of the nongrounding and the progressive divergence of interface metaphor from any reality congruence that is most difficult.

Hence it seems important, when considering the ways that metaphors structure our contemporary digital text production, to at once comprehend historical structuration—the historical archaeology that makes possible our present—but also to cut ourselves loose from such absolute determinism. This can be seen in the contradictions of software design. For instance, the designers of most word processing software were likely unaware of the history of colored paper in ancient

China or the background of the Fourdrinier machine. Instead, they might argue, they simply took a cue from the color of contemporary paper. In this latter sense, their approach is dehistoricized. It is an acontextual approach of the present. Yet, on the other hand, how has the present been produced except by historical progression and circumstance? To be ignorant of the histories that shape our present does not mean that one has, any less, been shaped by them.

Metaphor, in some ways, sculpts everything of which we speak. It is not possible to communicate without metaphor. Many of these metaphors are very distant from any literal overlay atop our digital text environments. Yet, at the same time, when metaphors have no literal correspondence, we should ask what this does to our development of text technologies.

It is also true that metaphors become routinized and condition our future possibilities. Once we had mice and windows and keyboards as *descriptive* terms, they mutated into *prescriptive* possibilities of technological and textual futures. Digital-textual metaphors are important because they shape how we *will* progress, and it can be very difficult to break free of metaphorical imprisonment. Digital-textual metaphor reflects back on the extradigital world.

The interesting undertaking, as this book has attempted, is to identify the moment when metaphor breaks. In every case of digital-textual metaphor there is a descriptive phase in which there are good reasons for the metaphor's application. However, there is also, next, an untethering phase in which the metaphor becomes unmoored. Finally, the metaphor becomes written as the standard and prescriptively categorizes future development. To understand the constraints on the digital-textual present, then, we must analyze where and when the metaphors break, which most of them do. So, while in many ways it can feel pedantic to pick such terms apart, it is actually a crucial part of understanding the technological choices we have made and *will continue to make*. For, often, our metaphors are a mere hair's breadth away from crumbling into nothing. It is these points and moments of fracture that reveal the slenderness of the metaphors on which our technologies depend; they are paper thin.

Chapter One

1. See William Goldbloom Bloch, *The Unimaginable Mathematics of Borges' Library of Babel* (Oxford: Oxford University Press, 2008); and Paul Gooding and Melissa Terras, "Inheriting Library Cards to Babel and Alexandria: Contemporary Metaphors for the Digital Library," *International Journal on Digital Libraries*, 18.3 (2017), 207–22, https://doi.org/10.1007/s00799-016-0194-2.

2. For a demonstration of this, see the digital recreation of the library: Jonathan Basile, "Library of Babel," 2023, https://libraryofbabel.info/, accessed 6 August 2023. Note that, if flicking to a "random" book, most of the text therein consists of unreadable and arbitrary strings.

3. Jonathan Basile, *Tar for Mortar: The Library of Babel and the Dream of Totality* (Santa Barbara, CA: Punctum Books, 2018), 21–22.

4. Jorge Luis Borges, "The Library of Babel," in *Collected Fictions*, trans. by Andrew Hurley (New York: Penguin, 1998), 113–14.

5. Jorge Luis Borges, "On Exactitude in Science," in *Collected Fictions*, 325.

6. Philip Langdale, "πfs: Never Worry about Data Again!," 2021, https://github.com/philipl/pifs, accessed 16 November 2021.

7. The history of the term "geek" is fascinating, taking a detour through circus sideshows. Mike Sugarbaker, "What Is a Geek?," *Gazebo (The Journal of Geek Culture)*, 1998, http://www.gibberish.com/gazebo/articles/geek3.html, ac-

cessed 30 October 2020; J. A. McArthur, "Digital Subculture: A Geek Meaning of Style," *Journal of Communication Inquiry*, 33.1 (2009), 58–70, https://doi.org/ 10.1177/0196859908325676.

8. Keith F. Lynch, "Converting Pi to Binary: DON'T DO IT," Comp.Risks, 2001, https://www.netfunny.com/rhf/jokes/01/Jun/pi.html, accessed 16 November 2021.

9. Keith F. Lynch, "Converting Pi to Binary: DON'T DO IT," Comp.Risks, 2001, https://www.netfunny.com/rhf/jokes/01/Jun/pi.html, accessed 16 November 2021.

10. For more on this, see Steven Connor, *Living by Numbers: In Defence of Quantity* (London: Reaktion Books, 2016), 12; and Michael Gavin, *Literary Mathematics: Quantitative Theory for Textual Studies*, Stanford Text Technologies (Stanford, CA: Stanford University Press, 2023).

11. Alexandra Gillespie, "The History of the Book," in *New Medieval Literatures*, vol. 9, ed. by David Lawton, Wendy Scase, and Rita Copeland (Turnhout, Belgium: Brepols, 2007), 245–86, https://www.brepolsonline.net/doi/10.1484/J .NML.2.302743.

12. Robert Darnton, "What Is the History of Books?," *Daedalus*, 111.3 (1982), 65–83.

13. Dennis Duncan and Adam Smyth, "Introduction," in *Book Parts*, ed. by Dennis Duncan and Adam Smyth (Oxford: Oxford University Press, 2019), 6.

14. Matthew Rubery, *The Untold Story of the Talking Book* (Cambridge, MA: Harvard University Press, 2016).

15. Wim van Mierlo, "Introduction," in *Textual Scholarship and the Material Book* (Amsterdam: Rodopi, 2007), 1–12, https://doi.org/10.1163/9789042028180 _002.

16. Another worthwhile study on this theme is Adrian Currie, "Of Records and Ruins: Metaphors about the Deep Past," *Journal of the Philosophy of History*, 17.1 (2023), 154–75, https://doi.org/10.1163/18722636-12341493.

17. Martin Paul Eve, "Jennifer Egan," in *Dictionary of Literary Biography: Twenty-First-Century American Novelists*, vol. 382, ed. by George P. Anderson (Columbia, SC: Bruccoli Clark Layman, 2018), 78.

18. Matthew G. Kirschenbaum, *Track Changes: A Literary History of Word Processing* (Cambridge, MA: The Belknap Press of Harvard University Press, 2016).

19. George Lakoff and Mark Johnson, *Metaphors We Live By* (Chicago: University Of Chicago Press, 1980), 97.

20. Stuart Hall, "Cultural Studies and Its Theoretical Legacies," in *Cultural Studies*, ed. by Lawrence Grossberg, Cary Nelson, and Paula A. Treichler (New York: Routledge, 1992), 282.

21. Jacques Derrida, *Writing and Difference*, trans. by Alan Bass, Routledge Classics (London: Routledge, 2005), 19.

22. Jeff Jarvis, *The Gutenberg Parenthesis: The Age of Print and Its Lessons for the Age of the Internet* (New York: Bloomsbury Academic, 2023), 14.

23. For more, see Jeffrey Pomerantz, *Metadata*, The MIT Press Essential Knowledge Series (Cambridge, MA: MIT Press, 2015); and Martin Paul Eve, "On the Political Aesthetics of Metadata," *Alluvium*, 5.1 (2016), https://doi.org /10.7766/alluvium.v5.1.04.

24. Lev Manovich, *The Language of New Media*, Leonardo (Cambridge, MA: MIT Press, 2002), 47.

25. Marianne van den Boomen, *Transcoding the Digital: How Metaphors Matter in New Media* (Amsterdam: Institute of Network Cultures, 2014), 12.

26. Marshall McLuhan, *Understanding Media: The Extensions of Man* (Cambridge, MA: MIT Press, 1994), 89.

27. Boomen, *Transcoding the Digital*, 14–15.

28. Matthew G. Kirschenbaum, *Bitstreams: The Future of Digital Literary Heritage* (Philadelphia: University of Pennsylvania Press, 2021), 102.

29. Friedrich A. Kittler, "There Is No Software," in *Literature, Media, Information Systems: Essays* ed. by John Johnston (Amsterdam: Overseas Publishers Association, 1997), 150.

30. Michel Foucault, "Of Other Spaces," trans. by Jay Miskowiec, *Diacritics*, 16.1 (1986), 22–27.

31. *Online Etymology Dictionary*, s.v. "virtual," https://www.etymonline .com/word/virtual, accessed 21 October 2021.

32. Thierry Bardini, *Bootstrapping: Douglas Engelbart, Coevolution, and the Origins of Personal Computing*, Writing Science (Stanford, CA: Stanford University Press, 2000), 165.

33. John Walker, "Through the Looking Glass," in *The Art of Human-Computer Interface Design*, ed. by Brenda Laurel (Reading, MA: Addison-Wesley, 1990), 443.

34. A. C. Kay, "User Interface: A Personal View," in Laurel, *The Art of Human-Computer Interface Design*, 199.

35. Kay, "User Interface," 199.

36. Bardini, *Bootstrapping*, 42.

37. Lakoff and Johnson, *Metaphors We Live By*, 3.

38. Lakoff and Johnson, 5.

39. Lakoff and Johnson, 9.

40. Lakoff and Johnson, 13.

41. Lakoff and Johnson, 28. Allen Newell, "Metaphors for Mind, Theories of Mind: Should the Humanities Mind?," in *The Boundaries of Humanity: Humans,*

Animals, Machines, ed. by James J. Sheehan and Morton Sosna (Berkeley, CA: University of California Press, 1991), 160 focuses on the difference between the computer as a metaphor for mind and the computer as offering a theory of mind. He explicitly objects to the treatment of science as metaphor.

42. Lakoff and Johnson, *Metaphors We Live By*, 95.

43. Lakoff and Johnson, 97.

44. Douglas Kellner, *Technology and Democracy: Toward a Critical Theory of Digital Technologies, Technopolitics, and Technocapitalism*, Medienkulturen im digitalen Zeitalter (Wiesbaden: Springer VS, 2021), 37. Indeed, the entire second chapter of Kellner's book provides a wide-ranging survey of the metaphors used in the digital environment.

45. Another interesting metaphorical conjunction is to be found in Leo Marx, *The Machine in the Garden: Technology and the Pastoral Ideal in America* (New York: Oxford University Press, 2000), 220, where the harmonization of machines with pastoral landscapes is theorized.

46. See also Sally Wyatt, "Metaphors in Critical Internet and Digital Media Studies," *New Media & Society*, 23.2 (2021), 406–16, https://doi.org/10.1177/1461444820929324.

47. See Jingfang Wu and Rong Chen, "Metaphors Ubiquitous in Computer and Internet Terminologies," *Journal of Arts and Humanities*, 10 (2013), 15. This very descriptive article is fine so far as it goes, although I was significantly under-awed by the conclusion that "new computer and Internet metaphorical terms have largely enriched people's vocabulary and brought people a lot of fun and enjoyment."

48. Lakoff and Johnson, *Metaphors We Live By*, 19.

49. Lakoff and Johnson, 71, 122–23.

50. Lakoff and Johnson, 41.

51. Lakoff and Johnson, 41.

52. Lakoff and Johnson, 112.

53. Theodor Holm Nelson, "The Right Way to Think about Software Design," in Laurel, *The Art of Human-Computer Interface Design*, 237.

54. Lakoff and Johnson, *Metaphors We Live By*, 44.

55. Nelson, "The Right Way to Think about Software Design," 237. Emphasis in original.

56. Lakoff and Johnson, *Metaphors We Live By*, 54.

57. Lakoff and Johnson, 55.

58. Michelle P. Brown, "The Triumph of the Codex: The Manuscript Book before 1100," in *A Companion to the History of the Book*, ed. by Simon Eliot and Jonathan Rose, Blackwell Companions to Literature and Culture, 48 (Malden, MA: Blackwell Publishers, 2007), 180.

59. Lakoff and Johnson, *Metaphors We Live By*, 157.

60. Susan Leigh Star, "Power, Technology and the Phenomenology of Conventions: On Being Allergic to Onions," *Sociological Review*, 38 (1990), 52, https://doi.org/10.1111/j.1467-954X.1990.tb03347.x.

61. Lakoff and Johnson, *Metaphors We Live By*, 147–48.

62. Lakoff and Johnson, 152.

63. Bardini, *Bootstrapping*, 157.

64. A. C. Kay, personal interview by Thierry Bardini, 1992.

65. Bardini, *Bootstrapping*, 157.

66. N. Katherine Hayles, *How We Became Posthuman: Virtual Bodies in Cybernetics, Literature, and Informatics* (Chicago: University Of Chicago Press, 1999), 198.

67. Hayles, 199.

68. Matthew G. Kirschenbaum, *Mechanisms: New Media and the Forensic Imagination* (Cambridge, MA: MIT Press, 2008), 17.

69. Nick Montfort, "Continuous Paper: The Early Materiality and Workings of Electronic Literature" (presented at the MLA Convention, Philadelphia, PA, 2004), https://nickm.com/writing/essays/continuous_paper_mla .html, accessed 15 March 2021.

70. See also Simone Murray, *Introduction to Contemporary Print Culture: Books as Media* (London: Routledge, 2021) for further unpicking of these layers.

71. Steven Connor, "CP: Or, A Few Don'ts by a Cultural Phenomenologist," *Parallax*, 5.2 (1999), 18, https://doi.org/10.1080/135346499249678.

72. Connor, 21.

73. Connor, 23.

74. Connor, 23.

75. Connor, 26.

76. Rita Felski, *The Limits of Critique* (Chicago: University of Chicago Press, 2015).

77. Connor, "CP," 26.

78. Connor, 28.

79. Safiya Umoja Noble, *Algorithms of Oppression: How Search Engines Reinforce Racism* (New York: New York University Press, 2018); and Marie Hicks, *Programmed Inequality: How Britain Discarded Women Technologists and Lost Its Edge in Computing* (Cambridge, MA: MIT Press, 2018).

80. Eric Chown and Fernando Nascimento, *Meaningful Technologies: How Digital Metaphors Change the Way We Think and Live* (Lever Press, 2023), 3, 9, https://doi.org/10.3998/mpub.12668201.

81. Matthew G. Kirschenbaum, *Track Changes*, 6.

82. Kirschenbaum, 7.

83. W. W. Greg, "On Certain False Dates in Shakespearian Quartos," *Library*, 34 (1908), 115.

Chapter Two

1. Raymond Gozzi, "The Power of Metaphor: In the Age of Electronic Media," *ETC: A Review of General Semantics*, 56.4 (2000), 380–404.

2. John Willinsky, Alex Garnett, and Angela Pan Wong, "Refurbishing the Camelot of Scholarship: How to Improve the Digital Contribution of the PDF Research Article," *Journal of Electronic Publishing*, 15.1 (2012), http://dx.doi.org /10.3998/3336451.0015.102.

3. David Greetham, "The Philosophical Discourse of [Textuality]," in *Reimagining Textuality: Textual Studies in the Late Age of Print*, ed. by Elizabeth Bergmann Loizeaux and Neil Fraistat (Madison: University of Wisconsin Press, 2002), 33.

4. Jef Raskin, "Viewpoint: Intuitive Equals Familiar," *Commun. ACM*, 37.9 (1994), 17, https://doi.org/10.1145/182987.584629.

5. Raskin, 17; see also Adream Blair-Early and Mike Zender, "User Interface Design Principles for Interaction Design," *Design Issues*, 24.3, (2008), 85–107.

6. Monica Landoni and Forbes Gibb, "The Role of Visual Rhetoric in the Design and Production of Electronic Books: The Visual Book," *Electronic Library*, 18.3 (2000), 190–201, https://doi.org/10.1108/02640470010337490; and Ruth Wilson and Monica Landoni, "Evaluating the Usability of Portable Electronic Books," in *Proceedings of the 2003 ACM Symposium on Applied Computing—SAC '03* (presented at the 2003 ACM symposium, Melbourne, Florida: ACM Press, 2003), 564, https://doi.org/10.1145/952532.952644.

7. Johanna Drucker, *SpecLab: Digital Aesthetics and Projects in Speculative Computing* (Chicago, IL: University of Chicago Press, 2009), 166.

8. Willinsky, Garnett, and Pan Wong, "Refurbishing the Camelot of Scholarship."

9. Alberto Manguel, *A Reader on Reading* (New Haven, CT: Yale University Press, 2010), 123.

10. Johanna Drucker, *The Century of Artists' Books* (New York: Granary Books, 1995), 123.

11. Henry Burton, *A Divine Tragedie Lately Acted, or A Collection of Sundry Memorable Examples of Gods Judgements upon Sabbath-Breakers, and Other like Libertines* (Amsterdam: J. F. Stam, 1636), H2r, cited and further remarked upon in *Renaissance Paratexts*, ed. by Helen Smith and Louise Wilson (Cambridge: Cambridge University Press, 2011), 8–9.

12. Shane Butler, *The Matter of the Page: Essays in Search of Ancient and Medieval Authors* (Madison: University of Wisconsin Press, 2011), 10.

13. At least part of the reason for PDF's eventual dominance must be attributed to the fact that Adobe had better font distribution deals in place than its rivals, leading to a cleaner look and feel to the format. By contrast, emergent markup forms did not try to replicate such aspects and so were less beholden to such constraints. As George White puts it, "Currently, the documents for which PDF offers the greatest advantage are those that use specialized fonts (e.g., math), which leads to the problem of licensing proprietary fonts for WWW distribution." George White, "Re: SGML Compliance and Future Directions," Com.Omnigroup.Omniweb-l—MarkMail (listserv), 1994, accessed 21 November 2019. PDF also won out over the print industry's "Tiff/IT" specification because it was able to incorporate a text underlay in its approach to hidden, searchable, readable verbal content beneath an image. For more on this, see Charles Bigelow, "The Font Wars, Part 1," *IEEE Annals of the History of Computing*, 42.1 (2020), 7–24, https://doi.org/10.1109/MAHC.2020.2971202; Charles Bigelow, "The Font Wars, Part 2," *IEEE Annals of the History of Computing*, 42.1 (2020), 25–40, https://doi.org/10.1109/MAHC.2020.2971745. There were also other formats, such as TeX, that were not strictly rivals here but that merit mention. See Barbara Beeton, Karl Berry, and David Walden, "TeX: A Branch in Desktop Publishing Evolution, Part 2," *IEEE Annals of the History of Computing*, 41.2 (2019), 29–41, https://doi.org/10.1109/MAHC.2019.2893731.

14. Jeanette Borzo, "Tools Resurrect Hope for Paperless Office Concept," Infoworld, 15.24 (14 June 1993), p. 24. This perhaps sits in tension with Friedrich A. Kittler's much-cited remark that "the general digitization of channels and information erases the differences among individual media." Friedrich A. Kittler, *Gramophone, Film, Typewriter*, trans. by Geoffrey Winthroup-Young and Michael Wutz (Stanford, CA: Stanford University Press, 1999), 1.

15. Ben Shneiderman and Catherine Plaisant, *Designing the User Interface: Strategies for Effective Human-Computer Interaction*, 4th ed. (Boston: Pearson, 2004), 540.

16. Thereby, they are participating in a relatively long history of evolving best practice in digital government document provision. John Carlo Bertot, "Challenges and Issues for Public Managers in the Digital Era," *Public Manager*, 27.4 (1998), 29–30.

17. National Health Service, "PDFs," *NHS Digital Service Manual*, 2019, https://beta.nhs.uk/service-manual, accessed 20 November 2019.

18. Jakob Nielsen, "Avoid PDF for On-Screen Reading," Nielsen Norman Group, 2001, https://www.nngroup.com/articles/avoid-pdf-onscreen-reading-original/, accessed 20 November 2019; and Jakob Nielsen, "PDF: Unfit for Human Consumption," Nielsen Norman Group, 2003, https://www.nngroup

.com/articles/pdf-unfit-for-human-consumption-original/, accessed 20 November 2019.

19. Giorgio Buccellati, *A Critique of Archaeological Reason: Structural, Digital, and Philosophical Aspects of the Excavated Record* (Cambridge: Cambridge University Press, 2017), 207, https://doi.org/10.1017/9781107110298.

20. Bardini, *Bootstrapping*, 137.

21. Wendy Hui Kyong Chun, "On 'Sourcery,' or Code as Fetish," *Configurations*, 16.3 (2008), 299–300, https://doi.org/10.1353/con.0.0064.

22. Roger Chartier, *Forms and Meanings: Texts, Performances, and Audiences from Codex to Computer* (Philadelphia: University of Pennsylvania Press, 1995), 14.

23. Chartier, 15.

24. Aaron Kitch, "Bastards and Broadsides in 'The Winter's Tale,'" *Renaissance Drama, New Series*, 30 (2001), 43–71; Douglas A. Brooks, ed., *Printing and Parenting in Early Modern England* (Aldershot: Ashgate, 2017), http://www.vle books.com/vleweb/product/openreader?id=none&isbn=9781351908849.

25. However, see Wendy Hui Kyong Chun, "The Enduring Ephemeral, or The Future Is a Memory," in *Media Archaeology: Approaches, Applications, and Implications*, ed. by Erkki Huhtamo and Jussi Parikka (Berkeley, CA: University of California Press, 2011), 184–206 on the distinction between memory and storage.

26. Butler, *The Matter of the Page*, 48; Brad Pasanek, *Metaphors of Mind: An Eighteenth-Century Dictionary* (Baltimore: Johns Hopkins University Press, 2015), 229; and Plato, *Phaedrus*, trans. by Christopher Rowe (London: Penguin, 2005), 275a.

27. Of course, woodblock printing and other techniques had been prominent across China and East Asia for many centuries before Gutenberg.

28. Pasanek, *Metaphors of Mind*, 230–31.

29. See Roger Luckhurst, *The Invention of Telepathy, 1870–1901* (Oxford: Oxford University Press, 2002) for more on this.

30. Johanna Drucker, "Graphical Readings and the Visual Aesthetics of Textuality," *Text*, 16 (2006), 274–75.

31. *Oxford English Dictionary Online*, s.v. "page, n.1," https://www.oed.com/view/Entry/135994, accessed 26 November 2019.

32. *Oxford English Dictionary Online*, s.v. "page, v.1," https://www.oed.com/view/Entry/135996, accessed 26 November 2019.

33. *Oxford English Dictionary Online*, s.v. "page, n.2," https://www.oed.com/view/Entry/135995, accessed 26 November 2019.

34. Dennis Tenen, *Plain Text: The Poetics of Computation* (Stanford, CA: Stanford University Press, 2017), 51–54. This is distinct from Tom Eyers's concept of the same name.

35. N. Katherine Hayles, *Writing Machines*, Mediawork Pamphlet (Cambridge, MA: MIT Press, 2002), 23.

36. Tenen, *Plain Text*, 53.

37. Tenen, *Plain Text*, 26. However, it is notable that one of the earliest experiments in "realistic," or mimetic, electronic book design, conducted by the British Library in 1997, was called "Turning the Pages" and aimed precisely to simulate this metaphor. See Yi-Chun Chu et al., "Realistic Books: A Bizarre Homage to an Obsolete Medium?," in *Proceedings of the 2004 Joint ACM/IEEE Conference on Digital Libraries—JCDL '04* (presented at the 2004 joint ACM/IEEE conference, Tucson, AZ, USA: ACM Press, 2004), 78, https://doi.org/10.1145/996350.996372; and Jennifer Pearson, George Buchanan, and Harold Thimbleby, "Designing for Digital Reading," *Synthesis Lectures on Information Concepts, Retrieval, and Services*, 5.4 (2013), 16–31, https://doi.org/10.2200/S00539ED1V01Y201310ICR029.

38. Drucker, "Graphesis,"13.

39. Drucker, *SpecLab*, 158.

40. Bonnie Mak, *How the Page Matters*, Studies in Book and Print Culture Series (Toronto: University of Toronto Press, 2011), 6, 8.

41. For more on Xerox Alto, see Robert F. Sproull, "The Xerox Alto Publishing Platform," *IEEE Annals of the History of Computing*, 40.3 (2018), 38–54, https://doi.org/10.1109/MAHC.2018.033841110.

42. Michael Heim, *Electric Language: A Philosophical Study of Word Processing* (New Haven, CT: Yale University Press, 1999), 130.

43. Jeff Jarvis, *The Gutenberg Parenthesis: The Age of Print and Its Lessons for the Age of the Internet* (New York: Bloomsbury Academic, 2023), 9.

44. Lev Manovich, *The Language of New Media*, Leonardo (Cambridge, MA: MIT Press, 2002), 74–76; see also Manguel, *A Reader on Reading*, 126.

45. Mak, *How the Page Matters*, 4.

46. Manuel Portela, *Scripting Reading Motions: The Codex and the Computer as Self-Reflexive Machines* (Cambridge, MA: MIT Press, 2013), 95.

47. Colin H. Roberts and Theodore C. Skeat, *The Birth of the Codex* (Oxford: Oxford University Press, 1987), 45–61; Michelle P. Brown, "The Triumph of the Codex: The Manuscript Book before 1100," in *A Companion to the History of the Book*, ed. by Simon Eliot and Jonathan Rose, Blackwell Companions to Literature and Culture, 48 (Malden, MA: Blackwell Publishers, 2007), 179; Simon Eliot and Jonathan Rose, eds., *A Companion to the History of the Book*, Blackwell Companions to Literature and Culture, 48 (Malden, MA: Blackwell Publishers, 2007); Eric G. Turner, *The Typology of the Early Codex* (Eugene, OR: Wipf & Stock, 2010); and Butler, *The Matter of the Page*, 8; for a dissenting view

of this lineage, see Miha Kovač et al., "What Is a Book?," *Publishing Research Quarterly*, 35.3 (2019), 313–26, https://doi.org/10.1007/s12109-019-09665-5.

48. Brown, "Triumph," 179; Christopher De Hamel, *The Book: The History of the Bible* (London: Phaidon Press, 2005); Michelle P. Brown, ed., *In the Beginning: Bibles before the Year 1000* (Washington, DC: Freer Gallery of Art and Arthur M. Sackler Gallery, Smithsonian Institution, 2006); and Mak, *How the Page Matters*, 4.

49. 1. "A codex is composed of many books; a book is composed of one scroll. It is called a codex (*codex*) by way of metaphor from the trunks (*codex*) of trees or vines, as if it were a wooden stock (*caudex*, i.e., an older form of the word *codex*), because it contains in itself a multitude of books, as it were of branches. 2. A scroll (*volumen*) is a book so called from rolling (*volvere*), as we speak of the scrolls of the Law and the scrolls of the Prophets among the Hebrews." Isidore et al., *The Etymologies of Isidore of Seville* (Cambridge: Cambridge University Press, 2006), 142.

50. Tim Oren, "Designing a New Medium," in *The Art of Human-Computer Interface Design*, ed. by Brenda Laurel (Reading, MA: Addison-Wesley, 1990), 469.

51. John Dagenais also reminds us that our understanding of earlier pages is shaped by future forms. "Most," he writes, "if not all of the ideas that we bring to our appreciation of the medieval page are shaped, almost unavoidably, by our prior familiarity with the printed page." John Dagenais, "Decolonizing the Medieval Page," in *The Future of the Page*, ed. by Peter Stoicheff and Andrew Taylor (Toronto: University of Toronto Press, 2004), 38.

52. Butler, *The Matter of the Page*, 9.

53. Brown, "Triumph," 180.

54. Matthew G. Kirschenbaum, *Track Changes: A Literary History of Word Processing* (Cambridge, MA: The Belknap Press of Harvard University Press, 2016), fig. 10.

55. Therese Fessenden, "Scrolling and Attention," Nielsen Norman Group, 2018, https://www.nngroup.com/articles/scrolling-and-attention/, accessed 4 March 2021.

56. Butler, *The Matter of the Page*, 68.

57. McKitterick, *Old Books, New Technologies*, 2.

58. D. F. McKenzie, "Computers and the Humanities: A Personal Synthesis of Conference Issues," in *Scholarship and Technology in the Humanities*, ed. by May Katzen (London: British Library Research Series, 1991), pp. 157–69, cited in McKitterick, 2.

59. Paul M. Leonardi, "Digital Materiality? How Artifacts without Matter, Matter," *First Monday*, 15.6 (2010), http://firstmonday.org/ojs/index.php/fm/

article/view/3036; Sydney J. Shep, "Digital Materiality," in *A New Companion to Digital Humanities* (Oxford: John Wiley & Sons, Ltd, 2015), 322–30, https://doi.org/10.1002/9781118680605.ch22.

60. Martin Paul Eve, "Scarcity and Abundance," in *The Bloomsbury Handbook of Electronic Literature*, ed. by Joseph Tabbi (London: Bloomsbury, 2017), 385.

61. Peter Suber, *Open Access*, Essential Knowledge Series (Cambridge, MA: MIT Press, 2012), 46–47, http://bit.ly/oa-book.

62. Thomas Jefferson, *The Writings of Thomas Jefferson*, ed. by H. A. Washington, vol. 6 (Washington, DC: The United States Congress, 1853), 180; Aaron Swartz, "Jefferson: Nature Wants Information to Be Free," in *The Boy Who Could Change the World*. (London: Verso, 2015), 24.

63. John Hartley et al., "Do We Need to Move from Communication Technology to User Community? A New Economic Model of the Journal as a Club," *Learned Publishing*, 32.1 (2019), 29, https://doi.org/10.1002/leap.1228.

64. This is despite ongoing debates over print fixity. See Adrian Johns, *The Nature of the Book* (Chicago: University of Chicago Press, 1998); Nicholas Hudson, "Challenging Eisenstein: Recent Studies in Print Culture," *Eighteenth-Century Life*, 26.2 (2002), 83–95; and Elizabeth L. Eisenstein, *The Printing Press as an Agent of Change: Communications and Cultural Transformations in Early-Modern Europe* (Cambridge: Cambridge University Press, 2009), https://doi.org/10.1017/CBO9781107049963.

65. Walter Benjamin, "The Work of Art in the Age of Mechanical Reproduction," in *Illuminations* (London: Pimlico, 1999), 218–19.

66. For more on how, in some senses, the PDF is thus not even a digital text, see Buccellati, *A Critique of Archaeological Reason*, 207–8.

67. John E. Warnock, "Simple Ideas That Changed Printing and Publishing," *Proceedings of the American Philosophical Society*, 156.4 (2012), 365.

68. For more on the DPI problem, see Paul McJones and Liz Bond Crews, "The Advent of Digital Typography," *IEEE Annals of the History of Computing*, 42.1 (2020), 41–50, https://doi.org/10.1109/MAHC.2019.2929883.

69. John E. Warnock and Charles Geschke, "Founding and Growing Adobe Systems, Inc.," *IEEE Annals of the History of Computing*, 41.3 (2019), 26, https://doi.org/10.1109/MAHC.2019.2923397. See also John E. Warnock, "The Origins of PostScript," *IEEE Annals of the History of Computing*, 40.3 (2018), 68–76, https://doi.org/10.1109/MAHC.2018.033841112.

70. Warnock, "Simple Ideas That Changed Printing and Publishing," 366.

71. Joseph A. Dane, *Blind Impressions: Methods and Mythologies in Book History*, Material Texts (Philadelphia: University of Pennsylvania Press, 2013), 16; and Joseph A. Dane, *Out of Sorts: On Typography and Print Culture*, Material Texts (Philadelphia: University of Pennsylvania Press, 2011), 9.

72. For more, see Warnock, "Simple Ideas That Changed Printing and Publishing," 368.

73. Frank J. Romano and Miranda Mitrano, *History of Desktop Publishing* (New Castle, DE: Oak Knoll Press, 2019), 157.

74. John E. Warnock, personal correspondence with Martin Paul Eve, "The Earliest 'Critique' of PDF," 24 November 2019.

75. The following history is derived from Laurens Leurs, "The History of PDF," 2008, https://www.prepressure.com/pdf/basics/history, accessed 13 November 2019; Willinsky, Garnett, and Pan Wong, "Refurbishing the Camelot of Scholarship"; and John E. Warnock's original specification document "The Camelot Project," PlanetPDF, 1991, https://planetpdf.com/planetpdf/pdfs/war nock_camelot.pdf, accessed 13 November 2019.

76. Warnock, personal correspondence with Eve.

77. Warnock, "The Camelot Project."

78. See Jarvis, *The Gutenberg Parenthesis.*

79. John B. Thompson, *Books in the Digital Age: The Transformation of Academic and Higher Education Publishing in Britain and the United States* (Cambridge: Polity Press, 2005), 411.

80. Warnock and Geschke, "Founding and Growing Adobe Systems, Inc.," 33.

81. Warnock, personal correspondence with Eve.

82. Thompson, *Books in the Digital Age*, 410; and Warnock, personal correspondence with Eve.

83. Kathleen Fitzpatrick, *Planned Obsolescence: Publishing, Technology, and the Future of the Academy* (New York: New York University Press, 2011), 94.

84. For some of these challenges, see Nelson H. F. Beebe, "BIBTEX for ACM Publications," 2010, 37.

85. However, in some industries, such as newspaper printing, the former may have played a greater role. For more on this, see Will Mari, *A Short History of Disruptive Journalism Technologies 1960–1990* (Milton: Routledge, 2019), 12, http://proxy.cm.umoncton.ca/login?url=https://ebookcentral.proquest.com/lib /umoncton-ebooks/detail.action?docID=5683704.

86. For perhaps isolationist political reasons, the USA did not adopt the A standards of paper used virtually everywhere else. Leon Wu, "The Article about Paper Sizes You Didn't Know You Needed," Medium, 3 October 2019, https://modus.medium.com/a4-vs-letter-why-size-matters-5477a647b1c2.

87. For more on the aspect ratio history of pages, see Peter Stoicheff and Andrew Taylor, "Introduction," in Stoicheff and Taylor, *The Future of the Page*, 6; and Sylvia Rodgers Albro, *Fabriano: City of Medieval and Renaissance Papermaking* (New Castle, DE: Oak Knoll Press, 2016), 83–84.

88. Bardini, *Bootstrapping*, 163.

89. These dimensions were originally related to the dimensions of human hands. See Manguel, *A Reader on Reading*, 122.

90. Butler, *The Matter of the Page*, 9.

91. Georg Christoph Lichtenberg, *Briefwechsel*, vol. 3, *1785—1792* (München: Beck, 1990), 274-75.

92. Robin Kinross, *A4 and Before: Towards a Long History of Paper Sizes*, KB Lecture, 6 (Wassenaar: NIAS, 2009).

93. Mark Bland, "The Appearance of the Text in Early Modern England," *Text*, 11 (1998), 92.

94. Dagenais, "Decolonizing the Medieval Page," 62.

95. For more on the early integration efforts between television and computers, see Douglas Crockford, "Integrating Computers and Television," in Laurel, *The Art of Human-Computer Interface Design*, 461-66.

96. James Monaco, *How to Read a Film: The World of Movies, Media, and Multimedia: Language, History, Theory*, 3rd ed. (New York: Oxford University Press, 2000), 107.

97. Gérard Genette, *Paratexts*, trans. by Jane E. Lewin (Cambridge: Cambridge University Press, 1997), 17.

98. Genette, 17.

99. Lucien Febvre and Henri-Jean Martin, *The Coming of the Book: The Impact of Printing 1450—1800*, Verso Classics (London: Verso, 2000), 17-18, 29-30; see Dane, *Out of Sorts*, 17-18 for a critique of Febvre and Martin, though.

100. For more on continuity in the history of publishing, see Dane, *Out of Sorts*, 11-14.

101. For more, see Simon Peter Rowberry, "The Ebook Imagination," *Digital Humanities Quarterly*, 16.1 (2022).

102. Phillip Barron, "E-Readers in the Classroom," *Transformations: The Journal of Inclusive Scholarship and Pedagogy*, 22.1 (2021), 134.

103. Jerome J. McGann, *The Textual Condition* (Princeton, NJ: Princeton University Press, 1991), 149.

Chapter Three

1. The definition and philosophy of what music comprises is complex and my statement here is reductive. See Theodore Gracyk and Andrew Kania, *The Routledge Companion to Philosophy and Music*, Routledge Philosophy Companions (London: Routledge, 2014).

2. Again, this is more complex than this statement can admit. See Luciano Floridi, *The Philosophy of Information* (Oxford: Oxford University Press, 2011).

3. Beatrice Warde, "The Crystal Goblet or Printing Should Be Invisible" (New York: The World Publishing Company, 1956), 17.

4. Laurie E. Maguire, *The Rhetoric of the Page* (Oxford: Oxford University Press, 2020), 5.

5. See, for instance, Craig Robertson and Deidre Lynch, "Pinning and Punching: A Provisional History of Holes, Paper, and Books," *Inscription: The Journal of Material Text—Theory, Practice, History*, 1.2 (2021), 13–23. For more on holes for binding and stab stitching, see Zachary Lesser, *Ghosts, Holes, Rips and Scrapes: Shakespeare in 1619, Bibliography in the Longue Durée* (Philadelphia: University of Pennsylvania Press, 2021), chap. 2.

6. Heather Wolfe, "On Curating Filing Holes," *Inscription: The Journal of Material Text—Theory, Practice, History*, 1.2 (2021), 27–47.

7. Beate Dobrusskin and Kirsten Glaus, *Katalog der Schadensbilder Spuren und Phänomene an Kunst und Kulturgut Papier, Dobrusskin, Beate; Glaus, Kirsten (2012). Catalogue of Damage Terminology for Works of Art and Cultural Property Paper [Textbook]*, trans. by Jean F. Rosston (Bern: Schriftenreihe Konservierung und Restaurierung der Hochschule der Künste Bern, 2012), https://arbor.bfh.ch/10329/.

8. Wolfe, "On Curating Filing Holes," 28.

9. Paul Reynolds, "A Glossary of Holes," *Inscription: The Journal of Material Text—Theory, Practice, History*, 1.2 (2021), 75–81.

10. Henry R. Woudhuysen, "Early Play Texts: Forms and Formes," in *In Arden: Editing Shakespeare: Essays in Honour of Richard Proudfoot*, ed. by Ann Thompson and Gordon McMullan (London: Arden Shakespeare, 2003), 51.

11. Woudhuysen, 51.

12. David McKitterick, "What Is the Use of Books without Pictures? Empty Space in Some Early Printed Books," *La Bibliofilía*, 116.1–3 (2014), 67–82. See also Phillipa Hardman, "Reading the Spaces: Pictorial Intentions in the Thornton MSS, Lincoln Cathedral MS 91, and BL MS Add. 31042," *Medium Aevum*, 63.2 (1994), 250–75; Phillipa Hardman, "Windows into the Text: Unfilled Spaces in Some Fifteenth-Century English Manuscript," in *Texts and Their Contexts: Papers from the Early Book Society*, ed. by John Scattergood and Julia Boffey (Dublin: Four Courts Press, 1997), 44–70; Phillipa Hardman, "Interpreting the Incomplete Scheme of Illustration in Cambridge, Corpus Christi College MS 61," *English Manuscript Studies 1100–1700*, 6 (1997), 52–69; Daniel Wakelin, "When Scribes Won't Write: Gaps in Middle English Books," *Studies in the Age of Chaucer*, 36.1 (2014), 249–78, https://doi.org/10.1353/sac.2014.0008; Daniel Wakelin, *Scribal Correction and Literary Craft: English Manuscripts 1375–1510*, Cambridge Studies in Medieval Literature (Cambridge: Cambridge University Press, 2014), https://doi.org/10.1017/CBO9781139923279; and Susanna

Fein, "Somer Soneday: Kingship, Sainthood, and Fortune in Oxford, Bodleian Library, MS Laud Misc. 108," in *The Texts and Contexts of Oxford, Bodleian Library, MS Laud Misc. 108* (Amsterdam: Brill, 2011), 275–97, https://brill.com/view/book/edcoll/9789004192249/Bej.9789004192065.i-342_015.xml.

13. For more on margins and marginalia, see William W. E. Slights, *Managing Readers: Printed Marginalia in English Renaissance Books* (Ann Arbor: University of Michigan Press, 2001). See also John Unsworth, "Scholarly Primitives: What Methods Do Humanities Researchers Have in Common, and How Might Our Tools Reflect This?" (presented at the Humanities Computing: formal methods, experimental practice, King's College London, 2000), http://www.people.virginia.edu/~jmu2m/Kings.5-00/primitives.html, accessed 24 December 2016; and Andrew Stauffer and Kristin Jensen, "About," Book Traces, 2023, https://booktraces-public.lib.virginia.edu/about/.

14. Henry de Montherlant, *Don Juan* (Paris: Editions Gallimard, 1958). See also Monique Masure-Williams, "In Defence of Henry de Montherlant's *Don Juan*," *CLA Journal*, 32.4 (1989), 466–83.

15. Piotr Stankiewicz, *Does Happiness Write Blank Pages? On Stoicism and Artistic Creativity* (Vernon Press, 2019).

16. Teju Cole, "Black Paper," in *Black Paper: Writing in a Dark Time* (Chicago: University of Chicago Press, 2021), 253.

17. Cole, 255.

18. Andrew Piper, Chad Wellmon, and Mohamed Cheriet, "The Page Image: Towards a Visual History of Digital Documents," *Book History*, 23.1 (2020), 365, https://doi.org/10.1353/bh.2020.0010.

19. Piper, Wellmon, and Cheriet, 384.

20. Sherif Abuelwafa et al., "Feature Learning for Footnote-Based Document Image Classification," in *Image Analysis and Recognition*, ed. by Fakhri Karray, Aurélio Campilho, and Farida Cheriet, Lecture Notes in Computer Science (Cham: Springer International Publishing, 2017), 645, https://doi.org/10.1007/978-3-319-59876-5_71.

21. Andrew Piper, "Deleafing: The History and Future of Losing Print," *Gramma: Journal of Theory and Criticism*, 21 (2013), 14–15, https://doi.org/10.26262/gramma.v21i0.6276.

22. Ryan Cordell, "'Q i-Jtb the Raven': Taking Dirty OCR Seriously," *Book History*, 20.1 (2017), 194, 196, https://doi.org/10.1353/bh.2017.0006.

23. Martin Paul Eve, "Textual Scholarship and Contemporary Literary Studies: Jennifer Egan's Editorial Processes and the Archival Edition of Emerald City," *Lit: Literature Interpretation Theory*, 31.1 (2020), 25–41, https://doi.org/10.1080/10436928.2020.1709713.

24. Rose Holley, "How Good Can It Get? Analysing and Improving OCR

Accuracy in Large Scale Historic Newspaper Digitisation Programs," *D-Lib Magazine*, 15.3/4 (2009), https://doi.org/10.1045/march2009-holley.

25. See Cordell, "'Q i-Jtb the Raven,'" 206–7.

26. For more on this, see Bronać Ferran, *The Smell of Ink and Soil. The Story of (Edition) Hansjörg Mayer* (Cologne: Walther Koenig, 2017).

27. Maguire, *The Rhetoric of the Page*, 18.

28. Herman Melville, *Moby-Dick: An Authoritative Text, Contexts, Criticism*, ed. by Hershel Parker, 3rd ed. (New York: W. W. Norton & Company, 2018), 157.

29. Melville, 151.

30. Thomas White, "Potential Lives: The Matter of Late Medieval Manuscripts" (unpublished doctoral thesis, Birkbeck, University of London, 2016), 80, http://vufind.lib.bbk.ac.uk/vufind/Record/560699, accessed 9 September 2021.

31. Helen Smith, "'A Unique Instance of Art': The Proliferating Surfaces of Early Modern Paper," *Journal of the Northern Renaissance*, 10 July 2017, para. 6, https://jnr2.hcommons.org/2017/4847.

32. Smith, paras. 2, 6; Jacques Derrida, *Paper Machine*, trans. by Rachel Bowlby, Cultural Memory in the Present (Stanford, CA: Stanford University Press, 2005); and William Shakespeare, *The Tragœdy of Othello, the Moore of Venice* (n.p.: Nicholas Okes for Thomas Walkley, 1622), K4r.

33. White, "Potential Lives," 80.

34. J. C. R. Licklider, *Libraries of the Future* (Cambridge, MA: MIT Press, 1965), 94. See also Thierry Bardini, *Bootstrapping: Douglas Engelbart, Coevolution, and the Origins of Personal Computing*, Writing Science (Stanford, CA: Stanford University Press, 2000), 84.

35. Matthew G. Kirschenbaum, *Track Changes: A Literary History of Word Processing* (Cambridge, MA: The Belknap Press of Harvard University Press, 2016), 47.

36. Robert S. Wahl, "The History of Punched Cards: Using Paper to Store Information," in *The Routledge Companion to Media Technology and Obsolescence*, ed. by Mark J. P. Wolf (New York: Routledge, 2019), 36.

37. The actual complexities of punched-card systems are beyond this paragraph's explanatory power. Different punched-card systems used different encodings, and they do not really correlate to binary encodings for different symbolic outcomes, but rather to numerical ones. Nonetheless, in many of these systems, the presence of a hole—really, an absence—can denote positivity.

38. Michel Pastoureau, *White: The History of a Color* (Princeton, NJ: Princeton University Press, 2023), 157.

39. Heidi Craig, "Rags, Ragpickers, and Early Modern Papermaking," *Literature Compass*, 16.5 (2019), e12523 (p. 4), https://doi.org/10.1111/lic3.12523. A

point also made by D. C. Coleman, *The British Paper Industry, 1495–1860 : A Study in Industrial Growth* (Oxford: Clarendon Press, 1975), 55.

40. Coleman, *The British Paper Industry*, 113–17.

41. Sylvia Rodgers Albro, *Fabriano: City of Medieval and Renaissance Papermaking* (New Castle, DE: Oak Knoll Press, 2016), 127.

42. Orietta Da Rold, *Paper in Medieval England: From Pulp to Fictions*, Cambridge Studies in Medieval Literature, 112 (Cambridge: Cambridge University Press, 2020), 187.

43. Joshua Calhoun, "The Word Made Flax: Cheap Bibles, Textual Corruption, and the Poetics of Paper," *PMLA*, 126.2 (2011), 331.

44. Jonathan Senchyne, *The Intimacy of Paper in Early and Nineteenth-Century American Literature*, Studies in Print Culture and the History of the Book (Amherst: University of Massachusetts Press, 2020), 142; John Power, *A Handy-Book about Books, for Book-Lovers, Book-Buyers, and Book-Sellers* (London: John Wilson, 1870), 135; "Black Paper and White Ink," *Baltimore Sun* (Baltimore, MD, 14 April 1855); "Black Paper and White Ink," *Miners' Journal, and Pottsville General Advertiser* (Pottsville, PA, 5 May 1855); "Black Paper and White Ink," *Athens Post* (Athens, TN, 27 April 1855); "Black Paper and White Ink," *Times & Sentinel Tri-Weekly* (Columbus, GA, 20 April 1855); "Black Paper and White Ink," *Philadelphia Public Ledger and Daily Transcript* (Philadelphia, PA, 13 April 1855).

45. Da Rold, *Paper in Medieval England*, 187. Italics mine.

46. Mark Kurlansky, *Paper: Paging through History* (New York: W. W. Norton & Company, 2016), 189.

47. Richard Leslie Hills, *Papermaking in Britain 1488–1988* (London: Bloomsbury Academic, 2015), 2.

48. For more on the spread of paper from China throughout the world, see Silvia Hufnagel, Þórunn Sigurðardóttir, and Davíð Ólafsson, eds., *Paper Stories—Paper and Book History in Early Modern Europe* (Berlin: De Gruyter, 2023), https://doi.org/10.1515/9783111162768.

49. Alexander Monro, *The Paper Trail: An Unexpected History of a Revolutionary Invention* (New York: Vintage Books, 2017); Dard Hunter, *Papermaking: The History and Technique of an Ancient Craft* (New York: Dover Publications, 1978), 5–6.

50. Tsuen-hsuin Tsien, *Paper and Printing*, Science and Civilisation in China, ed. by Joseph Needham, vol. 5, part 1 (1985; repr., Cambridge: Cambridge University Press, 2001), 2.

51. Tsuen-hsuin Tsien, *Written on Bamboo and Silk* (Chicago: University of Chicago Press, 1962).

52. Lothar Müller, *White Magic: The Age of Paper* (Cambridge: Polity Press, 2014), 5.

53. Tsien, *Paper and Printing*, 8–10. For more on the spread of paper in China, see Martin Kern, "Ritual, Text, and the Formation of the Canon: Historical Transitions of 'Wen' in Early China," *T'oung Pao*, 87.1/3 (2001), 89.

54. American Paper and Pulp Association, *The Dictionary of Paper, Including Pulp, Paperboard, Paper Properties, and Related Papermaking Terms*, 3rd ed. (New York: American Paper and Pulp Association, 1965), 246; Tsien, and *Paper and Printing*, 35.

55. Tsien, *Paper and Printing*, 53.

56. Tsien, 41. For more on Lun's role in light of new archaeological evidence, see T. H. Barrett, "The Woman Who Invented Notepaper: Towards a Comparative Historiography of Paper and Print," *Journal of the Royal Asiatic Society*, 21.2 (2011), 199–210.

57. Kurlansky, *Paper*, 37.

58. Tsien, *Paper and Printing*, 320–21.

59. Tsien, 74.

60. Hunter, *Papermaking*, 204.

61. Lionel Giles, "Dated Chinese Manuscripts in the Stein Collection," *Bulletin of the School of Oriental Studies, University of London*, 7.4 (1935), 813.

62. Kurlansky, *Paper*, 254.

63. Tsien, *Paper and Printing*, 76.

64. The entirety of this paragraph is indebted to Tsien, 76–77.

65. Gitta Salomon, "New Uses for Color," in *The Art of Human-Computer Interface Design*, ed. by Brenda Laurel (Reading, MA: Addison-Wesley, 1990), 272.

66. Müller, *White Magic*, 7. See Josef Karabacek, *Arab Paper*, trans. by Don Baker (London: Archetype, 2001).

67. White, "Potential Lives," 66.

68. Elaine Treharne and Claude Willan, *Text Technologies: A History*, Stanford Text Technologies (Stanford, CA: Stanford University Press, 2020), 69.

69. Craig, "Rags, Ragpickers, and Early Modern Papermaking."

70. Adam Smyth, *Material Texts in Early Modern England* (Cambridge: Cambridge University Press, 2018), 139, https://doi.org/10.1017/9781108367868. I was grateful to Craig, "Rags, Ragpickers, and Early Modern Papermaking," 8 for drawing this to my attention.

71. Müller, *White Magic*, 49.

72. Müller, 50.

73. Calhoun, "The Word Made Flax," 331–32.

74. Da Rold, *Paper in Medieval England*, 69.

75. Da Rold, 69.

76. Michel Pastoureau, *Black: The History of a Color* (Princeton, NJ: Princeton University Press, 2009), 118.

77. Elizabeth Savage, "Where Is the Colour in Book History?" (presented at the Frederik Muller Lezing, online, 10 September 2021), YouTube video, 1:07:45, https://www.youtube.com/watch?v=NbDIpNQEVhU.

78. Alvare de Semedo, *The History of That Great and Renowned Monarchy of China* (London: I. Crook, 1655), 34–35.

79. Pastoureau, *Black*, 119.

80. Pastoureau, 124. See Carlos M. N. Eire, *War against the Idols: The Reformation of Worship from Erasmus to Calvin* (Cambridge: Cambridge University Press, 1998), 69–72 for more on iconoclasm.

81. Michel Pastoureau, "L'incolore n'existe pas," in *Points de vue: Pour Philippe Junod*, ed. by Danielle Chaperon and Philippe Kaenel, Champs Visuels (Paris: L'Harmattan, 2003), 21–36. The following section is indebted to Pastoureau's little-known, French-language-only text on the history of colorlessness.

82. "Qui n'a pas de couleur bien déterminée, qui n'a pas de couleur propre, qui manque de teint." Pastoureau, "L'incolore n'existe pas," 22. Translation mine.

83. Pastoureau, "L'incolore n'existe pas," 22.

84. See Christine Mohrmann, "Observations sur la langue et le style de Saint Bernard," in *Sancti Bernardi opera*, vol. 2, ed. by Jean Leclercq and Henri Rochais (Rome: Editiones cistercienses, 1958), 9–33, cited in Pastoureau, "L'incolore n'existe pas," 23.

85. See Michel Pastoureau, "Les cisterciens et la couleur au XIIᵉ siècle," in *L'Ordre cistercien et le Berry*, ed. by Pierre-Gilles Girault (Bourges: Conseil général du Cher, 1998), 21–30, cited in Pastoureau, "L'incolore n'existe pas," 23–24. Translation mine.

86. Robert Grosseteste, "De Iride Seu de Iride et Speculo," in *Beitrage Zur Geschichte Der Philosophie Des Mittelalters*, vol. 9, ed. by Ludwig Baur (Münster: Aschendorff, 1912), 73; and John Pecham, "De Iride," in *John Pecham and the Science of Optics*, ed. by David C. Lindberg, Perspectiva Communis (Madison: University of Wisconsin Press, 1970), 114–23, cited in Pastoureau, "L'incolore n'existe pas," 25.

87. As a reminder, this argument continues to follow and is in some senses a translation of Pastoureau, "L'incolore n'existe pas."

88. Pastoureau, "L'incolore n'existe pas," 26.

89. Pastoureau, 27.

90. Jean-Claude Schmitt, *Les revenants. Les vivants et les morts dans la société médiévale* (Paris: Gallimard, 1994), 223–43, cited in Pastoureau, "L'incolore n'existe pas," 28.

91. These points are all from Pastoureau, "L'incolore n'existe pas," 28.

92. Most of this paragraph is indebted to Pastoureau, 29. See Moshe Barasch, *Light and Color in the Italian Renaissance Theory of Art* (New York: New York University Press, 1978) for more on the uptake of white as blankness.

93. Barasch, *Light and Color*, 18.

94. Leon Battista Alberti, *On Painting: A New Translation and Critical Edition*, ed. by Rocco Sinisgalli, trans. by Rocco Sinisgalli (Cambridge: Cambridge University Press, 2011), 31.

95. See Barasch, *Light and Color*, 172.

96. In Alberti, *On Painting*, 3–4, Rocco Sinisgalli proposes that although "the usual opinion is that the author wrote the text in Latin first and then translated it into the vernacular for the benefit of working-class painters who lacked a classical education," he believes the actual chain to be the other way around.

97. Barasch, *Light and Color*, 29.

98. Barasch, 40.

99. Barasch, 174.

100. "Perchè il bianco non è colore, ma è in potenzia ricettiva d'ogni colore." Jean Paul Richter, *The Literary Works of Leonardo Da Vinci* (London: Sampson Low, Marston, Searle, & Rivington, 1883), sec. 278. See also Barasch, *Light and Color*, 176, which cites Leonardo's *Treatise on Painting*, I have here Americanized the spelling of "color."

101. Isaac Newton, "Isaac Newton to Henry Oldenburg, 6 Feb, 1671/72," in *The Correspondence of Isaac Newton*, ed. by H. W. Turnbull et al, vol. 1 (Cambridge: Cambridge University Press, 1959), 98.

102. Alan E. Shapiro, "Artists' Colors and Newton's Colors," *Isis: A Journal of the History of Science Society*, 85.4 (1994), 614, https://doi.org/10.1086/356979.

103. See James Fox, *The World According to Colour: A Cultural History* (London: Allen Lane, 2021), 143.

104. Roy A. Sorensen, *Seeing Dark Things: The Philosophy of Shadows* (New York: Oxford University Press, 2008), 5.

105. Pastoureau, "L'incolore n'existe pas," 30.

106. Shapiro, "Artists' Colors and Newton's Colors," 616; and Pastoureau, "L'incolore n'existe pas," 31.

107. Fox, *The World According to Colour*, 22.

108. Alan L. Gilchrist, *Seeing Black and White* (Oxford: Oxford University Press, 2006), 9.

109. Hills, *Papermaking in Britain 1488–1988*, 5.

110. For example, Barbara A. Shailor, *The Medieval Book* (Toronto: University of Toronto Press, 1991), 9 describes MS 407 at the Beinecke Library, a fifteenth-century Italian manuscript, as "so fine it is virtually impossible to

distinguish hair side from flesh side; each page is supple, unblemished, and uniformly white." Cited in White, "Potential Lives," 72.

111. Karabacek, *Arab Paper*, 47ff cited in Müller, *White Magic*, 76; and Helen Loveday, *Islamic Paper: A Study of the Ancient Craft* (London: Archetype, 2001), 52f.

112. Müller, *White Magic*, 77.

113. Smith, A Unique Instance of Art,'" para. 36; Girolamo Ruscelli, *The Thyrde and Last Parte of the Secretes of the Reuerende Maister Alexis of Piemont*, trans. by William Ward (London: Rowland Hall for Nicholas England, 1562), H4r, cited in Smith.

114. Kurlansky, *Paper*, 171.

115. John Locke, *An Essay Concerning Human Understanding*, ed. by P. H Nidditch (Oxford: Clarendon, 1975), bk. II.i.2, 104, https://doi.org/10.1093/actrade/9780198243861.book.1, accessed 11 May 2021.

116. Müller, *White Magic*, 86–87.

117. In the Canadian context, the white sprice (*Picea glauca*) yielded a similar base white. Timo Särkkä, *Paper and the British Empire: The Quest for Imperial Raw Materials, 1861–1960*, Routledge Explorations in Economic History (Abingdon: Routledge, 2021), 55–56.

118. Hills, *Papermaking in Britain 1488–1988*, 131–33.

119. Ahmed S. M. Saleh et al., "Brown Rice versus White Rice: Nutritional Quality, Potential Health Benefits, Development of Food Products, and Preservation Technologies," *Comprehensive Reviews in Food Science and Food Safety*, 18.4 (2019), 1070–96, https://doi.org/10.1111/1541-4337.12449.

120. Gary Bryan Magee, *Productivity and Performance in the Paper Industry: Labour, Capital and Technology in Britain and America, 1860–1914* (Cambridge: Cambridge University Press, 2002), 180–81.

121. Georgina Wilson, "Surface Reading Paper as Feminist Bibliography," *Criticism*, 64.3 (2023), 372.

122. Gary Bryan Magee, "Competence or Omniscience? Assessing Entrepreneurship in the Victorian and Edwardian British Paper Industry," *Business History Review*, 71.2 (1997), 230–59, https://doi.org/10.2307/3116159.

123. R. H. Leach et al., *The Printing Ink Manual* (Boston: Springer US, 1988), 1, https://doi.org/10.1007/978-1-4684-6906-6.

124. Leach et al., 154.

125. Tsien, *Paper and Printing*, 5. That said, Thomas Christiansen, Marine Cotte, René Loredo-Portales, et al., "The Nature of Ancient Egyptian Copper-Containing Carbon Inks Is Revealed by Synchrotron Radiation Based X-Ray Microscopy," *Scientific Reports*, 7.1 (2017), 1–8, https://doi.org/10.1038/s41598-017-15652-7 points out that lead mixtures occurred earlier in this history than was until recently suspected.

126. Tsien, *Paper and Printing*, 236. The history of ink and substrate production has troubling links to the systemic exploitation of animals. For more on this, see Sarah Kay, "Legible Skins: Animals and the Ethics of Medieval Reading," *Postmedieval: A Journal of Medieval Cultural Studies*, 2.1 (2011), 13–32, https://doi.org/10.1057/pmed.2010.48.

127. Zora Neale Hurston, "How It Feels to Be Colored Me," *World Tomorrow*, May 1928, 215–16. Some of the specifics of how race and print culture interact are better handled in Brigitte Fielder and Jonathan Senchyne, eds., *Against a Sharp White Background: Infrastructures of African American Print* (Madison: University of Wisconsin Press, 2019) than I can cover adequately here.

128. Tsien, *Paper and Printing*, 238.

129. Tsien, *Written on Bamboo and Silk*, 168; Tsien, *Paper and Printing*, 239.

130. Tsien, *Paper and Printing*, 246–47.

131. Thomas Christiansen, Marine Cotte, Wout de Nolf, et al., "Insights into the Composition of Ancient Egyptian Red and Black Inks on Papyri Achieved by Synchrotron-Based Microanalyses," *Proceedings of the National Academy of Sciences*, 117.45 (2020), 27825–35, https://doi.org/10.1073/pnas.2004534117.

132. Thomas Christiansen, "Manufacture of Black Ink in the Ancient Mediterranean," *Bulletin of the American Society of Papyrologists*, 54 (2017), 167, https://doi.org/10.2143/BASP.54.0.3239877.

133. Zerdoun Bat-Yehouda Monique, *Les encres noires au Moyen Age* (Paris: CNRS Editions, 2003), 23.

134. Christiansen, "Manufacture of Black Ink," 169–70.

135. Monique, *Les encres noires au Moyen Age*, 145.

136. Martin Levey, "Some Black Inks in Early Mediaeval Jewish Literature," *Chymia*, 9 (1964), 27–31, https://doi.org/10.2307/27757229.

137. Monique, *Les encres noires au Moyen Age*, 109–10.

138. Monique, 75–76.

139. White, "Potential Lives," 71.

140. Courtney J. Campbell, Allegra Giovine, and Jennifer Keating, "Introduction: Confronting Emptiness in History," in *Empty Spaces: Perspectives on Emptiness in Modern History*, ed. by Courtney J. Campbell, Allegra Giovine, and Jennifer Keating (London: University of London Press, 2019), 1, https://www.jstor.org/stable/j.ctvp2n2r8.6, accessed 9 March 2021.

141. W. E. B. Du Bois, "Jefferson Davis as a Representative of Civilization," 1890, Special Collections and University Archives, University of Massachusetts Amherst Libraries, W. E. B. Du Bois Papers (MS 312), http://credo.library.umass.edu/view/full/mums312-b196-i029, accessed 4 May 2021.

142. Eric Gardner, *Black Print Unbound: The Christian Recorder, African*

American Literature, and Periodical Culture (New York: Oxford University Press, 2015), 171.

143. Jennifer DeVere Brody, "The Blackness of Blackness . . . Reading the Typography of 'Invisible Man,'" *Theatre Journal*, 57.4 (2005), 681. See also George Hutchinson and John K. Young, "Introduction," in *Publishing Blackness: Textual Constructions of Race since 1850*, ed. by George Hutchinson and John K. Young, Editorial Theory and Literary Criticism (Ann Arbor: University of Michigan Press, 2013), 3.

144. Theodore W. Allen, *The Invention of the White Race*, vol. 1, *Racial Oppression And Social Control* (London: Verso, 2012), 9.

145. Eric Arnesen, "Whiteness and the Historians' Imagination," *International Labor and Working-Class History*, 60 (2001), 3-32; and Eric Kaufmann, "The Dominant Ethnic Moment: Towards the Abolition of 'Whiteness'?," *Ethnicities*, 6.2 (2006), 231-53, https://doi.org/10.1177/1468796806063754.

146. Susan Murray, *Bright Signals: A History of Color Television* (Durham, NC: Duke University Press, 2018), 1.

147. Murray, 3.

148. Albert Abramson, *The History of Television, 1880 to 1941* (Jefferson, NC: McFarland, 1987), 1.

149. Abramson, 4.

150. Laurent Mannoni, *The Great Art of Light and Shadow: Archaeology of the Cinema* (Exeter: University of Exeter Press, 2000), 33-34. The history of the magic lantern was also covered extensively between 1978-2014 in the *New Magic Lantern Journal*, See also Koen Vermeir, "The Magic of the Magic Lantern (1660-1700): On Analogical Demonstration and the Visualization of the Invisible," *British Journal for the History of Science*, 38.2 (2005), 128.

151. Mannoni, *The Great Art of Light and Shadow*, 28.

152. Mannoni, 43.

153. Christiaan Huygens, *Correspondance*, vol. 4 (The Hague: Société Hollandaise des Sciences, 1888), 125, cited by Mannoni, *The Great Art of Light and Shadow*, 45.

154. Mannoni, *The Great Art of Light and Shadow*, 13.

155. Jan E. Purkinje, *Beobachtungen und Versuche zur Physiologie der Sinne. Beiträge zur Kenntniss des Sehens in Subjectiver Hinsicht* (Prague: Calve, 1823); John Geiger, *Chapel of Extreme Experience: A Short History of Stroboscopic Light and the Dream Machine* (Brooklyn, NY: Soft Skull Press, 2003), 12; Nicholas J. Wade, Josef Brožek, and Jiří Hoskovec, *Purkinje's Vision: The Dawning of Neuroscience* (Mahwah, NJ: Lawrence Erlbaum Associates, 2001), 47-48; and Peter Mark Roget, "V. Explanation of an Optical Deception in the Appear-

ance of the Spokes of a Wheel Seen through Vertical Apertures," *Philosophical Transactions of the Royal Society of London*, 115 (1825), 131–40, https://doi.org/10.1098/rstl.1825.0007.

156. Joseph Plateau, "des illusions d'optique sur lesquelles se fonde le petit appareil appelé récemment Phénakistiscope," *Ann Chimie Phys*, 53 (1833), 304–8.

157. For more on this history, see Nicholas J. Wade, "Toying with Science," *Perception*, 33.9 (2004), 1025–32, https://doi.org/10.1068/p3309ed.

158. Simon Stampfer, *Die stroboscopischen Scheiben; oder, Optischen Zauberscheiben: Deren Theorie und wissenschaftliche Anwendung* (Vienna: Trentsensky & Vieweg, 1833).

159. William A. Belson, "The Effect of Television on Cinema Going," *Audio Visual Communication Review*, 6.2 (1958), 131–39. See also Vincent Porter, "The Three Phases of Film and Television," *Journal of Film and Video*, 36.1 (1984), 5–21.

160. Abramson, *History of Television*, 38–39.

161. For more on this, see Mark J. P. Wolf, "Farewell to the Phosphorescent Glow: The Long Life of the Cathode-Ray Tube," in Wolf, *The Routledge Companion to Media Technology and Obsolescence*, 118–35.

162. Ian Sinclair, "Elements of Television," in *Electronics Simplified*, ed. by Ian Sinclair, 3rd ed. (Oxford: Newnes, 2011), 137–65, https://doi.org/10.1016/B978-0-08-097063-9.10008-1.

163. D. F. McKenzie, *"What's Past Is Prologue": The Bibliographical Society and History of the Book* (London: Hearthstone Publications, 1993), 23. See also Simone Murray, *Introduction to Contemporary Print Culture: Books as Media* (London: Routledge, 2021), 4.

164. Müller, *White Magic*, 76.

165. Mark Robin Campbell, "John Cage's 4′33″: Using Aesthetic Theory to Understand a Musical Notion," *Journal of Aesthetic Education*, 26.1 (1992), 83, https://doi.org/10.2307/3332730.

166. Craig Dworkin, *No Medium* (Cambridge, MA: MIT Press, 2015), 145–73.

167. John Cage, *Silence: Lectures and Writings*, 50th anniversary ed. (Middletown, CT: Wesleyan University Press, 2011), 96.

168. Douglas Kahn, "John Cage: Silence and Silencing," *Musical Quarterly*, 81.4 (1997), 556–98.

169. Sorensen, *Seeing Dark Things*, 267.

170. For more on this, see Will Hill, *Space as Language: The Properties of Typographic Space* (Cambridge: Cambridge University Press, 2023), https://www.cambridge.org/core/elements/space-as-language/1BC7F7D5349DE22E88310CE06AB6F516.

171. "John Cage, *4'33" (In Proportional Notation)*, 1952/1953, MoMA: The Museum of Modern Art website, https://www.moma.org/collection/works/163616, accessed 8 March 2021.

172. Kyle Gann, *No Such Thing as Silence: John Cage's 4'33"* (New Haven, CT: Yale University Press, 2010), 167.

173. Gann, 128. This is also remarked upon by Dworkin, *No Medium*, 121.

174. Edith Wylder, "Emily Dickinson's Punctuation: The Controversy Revisited," *American Literary Realism*, 36.3 (2004), 206-7.

175. Ena Jung, "The Breath of Emily Dickinson's Dashes," *Emily Dickinson Journal*, 24.2 (2015), 1, https://doi.org/10.1353/edj.2015.0018.

176. See Richard Gillam, *Unicode Demystified: A Practical Programmer's Guide to the Encoding Standard* (Boston, MA: Addison-Wesley, 2003).

177. Gillam, 59.

178. James Mission, "Signifying Nothing: Following a Hole through Three Text Technologies," *Inscription: The Journal of Material Text—Theory, Practice, History*, 1.2 (2021), 68.

179. J. L. Austin, *How to Do Things with Words* (Oxford: Clarendon Press, 1962), 5-7.

180. John R. Searle, "A Taxonomy of Illocutionary Acts," in *Language, Mind, and Knowledge*, ed. by K. Gunderson (Minneapolis: University of Minnesota Press, 1975), 350-69.

181. For more on this, see Dennis Tenen, *Plain Text: The Poetics of Computation* (Stanford, CA: Stanford University Press, 2017).

182. David Nofre, Mark Priestley, and Gerard Alberts, "When Technology Became Language: The Origins of the Linguistic Conception of Computer Programming, 1950-1960," *Technology and Culture*, 55.1 (2014), 40-75, https://doi.org/10.1353/tech.2014.0031.

183. Nofre, Priestley, and Alberts, 40.

184. Jeffrey M. Binder, "Romantic Disciplinarity and the Rise of the Algorithm," *Critical Inquiry*, 46.4 (2020), 817, https://doi.org/10.1086/709225.

185. Roger Chartier, "Languages, Books, and Reading from the Printed Word to the Digital Text," trans. by Teresa Lavender Fagan, *Critical Inquiry*, 31.1 (2004), 137, https://doi.org/10.1086/427305.

186. Daniel Temkin, "Coding in Indigenous African Languages," *Esoteric.Codes*, 18 August 2021, https://esoteric.codes/blog/african-programming-languages.

187. Chartier, "Languages, Books, and Reading," 137-38.

188. Friedrich A. Kittler, *Gramophone, Film, Typewriter*, trans. by Geoffrey Winthroup-Young and Michael Wutz (Stanford, CA: Stanford University Press, 1999), 191.

189. Marshall McLuhan, *Understanding Media: The Extensions of Man* (Cambridge, MA: MIT Press, 1994), 260.

190. Kittler, *Gramophone, Film, Typewriter*, 201, 210.

191. John F. Kihlstrom and Lillian Park, "Cognitive Psychology: Overview," in *Reference Module in Neuroscience and Biobehavioral Psychology* (Amsterdam: Elsevier, 2018), B9780128093245217000 (pp. 10–11), https://doi.org/10.1016/B978-0-12-809324-5.21702-1; J. A. Lucy, "Sapir-Whorf Hypothesis," in *International Encyclopedia of the Social & Behavioral Sciences* (Amsterdam: Elsevier, 2001), 13486–90, https://doi.org/10.1016/B0-08-043076-7/03042-4.

192. Laura M. Ahearn, *Living Language: An Introduction to Linguistic Anthropology*, 2nd ed. (Malden, MA: Wiley-Blackwell, 2017), 91.

193. Ted Chiang, *Stories of Your Life and Others: Ted Chiang* (London: Picador, 2015). See also Francesco Sticchi, "From Spinoza to Contemporary Linguistics: Pragmatic Ethics in Denis Villeneuve's *Arrival*," *Revue canadienne d'études cinématographiques / Canadian Journal of Film Studies*, 27.2 (2018), 63.

194. Kittler, *Gramophone, Film, Typewriter*, 206.

195. Bardini, *Bootstrapping*, 45; and D. C. Engelbart, *Augmenting Human Intellect: A Conceptual Framework* (Menlo Park, CA: Air Force Office of Scientific Research, 1962), 24.

196. A. Frutiger, "The IBM SELECTRIC Composer: The Evolution of Composition Technology," *IBM Journal of Research and Development*, 12.1 (1968), 10, https://doi.org/10.1147/rd.121.0009.

197. Alan C. Lloyd, "Typewriters That Think," *Business Education World*, 27 (1947), 453–54. See also Dave Morton, "Working Notes: 36.1 (Dead Medium: The Auto-Typist)," *The Dead Media Project*, http://www.deadmedia.org/notes/36/361.html, accessed 26 August 2021.

198. Lloyd, "Typewriters That Think,"454.

199. Ivan Raykoff, *Dreams of Love: Playing the Romantic Pianist* (Oxford: Oxford University Press, 2014), 22.

200. Edward Tenner, *Our Own Devices: The Past and Future of Body Technology* (New York: Alfred A. Knopf, 2003), 161.

201. Raykoff, *Dreams of Love*, 23.

202. John Tresch, *The Romantic Machine: Utopian Science and Technology after Napoleon* (Chicago: University of Chicago Press, 2012), 223–26.

203. "Young and Delcambre's Type-Composing Machine," *Mechanics' Magazine*, 36.985 (1842), 497–500.

204. "Rosenberg's Type-Composing and Distributing Machines," *Mechanics' Magazine*, 36.1003 (1842), 401–8. Most of these examples come from Raykoff, *Dreams of Love*, 31. In turn, Raykoff is citing Michael H. Adler, *The*

Writing Machine: History of the Typewriter (London: Allen & Unwin, 1973), 48–49, 67, 75, 86, 91, 104–6, 107, 126, 212–13.

205. James A. Secord, *Victorian Sensation: The Extraordinary Publication, Reception, and Secret Authorship of Vestiges of the Natural History of Creation* (Chicago: University of Chicago Press, 2003), 117–18.

206. Raykoff, *Dreams of Love*, 31. See also Richard N. Current, "The Original Typewriter Enterprise 1867–1873," *Wisconsin Magazine of History*, 32.4 (1949), 391–407.

207. Everett M. Rogers, *Diffusion of Innovations*, 3rd ed. (New York: Free Press, 1983), 9.

208. Graham Lawton, "The Truth about the QWERTY Keyboard," *New Scientist*, 25 April 2019, https://www.newscientist.com/article/2200664-the-truth-about-the-qwerty-keyboard/, accessed 27 August 2021.

209. Jan Noyes, "The QWERTY Keyboard: A Review," *International Journal of Man-Machine Studies*, 18.3 (1983), 266, https://doi.org/10.1016/S0020-7373(83)80010-8.

210. Bardini, *Bootstrapping*, 71.

211. Don Ihde, *Embodied Technics* (Birkerød: Automatic Press/VIP, 2010), 17–36.

212. Thomas W. Patteson, "Player Piano," in *Oxford Handbooks Online: Scholarly Research Reviews* (Oxford: Oxford University Press, 2014), https://doi.org/10.1093/oxfordhb/9780199935321.013.16. Much of this section is indebted to Patteson.

213. *The Pneumatics of Hero of Alexandria*, trans. by Bennet Woodcroft, History of Science Library Primary Sources (London: Taylor Walton and Maberly, 1971); and Hugo Leichtentritt, "Mechanical Music in Olden Times," *Musical Quarterly*, 20.1 (1934), 15–26.

214. Teun Koetsier, "On the Prehistory of Programmable Machines: Musical Automata, Looms, Calculators," *Mechanism and Machine Theory*, 36.5 (2001), 590–91, https://doi.org/10.1016/S0094-114X(01)00005-2.

215. Patteson, "Player Piano."

216. Lisa Gitelman, "Media, Materiality, and the Measure of the Digital: Or, the Case of Sheet Music and the Problem of Piano Rolls," in *Memory Bytes: History, Technology, and Digital Culture*, ed. by Lauren Rabinovitz and Abraham Geil (Durham: Duke University Press, 2004), 201.

217. Matthew G. Kirschenbaum, *Mechanisms: New Media and the Forensic Imagination* (Cambridge, MA: MIT Press, 2008).

218. Gitelman, "Media, Materiality, and the Measure of the Digital," 210.

219. Mark Seltzer, *Bodies and Machines* (New York: Routledge, 1992), 10.

220. D. C. Engelbart, "The Augmented Knowledge Workshop," in *A History of Personal Workstations*, ed. by A. Goldberg (New York: ACM Press, 1988), 200.

221. Bardini, *Bootstrapping*, 68–69.

222. Bardini, 60.

223. Bardini, 69.

224. Friedrich A. Kittler, *Discourse Networks 1800/1900*, trans. by Michael Metteer and Chris Cullens (Stanford, CA: Stanford University Press, 1990), 195.

225. Brenda Laurel, ed., *The Art of Human-Computer Interface Design* (Reading, MA: Addison-Wesley, 1990), xii.

226. Paul A. David, "Clio and the Economics of QWERTY," *American Economic Review*, 75.2 (1985), 334.

227. N. Katherine Hayles, *How We Became Posthuman: Virtual Bodies in Cybernetics, Literature, and Informatics* (Chicago: University of Chicago Press, 1999), 199.

228. Gitelman, "Media, Materiality, and the Measure of the Digital," 211.

229. Gitelman, 212.

230. Matthew G. Kirschenbaum, *Bitstreams: The Future of Digital Literary Heritage* (Philadelphia: University of Pennsylvania Press, 2021), ix.

231. Wendy Hui Kyong Chun, "The Enduring Ephemeral, or The Future Is a Memory," in *Media Archaeology: Approaches, Applications, and Implications*, ed. by Erkki Huhtamo and Jussi Parikka (Berkeley: University of California Press, 2011), 184.

232. In this sense, this chapter disagrees with Marianne van den Boomen, *Transcoding the Digital: How Metaphors Matter in New Media* (Amsterdam: Institute of Network Cultures, 2014), 32. There, she argues that the computer is not just a pianola, with automagically moving keys. I have suggested, here, how playback and musical serial progression could be key for our understanding of contemporary text editing.

Chapter Four

1. Antti Silvast and Markku Reunanen, "Multiple Users, Diverse Users: Appropriation of Personal Computers by Demoscene Hackers," in *Hacking Europe: From Computer Cultures to Demoscenes*, ed. by Gerard Alberts (New York: Springer, 2014), 151.

2. For more on this, see Martin Paul Eve, *Warez: The Infrastructure and Aesthetics of Piracy* (New York: Punctum Books, 2021).

3. I first covered this phenomenon in Eve, *Warez*; and Martin Paul Eve, *The Digital Humanities and Literary Studies* (Oxford: Oxford University Press, 2021).

4. K. David Harrison and Gregory Anderson, letter to Deborah Anderson,

"Review of Proposal for Encoding Warang Chiti (Ho Orthography) in Unicode," 22 April 2007, https://www.unicode.org/L2/L2007/07137-warang-chiti-review.pdf.

5. Sharjeel Imam (@_imaams), "Digital Colonialism: 1. All Latin Alphabets and Symbols Are Denoted in Unicode by the Range of 0 to 500 in One Single Block. But Urdu-Arabic Alphabets Are Scattered in Five Different Blocks Ranging 1500 to around 64000," Twitter, 24 November 2017, https://twitter.com/_imaams/status/934109280285765632.

6. Don Osborn, *African Languages in a Digital Age: Challenges and Opportunities for Indigenous Language Computing* (Cape Town: HSRC Press, 2010), 59–60.

7. Domenico Fiormonte, "Towards a Cultural Critique of the Digital Humanities," *Historical Social Research / Historische Sozialforschung*, 37.3 (2012), 64.

8. Bernhard Rieder, *Engines of Order: A Mechanology of Algorithmic Techniques* (Amsterdam: Amsterdam University Press, 2020), 63; Gilbert Simondon, *On the Mode of Existence of Technical Objects* (Minneapolis, MN: Univocal Pub, 2016), 56.

9. Madelyn Bacon, "What Is STIX (Structured Threat Information EXpression)?—Definition from WhatIs.Com," SearchSecurity, 2015, https://www.techtarget.com/searchsecurity/definition/STIX-Structured-Threat-Information-eXpression, accessed 14 April 2022.

10. Jonathan Chan, "UPDATE: U+237C ⍼ &angzarr," ⟨ortho/normal⟩ (blog), 6 June 2023, https://ionathan.ch//2023/06/06/angzarr.html.

11. Jonathan Chan, "U+237C ⍼ RIGHT ANGLE WITH DOWNWARDS ZIGZAG ARROW," ⟨ortho/normal⟩ (blog), 9 April 2022, https://ionathan.ch//2022/04/09/angzarr.html.

12. Barbara Beeton, "Answer to 'What Is ⍼ Used For?,'" TeX—LaTeX Stack Exchange, 13 April 2022, https://tex.stackexchange.com/a/640596.

13. Timothy Gowers (@wtgowers), "@martin_eve None at All I'm Afraid, Though It Somewhat Resembles a Mark Some People Put at the End of a Proof by Contradiction," Twitter, 2022, https://twitter.com/wtgowers/status/1514674839688298498, accessed 11 July 2022.

14. Chan, "U+237C ⍼."

15. Aart, "Answer to 'What Is ⍼ Used For?,'" Mathematics Stack Exchange, 2022, https://math.stackexchange.com/a/4426967, accessed 14 April 2022.

16. Susan Leigh Star, "The Ethnography of Infrastructure," *American Behavioral Scientist*, 43.3 (1999), 377, https://doi.org/10.1177/00027649921955326.

17. Star, 379.

18. Star, 380.

19. Star, 381–82.

20. This is also a theme pursued prominently in Bill Brown, "Thing Theory," *Critical Inquiry*, 28.1 (2001), 4; and Terry Winograd and Fernando Flores, *Understanding Computers and Cognition: A New Foundation for Design*, 24th printing (Boston: Addison-Wesley, 2008), 77–78.

21. Star, "The Ethnography of Infrastructure," 384–87.

22. Star, 387–88.

23. Star, 388. For an actual history of this subject, see Joanna Bourke, *Rape: A History from 1860 to the Present Day* (London: Virago, 2010).

24. For a strong previous effort at such an analysis, see Louise Amoore, "Cloud Geographies: Computing, Data, Sovereignty," *Progress in Human Geography*, 42.1 (2018), 4–24, https://doi.org/10.1177/0309132516662147.

25. Geoffrey C. Bowker and Susan Leigh Star, *Sorting Things Out: Classification and Its Consequences*, Inside Technology (Cambridge, MA: MIT Press, 1999), 13–14.

26. Randall Monroe, "Standards," *xkcd*, 2011, https://xkcd.com/927/, accessed 10 September 2021.

27. See Richard Gillam, *Unicode Demystified: A Practical Programmer's Guide to the Encoding Standard* (Boston: Addison-Wesley, 2003).

28. Florian Coulmas, *Writing Systems: An Introduction to Their Linguistic Analysis* (Cambridge: Cambridge University Press, 2003), 201.

29. David Diringer, *The Alphabet: A Key to the History of Mankind* (London: Hutchinson's Scientific and Technical Publications, 1948), 578.

30. Coulmas, *Writing Systems*, 201.

31. Coulmas, 201.

32. That said, alphabetical ordering was also rare in the Middle Ages in Europe. See Dennis Duncan, *Index, A History of the: A Bookish Adventure* (London: Allen Lane, 2021), 23–27.

33. Thomas S. Mullaney, *The Chinese Typewriter: A History* (Cambridge, MA: MIT Press, 2017), 11. Italics removed from the original.

34. "Unicode 13.0 Versioned Charts Index," 2020, https://www.unicode.org/charts/PDF/Unicode-13.0/, accessed 6 October 2021.

35. "IRG Meeting No. 45 Website," 2015, https://appsrv.cse.cuhk.edu.hk/~irg/irg/irg45/IRG45.htm, accessed 6 October 2021.

36. Ermanen, "Is the Kanji/Kokuji 'Taito' (たいと) with 84 Strokes Legitimate and Ever Used?," Japanese Language Stack Exchange, 20 December 2014, https://japanese.stackexchange.com/q/20980.

37. Ashwin Purohit, "How Many Chinese Characters and Words Are in Use?," Ashwin Purohit (website), 2014, https://puroh.it/how-many-chinese-characters-and-words-are-in-use/, accessed 7 October 2021.

38. Ed Felten, "Taking Stevens Seriously," *Freedom to Tinker: Research and*

Expert Commentary on Digital Technologies in Public Life (blog),17 July 2006, https://freedom-to-tinker.com/2006/07/17/taking-stevens-seriously.

39. Domenico Fiormonte, "Digital Humanities and the Geopolitics of Knowledge," *Digital Studies/Le Champ Numérique*, 7.1 (2017), 5, https://doi.org /10.16995/dscn.274.

40. Andrew Blum, *Tubes: Behind the Scenes at the Internet* (London: Penguin, 2013), 124.

41. Kenneth Finnegan, "Creating an Autonomous System for Fun and Profit," *The Life of Kenneth* (blog), 15 November 2017, https://blog.thelifeofkenneth.com /2017/11/creating-autonomous-system-for-fun-and.html.

42. Finnegan.

43. William B. Norton, *The 2014 Internet Peering Playbook: Connecting to the Core of the Internet* (Palo Alto, CA: DrPeering Press, 2014).

44. Benedict Anderson, *Imagined Communities: Reflections on the Origin and Spread of Nationalism*, rev. ed (London: Verso, 2006), 3.

45. Anderson, 4.

46. Anderson, 6.

47. Anderson, 6.

48. Anderson, 7.

49. See, for example, Tim Worstall, "'I'll Believe Corporations Are People When Texas Executes One': What Is This Foolishness From Robert Reich?," *Forbes*, 17 November 2012, https://www.forbes.com/sites/timworstall/2012/11/ 17/ill-believe-corporations-are-people-when-texas-executes-one-what-is-this -foolishness-from-robert-reich.

50. Adam Winkler, "'Corporations Are People' Is Built on an Incredible 19th-Century Lie," *Atlantic*, 5 March 2018, https://www.theatlantic.com/busi ness/archive/2018/03/corporations-people-adam-winkler/554852/; Santa Clara County v. Southern Pacific Railroad Co., 118 U.S. 394 (1886).

51. Burwell v. Hobby Lobby Stores, Inc., 573 U.S. 682 (2014); Citizens United v. FEC, 558 U.S. 310 (2010).

52. Mark McGurl, *Everything and Less: The Novel in the Age of Amazon* (London: Verso, 2021), 9.

53. "Overview of the Privacy Act of 1974," US Department of Justice Archives website, 2014, https://www.justice.gov/archives/opcl/definitions, accessed 16 October 2021.

54. John Plunkett, "Carphone Axes Big Brother Deal," *Guardian*, 18 January 2007, https://www.theguardian.com/media/2007/jan/18/business.market ingandpr.

55. Stewart Lee. Oral remarks made during his 41st Best Stand Up Ever tour in 2008.

56. Martin Paul Eve, "Scarcity and Abundance," in *The Bloomsbury Handbook of Electronic Literature*, ed. by Joseph Tabbi (London: Bloomsbury, 2017), 385–98.

57. Laura DeNardis, *Protocol Politics: The Globalization of Internet Governance* (Cambridge, MA: MIT Press, 2009), 1–6.

58. Milton Mueller, *Ruling the Root: Internet Governance and the Taming of Cyberspace* (Cambridge, MA: MIT Press, 2002), 11.

59. Janet Abbate, *Inventing the Internet* (Cambridge, MA: MIT Press, 2000).

60. Mueller, *Ruling the Root*, 1–3.

61. Mueller, 3.

62. Mueller, 4.

63. Mueller, 5.

64. Mo Krochmal, "Magaziner, Lessig Spar over Domain Name Plan," *TechNWeb News*, 11 June 1998.

65. See Ray Hunt, "Transmission Control Protocol/Internet Protocol (TCP/IP)," in *Encyclopedia of Information Systems*, ed. by Hossein Bidgoli (New York: Elsevier, 2003), 489–510, https://doi.org/10.1016/B0-12-227240-4/00187-8.

66. Bruce Davie, "It's Time to Decentralize the Internet, Again: What Was Distributed Is Now Centralized by Google, Facebook, Etc," *Register*, 11 August 2021, https://www.theregister.com/2021/08/11/decentralized_internet.

67. Mueller, *Ruling the Root*, 6.

68. See Don Tapscott and Alex Tapscott, *The Blockchain Revolution: How the Technology behind Bitcoin Is Changing Money, Business, and the World* (New York: Penguin, 2016).

69. Yanmaani, "Proof of Stake Is a Scam and the People Promoting It Are Scammers," *Yanmaani's Blog*, 9 November 2021, https://yanmaani.github.io/proof-of-stake-is-a-scam-and-the-people-promoting-it-are-scammers.

70. This example is drawn from Antsstyle, "Why NFTs Are Bad: The Long Version," *Medium*, 24 October 2021, https://antsstyle.medium.com/why-nfts-are-bad-the-long-version-2c16dae145e2.

71. Antsstyle.

72. Richard M. Stallman, "Did You Say 'Intellectual Property'? It's a Seductive Mirage," Gnu.Org, 2015, https://www.gnu.org/philosophy/not-ipr.en.html, accessed 2 August 2015.

73. For more on identity, see my previous book, *Password* (New York: Bloomsbury, 2016).

74. "Tim Berners-Lee Sells Web Source Code NFT for $5.4m," BBC News, 30 June 2021, https://www.bbc.com/news/technology-57666335.

75. Satoshi Nakamoto, "Bitcoin: A Peer-to-Peer Electronic Cash System," *Decentralized Business Review*, 2008.

76. Markus Jakobsson and Ari Juels, "Proofs of Work and Bread Pudding Protocols," in *Secure Information Networks: Communications and Multimedia Security IFIP TC6/TC11 Joint Working Conference on Communications and Multimedia Security (CMS'99) September 20–21, 1999, Leuven, Belgium*, ed. by Bart Preneel, IFIP—The International Federation for Information Processing (Boston: Springer US, 1999), 258–72, https://doi.org/10.1007/978-0-387-35568-9_18; and Cynthia Dwork and Moni Naor, "Pricing via Processing or Combatting Junk Mail," in *Advances in Cryptology—CRYPTO' 92*, ed. by Ernest F. Brickell, Lecture Notes in Computer Science (Berlin: Springer, 1993), 139–47, https://doi.org/10.1007/3-540-48071-4_10.

77. See Arvind Narayanan et al., *Bitcoin and Cryptocurrency Technologies: A Comprehensive Introduction* (Princeton, NJ: Princeton University Press, 2016), chap. 2.

78. See Alex de Vries, "Renewable Energy Will Not Solve Bitcoin's Sustainability Problem," *Joule*, 3.4 (2019), 893–98, https://doi.org/10.1016/j.joule.2019.02.007.

79. Alex de Vries and Christian Stoll, "Bitcoin's Growing E-Waste Problem," *Resources, Conservation and Recycling*, 175 (2021), 105901, https://doi.org/10.1016/j.resconrec.2021.105901.

80. "Bitcoin Energy Consumption Index," Digiconomist, https://digiconomist.net/bitcoin-energy-consumption/, accessed 26 October 2021.

81. De Vries and Stoll, "Bitcoin's Growing E-Waste Problem."

82. Yanmaani, "Proof of Stake Is a Scam."

83. Christian Stoll, Lena Klaaßen, and Ulrich Gallersdörfer, "The Carbon Footprint of Bitcoin," *Joule*, 3.7 (2019), 1647–61, https://doi.org/10.1016/j.joule.2019.05.012.

84. David Thomas, "Policy Reform Required as Swedish Director Generals Look to Ban Proof-of-Work Mining," BeInCrypto, 7 November 2021, https://beincrypto.com/?p=166381.

85. Hamza Abusalah et al., "Beyond Hellman's Time-Memory Trade-Offs with Applications to Proofs of Space," in *Advances in Cryptology—ASIACRYPT 2017*, ed. by Tsuyoshi Takagi and Thomas Peyrin, Lecture Notes in Computer Science (Cham: Springer International Publishing, 2017), 357–79, https://doi.org/10.1007/978-3-319-70697-9_13.

86. Merlinda Andoni et al., "Blockchain Technology in the Energy Sector: A Systematic Review of Challenges and Opportunities," *Renewable and Sustainable Energy Reviews*, 100 (2019), 143–74, https://doi.org/10.1016/j.rser.2018.10.014.

87. Jorge Stolfi, "Bitcoin Is a Ponzi," State University of Campinas, 2 January 2021, https://ic.unicamp.br/~stolfi/bitcoin/2020-12-31-bitcoin-ponzi.html, accessed.

88. Cong T. Nguyen et al., "Proof-of-Stake Consensus Mechanisms for Future Blockchain Networks: Fundamentals, Applications and Opportunities," *IEEE Access*, 7 (2019), 85727–45, https://doi.org/10.1109/ACCESS.2019 .2925010.

89. For more, see Robert K. Merton, "The Matthew Effect in Science," *Science*, 159.3810 (1968), 56–63.

90. Much of this is derived from Antsstyle, "Why NFTs Are Bad."

91. Alexander Savelyev, *Contract Law 2.0: "Smart" Contracts as the Beginning of the End of Classic Contract Law* (Rochester, NY: Social Science Research Network, 14 December 2016), https://doi.org/10.2139/ssrn.2885241.

92. Karl Marx, *Capital*, vol. 1 (London: Penguin, 1992), 163.

93. "Squid Game Cryptocurrency Rockets in First Few Days of Trading," BBC News, 29 October 2021, https://www.bbc.com/news/business-59059097.

94. MacKenzie Sigalos, "'Squid Game' Crypto Token Cost One Shanghai Investor His Life Savings of $28,000 after Coin Plunged to Near Zero," CNBC, 2 November 2021, https://www.cnbc.com/2021/11/02/squid-game-token-cost -one-investor-28000-after-coin-plunged.html.

95. For more on how digital metaphors have shaped the legal sphere, see I. Glenn Cohen and Jonathan H. Blavin, "Gore, Gibson, and Goldsmith: The Evolution of Internet Metaphors in Law and Commentary," *Harvard Journal of Law & Technology*, 16.1 (2002), 265–85.

96. Lawrence Lessig, *Code: Version 2.0* (New York: Basic Books, 2006), 2–3.

97. Lessig, 15–16.

98. Michael Clarke and Laura Ricci, *Open Access EBook Supply Chain Maps for Distribution and Usage Reporting* (Zenodo, 9 April 2021), https://doi.org/10 .5281/zenodo.4681871.

99. S. Nazrul Islam and John Winkel, "Climate Change and Social Inequality," *DESA Working Papers*, 152, 2017.

100. See, for instance, Jacob Katz Cogan, "The Look Within: Property, Capacity, and Suffrage in Nineteenth-Century America," *Yale Law Journal*, 107.2 (1997), 473–98, https://doi.org/10.2307/797262.

Chapter Five

1. For more, see Matthew Rubery, *The Untold Story of the Talking Book* (Cambridge, MA: Harvard University Press, 2016).

2. Matthew G. Kirschenbaum, *Bitstreams: The Future of Digital Literary Heritage* (Philadelphia: University of Pennsylvania Press, 2021), 102.

3. Charles Howard Hinton, *The Fourth Dimension* (New York: Arno Press, 1976); and Mark Blacklock, *The Emergence of the Fourth Dimension: Higher Spatial Thinking in the Fin de Siècle* (Oxford: Oxford University Press, 2018).

4. Much of this section is indebted to Blacklock, *The Emergence of the Fourth Dimension* for the basic background about and emergence of higher-dimensional thinking.

5. David Harvey, "The Geopolitics of Capitalism," in *Social Relations and Spatial Structures*, ed. by Derek Gregory and John Urry, Critical Human Geography (London: Macmillan Education UK, 1985), 141, https://doi.org/10.1007/978-1-349-27935-7_7.

6. Michel Foucault, "The Eye of Power," in *Power/Knowledge: Selected Interviews and Other Writings, 1972–1977*, ed. and trans. by Colin Gordon (Brighton: Harvester Press, 1980), 149–50.

7. For more on this, see Alice Jenkins, *Space and the "March of Mind": Literature and the Physical Sciences in Britain, 1815–1850* (Oxford: Oxford University Press, 2007); and Graham Bird, "Kant's Transcendental Aesthetic," *British Journal for the History of Philosophy*, 7.1 (1999), 147–53.

8. Jerrold Levinson and Philip Alperson, "What Is a Temporal Art?," in *Musical Concerns* (Oxford: Oxford University Press, 2015), https://doi.org/10.1093/acprof:oso/9780199669660.003.0013.

9. See Blacklock, *The Emergence of the Fourth Dimension*, chap. 4.

10. Blacklock has also written a novel that charts Hinton's life. See Mark Blacklock, *Hinton* (London: Granta, 2020).

11. Library of Congress, "Microsoft Office Word 97–2003 Binary File Format (.Doc)," Sustainability of Digital Formats: Planning for Library of Congress Collections website, 2019, https://www.loc.gov/preservation/digital/formats/fdd/fdd000509.shtml, accessed 11 November 2021.

12. Gary Kessler, "File Signatures," GaryKessler.net, 2021, https://www.garykessler.net/library/file_sigs.html, accessed 11 November 2021.

13. Microsoft, "[MS-DOC]: FibRgFcLcb2002," 2021, https://docs.microsoft.com/en-us/openspecs/office_file_formats/ms-doc/fce09f81-704b-460d-9bca-f7dc121aed66, accessed 11 November 2021.

14. Merve Emre, *Paraliterary: The Making of Bad Readers in Postwar America* (Chicago: University of Chicago Press, 2017).

15. Kenneth Burke, *Counter-Statement* (Berkeley: University of California Press, 1968), 70.

16. Emre, *Paraliterary*, 3.

17. Daniel Aleksandersen, "Windows 11 Blocks Edge Browser Competitors from Opening Links," *Ctrl Blog*, last updated 13 December 2021, https://www.ctrl.blog/entry/microsoft-edge-protocol-competition.html.

18. Brad Jones, "The Rise and Fall of Internet Explorer," Digital Trends, 2015, https://www.digitaltrends.com/computing/the-rise-and-fall-of-internet-explorer/, accessed 12 November 2021.

19. See Mark McGurl, *Everything and Less: The Novel in the Age of Amazon* (London: Verso, 2021).

20. Although see Alvaro Videla, "Programming Languages Are Not Languages," Medium, 1 September 2018, https://old-sound.medium.com/programming-languages-are-not-languages-c6f161a78c44.

21. Louis Althusser et al., *Reading Capital: The Complete Edition*, trans. by Ben Brewster and David Fernbach (London: Verso, 2015), 32. Emphasis in original.

22. Althusser et al., 27.

23. See Cynthia Running-Johnson, "Reading Life Signs in Jean Genet's 'Atelier d'Alberto Giacometti' and 'Ce qui est resté d'un Rembrandt...,'" *L'Esprit Créateur*, 35.1 (1995), 20–29; Jacques Derrida, *Glas*, trans. by John P. Leavey Jr. and Richard Rand (Lincoln: University of Nebraska Press, 1986); and Roland Barthes, *S/Z* (Oxford: John Wiley & Sons, 2009).

24. John Hollander, "It All Depends," *Social Research*, 58.1 (1991), 44.

25. Hollander, 34.

26. Steven Connor, *The Madness of Knowledge: On Wisdom, Ignorance and Fantasies of Knowing* (London: Reaktion Books, 2019), 242–43.

27. Mary Douglas, "The Idea of a Home: A Kind of Space," *Social Research*, 58.1 (1991), 289.

28. Hollander, "It All Depends," 37.

29. John Berger, *And Our Faces, My Heart, Brief as Photos* (London: Writers and Readers Publishing Cooperative, 1984), 55.

30. Nigel Rapport and Andrew Dawson, eds., *Migrants of Identity: Perceptions of Home in a World of Movement* (Oxford: Berg, 1998), 6–7.

31. Rapport and Dawson, 7.

32. Aviezer Tucker, "In Search of Home," *Journal of Applied Philosophy*, 11.2 (1994), 184, https://doi.org/10.1111/j.1468-5930.1994.tb00107.x.

33. Shelley Mallett, "Understanding Home: A Critical Review of the Literature," *Sociological Review*, 52.1 (2004), 69, https://doi.org/10.1111/j.1467-954X.2004.00442.x.

34. Doreen Massey, "Double Articulation: A Place in the World," in *Displacements: Cultural Identities in Question*, ed. by Angelika Bammer (Bloomington: Indiana University Press, 1994), 119.

35. For more, see Owen Clayton, ed., *Representing Homelessness*, Proceedings of the British Academy (Oxford: Oxford University Press, 2022).

36. Andrew Mercado, *Super Aussie Soaps—Behind the Scenes of Australia's Best Loved TV Shows* (Melbourne: Pluto Press Australia Limited, 2004), 251.

37. Jessa Lingel, *The Gentrification of the Internet: How to Reclaim Our Digital Freedom* (Berkeley: University of California Press, 2021).

38. Gina M. Pérez, *The Near Northwest Side Story: Migration, Displacement, and Puerto Rican Families* (Berkeley: University of California Press, 2004), 139.

39. Lingel, *The Gentrification of the Internet*, 10.

40. Lingel, 10.

41. For more on this, see Julia Bell, *Radical Attention* (London: Peninsula Press, 2020).

42. Lingel, *The Gentrification of the Internet*, 11–14.

43. Lingel, 15.

44. For more on platformization, see Penny C. S. Andrews, "The Platformization of Open," in *Reassembling Scholarly Communications: Histories, Infrastructures, and Global Politics of Open Access*, ed. by Martin Paul Eve and Jonathan Gray (Cambridge, MA: MIT Press, 2020).

45. Lingel, *The Gentrification of the Internet*, 15.

46. "About the WordPress Foundation," WordPress Foundation, 2021, https://wordpressfoundation.org/, accessed 10 December 2021.

47. For more on this, see Sabina Leonelli, *Philosophy of Open Science* (Cambridge: Cambridge University Press, 2023), https://doi.org/10.1017/9781009416368.

48. "Philosophy," WordPress Foundation, 2010, https://wordpressfoundation.org/philosophy/, accessed 10 December 2021.

49. For my previous work on this, see Martin Paul Eve, *Open Access and the Humanities: Contexts, Controversies and the Future* (Cambridge: Cambridge University Press, 2014), https://doi.org/10.1017/CBO9781316161012.

50. William H. Oakland, "Theory of Public Goods," in *Handbook of Public Economics*, vol. 2, ed. by Alan J. Auerbach and Martin S. Feldstein, Handbooks in Economics (Amsterdam: Elsevier, 1985), 485. See also Paul A. Samuelson, "The Pure Theory of Public Expenditure," *Review of Economics and Statistics*, 36.4 (1954), 387–89, https://doi.org/10.2307/1925895.

51. Oakland, "Theory of Public Goods," 2:485.

52. Oakland, 2: 485.

53. Timothy Morton, *Hyperobjects: Philosophy and Ecology for the End of the World* (Minneapolis: University of Minnesota Press, 2013).

54. Marilys Guillemin and Lynn Gillam, "Ethics, Reflexivity, and 'Ethically Important Moments' in Research," *Qualitative Inquiry*, 10.2 (2004), 266, https://doi.org/10.1177/1077800403262360. See also Paul A. Komesaroff, "From Bioethics to Microethics: Ethical Debate and Clinical Medicine," in *Troubled Bodies: Critical Perspectives on Postmodernism, Medical Ethics, and the Body*, ed. by Paul A. Komesaroff (Durham, NC: Duke University Press, 1995), 62–86, https://doi.org/10.1515/9780822379782-004.

55. Perry Hendricks, "The Axiology of Abortion: Should We Hope Pro-

Choicers or Pro-Lifers Are Right?," *Ergo*, 7.29 (2021), 774, https://doi.org/10.39 98/ergo.1126.

56. "Right to Participate in Cultural Life," UNESCO, 2019, https://en .unesco.org/human-rights/cultural-life, accessed 11 December 2021.

57. Kate Nash, "The Cultural Politics of Human Rights and Neoliberalism," *Journal of Human Rights*, 18.5 (2019), 490–505, https://doi.org/10.1080/14754835 .2019.1653174.

58. I am indebted, for much of this section, to the work of my former PhD student Stuart Lawson. Stuart Lawson, "Open Access Policy in the UK: From Neoliberalism to the Commons" (unpublished doctoral thesis, Birkbeck, University of London, 2019), https://hcommons.org/deposits/item/hc:23661/, accessed 1 June 2019.

59. Karl Popper, *The Logic of Scientific Discovery* (London: Routledge, 2010), 10.

60. Karl Popper, *The Open Society and Its Enemies*, vol. 1, *The Spell of Plato* (Abingdon: Routledge, 2003), 29.

61. Popper, 1:62–63.

62. Karl Popper, *Conjectures and Refutations: The Growth of Scientific Knowledge*, Routledge Classics (London: Routledge, 2002), 452.

63. Popper, 453.

64. Popper, *The Open Society and Its Enemies*, 1:132–35.

65. Lawson, "Open Access Policy in the UK," 109.

66. Karl Popper, *The Open Society and Its Enemies*, vol. 2, *Hegel and Marx* (Abingdon: Routledge, 2003), 135.

67. Popper, *The Open Society and Its Enemies*, 1:117.

68. Popper, *The Open Society and Its Enemies*, 2:135.

69. Friedrich Hayek, *The Road to Serfdom* (Abingdon: Routledge, 2001), 1–5. The point about Hayek's historicism comes from Lawson, "Open Access Policy in the UK," 98.

70. Friedrich Hayek, *The Constitution of Liberty* (Abingdon: Routledge, 2006), 12.

71. Hayek, 19.

72. André Azevedo Alves and John Meadowcroft, "Hayek's Slippery Slope, the Stability of the Mixed Economy and the Dynamics of Rent Seeking," *Political Studies*, 62.4 (2014), 857, https://doi.org/10.1111/1467-9248.12043.

73. See William Davies, *The Limits of Neoliberalism: Authority, Sovereignty and the Logic of Competition* (Thousand Oaks, CA: SAGE, 2014).

74. Mitja Sardoč, "The Language of Neoliberalism in Education," in *The Impacts of Neoliberal Discourse and Language in Education: Critical Perspectives on a Rhetoric of Equality, Well-Being, and Justice*, ed. by Mitja Sardoč, Rout-

ledge Studies in Education, Neoliberalism, and Marxism (New York: Routledge, 2021), 5.

75. Stephen J. Ball, *The Education Debate* (Bristol: Policy, 2008), 1.

76. Kelly L. Grotke and Stephen Hastings-King, "Historical Genesis of the Relation between Science, Numbers and Politics—Part I Introduction," in *Science, Numbers and Politics*, ed. by Markus J. Prutsch (New York: Springer Berlin Heidelberg, 2019), 22.

77. Steven Connor, *Living by Numbers: In Defence of Quantity* (London: Reaktion Books, 2016), 12.

Chapter Six

1. Thomas D. Erickson, "Working with Interface Metaphors," in *The Art of Human-Computer Interface Design*, ed. by Brenda Laurel (Reading, MA: Addison-Wesley, 1990), 71.

2. See Thierry Bardini, *Bootstrapping: Douglas Engelbart, Coevolution, and the Origins of Personal Computing*, Writing Science (Stanford, CA: Stanford University Press, 2000), 81–102.

3. John Markoff, "Computer Visionary Who Invented the Mouse," *New York Times*, 3 July 2013, https://www.nytimes.com/2013/07/04/technology/douglas-c-engelbart-inventor-of-the-computer-mouse-dies-at-88.html.

4. Bardini, *Bootstrapping*, 95.

5. For more on the complexities, see Daniel Donahoo, "Why the A Magazine Is an iPad That Does Not Work Video Is Ridiculous," *Wired*, 14 October 2011, https://www.wired.com/2011/10/why-the-a-magazine-is-an-ipad-that-does-not-work-video-is-ridiculous.

6. Jimmy Maher, "Doing Windows, Part 2: From Interface Manager to Windows The Digital Antiquarian," *The Digital Antiquarian* (blog), 2018, https://www.filfre.net/2018/06/doing-windows-part-2-from-interface-manager-to-windows/, accessed 12 December 2021.

7. Maher, "Doing Windows, Part 2."

8. B. Lampson, personal interview by Thierry Bardini, 1997; and Bardini, *Bootstrapping*, 126.

9. Scientific Data Systems, "SDS 940 Time-Sharing Computer System Manual," 1966, 7.

10. The most well-known historical account of this phenomenon is, of course, Walter J Ong, *Orality and Literacy: The Technologizing of the Word* (London: Routledge, 2002).

11. For more, see Maria Teresa Zanola, "Les anglicismes et le français du XXIe siècle : La fin du franglais?," *Synergies*, 4, 2008, 87–96. A whole industry satirizing such cultures has sprung up. See Miles Kington, *Le bumper book de*

franglais (Brecon: Old Street, 2011), https://archive.org/details/lebumperbook defrooooking_h5x9.

12. Jeremy Reimer, "A History of the GUI," *Ars Technica*, 5 May 2005, https://arstechnica.com/features/2005/05/gui.

13. "Desktop Metaphor," 2001, https://web.archive.org/web/20010222011552/http://www.csdl.tamu.edu/~lof0954/academic/cpsc610/hw2-3.htm, accessed 14 December 2021.

14. Yoni Heisler, "The Most Viewed Photo in the History of the World," BGR, 2015, https://bgr.com/general/most-viewed-photograph-windows-xp/, accessed 15 December 2021.

15. "Bliss by Charles O'Rear—Iconic Photograph," Amateur Photographer, 28 May 2012, https://www.amateurphotographer.co.uk/iconic-images/bliss-by-charles-orear-iconic-photograph-13083.

16. Cynthia Sweeney, "Say Goodbye to 'Bliss,'" *Napa Valley Register*, 26 March 2014, https://napavalleyregister.com/star/lifestyles/say-goodbye-to-bliss/article_2c485132-b504-11e3-85ef-0019bb2963f4.html.

17. Raymond Chen, "Windows Brings out the Rorschach Test in Everyone," *The Old New Thing*, (blog), Microsoft, August 25, 2003, https://devblogs.microsoft.com/oldnewthing/20030825-00/?p=42803, accessed 15 December 2021.

18. Carolyn Younger, "Windows XP Desktop Screen Is a Napa Image," *Napa Valley Register*, 18 January 2010, https://napavalleyregister.com/news/local/windows-xp-desktop-screen-is-a-napa-image/article_7703c8b2-03e9-11df-bb34-001cc4c03286.html.

19. Rachel DeSantis, "Inside the Real-Life Love Story That Inspired Microsoft's 'Bliss,' the Most Viewed Photo Ever," PEOPLE.Com, 14 April 2021, https://people.com/human-interest/how-an-unlikely-love-story-inspired-bliss-famous-microsoft-photo.

20. Bardini, *Bootstrapping*, 151.

21. For instance, the Android subsystem that handles the display screen is called SurfaceFlinger.

22. Jennifer G. Steiner and Daniel E. Geer Jr., "Network Services in the Athena Environment," *Proceedings of the Winter 1988 Usenix Conference*, 1988.

23. Fred Moody, *I Sing the Body Electronic: A Year with Microsoft on the Multimedia Frontier* (New York: Penguin Books, 1996), 15.

24. See, for instance Derek Parfit, "Personal Identity," *Philosophical Review*, 80.1 (1971), 3–27.

25. Ludwig Wittgenstein, *Philosophical Investigations: The German Text, with a Revised English Translation* (Oxford: Blackwell, 2001), sec. 80.

26. Lucy, "Inside the Mac OS X Kernel" (presented at the 24th Chaos Communication Congress 24C3, Berlin, 2007), 5.

27. Erickson, "Working with Interface Metaphors," 65.

28. Moody, *I Sing the Body Electronic*, 57.

29. Tim Nudd, "Apple's 'Get a Mac,' the Complete Campaign," AdWeek, 2011, https://www.adweek.com/creativity/apples-get-mac-complete-campaign-130552/, accessed 31 January 2022.

30. Matthew Russell, "What Is Quartz (or Why Can't Windows Do That)," O'Reilly Media, 2013, https://web.archive.org/web/20130527151142/http://oreilly.com/pub/a/mac/2005/10/11/what-is-quartz.html, accessed 13 January 2022.

31. Apple, "Human Interface Guidelines," Apple Developer, 2022, https://developer.apple.com/design/human-interface-guidelines/macos/overview/themes/#//apple_ref/doc/uid/TP40002723-TPXREF101, accessed 13 January 2022.

32. David Muggleton and Rupert Weinzierl, *The Post-Subcultures Reader* (Oxford: Berg, 2003), 4–5.

33. Bruce Tognazzini, "Consistency," in Laurel, *The Art of Human-Computer Interface Design*, 77.

34. Verhaert, "User Inyerface: A Worst-Practice UI Experiment," 2023, https://userinyerface.com/. For more on this, see Martin Paul Eve, *Password* (New York: Bloomsbury, 2016).

35. "<blink>: The Blinking Text Element—HTML: HyperText Markup Language," MDN Web Docs, Mozilla, 2022, https://developer.mozilla.org/en-US/docs/Web/HTML/Element/blink.

36. Shannon Mattern, *A City Is Not a Computer: Other Urban Intelligences*, Places Books (Princeton, NJ: Princeton University Press, 2021). See also Ranjodh Singh Dhaliwal, "On Addressability, or What Even Is Computation?," *Critical Inquiry*, 49.1 (2022), 1–27, https://doi.org/10.1086/721167.

37. Raphael Lyne, *Memory and Intertextuality in Renaissance Literature* (Cambridge: Cambridge University Press, 2016), 26–27.

38. Lyne, 27.

39. Carl DiSalvo, *Design as Democratic Inquiry: Putting Experimental Civics into Practice* (Cambridge, MA: MIT Press, 2022), 15–33.

40. See Gabriella Coleman, *Coding Freedom: The Ethics and Aesthetics of Hacking* (Princeton, NJ: Princeton University Press, 2012); and Gabriella Coleman, "The Political Agnosticism of Free and Open Source Software and the Inadvertent Politics of Contrast," *Anthropological Quarterly*, 77.3 (2004), 507–19, https://doi.org/10.2307/3318232.

41. For more on the carnivalesque, see Mikhail Bakhtin, *Rabelais and His World* (Bloomington: Indiana University Press, 1984).

42. Grahame String Weinbren, "Mastery: Computer Games, Intuitive Interfaces, and Interactive Multimedia," *Leonardo*, 28.5 (1995), 404, https://doi .org/10.2307/1576225.

43. Kristine Jorgensen, *Gameworld Interfaces* (Cambridge, MA: MIT Press, 2013), 4.

44. Cathie Marache-Francisco and Eric Brangier, "Gamification and Human-Machine Interaction: A Synthesis," *Le travail humain*, 78.2 (2015), 165, https://doi.org/10.3917/th.782.0165.

45. Marache-Francisco and Brangier, 166.

46. Jorgensen, *Gameworld Interfaces*, 19.

47. Matthew G. Kirschenbaum, "Hello Worlds," *Chronicle of Higher Education*, 23 January 2009, https://www.chronicle.com/article/Hello-Worlds/5476; and Roopika Risam, *New Digital Worlds: Postcolonial Digital Humanities in Theory, Praxis, and Pedagogy* (Evanston, IL: Northwestern University Press, 2018), 33–34. See also David West, *Object Thinking* (Redmond, WA: Microsoft Press, 2004).

48. Jorgensen, *Gameworld Interfaces*, 4; Andrew Baerg, "WIMPing Out," *Symplokē*, 22.1–2 (2014), 309, https://doi.org/10.5250/symploke.22.1-2.0307.

49. For more, see the playful Jacques Derrida, "The Law of Genre," trans. by Avital Ronell, *Critical Inquiry*, 7.1 (1980), 55–81.

50. D. Christopher Ralston and Justin Ho, "Introduction: Philosophical Reflections on Disability," in *Philosophical Reflections on Disability*, ed. by D. Christopher Ralston and Justin Ho, Philosophy and Medicine (Dordrecht: Springer Verlag, 2010), 1–16.

51. Tom Shakespeare et al., "Models," in *Encyclopedia of Disability*, ed. by Gary L. Albrecht (Thousand Oaks, CA: Sage Publications, 2006), 1103.

52. Rosemarie Garland-Thomson, "Feminist Disability Studies," *Signs: Journal of Women in Culture and Society*, 30.2 (2005), 1567–68, https://doi.org /10.1086/423352.

53. Rachel Carroll, "'Making the Blood Flow Backwards': Disability, Heterosexuality and the Politics of Representation in Julian Barnes's *The Sense of an Ending*," *Textual Practice*, 2014, 155–72, https://doi.org/10.1080/0950236X .2014.955818.

54. Marshall McLuhan, Quentin Fiore, and Jerome Agel, *The Medium Is the Massage* (Gingko Press, 1967), http://archive.org/details/pdfy-vNiFct6b-L5ucJEa.

55. Alan Liu, *Local Transcendence: Essays on Postmodern Historicism and the Database* (Chicago: University of Chicago Press, 2008), 214–15. I first covered this distinction in Liu in Martin Paul Eve, "Review of Alan Liu, Local

Transcendence: Essays on Postmodern Historicism and the Database," *Textual Practice*, 24.6 (2010), 1117–19, https://doi.org/10.1080/0950236X.2010.521676.

56. Much of this section is indebted to Digital Education Strategies, the Chang School, and Greg Gay, "The Evolution of Web Accessibility," in *Professional Web Accessibility Auditing Made Easy* (Toronto: Ryerson University Press, 2019), https://pressbooks.library.ryerson.ca/pwaa/chapter/the-evolution-of-web-accessibility/, accessed 10 January 2022.

57. Laurel, *The Art of Human-Computer Interface Design*.

58. S. Joy Mountford and William W. Gaver, "Talking and Listening to Computers," in Laurel, *The Art of Human-Computer Interface Design*, 334; Gitta Salomon, "New Uses for Color," in Laurel, *The Art of Human-Computer Interface Design*, 271.

59. S. Joy Mountford, "Technique and Technology," in Laurel, *The Art of Human-Computer Interface Design*, 249.

60. Again, see Digital Education Strategies, the Chang School, and Gay, "The Evolution of Web Accessibility."

61. For more on this, see Randall Owen and Sarah Parker Harris, "'No Rights without Responsibilities': Disability Rights and Neoliberal Reform under New Labour," *Disability Studies Quarterly*, 32.3 (2012), https://doi.org/10.18061/dsq.v32i3.3283; Teodor Mladenov, "Neoliberalism, Postsocialism, Disability," *Disability & Society*, 30.3 (2015), 445–59, https://doi.org/10.1080/09687599.2015.1021758; Dikaios Sakellariou and Elena S. Rotarou, "The Effects of Neoliberal Policies on Access to Healthcare for People with Disabilities," *International Journal for Equity in Health*, 16.1 (2017), 1–8, https://doi.org/10.1186/s12939-017-0699-3; and Goodley and Rebecca Lawthom, "Critical Disability Studies, Brexit and Trump: A Time of Neoliberal–Ableism," *Rethinking History*, 23.2 (2019), 233–51, https://doi.org/10.1080/13642529.2019.1607476.

62. Mehrunisha Suleman, "6 out of 10 People Who Have Died from COVID-19 Are Disabled," 2021, https://www.health.org.uk/news-and-comment/news/6-out-of-10-people-who-have-died-from-covid-19-are-disabled, accessed 18 January 2022.

63. Catherine E. Barrett et al., "Risk for Newly Diagnosed Diabetes >30 Days After SARS-CoV-2 Infection among Persons Aged <18 Years—United States, March 1, 2020–June 28, 2021," *MMWR (Morbidity and Mortality Weekly Report)*, 71.2 (2022), 59–65, https://doi.org/10.15585/mmwr.mm7102e2.

64. Lynne Segal, *Out of Time: The Pleasures and the Perils of Ageing* (London: Verso Books, 2013), 260.

65. Sarah Lamb, "Beyond the View of the West," in *Routledge Handbook of Cultural Gerontology*, ed. by Julia Twigg (London: Routledge, 2015), 37.

66. Margaret Morganroth Gullette, "Aged by Culture," in Twigg, *Routledge Handbook of Cultural Gerontology*, 21–28.

67. For more on symbolic economy and power, see Pierre Bourdieu, "Social Space and Symbolic Power," *Sociological Theory*, 7.1 (1989), 14–25, https://doi.org/10.2307/202060. See also Anne Jourdain, "Analysing the Symbolic Economy with Pierre Bourdieu: The World of Crafts," *Forum for Social Economics*, 47.3–4 (2018), 342–61, https://doi.org/10.1080/07360932.2015.1075895.

68. For some of the foundational texts in critical literary disability studies, see Rosemarie Garland-Thomson, *Extraordinary Bodies: Figuring Physical Disability in American Culture and Literature* (New York: Columbia University Press, 2017); David T. Mitchell and Sharon L. Snyder, *Narrative Prosthesis: Disability and the Dependencies of Discourse*, Corporealities (Ann Arbor: University of Michigan Press, 2001); Ato Quayson, *Aesthetic Nervousness: Disability and the Crisis of Representation* (New York: Columbia University Press, 2007); and Michael Bérubé, *The Secret Life of Stories: From Don Quixote to Harry Potter, How Understanding Intellectual Disability Transforms the Way We Read* (New York: New York University Press, 2016).

69. Harlan Hahn, "The Politics of Physical Differences: Disability and Discrimination," *Journal of Social Issues*, 44.1 (1988), 43, https://doi.org/10.1111/j.1540-4560.1988.tb02047.x.

70. Elizabeth F. Emens, "Framing Disability," *University of Illinois Law Review*, 5, 2012, 1406.

71. Ferdinand de Saussure, *Course in General Linguistics*, trans. by Roy Harris, Reprint edition (LaSalle, IL: Open Court, 1998).

72. For more, see Matthew G. Kirschenbaum, *Mechanisms: New Media and the Forensic Imagination* (Cambridge, MA: MIT Press, 2008); and Matthew G. Kirschenbaum, "Extreme Inscription: Towards a Grammatology of the Hard Drive," *Text Technology*, 2, 2004, 91–125.

Chapter Seven

1. Colin Warn, "Coding Is 90% Google Searching—A Brief Note for Beginners," Medium, 4 July 2019, 90, https://medium.com/@DJVeaux/coding-is-90-google-searching-a-brief-note-for-beginners-f2f1161876b1.

2. Paul Gooding and Melissa Terras, "Inheriting Library Cards to Babel and Alexandria: Contemporary Metaphors for the Digital Library," *International Journal on Digital Libraries*, 18.3 (2017), 208, https://doi.org/10.1007/s00799-016-0194-2. Other studies of metaphor in the digital library space include Catherine Kennedy, "Metaphor: Library" (unpublished master's thesis, University of Cape Town, 2007), https://open.uct.ac.za/handle/11427/8071, accessed 4 October 2022; Jeffrey Pomerantz and Gary Marchionini, "The Digital Library as

Place," *Journal of Documentation*, 63.4 (2007), 505–33, https://doi.org/10.1108/00220410710758995; and Moira Smith and Paul Yachnes, "Scholar's Playground or Wisdom's Temple? Competing Metaphors in a Library Electronic Text Center," *Library Trends*, 46.4 (1998), 718–31.

3. Joan Giesecke, "Finding the Right Metaphor: Restructuring, Realigning, and Repackaging Today's Research Libraries," *Journal of Library Administration*, 51.1 (2010), 54–65, https://doi.org/10.1080/01930826.2011.531641.

4. Kennedy, "Metaphor: Library," 1.

5. Robert F. Nardini, "A Search for Meaning: American Library Metaphors, 1876–1926," *Library Quarterly: Information, Community, Policy*, 71.2 (2001), 113.

6. Mark S. Ackerman, "Metaphors along the Information Highway," in *Proceedings of the Symposium on Directions and Impacts of Advanced Computing (DIAC 94)* (Cambridge, MA, 1994), 3, http://www.douri.sh/classes/ics234cw04/ackerman.pdf.

7. Ulrike Felt, "Sociotechnical Imaginaries of 'the Internet,' Digital Health Information and the Making of Citizen-Patients," in *Science and Democracy: Making Knowledge and Making Power in the Biosciences and Beyond*, ed. by Stephen Hilgartner, Clark Miller, and Rob Hagendijk (New York: Routledge, Taylor & Francis Group, 2015), 176–97.

8. For another set of thoughts on how digital libraries are shaped by metaphor, see part 1 of Mark Stefik, ed., *Internet Dreams: Archetypes, Myths, and Metaphors* (Cambridge, MA: MIT Press, 2001).

9. Much of this chapter is indebted to Stuart Lawson, "The Political Histories of UK Public Libraries and Access to Knowledge," in *Reassembling Scholarly Communications: Histories, Infrastructures, and Global Politics of Open Access*, ed. by Martin Paul Eve and Jonathan Gray (Cambridge, MA: MIT Press, 2020), 161–72.

10. Caroline Bassett, "Feminism, Refusal, Artificial Writing," *Transmediale*, 2021, https://202122.transmediale.de/almanac/feminism-refusal-artificial-writing, accessed 18 March 2023; Wendy Hui Kyong Chun, "On 'Sourcery,' or Code as Fetish," *Configurations*, 16.3 (2008), 299–324, https://doi.org/10.1353/con.0.0064; and David M. Berry and Anders Fagerjord, *Digital Humanities: Knowledge and Critique in a Digital Age* (Cambridge: Polity, 2017).

11. Idealistic notions of what libraries are and what they do, however, have been a longstanding feature of their constitution. See S. R. Ranganathan, *The Five Laws of Library Science* (Madras, London: The Madras Library Association, 1931), https://catalog.hathitrust.org/Record/001661182.

12. Thomas Kelly, *History of Public Libraries in Great Britain, 1845–1975* (London: Library Association Publishing, 1977), 3–4.

13. Alistair Black, *The Public Library in Britain, 1914–2000* (London: The British Library, 2000), 115.

14. Miron Grindea, ed., *The London Library* (Ipswich: Boydell Press, 1978), 3, http://archive.org/details/londonlibrary0000unse, accessed 9 May 2022.

15. On this, I recommend the work of Janneke Adema and Sam Moore. Janneke Adema and Samuel A. Moore, "Collectivity and Collaboration: Imagining New Forms of Communality to Create Resilience in Scholar-Led Publishing," *Insights*, 31.1 (2018), https://doi.org/10.1629/uksg.399; and Samuel Moore, "Common Struggles: Policy-Based vs. Scholar-Led Approaches to Open Access in the Humanities" (unpublished doctoral thesis, King's College London, 2019), https://hcommons.org/deposits/item/hc:24135/, accessed 6 June 2019.

16. See, for example Balázs Bodó, "The Genesis of Library Genesis: The Birth of a Global Scholarly Shadow Library," in *Shadow Libraries: Access to Educational Materials in Global Higher Education*, ed. by Joe Karaganis (Cambridge, MA: MIT Press, 2018), 25–52.

17. For more on the overused but nonetheless helpful term "neoliberalism," see William Davies, *The Limits of Neoliberalism: Authority, Sovereignty and the Logic of Competition* (Thousand Oaks, CA: SAGE, 2014); Wendy Brown, *Undoing the Demos: Neoliberalism's Stealth Revolution* (New York: Zone Books, 2015); and Wendy Brown, *In the Ruins of Neoliberalism: The Rise of Antidemocratic Politics in the West*, The Wellek Library Lectures (New York: Columbia University Press, 2019).

18. For more, see Martin Paul Eve, *Open Access and the Humanities: Contexts, Controversies and the Future* (Cambridge: Cambridge University Press, 2014), https://doi.org/10.1017/CBO9781316161012.

19. For more, see Vincent Larivière, Stefanie Haustein, and Philippe Mongeon, "The Oligopoly of Academic Publishers in the Digital Era," *PLOS ONE*, 10.6 (2015), e0127502, https://doi.org/10.1371/journal.pone.0127502.

20. Michael Bhaskar, *The Content Machine: Towards a Theory of Publishing From the Printing Press to the Digital Network* (New York: Anthem Press, 2013).

21. I cover this more thoroughly in Eve, *Open Access and the Humanities*.

22. Samuel Moore et al., "Excellence R Us: University Research and the Fetishisation of Excellence," *Palgrave Communications*, 3 (2017). https://doi.org/10.1057/palcomms.2016.105.

23. Adam Eyre-Walker and Nina Stoletzki, "The Assessment of Science: The Relative Merits of Post-Publication Review, the Impact Factor, and the Number of Citations," *PLOS Biology*, 11.10 (2013), e1001675, https://doi.org/10.1371/journal.pbio.1001675.

24. Jian Wang, Reinhilde Veugelers, and Paula E. Stephan, *Bias against Novelty in Science: A Cautionary Tale for Users of Bibliometric Indicators* (Rochester,

NY: Social Science Research Network, 1 December 2015), https://doi.org/10
.2139/ssrn.2710572.

25. Juan Miguel Campanario, "Consolation for the Scientist: Sometimes
It Is Hard to Publish Papers That Are Later Highly-Cited," *Social Studies of
Science*, 23.2 (1993), 342–62; Juan Miguel Campanario, "Have Referees Rejected
Some of the Most-Cited Articles of All Times?," *Journal of the American Society
for Information Science*, 47.4 (1996), 302–10, https://doi.org/10.1002/(SICI)1097
-4571(199604)47:4<302::AID-ASI63.0.CO;2-0; and Juan Miguel Campanario
and Erika Acedo, "Rejecting Highly Cited Papers: The Views of Scientists Who
Encounter Resistance to Their Discoveries from Other Scientists," *Journal of
the American Society for Information Science and Technology*, 58.5 (2007), 734–43,
https://doi.org/10.1002/asi.20556.

26. Michele Pagano, "American Idol and NIH Grant Review," *Cell*, 126.4
(2006), 637–38, https://doi.org/10.1016/j.cell.2006.08.004; Leslie C. Costello,
"Perspective: Is NIH Funding the 'Best Science by the Best Scientists'? A Critique of the NIH R01 Research Grant Review Policies," *Academic Medicine*,
85.5 (2010), 775–79, https://doi.org/10.1097/ACM.0b013e3181d74256; Mark D.
Lindner and Richard K. Nakamura, "Examining the Predictive Validity of
NIH Peer Review Scores," ed. by Neil R. Smalheiser, *PLOS ONE*, 10.6 (2015),
e0126938, https://doi.org/10.1371/journal.pone.0126938; Ferric C Fang, Anthony Bowen, and Arturo Casadevall, "NIH Peer Review Percentile Scores
Are Poorly Predictive of Grant Productivity," *ELife*, 5 (2016), e13323, https://
doi.org/10.7554/eLife.13323; and Weishi Meng, "Peer Review: Is NIH Rewarding Talent?," *Science Transparency*, 10 January 2016, https://scienceretractions
.wordpress.com/2016/01/10/peer-review-is-nih-rewarding-talent.

27. Maggie Fieldhouse and Audrey Marshall, *Collection Development in the
Digital Age* (London: Facet Publishing, 2011).

28. "Facts and Figures of the British Library," The British Library (website),
https://www.bl.uk/about-us/our-story/facts-and-figures-of-the-british-library,
accessed 10 March 2020.

29. See Roger C. Schonfeld et al., "The Internet Archive Loses on Controlled Digital Lending," *The Scholarly Kitchen*, 28 March 2023, https://
scholarlykitchen.sspnet.org/2023/03/28/internet-archive-controlled-digital
-lending.

30. David R. Hansen and Kyle K. Courtney, "A White Paper on Controlled
Digital Lending of Library Books" (LawArXiv, 2018), https://doi.org/10.31228
/osf.io/7fdyr.

31. Electronic Frontier Foundation, "Digital Rights Management: A Failure
in the Developed World, a Danger to the Developing World," EFF, 23 March

2005, https://www.eff.org/wp/digital-rights-management-failure-developed-world-danger-developing-world.

32. Electronic Frontier Foundation.

33. United States District Court, "Memorandum Order, in MPAA v. Reimerdes, Corley and Kazan," 2000, https://cyber.harvard.edu/openlaw/DVD/filings/NY/0202-mem-order.html, accessed 21 September 2022.

34. For an example of a non-English programming language, in this case Paleo-Hebrew, see Elon Litman, "Genesis," GitHub, 2022, https://github.com/elonlit/Genesis, accessed 21 September 2022.

35. L. Jean Camp and K. Lewis, "Code as Speech: A Discussion of Bernstein v. USDOJ, Karn v. USDOS, and Junger v. Daley in Light of the U.S. Supreme Court's Recent Shift to Federalism," KSG Faculty Research Working Papers Series RWP01-007, February 2001, 2, https://www.hks.harvard.edu/publications/code-speech.

36. Camp and Lewis, 3.

37. Whitfield Diffie and Susan Landau, "The Export of Cryptography in the 20th and the 21st Centuries," in *The History of Information Security*, ed. by Karl De Leeuw and Jan Bergstra (Amsterdam: Elsevier Science B.V., 2007), 725–36, https://doi.org/10.1016/B978-044451608-4/50027-4.

38. Cypherspace, "Munitions T-Shirt," http://www.cypherspace.org/adam/rsa/uk-shirt.html, accessed 23 September 2022.

39. For more, see Martin Paul Eve, *Password* (New York: Bloomsbury, 2016).

40. Joseph Cox, "Why You Don't Roll Your Own Crypto," *Vice*, 10 December 2015, https://www.vice.com/en/article/wnx8nq/why-you-dont-roll-your-own-crypto.

41. Seth Kenlon, "Understanding Linus's Law for Open Source Security," Opensource.com, 21 February 2021, https://opensource.com/article/21/2/open-source-security.

42. Monica Chin, "How a University Got Itself Banned from the Linux Kernel," *The Verge*, 30 April 2021, https://www.theverge.com/2021/4/30/22410164/linux-kernel-university-of-minnesota-banned-open-source.

43. Qiushi Wu and Kangjie Lu, "On the Feasibility of Stealthily Introducing Vulnerabilities in Open-Source Software via Hypocrite Commits," 2021, https://linuxreviews.org/images/d/d9/OpenSourceInsecurity.pdf.

44. Chin, "How a University Got Itself Banned."

45. Bruce Schneier, "Essays: Did NSA Put a Secret Backdoor in New Encryption Standard?," *Schneier on Security*, 15 November 2007, https://www.schneier.com/essays/archives/2007/11/did_nsa_put_a_secret.html.

46. Kathleen Fitzpatrick, *Planned Obsolescence: Publishing, Technology, and the Future of the Academy* (New York: New York University Press, 2011), 38.

47. For more on this, see Thomas M. Leitch, *Wikipedia U: Knowledge, Authority, and Liberal Education in the Digital Age*, Tech.Edu: A Hopkins Series on Education and Technology (Baltimore, MD: Johns Hopkins University Press, 2014); and Nathaniel Tkacz, *Wikipedia and the Politics of Openness* (Chicago: University of Chicago Press, 2014).

48. Reid Priedhorsky et al., "Creating, Destroying, and Restoring Value in Wikipedia," in *Proceedings of the 2007 International ACM Conference on Supporting Group Work—GROUP '07* (presented at the 2007 international ACM conference, Sanibel Island, Florida, USA: ACM Press, 2007), 259, https://doi .org/10.1145/1316624.1316663.

49. Elinor Mills, "Security Researcher: I Keep Getting Detained by Feds," CNET, 18 November 2010, https://www.cnet.com/news/privacy/security -researcher-i-keep-getting-detained-by-feds.

50. Kim Zetter, "Another Hacker's Laptop, Cellphones Searched at Border," *Wired*, 18 November 2010, https://www.wired.com/2010/11/hacker-border -search.

51. The following paragraphs are indebted to previous work in Martin Paul Eve, *The Digital Humanities and Literary Studies* (Oxford: Oxford University Press, 2022), 47.

52. Jason David Hall, "Popular Prosody: Spectacle and the Politics of Victorian Versification," *Nineteenth-Century Literature*, 62.2 (2007), 222–49, https: //doi.org/10.1525/ncl.2007.62.2.222.

53. For more on this, see Simone Natale, *Deceitful Media: Artificial Intelligence and Social Life after the Turing Test* (Oxford: Oxford University Press, 2021).

54. Ben Tarnoff, "Weizenbaum's Nightmares: How the Inventor of the First Chatbot Turned against AI," *Guardian*, 25 July 2023, https://www.theguardian .com/technology/2023/jul/25/joseph-weizenbaum-inventor-eliza-chatbot -turned-against-artificial-intelligence-ai.

55. See Leah Henrickson, *Reading Computer-Generated Texts* (Cambridge: Cambridge University Press, 2021), https://doi.org/10.1017/9781108906463.

56. Jon Stokes, "Please Stop Talking about The ELIZA Chatbot," Return, 23 February 2023, https://www.return.life/p/please-stop-talking-about-the-eliza -chatbot.

57. Emily M. Bender et al., "On the Dangers of Stochastic Parrots: Can Language Models Be Too Big? 🦜," in *Proceedings of the 2021 ACM Conference on Fairness, Accountability, and Transparency* (presented at the FAccT '21:

2021 ACM Conference on Fairness, Accountability, and Transparency, Virtual Event Canada: ACM, 2021), 610–23, https://doi.org/10.1145/3442188.3445922. See also Yoav Goldberg, "A Criticism of 'On the Dangers of Stochastic Parrots: Can Language Models Be Too Big?,'" GitHub Gist, 23 January 2021, https://gist.github.com/yoavg/9fc9be2f98b47c189a513573d902fb27.

58. For more, see Richard Jean So, "All Models Are Wrong," *PMLA*, 132.3 (2017), 668–73.

59. The best explanation of the most recent evolution of language generation models is given, in my view, by Stephen Wolfram. Stephen Wolfram, "What Is ChatGPT Doing . . . and Why Does It Work?," Stephen Wolfram: Writings, 14 February 2023, https://writings.stephenwolfram.com/2023/02/what-is-chatgpt-doing-and-why-does-it-work.

60. Tiffany C. Li, "Algorithmic Destruction" *SMU Law Review*, 75.3 (2022), https://doi.org/10.2139/ssrn.4066845.

61. Li.

62. This is a contentious point. See Noam Chomsky, Ian Roberts, and Jeffrey Watumull, "The False Promise of ChatGPT," *New York Times*, 8 March 2023, https://www.nytimes.com/2023/03/08/opinion/noam-chomsky-chatgpt-ai.html.

63. Martin Paul Eve, "The Great Automatic Grammatizator: Writing, Labour, Computers," *Critical Quarterly*, 59.3, 39, https://doi.org/10.1111/criq.12359.

64. Eve, 45.

65. For more on GPT-3, see Katherine Elkins and Jon Chun, "Can GPT-3 Pass a Writer's Turing Test?," *Journal of Cultural Analytics*, 5.2 (2020), 17212, https://doi.org/10.22148/001c.17212; and Robert Dale, "GPT-3: What's It Good For?," *Natural Language Engineering*, 27.1 (2021), 113–18, https://doi.org/10.1017/S1351324920000601.

66. Ted Underwood, "The Empirical Triumph of Theory," *Again Theory: A Forum on Language, Meaning, and Intent in a Time of Stochastic Parrots* (blog), 29 June 2023, https://critinq.wordpress.com/2023/06/29/the-empirical-triumph-of-theory.

67. Roland Barthes, "The Death of the Author," in *Image, Music, Text*, trans. by Stephen Heath (London: Fontana Press, 1987), 142–48; Michel Foucault, "What Is an Author?," in *The Essential Works of Michel Foucault, 1954–1984*, vol. 2 (London: Penguin, 2000), 205–22; Sean Burke, *The Death and Return of the Author: Criticism and Subjectivity in Barthes, Foucault and Derrida* (Edinburgh: Edinburgh University Press, 2008).

68. Daniel Schönberger, "Deep Copyright: Up—And Downstream Questions Related to Artificial Intelligence (AI) and Machine Learning (ML)" (Rochester, NY, 9 January 2018), 13, https://papers.ssrn.com/abstract=3098315.

69. Theodoros Chiou, "Copyright Lessons on Machine Learning: What Impact on Algorithmic Art?," *JIPITEC*, 10.3 (2020), https://www.jipitec.eu/issues/jipitec-10-3-2019/5025.

70. Matthew Stewart, "The Most Important Supreme Court Decision For Data Science and Machine Learning," Medium, 31 October 2019, https://towardsdatascience.com/the-most-important-supreme-court-decision-for-data-science-and-machine-learning-44cfc1c1bcaf.

71. Also, of important note, nonhuman agents cannot hold copyright. This can, however, be complex. See Andrés Guadamuz, "The Monkey Selfie: Copyright Lessons for Originality in Photographs and Internet Jurisdiction," *Internet Policy Review*, 5.1 (2016), https://policyreview.info/articles/analysis/monkey-selfie-copyright-lessons-originality-photographs-and-internet-jurisdiction.

72. US Copyright Office Review Board, letter to Ryan Abbott, "Second Request for Reconsideration for Refusal to Register a Recent Entrance to Paradise (Correspondence ID 1–3ZPC6C3; SR# 1–7100387071)," 14 February 2022, https://www.copyright.gov/rulings-filings/review-board/docs/a-recent-entrance-to-paradise.pdf.

73. Robert A. Gonsalves, "Who Owns AI-Generated Art?," Medium, 1 March 2022, https://robgon.medium.com/who-owns-ai-generated-art-3b38626e8b33.

74. For more, see Catherine D'Ignazio and Lauren F. Klein, *Data Feminism*, Strong Ideas Series (Cambridge, MA: MIT Press, 2020).

75. Bethany Nowviskie, "Reconstitute the World: Machine-Reading Archives of Mass Extinction," Bethany Nowviskie (website), 12 June 2018, http://nowviskie.org/2018/reconstitute-the-world/. Emphasis in original.

76. Ranganathan, *The Five Laws of Library Science.*

77. See also Matthew Kirschenbaum, "Prepare for the Textpocalypse," *Atlantic*, 8 March 2023, https://www.theatlantic.com/technology/archive/2023/03/ai-chatgpt-writing-language-models/673318.

78. Veniamin Veselovsky, Manoel Horta Ribeiro, and Robert West, "Artificial Artificial Artificial Intelligence: Crowd Workers Widely Use Large Language Models for Text Production Tasks" (arXiv, 2023), https://doi.org/10.48550/arXiv.2306.07899.

79. See Safiya Umoja Noble, *Algorithms of Oppression: How Search Engines Reinforce Racism* (New York: New York University Press, 2018).

80. William MacAskill, *What We Owe the Future*, 1st ed. (New York: Hachette Book Group, Inc, 2022).

81. Ray Kurzweil, "The Future of Machine–Human Intelligence," *Futurist*, 2006, 39–46.

82. Guardian Staff and Agency, "Google Fires Software Engineer Who

Claims AI Chatbot Is Sentient," *Guardian*, 23 July 2022, https://www.theguar
dian.com/technology/2022/jul/23/google-fires-software-engineer-who-claims
-ai-chatbot-is-sentient.

83. Jon Henley, "Chess Robot Grabs and Breaks Finger of Seven-Year-Old
Opponent," *Guardian*, 24 July 2022, https://www.theguardian.com/sport/2022
/jul/24/chess-robot-grabs-and-breaks-finger-of-seven-year-old-opponent
-moscow.

84. Isaac Asimov, *I, Robot* (London: Harper Voyager, 2018).

85. Alex Blechman (@AlexBlechman), "Sci-Fi Author: In My Book I Invented the Torment Nexus as a Cautionary Tale Tech Company: At Long Last,
We Have Created the Torment Nexus from Classic Sci-Fi Novel Don't Create
The Torment Nexus," Twitter, 8 November 2021, https://twitter.com/AlexBlech
man/status/1457842724128833538.

86. Faiz Siddiqui, "Elon Musk Debuts Tesla Robot, Optimus, Calling It
a 'Fundamental Transformation,'" *Washington Post*, 1 October 2022, https://
www.washingtonpost.com/technology/2022/09/30/elon-musk-tesla-bot.

87. Other similar, but not quite the same, terms that have been deployed
include "epistemic imperialism." See Lucas B. Mazur, "The Epistemic Imperialism of Science. Reinvigorating Early Critiques of Scientism," *Frontiers in
Psychology*, 11 (2021), https://www.frontiersin.org/articles/10.3389/fpsyg.2020
.609823.

88. See, for instance, Edward Demenchonok, "From Power Politics to the
Ethics of Peace," in *Philosophy after Hiroshima*, ed. by Edward Demenchonok
(Newcastle upon Tyne: Cambridge Scholars, 2010), 10–12.

89. Emily M. Bender and Alex Hanna, "AI Causes Real Harm. Let's Focus
on That over the End-of-Humanity Hype," *Scientific American*, 12 August 2023,
https://www.scientificamerican.com/article/we-need-to-focus-on-ais-real
-harms-not-imaginary-existential-risks.

90. Mike Godwin, "Meme, Counter-Meme," *Wired*, 1 October 1994, http://
www.wired.com/wired/archive/2.10/godwin.if_pr.html.

91. For a thoughtful and evolving stance on this, see Nature Portfolio,
"Artificial Intelligence (AI)," 2023, https://www.nature.com/nature-portfolio/
editorial-policies/ai, accessed 30 June 2023.

92. Stephen Politzer-Ahles, Teresa Girolamo, and Samantha Ghali, "Preliminary Evidence of Linguistic Bias in Academic Reviewing," *Journal of English for Academic Purposes*, 47 (2020), 100895, https://doi.org/10.1016/j.jeap
.2020.100895; and Mario S. Di Bitetti and Julián A. Ferreras, "Publish (in English) or Perish: The Effect on Citation Rate of Using Languages Other than
English in Scientific Publications," *Ambio*, 46.1 (2017), 121–27, https://doi.org/
10.1007/s13280-016-0820-7.

93. Much of this section is indebted to Joanna Bourke, *Birkbeck: 200 Years of Radical Learning for Working People*, History of Universities Series (New York: Oxford University Press, 2022).

94. Edward William Grinfield, *A Reply to Mr. Brougham's "Practical Observations upon the Education of the People; Addressed to the Working Classes and Their Employers"* (London: C. & J. Rivington, 1825), iv, cited in Bourke, *Birkbeck*, 3.

95. "Postscript," *Saint James' Chronicle*, 2 August 1825, cited in Bourke, *Birkbeck*, 6.

96. Bourke, *Birkbeck*, 31.

97. Bourke, 31.

98. Bourke, 37.

99. Bourke, 37.

100. Bourke, 37.

101. See Steven Connor, *The Madness of Knowledge: On Wisdom, Ignorance and Fantasies of Knowing* (London: Reaktion Books, 2019).

102. Chris Baggs, "'The Whole Tragedy of Leisure in Penury': The South Wales Miners' Institute Libraries during the Great Depression," *Libraries & Culture*, 39.2 (2004), 115–36.

103. This history is drawn from Lawson, "The Political Histories of UK Public Libraries," 164–65.

104. Elizabeth B. Fitzpatrick, "The Public Library as Instrument of Colonialism: The Case of the Netherlands East Indies," *Libraries & the Cultural Record*, 43.3 (2008), 270–85; and L. Sulistyo-Basuki, "The Rise and Growth of Libraries in Pre-War Indonesia," *Library History*, 14.1 (1998), 55–64, https://doi.org/10.1179/lib.1998.14.1.55.

105. Sterling Joseph Coleman, "The British Council and Unesco in Ethiopia: A Comparison of Linear and Cyclical Patterns of Librarianship Development," *Library History*, 21.2 (2005), 121–30, https://doi.org/10.1179/002423005x44952.

106. Elizabeth B. Fitzpatrick, "The Public Library as Instrument of Colonialism."

107. Lawson, "The Political Histories of UK Public Libraries," 165; and George Roe, "Challenging the Control of Knowledge in Colonial India: Political Ideas in the Work of S. R. Ranganathan," *Library & Information History*, 26.1 (2010), 19, https://doi.org/10.1179/175834909X12593371068342.

108. Lawson, "The Political Histories of UK Public Libraries," 165; Jashu Patel and Krishan Kumar, *Libraries and Librarianship in India* (Westport, CT: Greenwood Press, 2001), 2–14; and Roe, "Challenging the Control of Knowledge."

109. Roe, "Challenging the Control of Knowledge," 165; Jennifer Cram, "Colonialism and Libraries in Third World Africa," *Australian Library Jour-*

nal, 42.1 (1993), 13–20, https://doi.org/10.1080/00049670.1993.10755621; Gabe Ignatow, "What Has Globalization Done to Developing Countries' Public Libraries?," *International Sociology*, 26.6 (2011), 746–68, https://doi.org/10.1177/0268580910393373; Adakole Ochai, "The Purpose of the Library in Colonial Tropical Africa: An Historical Survey," *International Library Review*, 16.3 (1984), 309–15, https://doi.org/10.1016/0020-7837(84)90007-4; Amusi Odi, "The Colonial Origins of Library Development in Africa: Some Reflections on Their Significance," *Libraries & Culture*, 26.4 (1991), 594–604; and Kate Parry, "Libraries in Uganda: Not Just Linguistic Imperialism," *Libri*, 61.4 (2011), 328–37, https://doi.org/10.1515/libr.2011.027.

110. Jeff Atwood, "Help Name Our Website," *Coding Horror*, 6 April 2008, https://blog.codinghorror.com/help-name-our-website.

111. Jeff Atwood, "What Does Stack Overflow Want to Be When It Grows Up?," *Coding Horror*, 22 October 2018, https://blog.codinghorror.com/what-does-stack-overflow-want-to-be-when-it-grows-up.

112. Fitzpatrick, *Planned Obsolescence*; and Atwood, "What Does Stack Overflow Want to Be When It Grows Up?"

113. Atwood, "What Does Stack Overflow Want to Be When It Grows Up?"

114. Atwood.

115. Richard Hall, "On the University as Anxiety Machine," *Richard Hall's Space*, 19 March 2014, http://www.richard-hall.org/2014/03/19/on-the-university-as-anxiety-machine; J. D. Taylor, "Spent? Capitalism's Growing Problem with Anxiety," *ROAR Magazine*, 14 March 2014, https://roarmag.org/essays/neoliberal-capitalism-anxiety-depression-insecurity; Lawrence D. Berg, Edward H. Huijbens, and Henrik Gutzon Larsen, "Producing Anxiety in the Neoliberal University," *The Canadian Geographer / Le géographe canadien*, 60.2 (2016), 168–80, https://doi.org/10.1111/cag.12261.

116. For one of the most nauseating examples, see Sofia Pellaschiar, *A Hug in a Book: Everyday Self-Care and Comforting Rituals* (Pop Press, 2022).

117. Samuel Moore, "The 'Care-Full' Commons: Open Access and the Care of Commoning," in *The Commons and Care*, ed. by Joe Deville, Samuel Moore, and Tahani Nadim (Birmingham: Post Office Press and Rope Press, 2018), 16–25, https://hcommons.org/deposits/item/hc:19817; Valeria Graziano, Marcell Mars, and Tomislav Medak, "Introduction to Pirate Care," *Pirate Care Syllabus*, 2020, https://syllabus.pirate.care/topic/piratecareintroduction/, accessed 18 September 2021.

118. Deville, Moore, and Nadim, *The Commons and Care*.

119. Eve, *Open Access and the Humanities*, chap. 2.

Chapter Eight

1. Jorge Luis Borges, "The Sacred Unreadable Artifact," in *Collected Fictions*, trans. by Andrew Hurley (New York: Penguin, 1998), 654–57.

2. See the excellent Paul Gooding and Melissa Terras, "Introduction," in *Electronic Legal Deposit: Shaping the Library Collections of the Future*, ed. by Paul Gooding and Melissa Terras (London: Facet Publishing, 2020), xxiii–xxx.

3. Svend Larsen, "Preserving the Digital Heritage: New Legal Deposit Act in Denmark," *Alexandria: The Journal of National and International Library and Information Issues*, 17.2 (2005), 86, https://doi.org/10.1177/095574900501700204.

4. Gooding and Terras, "Introduction," xxiv.

5. "About Us," UK Web Archive, 2021, https://www.webarchive.org.uk/en/ukwa/about, accessed 10 February 2022.

6. "FAQ," UK Web Archive, 2021, https://www.webarchive.org.uk/en/ukwa/info/faq, accessed 10 February 2022.

7. Mike Taylor, "Heaven Protect Us from a 'UK National Licence,'" *Sauropod Vertebra Picture of the Week* (blog), 1 April 2015, https://svpow.com/2015/04/01/heaven-help-us-from-a-uk-national-licence; Martin Paul Eve, "If We Choose to Align Open Access to Research with Geo-Political Borders We Negate the Moral Value of Open Access," *LSE Impact Blog*, 11 November 2019, https://blogs.lse.ac.uk/impactofsocialsciences/2019/11/11/if-we-choose-to-align-open-access-to-research-with-geo-political-borders-we-negate-the-moral-value-of-open-access.

8. Bernhard Rieder, *Engines of Order: A Mechanology of Algorithmic Techniques* (Amsterdam: Amsterdam University Press, 2020), 63.

9. Isabel Galina Russell, Jo Ana Morfin, and Ana Yuri Ramírez-Molina, "E-Legal Deposit at the Biblioteca Nacional de México (National Library of Mexico)," in Gooding and Terras, *Electronic Legal Deposit*, 57–76; Eva Lis-Green and Göran Konstenius, "Electronic Legal Deposit in Sweden: The Evolution of Digital Publications and Legislative Systems," in Gooding and Terras, *Electronic Legal Deposit*, 99–118; and Collence T. Chisita, Blessing Chiparausha, and Danmore Maboreke, "Bibliographic Control in Zimbabwe: The Conundrum of Legal Deposit in the Age of Digital Technologies," in Gooding and Terras, *Electronic Legal Deposit*, 90.

10. Chisita, Chiparausha, and Maboreke, "Bibliographic Control in Zimbabwe," 80.

11. Chisita, Chiparausha, and Maboreke, 80.

12. Jules Larivière, "Guidelines for Legal Deposit Legislation: A Revised, Enlarged and Updated Edition of the 1981 Publication by Dr. Jean LUNN IFLA Committee on Cataloguing" (UNESCO, 2000).

13. James Cummings, "The Materiality of Markup and the Text Encoding

Initiative," in *Digitizing Medieval and Early Modern Material Culture*, ed. by Brent Nelson and Melissa M. Terras (Toronto: Arizona Center for Medieval and Renaissance Studies, 2012), 49–81.

14. Marshall McLuhan, Quentin Fiore, and Jerome Agel, *The Medium Is the Massage* (Gingko Press, 1967), http://archive.org/details/pdfy-vNiFct6b-L5ucJEa.

15. Helen Speight, "Rachel Speght's Polemical Life," *Huntington Library Quarterly*, 65.3/4 (2002), 449–63; and Lisa J. Schnell, "Muzzling the Competition: Rachel Speght and the Economics of Print," in *Debating Gender in Early Modern England, 1500–1700*, ed. by Cristina Malcolmson and Mihoko Suzuki, Early Modern Cultural Studies (New York: Palgrave Macmillan US, 2002), 57–77, https://doi.org/10.1057/9780230107540_4.

16. For example, see Cis van Heertum, "A Hostile Annotation of Rachel Speght's *A Mouzell for Melastomus* (1617)," *English Studies*, 68.6 (1987), 490–96, https://doi.org/10.1080/00138388708598539.

17. That said, of note is the recent ongoing court case in which the Internet Archive lost the right to format shift physical items that it had purchased into a digital format. Hachette Book Group, Inc. et al. v. Internet Archive, et al., 20-cv-4160 (JGK) (S.D.N.Y. Mar. 24, 2023).

18. Friedrich A. Kittler, "There Is No Software," in *Literature, Media, Information Systems: Essays*, ed. by John Johnston (Amsterdam: Overseas Publishers Association, 1997), 147–55.

19. Rieder, *Engines of Order*, 53.

20. For more on this, see Peter De Bolla, *The Architecture of Concepts: The Historical Formation of Human Rights* (New York: Fordham University Press, 2013).

21. Kathleen Fitzpatrick, *Planned Obsolescence: Publishing, Technology, and the Future of the Academy* (New York: New York University Press, 2011).

22. Ann Elizabeth Wiener, "What's That Smell You're Reading?," *Science History Institute*, 27 March 2018, https://www.sciencehistory.org/distillations/whats-that-smell-youre-reading. See also John Francis Xavier O'Conor, *Facts about Bookworms: Their History in Literature and Work in Libraries* (New York: F. P. Harper, 1898).

23. Bec Crew, "How Book Scorpions Tend to Your Dusty Tomes," *Scientific American Blog Network*, 25 August 2014, https://blogs.scientificamerican.com/running-ponies/how-book-scorpions-tend-to-your-dusty-tomes.

24. Wiener, "What's That Smell You're Reading?"

25. Google, "About Google, Our Culture & Company News," 2020, https://about.google., accessed 7 March 2020.

26. Rachel Coldicutt, "Just Enough Internet: Why Public Service Internet Should Be a Model of Restraint," Doteveryone, 21 October 2019, https://doteveryone.org.uk/2019/10/just-enough-internet.

27. Tom Scott, "Data Ethics & Design Implications for Wellcome Collection's Digital Platform," Medium, 16 July 2020, https://stacks.wellcomecollection.org/data-ethics-design-implications-for-wellcome-collections-digital-platform-64878cbe31d6.

28. Catherine D'Ignazio and Lauren F. Klein, *Data Feminism*, Strong Ideas Series (Cambridge, MA: MIT Press, 2020).

29. "Facts and Figures of the British Library," The British Library (website), https://www.bl.uk/about-us/our-story/facts-and-figures-of-the-british-library, accessed 10 March 2020.

30. Tom Arrow, Jenny Molloy, and Peter Murray-Rust, "A Day in the Life of *a Content Miner and Team*," *Insights: The UKSG Journal*, 29.2 (2016), 208–11, https://doi.org/10.1629/uksg.310; Peter Murray-Rust, "What Is TextAndData/ContentMining?," *Petermr's Blog*, 11 July 2017, https://blogs.ch.cam.ac.uk/pmr/2017/07/11/what-is-textanddatacontentmining/.

31. John R. Searle, *The Construction of Social Reality* (New York: Free Press, 1997), 1.

32. Josef Moural, "Searle's Theory of Institutional Facts: A Program of Critical Revision," in *Speech Acts, Mind, and Social Reality: Discussions with John R. Searle*, ed. by Günther Grewendorf and Georg Meggle, Studies in Linguistics and Philosophy (Dordrecht: Springer Netherlands, 2002), 272, https://doi.org/10.1007/978-94-010-0589-0_18.

33. Searle, *The Construction of Social Reality*, 2.

34. John R. Searle, *Making the Social World: The Structure of Human Civilization* (Oxford: Oxford University Press, 2010), 63.

35. Searle, *Making the Social World*, 101. See also Gregory J. Lobo, "A Critique of Searle's Linguistic Exceptionalism," *Philosophy of the Social Sciences*, 51.6 (2021), 555–73, https://doi.org/10.1177/0048393121995581.

36. G. Aad, B. Abbott, J. Abdallah, O. Abdinov, R. Aben, M. Abolins, et al., "Combined Measurement of the Higgs Boson Mass in p p Collisions at s = 7 and 8 TeV with the ATLAS and CMS Experiments," *Physical Review Letters*, 114.19 (2015), https://doi.org/10.1103/PhysRevLett.114.191803.

37. John Daintith, ed., *A Dictionary of Chemistry*, 6th ed. (New York: Oxford University Press, 2008), 409.

38. Seymour H. Mauskopf, "Chemical Revolution," in *Reader's Guide to the History of Science*, ed. by Arne Hessenbruch (London: Fitzroy Dearborn, 2000), 128.

39. James Bryant Conant, ed., *The Overthrow of the Phlogiston Theory: The Chemical Revolution of 1775–1789* (Cambridge, MA: Harvard University Press, 1964), 13.

40. Seymour Mauskop, "Richard Kirwan's Phlogiston Theory: Its Success and Fate," *Ambix*, 49.3 (2002), 187, https://doi.org/10.1179/amb.2002.49.3.185.

41. Thomas S. Kuhn, *The Structure of Scientific Revolutions*, 3rd ed. (Chicago: University of Chicago Press, 1996), 53.

42. Olga Kirillova, "The Chemical Theory of Phlogiston in the Cultural Economy of Fire: From the Enlightenment to Contemporary Times," *Stasis*, 11.1 (2021), 75–111, https://doi.org/10.33280/2310-3817-21-11-1-75-111; John Stewart, "The Reality of Phlogiston in Great Britain," *HYLE—International Journal for Philosophy of Chemistry*, 18.2 (2012), 175–94.

43. For more on the history of the Statute of Anne, see "The Statute of Anne; April 10, 1710," The Avalon Project, 2008, http://avalon.law.yale.edu/18th_century/anne_1710.asp, accessed 28 April 2019; Ronan Deazley, "Commentary on the Statute of Anne 1710," Primary Sources on Copyright (1450–1900) (website), ed. by Lionel Bently and Martin Kretschmer, 2008, https://www.copyrighthistory.org/cam/tools/request/showRecord.php?id=commentary_uk_1710; William Cornish, "The Statute of Anne 1709–10: Its Historical Setting," in *Global Copyright: Three Hundred Years since the Statute of Anne, from 1709 to Cyberspace*, ed. by Lionel Bently, Uma Suthersanen, and Paul Torresmans (Cheltenham: Edward Elgar Publishing, 2010), 14–25, https://doi.org/10.4337/9781849806428.00010; Ronan Deazley, "What's New about the Statute of Anne? Or Six Observations in Search of an Act," in Bently, Suthersanen, and Torresmans, *Global Copyright*, 26–33; Oren Bracha, "The Statute of Anne: An American Mythology," *Houston Law Review*, 47.4 (2010), 877–918; and John Willinsky, *The Intellectual Properties of Learning: A Prehistory from Saint Jerome to John Locke* (Chicago: University of Chicago Press, 2017).

44. Bryan A. Garner, *Black's Law Dictionary, Abridged*, 9th ed. (Toronto: West, 2010), 669.

45. Garner, 670.

46. See, for instance, Moritz Schlick, "Facts and Propositions," *Analysis*, 2.5 (1935), 65–70, https://doi.org/10.2307/3326403 for a classic example of the form.

47. Charles Oppenheim, Adrienne Muir, and Naomi Korn, *Information Law: Compliance for Librarians, Information Professionals and Knowledge Managers* (London: Facet Publishing, 2020), 2, http://ebookcentral.proquest.com/lib/bbk/detail.action?docID=6235937.

48. See Marc Lucht and Donna Yarri, eds., *Kafka's Creatures: Animals, Hybrids, and Other Fantastic Beings* (Lanham, MD: Lexington Books, 2010); and Naama Harel, "De-Allegorizing Kafka's Ape: Two Animalistic Contexts," in

Kafka's Creatures: Animals, Hybrids, and Other Fantastic Beings, ed. by Marc Lucht and Donna Yarri (Lanham, MD: Lexington Books, 2010), 53–66.

49. Ernest Hemingway, *The Old Man and the Sea* (New York: Scribner, 1996).

50. Hemingway, 10, 22.

51. Hemingway, 22.

52. Alfred Edward Housman, "How Clear, How Lovely Bright," in *More Poems* (London: A. A. Knopf, 1936), 26–27.

53. James J Rucker et al., "The Effects of Psilocybin on Cognitive and Emotional Functions in Healthy Participants: Results from a Phase 1, Randomised, Placebo-Controlled Trial Involving Simultaneous Psilocybin Administration and Preparation," *Journal of Psychopharmacology*, 36.1 (2022), 114–25, https://doi.org/10.1177/02698811211064720.

54. Custom Dynamics, LLC v. Radiantz Led Lighting, Inc., 535 F. Supp. 2d 542 (E.D.N.C. 2008).

55. For commentary on how this focus on originality is changing, see Martin Paul Eve et al., *Reading Peer Review: PLOS ONE and Institutional Change in Academia* (Cambridge: Cambridge University Press, 2021).

56. Vincent Larivière, Stefanie Haustein, and Philippe Mongeon, "The Oligopoly of Academic Publishers in the Digital Era," *PLOS ONE*, 10.6 (2015), e0127502, https://doi.org/10.1371/journal.pone.0127502. See Robert-Jan Smits and Rachael Pells, *Plan S for Shock: Science, Shock, Solution, Speed* (London: Ubiquity Press, 2022), https://doi.org/10.5334/bcq for how this is changing.

57. This section is derived from Martin Paul Eve, "Lessons from the Library: Extreme Minimalist Scaling at Pirate Ebook Platforms," *Digital Humanities Quarterly*, 2022.

58. Balázs Bodó, "The Genesis of Library Genesis: The Birth of a Global Scholarly Shadow Library," in *Shadow Libraries: Access to Educational Materials in Global Higher Education*, ed. by Joe Karaganis (Cambridge, MA: MIT Press, 2018), 25.

59. u/shrine, "Library Genesis Project Update: 2.5 Million Books Seeded with the World, 80 Million Scientific Articles Next," Reddit—r/DataHoarder, 20 December 2019, https://www.reddit.com/r/DataHoarder/comments/ed9byj/library_genesis_project_update_25_million_books.

60. Maslow's hierarchy has been subject to many criticisms and revisions over the years. See, for instance, Louis Tay and Ed Diener, "Needs and Subjective Well-Being around the World," *Journal of Personality and Social Psychology*, 101.2 (2011), 354–65, https://doi.org/10.1037/a0023779.

61. See Maureen N. McLane, *Romanticism and the Human Sciences: Poetry, Population, and the Discourse of the Species*, Cambridge Studies in Romanticism, 41 (Cambridge: Cambridge University Press, 2000), 84–108, for example, for an

exploration of how *Frankenstein* can be read as an exploration of the Malthus-Godwin debate on human nature.

62. See, for instance Evanthia Samaras, "Researching Malware at the British Library," Digital Preservation Coalition, last updated 4 October 2018, https://www.dpconline.org/blog/researching-malware-at-the-british-library.

63. Jonathan Farbowitz, "More Than Digital Dirt: Preserving Malware in Archives, Museums, and Libraries" (New York University, 2016), http://archive.org/details/16sThesisFarbowitzFinal, accessed 18 April 2022.

64. Jussi Parikka, *Digital Contagions: A Media Archaeology of Computer Viruses* (New York: Peter Lang, 2016), xiii–xiv.

65. Sara Reardon, "'Forgotten' NIH Smallpox Virus Languishes on Death Row," *Nature*, 514.7524 (2014), 544, https://doi.org/10.1038/514544a.

66. John O. Agwunobi, "Should the US and Russia Destroy Their Stocks of Smallpox Virus?," *BMJ : British Medical Journal*, 334.7597 (2007), 775, https://doi.org/10.1136/bmj.39156.490799.BE.

67. For more on the emergence of the "cloud" terminology, see Tung-Hui Hu, *A Prehistory of the Cloud* (Cambridge, MA: MIT Press, 2015).

68. Monica E. Ortiz and Drew Endy, "Engineered Cell-Cell Communication via DNA Messaging," *Journal of Biological Engineering*, 6.1 (2012), 16, https://doi.org/10.1186/1754-1611-6-16.

69. Fatima Akram et al., "Trends to Store Digital Data in DNA: An Overview," *Molecular Biology Reports*, 45.5 (2018), 1479–90, https://doi.org/10.1007/s11033-018-4280-y; and Luis Ceze, Jeff Nivala, and Karin Strauss, "Molecular Digital Data Storage Using DNA," *Nature Reviews Genetics*, 20.8 (2019), 456–66, https://doi.org/10.1038/s41576-019-0125-3.

70. Elie Dolgin, "The Secret Social Lives of Viruses," *Nature*, 570.7761 (2019), 290–92, https://doi.org/10.1038/d41586-019-01880-6.

71. Michael McCabe, "AIDS and the God of Wrath," *Furrow*, 38.8 (1987), 512–21. See also Mark R. Kowalewski, "Religious Constructions of the AIDS Crisis," *Sociological Analysis*, 51.1 (1990), 91–96, https://doi.org/10.2307/3711343; Rachel Spronk, "The Disease Immorality: Narrating Aids as 'Sign of the Times' in Middle-Class Nairobi," *Etnofoor*, 13.1 (2000), 67–86.

72. Parikka, *Digital Contagions*, xxii.

73. See, for instance Adrienne Mayor, *Greek Fire, Poison Arrows, and Scorpion Bombs: Biological and Chemical Warfare in the Ancient World* (Woodstock: Overlook, 2003).

74. Anshula Sharma et al., "Next Generation Agents (Synthetic Agents): Emerging Threats and Challenges in Detection, Protection, and Decontamination," *Handbook on Biological Warfare Preparedness* (2020), 217–56, https://doi.org/10.1016/B978-0-12-812026-2.00012-8.

75. Roger Collier, "NHS Ransomware Attack Spreads Worldwide," *CMAJ : Canadian Medical Association Journal*, 189.22 (2017), E786–87, https://doi.org/10.1503/cmaj.1095434; and Stacy Weiner, "The Growing Threat of Ransomware Attacks on Hospitals," AAMC, 20 July 2021, https://www.aamc.org/news-insights/growing-threat-ransomware-attacks-hospitals.

76. Jussi Parikka and Tony D. Sampson, eds., *The Spam Book: On Viruses, Porn, and Other Anomalies from the Dark Side of Digital Culture*, Hampton Press Communication Series : Communication Alternatives (Cresskill, NJ: Hampton Press, 2009), 4.

77. Microsoft, "Consumer Antivirus Software Providers for Windows," 2022, https://support.microsoft.com/en-gb/windows-antivirus-providers, accessed 19 April 2022.

78. See, for instance, Google, "KCTF," 2022, https://github.com/google/kctf, accessed 19 April 2022.

79. Aaron Yi Ding, Gianluca Limon De Jesus, and Marijn Janssen, "Ethical Hacking for Boosting IoT Vulnerability Management: A First Look into Bug Bounty Programs and Responsible Disclosure," in *Proceedings of the Eighth International Conference on Telecommunications and Remote Sensing*, ICTRS '19 (New York: Association for Computing Machinery, 2019), 49–55, https://doi.org/10.1145/3357767.3357774.

80. This section draws extensively on Martin Paul Eve, *Warez: The Infrastructure and Aesthetics of Piracy* (New York: Punctum Books, 2021), 47–51.

81. Robert V. Kozinets, *Netnography: Ethnographic Research in the Age of the Internet*, 1st ed. (Thousand Oaks, CA: Sage Publications Ltd, 2010), 153.

82. Amy Bruckman, "Teaching Students to Study Online Communities Ethically," *Journal of Information Ethics*, 15.2 (2006), 89.

83. Kozinets, *Netnography*, 145.

84. Kozinets, 144.

85. Kevin D. Mitnick and William L. Simon, *Ghost in the Wires: My Adventures as the World's Most Wanted Hacker* (New York: Little, Brown and Company, 2011).

86. Sally Morris et al., *The Handbook of Journal Publishing* (Cambridge: Cambridge University Press, 2013), 152.

87. Most of this section is deeply indebted to Geoffrey Bilder, *Disambiguation without De-Duplication: Modeling Authority and Trust in the ORCID System* (Crossref, 16 March 2011), 25.

88. Bilder, 4.

89. Nate Anderson, "Confirmed: US and Israel Created Stuxnet, Lost Control of It," *Ars Technica*, June 1, 2012, https://arstechnica.com/tech-policy/2012/06/confirmed-us-israel-created-stuxnet-lost-control-of-it.

90. Wachowski, Lana (as Larry), and Lilly (as Andy) Wachowski, dirs., *The Matrix* (Warner Bros, 1999).

91. Fitzpatrick, *Planned Obsolescence*.

92. Peter Kidd, "Nobody Cares about Your Blog!," *Medieval Manuscripts Provenance* (blog), 24 December 2022, https://mssprovenance.blogspot.com/2022/12/nobody-cares-about-your-blog.html.

93. Author Ellie Kincaid, "University to Investigate Adjunct Professor after Allegations of Plagiarism—and Legal Threats," *Retraction Watch*, 30 December 2022, https://retractionwatch.com/2022/12/30/university-to-investigate-adjunct-professor-after-allegations-of-plagiarism-and-legal-threats.

94. Peter Kidd, "The RECEPTIO-Rossi Affair VI: The Backstory," *Medieval Manuscripts Provenance* (blog), 28 December 2022, https://mssprovenance.blogspot.com/2022/12/the-receptio-rossi-affair-vi-backstory.html.

Chapter Nine

1. Merlin Sheldrake, *Entangled Life: How Fungi Make Our Worlds, Change Our Minds, and Shape Our Futures* (London: Vintage, 2021).

2. Richard C. Lewontin, *The Triple Helix: Gene, Organism, and Environment* (Cambridge, MA: Harvard University Press, 2001), 3.

3. Theodor Holm Nelson, "The Right Way to Think about Software Design," in *The Art of Human-Computer Interface Design*, ed. by Brenda Laurel (Reading, MA: Addison-Wesley, 1990), 237.

Aad, G., B. Abbott, J. Abdallah, O. Abdinov, R. Aben, M. Abolins, et al., "Combined Measurement of the Higgs Boson Mass in p p Collisions at s = 7 and 8 TeV with the ATLAS and CMS Experiments," *Physical Review Letters*, 114.19 (2015). https://doi.org/10.1103/PhysRevLett.114.191803.

Aart, "Answer to 'What Is £ Used For?,'" Mathematics Stack Exchange, 2022 https://math.stackexchange.com/a/4426967. Accessed 14 April 2022.

Abbate, Janet, *Inventing the Internet* (Cambridge, MA: MIT Press, 2000).

Abramson, Albert, *The History of Television, 1880 to 1941* (Jefferson, NC: McFarland, 1987).

Abuelwafa, Sherif, Mohamed Mhiri, Rachid Hedjam, Sara Zhalehpour, Andrew Piper, Chad Wellmon, et al., "Feature Learning for Footnote-Based Document Image Classification," in *Image Analysis and Recognition*, ed. by Fakhri Karray, Aurélio Campilho, and Farida Cheriet, Lecture Notes in Computer Science (Cham: Springer International Publishing, 2017), 643–50. https://doi.org/10.1007/978-3-319-59876-5_71.

Abusalah, Hamza, Joël Alwen, Bram Cohen, Danylo Khilko, Krzysztof Pietrzak, and Leonid Reyzin, "Beyond Hellman's Time-Memory Trade-Offs with Applications to Proofs of Space," in *Advances in Cryptology—ASIACRYPT 2017*, ed. by Tsuyoshi Takagi and Thomas Peyrin, Lecture

Notes in Computer Science (Cham: Springer International Publishing, 2017), 357–79. https://doi.org/10.1007/978-3-319-70697-9_13.

Ackerman, Mark S., "Metaphors along the Information Highway," in *Proceedings of the Symposium on Directions and Impacts of Advanced Computing (DIAC 94)* (Cambridge, MA, 1994), 1–5. http://www.douri.sh/classes/ics234cw04/ackerman.pdf.

Adema, Janneke, and Samuel A. Moore, "Collectivity and Collaboration: Imagining New Forms of Communality to Create Resilience in Scholar-Led Publishing," *Insights* 31.1 (2018). https://doi.org/10.1629/uksg.399.

Adler, Michael H., *The Writing Machine: History of the Typewriter*. London: Allen & Unwin, 1973.

Agwunobi, John O., "Should the US and Russia Destroy Their Stocks of Smallpox Virus?" *BMJ : British Medical Journal* 334 (2007), 775. https://doi.org/10.1136/bmj.39156.490799.BE.

Ahearn, Laura M., *Living Language: An Introduction to Linguistic Anthropology*, 2nd ed. (Malden, MA: Wiley-Blackwell, 2017).

Akram, Fatima, Ikram ul Haq, Haider Ali, and Aiman Tahir Laghari, "Trends to Store Digital Data in DNA: An Overview," *Molecular Biology Reports* 45.5 (2018): 1479–90. https://doi.org/10.1007/s11033-018-4280-y.

Alberti, Leon Battista, *On Painting: A New Translation and Critical Edition*, ed. by Rocco Sinisgalli, trans. by Rocco Sinisgalli (Cambridge: Cambridge University Press, 2011).

Aleksandersen, Daniel, "Windows 11 Blocks Edge Browser Competitors from Opening Links," *Ctrl Blog*, last updated 13 December 2021. https://www.ctrl.blog/entry/microsoft-edge-protocol-competition.html.

Allen, Theodore W., *The Invention of the White Race*, vol. 1, *Racial Oppression And Social Control*, London: Verso, 2012.

Althusser, Louis, Étienne Balibar, Roger Establet, Pierre Machery, and Jacques Rancière, *Reading Capital: The Complete Edition*, trans. by Ben Brewster and David Fernbach (London: Verso, 2015).

Alves, André Azevedo, and John Meadowcroft, "Hayek's Slippery Slope, the Stability of the Mixed Economy and the Dynamics of Rent Seeking," *Political Studies*, 62.4 (2014), 843–61. https://doi.org/10.1111/1467-9248.12043.

Amateur Photographer, "Bliss by Charles O'Rear—Iconic Photograph," 28 May 2012. https://www.amateurphotographer.co.uk/iconic-images/bliss-by-charles-orear-iconic-photograph-13083.

American Paper and Pulp Association, *The Dictionary of Paper, Including Pulp, Paperboard, Paper Properties, and Related Papermaking Terms*, 3rd ed. (New York: American Paper and Pulp Association, 1965).

Amoore, Louise, "Cloud Geographies: Computing, Data, Sovereignty," *Progress*

in Human Geography, 42.1 (2018), 4–24. https://doi.org/10.1177/030913251666
2147.

Anderson, Benedict, *Imagined Communities: Reflections on the Origin and Spread of Nationalism*, rev. ed (London: Verso, 2006).

Anderson, Nate, "Confirmed: US and Israel Created Stuxnet, Lost Control of It," *Ars Technica*, 1 June 2012. https://arstechnica.com/tech-policy/2012/06/confirmed-us-israel-created-stuxnet-lost-control-of-it/.

Andoni, Merlinda, Valentin Robu, David Flynn, Simone Abram, Dale Geach, David Jenkins, et al., "Blockchain Technology in the Energy Sector: A Systematic Review of Challenges and Opportunities," *Renewable and Sustainable Energy Reviews*, 100 (2019), 143–74. https://doi.org/10.1016/j.rser.2018.10.014.

Andrew Baerg, "WIMPing Out," *Symplokē*, 22.1–2 (2014), 307–10. https://doi.org/10.5250/symploke.22.1-2.0307.

Andrews, Penny C. S., "The Platformization of Open," in Eve and Grays, *Reassembling Scholarly Communications*, 265–76.

Antsstyle, "Why NFTs Are Bad: The Long Version," Medium, 24 October 2021. https://antsstyle.medium.com/why-nfts-are-bad-the-long-version-2c16dae145e2.

Apple, "Human Interface Guidelines," Apple Developer, 2022 https://developer.apple.com/design/human-interface-guidelines/macos/overview/themes/#//apple_ref/doc/uid/TP40002723-TPXREF101. Accessed 13 January 2022.

Arnesen, Eric, "Whiteness and the Historians' Imagination," *International Labor and Working-Class History*, 60 (2001), 3–32.

Arrow, Tom, Jenny Molloy, and Peter Murray-Rust, "A Day in the Life of a Content Miner and Team," *Insights: The UKSG Journal*, 29.2 (2016), 208–11. https://doi.org/10.1629/uksg.310.

Asimov, Isaac, *I, Robot* (London: Harper Voyager, 2018).

Atwood, Jeff, "Help Name Our Website," *Coding Horror*, 6 April 2008. https://blog.codinghorror.com/help-name-our-website/.

———, "What Does Stack Overflow Want to Be When It Grows Up?," *Coding Horror*, 22 October 2018. https://blog.codinghorror.com/what-does-stack-overflow-want-to-be-when-it-grows-up/.

Austin, J. L., *How to Do Things with Words* (Oxford: Clarendon Press, 1962).

Avalon Project, The, "The Statute of Anne; April 10, 1710," 2008. http://avalon.law.yale.edu/18th_century/anne_1710.asp. Accessed 28 April 2019.

Bacon, Madelyn, "What Is STIX (Structured Threat Information EXpression)?—Definition from WhatIs.Com," SearchSecurity, 2015. https://www.techtarget.com/searchsecurity/definition/STIX-Structured-Threat-Information-eXpression. Accessed 14 April 2022.

Baggs, Chris, "'The Whole Tragedy of Leisure in Penury': The South Wales Miners' Institute Libraries during the Great Depression," *Libraries & Culture*, 39.2 (2004), 115–36.

Bakhtin, Mikhail, *Rabelais and His World* (Bloomington, IN: Indiana University Press, 1984).

Ball, Stephen J., *The Education Debate* (Bristol: Policy, 2008).

Barasch, Moshe, *Light and Color in the Italian Renaissance Theory of Art* (New York: New York University Press, 1978).

Bardini, Thierry, *Bootstrapping: Douglas Engelbart, Coevolution, and the Origins of Personal Computing*, Writing Science (Stanford, CA: Stanford University Press, 2000).

Barrett, Catherine E., Alain K. Koyama, Pablo Alvarez, Wilson Chow, Elizabeth A. Lundeen, Cria G. Perrine, et al., "Risk for Newly Diagnosed Diabetes >30 Days After SARS-CoV-2 Infection among Persons Aged <18 Years—United States, March 1, 2020–June 28, 2021," *MMWR (Morbidity and Mortality Weekly Report)*, 71.2 (2022), 59–65. https://doi.org/10.15585/mmwr.mm7102e2.

Barrett, T. H., "The Woman Who Invented Notepaper: Towards a Comparative Historiography of Paper and Print," *Journal of the Royal Asiatic Society*, 21.2 (2011), 199–210.

Barron, Phillip, "E-Readers in the Classroom," *Transformations: The Journal of Inclusive Scholarship and Pedagogy*, 22.1 (2021), 133–38.

Barthes, Roland, "The Death of the Author," in *Image, Music, Text*, trans. by Stephen Heath (London: Fontana Press, 1987), 142–48.

———, *S/Z* (Oxford: John Wiley & Sons, 2009).

Basile, Jonathan, *Tar for Mortar: The Library of Babel and the Dream of Totality* (Santa Barbara, CA: Punctum Books, 2018).

Bassett, Caroline, "Feminism, Refusal, Artificial Writing," Transmediale, 2021. https://202122.transmediale.de/almanac/feminism-refusal-artificial-writing. Accessed 18 March 2023.

BBC News, "Squid Game Cryptocurrency Rockets in First Few Days of Trading," 29 October 2021. https://www.bbc.com/news/business-59059097.

BBC News, "Tim Berners-Lee Sells Web Source Code NFT for $5.4m," 30 June 2021. https://www.bbc.com/news/technology-57666335.

Beebe, Nelson H. F., "BIBTEX for ACM Publications," 2010, 37.

Beeton, Barbara, "Answer to 'What Is $ Used For?,'" TeX—LaTeX Stack Exchange, 13 April 2022. https://tex.stackexchange.com/a/640596.

Beeton, Barbara, Karl Berry, and David Walden, "TeX: A Branch in Desktop Publishing Evolution, Part 2," *IEEE Annals of the History of Computing*, 41.2 (2019), 29–41. https://doi.org/10.1109/MAHC.2019.2893731.

Bell, Julia, *Radical Attention* (London: Peninsula Press, 2020).

Belson, William A., "The Effect of Television on Cinema Going," *Audio Visual Communication Review*, 6.2 (1958), 131–39.

Bender, Emily M., Timnit Gebru, Angelina McMillan-Major, and Shmargaret Shmitchell, "On the Dangers of Stochastic Parrots: Can Language Models Be Too Big? 🦜," in *Proceedings of the 2021 ACM Conference on Fairness, Accountability, and Transparency* (presented at the FAccT '21: 2021 ACM Conference on Fairness, Accountability, and Transparency, Virtual Event Canada: ACM, 2021), 610–23. https://doi.org/10.1145/3442188.3445922.

Bender, Emily M., and Alex Hanna, "AI Causes Real Harm. Let's Focus on That over the End-of-Humanity Hype," *Scientific American*, 12 August 2023. https://www.scientificamerican.com/article/we-need-to-focus-on-ais-real-harms-not-imaginary-existential-risks/.

Benjamin, Walter, "The Work of Art in the Age of Mechanical Reproduction," in *Illuminations* (London: Pimlico, 1999), 211–44.

Bently, Lionel, Uma Suthersanen, and Paul Torresmans, eds., *Global Copyright: Three Hundred Years since the Statute of Anne, from 1709 to Cyberspace* (Cheltenham: Edward Elgar Publishing, 2010), 26–33. https://doi.org/10.4337/9781849806428.00010.

Berg, Lawrence D., Edward H. Huijbens, and Henrik Gutzon Larsen, "Producing Anxiety in the Neoliberal University: Producing Anxiety," *The Canadian Geographer / Le géographe canadien*, 60.2 (2016), 168–80. https://doi.org/10.1111/cag.12261.

Berger, John, *And Our Faces, My Heart, Brief as Photos* (London: Writers and Readers Publishing Cooperative, 1984).

Berry, David M., and Anders Fagerjord, *Digital Humanities: Knowledge and Critique in a Digital Age* (Cambridge: Polity, 2017).

Bertot, John Carlo, "Challenges and Issues for Public Managers in the Digital Era," *Public Manager*, 27.4 (1998), 27–31.

Bérubé, Michael, *The Secret Life of Stories: From Don Quixote to Harry Potter, How Understanding Intellectual Disability Transforms the Way We Read* (New York: New York University Press, 2016).

Bhaskar, Michael, *The Content Machine: Towards a Theory of Publishing from the Printing Press to the Digital Network* (New York: Anthem Press, 2013).

Bigelow, Charles, "The Font Wars, Part 1," *IEEE Annals of the History of Computing*, 42.1 (2020), 7–24. https://doi.org/10.1109/MAHC.2020.2971202.

———, "The Font Wars, Part 2," *IEEE Annals of the History of Computing*, 42.1 (2020), 25–40. https://doi.org/10.1109/MAHC.2020.2971745.

Bilder, Geoffrey, *Disambiguation without De-Duplication: Modeling Authority and Trust in the ORCID System* (Crossref, 16 March 2011), 25.

Binder, Jeffrey M., "Romantic Disciplinarity and the Rise of the Algorithm," *Critical Inquiry*, 46.4 (2020), 813–34. https://doi.org/10.1086/709225.

Bird, Graham, "Kant's Transcendental Aesthetic," *British Journal for the History of Philosophy*, 7.1 (1999), 147–53.

Black, Alistair, *The Public Library in Britain, 1914–2000* (London: The British Library, 2000).

Blacklock, Mark, *The Emergence of the Fourth Dimension: Higher Spatial Thinking in the Fin de Siècle* (Oxford: Oxford University Press, 2018).

———, *Hinton* (London: Granta, 2020).

Blair-Early, Adream, and Mike Zender, "User Interface Design Principles for Interaction Design," *Design Issues*, 24.3 (2008), 85–107.

Bland, Mark, "The Appearance of the Text in Early Modern England," *Text*, 11 (1998), 91–154.

Bloch, William Goldbloom, *The Unimaginable Mathematics of Borges' Library of Babel* (Oxford: Oxford University Press, 2008).

Blum, Andrew, *Tubes: Behind the Scenes at the Internet* (London: Penguin, 2013).

Bodó, Balázs, "The Genesis of Library Genesis: The Birth of a Global Scholarly Shadow Library," in *Shadow Libraries: Access to Educational Materials in Global Higher Education*, ed. by Joe Karaganis (Cambridge, MA: MIT Press, 2018), 25–52.

Boomen, Marianne van den, *Transcoding the Digital: How Metaphors Matter in New Media* (Amsterdam: Institute of Network Cultures, 2014).

Borges, Jorge Luis, *Collected Fictions*, trans. by Andrew Hurley (New York: Penguin, 1998).

———, "The Library of Babel," in *Collected Fictions*, 113–14.

———, "On Exactitude in Science," in *Collected Fictions*, 325.

———, "The Sacred Unreadable Artifact," in *Collected Fictions*, 654–57.

Borzo, Jeanette, "Tools Resurrect Hope for Paperless Office Concept," Infoworld, 15.24 (14 June 1993).

Bourdieu, Pierre, "Social Space and Symbolic Power," *Sociological Theory*, 7.1 (1989), 14–25. https://doi.org/10.2307/202060.

Bourke, Joanna, *Birkbeck: 200 Years of Radical Learning for Working People*, History of Universities Series (New York: Oxford University Press, 2022).

———, *Rape: A History from 1860 to the Present Day* (London: Virago, 2010).

Bowker, Geoffrey C., and Susan Leigh Star, *Sorting Things Out: Classification and Its Consequences*, Inside Technology (Cambridge, MA: MIT Press, 1999).

Bracha, Oren, "The Statute of Anne: An American Mythology," *Houston Law Review*, 47.4 (2010), 877–918.

Brody, Jennifer DeVere, "The Blackness of Blackness . . . Reading the Typography of 'Invisible Man,'" *Theatre Journal*, 57.4 (2005), 679–98.

Brooks, Douglas A., ed., *Printing and Parenting in Early Modern England* (Aldershot: Ashgate, 2017). http://www.vlebooks.com/vleweb/product/openreader ?id=none&isbn=9781351908849. Accessed 14 December 2019.

Brown, Bill, "Thing Theory," *Critical Inquiry*, 28.1 (2001), 1–22.

Brown, Michelle P., ed., *In the Beginning: Bibles before the Year 1000* (Washington, DC: Freer Gallery of Art and Arthur M. Sackler Gallery, Smithsonian Institution, 2006).

———, "The Triumph of the Codex: The Manuscript Book before 1100," in Eliot and Rose, *A Companion to the History of the Book*, 179–93.

Brown, Wendy, *In the Ruins of Neoliberalism: The Rise of Antidemocratic Politics in the West*, The Wellek Library Lectures (New York: Columbia University Press, 2019).

———, *Undoing the Demos: Neoliberalism's Stealth Revolution* (New York: Zone Books, 2015).

Bruckman, Amy, "Teaching Students to Study Online Communities Ethically," *Journal of Information Ethics*, 15.2 (2006), 82–98.

Buccellati, Giorgio, *A Critique of Archaeological Reason: Structural, Digital, and Philosophical Aspects of the Excavated Record* (Cambridge: Cambridge University Press, 2017). https://doi.org/10.1017/9781107110298.

Burke, Kenneth, *Counter-Statement* (Berkeley: University of California Press, 1968).

Burke, Sean, *The Death and Return of the Author: Criticism and Subjectivity in Barthes, Foucault and Derrida* (Edinburgh: Edinburgh University Press, 2008).

Burton, Henry, *A Divine Tragedie Lately Acted, or A Collection of Sundry Memorable Examples of Gods Judgements upon Sabbath-Breakers, and Other like Libertines* (Amsterdam: J. F. Stam, 1636).

Burwell v. Hobby Lobby Stores, Inc., 573 U.S. 682 (2014).

Butler, Shane, *The Matter of the Page: Essays in Search of Ancient and Medieval Authors* (Madison: University of Wisconsin Press, 2011).

Cage, John, *4'33" (In Proportional Notation)*, 1952/1953, MoMA: The Museum of Modern Art website. https://www.moma.org/collection/works/163616. Accessed 8 March 2021.

———, *Silence: Lectures and Writings*, 50th anniversary ed. (Middletown, CT: Wesleyan University Press, 2011).

Calhoun, Joshua, "The Word Made Flax: Cheap Bibles, Textual Corruption, and the Poetics of Paper," *PMLA*, 126.2 (2011), 327–44.

Camp, L. Jean, and K. Lewis, "Code as Speech: A Discussion of Bernstein v. USDOJ, Karn v. USDOS, and Junger v. Daley in Light of the U.S. Supreme Court's Recent Shift to Federalism," KSG Faculty Research Working Papers

Series RWP01-007, February 2001. https://www.hks.harvard.edu/publica tions/code-speech.

Campanario, Juan Miguel, "Consolation for the Scientist: Sometimes It Is Hard to Publish Papers That Are Later Highly-Cited," *Social Studies of Science*, 23.2 (1993), 342–62.

———, "Have Referees Rejected Some of the Most-Cited Articles of All Times?," *Journal of the American Society for Information Science*, 47.4 (1996), 302–10. https://doi.org/10.1002/(SICI)1097-4571(199604)47:4<302::AID-AS I6>3.0.CO;2-0.

Campanario, Juan Miguel, and Erika Acedo, "Rejecting Highly Cited Papers: The Views of Scientists Who Encounter Resistance to Their Discoveries from Other Scientists," *Journal of the American Society for Information Science and Technology*, 58.5 (2007), 734–43. https://doi.org/10.1002/asi.20556.

Campbell, Courtney J., Allegra Giovine, and Jennifer Keating, "Introduction: Confronting Emptiness in History," in *Empty Spaces: Perspectives on Emptiness in Modern History*, ed. by Courtney J. Campbell, Allegra Giovine, and Jennifer Keating (London: University of London Press, 2019), 1–13. https:// www.jstor.org/stable/j.ctvp2n2r8.6. Accessed 9 March 2021.

Campbell, Mark Robin, "John Cage's 4'33": Using Aesthetic Theory to Understand a Musical Notion," *Journal of Aesthetic Education*, 26.1 (1992), 83–91. https://doi.org/10.2307/3332730.

Carroll, Rachel, "'Making the Blood Flow Backwards': Disability, Heterosexuality and the Politics of Representation in Julian Barnes's *The Sense of an Ending*," *Textual Practice*, 24 November 2014, 155–72. https://doi.org/10.1080 /0950236X.2014.955818.

Ceze, Luis, Jeff Nivala, and Karin Strauss, "Molecular Digital Data Storage Using DNA," *Nature Reviews Genetics*, 20.8 (2019), 456–66. https://doi.org/ 10.1038/s41576-019-0125-3.

Chan, Jonathan, "UPDATE: U+237C ⍼ &angzarr," ⟨ortho/normal⟩ (blog), 6 June 2023. https://ionathan.ch//2023/06/06/angzarr.html.

———, "U+237C ⍼ RIGHT ANGLE WITH DOWNWARDS ZIGZAG ARROW," ⟨ortho/normal⟩ (blog), 9 April 2022. https://ionathan.ch//2022/04/09/angzarr .html.

Chartier, Roger, *Forms and Meanings: Texts, Performances, and Audiences from Codex to Computer* (Philadelphia: University of Pennsylvania Press, 1995).

———, "Languages, Books, and Reading from the Printed Word to the Digital Text," trans. by Teresa Lavender Fagan, *Critical Inquiry*, 31.1 (2004), 133–52. https://doi.org/10.1086/427305.

Chen, Raymond, "Windows Brings out the Rorschach Test in Everyone," *The*

Old New Thing (blog), Microsoft, 25 August 2003. https://devblogs.microsoft
.com/oldnewthing/20030825-00/?p=42803.

Chiang, Ted, *Stories of Your Life and Others: Ted Chiang* (London: Picador, 2015).

Chin, Monica, "How a University Got Itself Banned from the Linux Kernel,"
The Verge, 30 April 2021. https://www.theverge.com/2021/4/30/22410164/
linux-kernel-university-of-minnesota-banned-open-source.

Chiou, Theodoros, "Copyright Lessons on Machine Learning: What Impact on
Algorithmic Art?," *JIPITEC*, 10.3 (2020). https://www.jipitec.eu/issues/
jipitec-10-3-2019/5025.

Chisita, Collence T., Blessing Chiparausha, and Danmore Maboreke, "Bibliographic Control in Zimbabwe: The Conundrum of Legal Deposit in the
Age of Digital Technologies," in Gooding and Terras, *Electronic Legal Deposit*, 77–98.

Chomsky, Noam, Ian Roberts, and Jeffrey Watumull, "The False Promise of
ChatGPT," *New York Times*, 8 March 2023. https://www.nytimes.com/2023
/03/08/opinion/noam-chomsky-chatgpt-ai.html.

Chown, Eric, and Fernando Nascimento, *Meaningful Technologies: How Digital
Metaphors Change the Way We Think and Live* (Lever Press, 2023). https://doi
.org/10.3998/mpub.12668201.

Christiansen, Thomas, "Manufacture of Black Ink in the Ancient Mediterranean," *Bulletin of the American Society of Papyrologists*, 54 (2017), 167–95.
https://doi.org/10.2143/BASP.54.0.3239877.

Christiansen, Thomas, Marine Cotte, René Loredo-Portales, Poul Erik Linde-
lof, Kell Mortensen, Kim Ryholt, et al., "The Nature of Ancient Egyptian
Copper-Containing Carbon Inks Is Revealed by Synchrotron Radiation
Based X-Ray Microscopy," *Scientific Reports*, 7.1 (2017), 1–8. https://doi.org/
10.1038/s41598-017-15652-7.

Christiansen, Thomas, Marine Cotte, Wout de Nolf, Elouan Mouro, Juan
Reyes-Herrera, Steven de Meyer, et al., "Insights into the Composition of
Ancient Egyptian Red and Black Inks on Papyri Achieved by Synchrotron-
Based Microanalyses," *Proceedings of the National Academy of Sciences*,
117.45 (2020), 27825–35. https://doi.org/10.1073/pnas.2004534117.

Chu, Yi-Chun, David Bainbridge, Matt Jones, and Ian H. Witten, "Realistic
Books: A Bizarre Homage to an Obsolete Medium?," in *Proceedings of the
2004 Joint ACM/IEEE Conference on Digital Libraries—JCDL '04* (presented
at the 2004 joint ACM/IEEE conference, Tucson, AZ, USA: ACM Press,
2004), 78. https://doi.org/10.1145/996350.996372.

Chun, Wendy Hui Kyong, "The Enduring Ephemeral, or The Future Is a
Memory," in *Media Archaeology: Approaches, Applications, and Implications*,

ed. by Erkki Huhtamo and Jussi Parikka (Berkeley: University of California Press, 2011), 184–206.

———, "On 'Sourcery,' or Code as Fetish," *Configurations*, 16.3 (2008), 299–324. https://doi.org/10.1353/con.0.0064.

Citizens United v. FEC, 558 U.S. 310 (2010).

Clarke, Michael, and Laura Ricci, *Open Access EBook Supply Chain Maps for Distribution and Usage Reporting* (Zenodo, 9 April 2021). https://doi.org/10.5281/zenodo.4681871.

Clayton, Owen, ed., *Representing Homelessness*, Proceedings of the British Academy (Oxford: Oxford University Press, 2022).

Cogan, Jacob Katz, "The Look Within: Property, Capacity, and Suffrage in Nineteenth-Century America," *Yale Law Journal*, 107.2 (1997), 473–98. https://doi.org/10.2307/797262.

Cohen, I. Glenn, and Jonathan H. Blavin, "Gore, Gibson, and Goldsmith: The Evolution of Internet Metaphors in Law and Commentary," *Harvard Journal of Law & Technology*, 16.1 (2002), 265–85.

Coldicutt, Rachel, "Just Enough Internet: Why Public Service Internet Should Be a Model of Restraint," Doteveryone, 21 October 2019. https://doteveryone.org.uk/2019/10/just-enough-internet.

Cole, Teju, "Black Paper," in *Black Paper: Writing in a Dark Time* (Chicago: University of Chicago Press, 2021), 253–58.

Coleman, D. C., *The British Paper Industry, 1495–1860 : A Study in Industrial Growth* (Oxford: Clarendon Press, 1975).

Coleman, Gabriella, *Coding Freedom: The Ethics and Aesthetics of Hacking* (Princeton, NJ: Princeton University Press, 2012).

———, "The Political Agnosticism of Free and Open Source Software and the Inadvertent Politics of Contrast," *Anthropological Quarterly*, 77.3 (2004), 507–19. https://doi.org/10.2307/3318232.

Coleman, Sterling Joseph, "The British Council and Unesco in Ethiopia: A Comparison of Linear and Cyclical Patterns of Librarianship Development," *Library History*, 21.2 (2005), 121–30. https://doi.org/10.1179/002423005x44952.

Collier, Roger, "NHS Ransomware Attack Spreads Worldwide," *CMAJ : Canadian Medical Association Journal*, 189.22 (2017), E786–87. https://doi.org/10.1503/cmaj.1095434.

Conant, James Bryant, ed., *The Overthrow of the Phlogiston Theory: The Chemical Revolution of 1775–1789* (Cambridge, MA: Harvard University Press, 1964).

Connor, Steven, "CP: Or, A Few Don'ts by a Cultural Phenomenologist," *Parallax*, 5.2 (1999), 17–31. https://doi.org/10.1080/135346499249678.

———, *Living by Numbers: In Defence of Quantity* (London: Reaktion Books, 2016).

———, *The Madness of Knowledge: On Wisdom, Ignorance and Fantasies of Knowing* (London: Reaktion Books, 2019).

Cordell, Ryan, "'Q i-Jtb the Raven': Taking Dirty OCR Seriously," *Book History*, 20.1 (2017), 188–225. https://doi.org/10.1353/bh.2017.0006.

Cornish, William, "The Statute of Anne 1709–10: Its Historical Setting," in Bently, Suthersanen, and Torremans, *Global Copyright*, 14–25.

Costello, Leslie C., "Perspective: Is NIH Funding the 'Best Science by the Best Scientists'? A Critique of the NIH R01 Research Grant Review Policies," *Academic Medicine*, 85.5 (2010), 775–79. https://doi.org/10.1097/ACM.0b01 3e3181d74256.

Coulmas, Florian, *Writing Systems: An Introduction to Their Linguistic Analysis* (Cambridge: Cambridge University Press, 2003).

Cox, Joseph, "Why You Don't Roll Your Own Crypto," *Vice*, 10 December 2015. https://www.vice.com/en/article/wnx8nq/why-you-dont-roll-your-own -crypto.

Craig, Heidi, "Rags, Ragpickers, and Early Modern Papermaking," *Literature Compass*, 16.5 (2019), e12523. https://doi.org/10.1111/lic3.12523.

Cram, Jennifer, "Colonialism and Libraries in Third World Africa," *Australian Library Journal*, 42.1 (1993), 13–20. https://doi.org/10.1080/00049670.1993.10 755621.

Crew, Bec, "How Book Scorpions Tend to Your Dusty Tomes," *Scientific American Blog Network*, 25 August 2014. https://blogs.scientificamerican.com/ running-ponies/how-book-scorpions-tend-to-your-dusty-tomes/.

Crockford, Douglas, "Integrating Computers and Television," in Laurel, *The Art of Human-Computer Interface Design*, 461–66.

Cummings, James, "The Materiality of Markup and the Text Encoding Initiative," in *Digitizing Medieval and Early Modern Material Culture*, ed. by Brent Nelson and Melissa M. Terras (Toronto: Arizona Center for Medieval and Renaissance Studies, 2012), 49–81.

Current, Richard N., "The Original Typewriter Enterprise 1867–1873," *Wisconsin Magazine of History*, 32.4 (1949), 391–407.

Currie, Adrian, "Of Records and Ruins: Metaphors about the Deep Past," *Journal of the Philosophy of History*, 17.1 (2023), 154–75. https://doi.org/10.1163/ 18722636-12341493.

Custom Dynamics, LLC v. Radiantz Led Lighting, Inc., 535 F. Supp. 2d 542 (EDNC 2008).

Cypherspace, "Munitions T-Shirt." http://www.cypherspace.org/adam/rsa/uk -shirt.html. Accessed 23 September 2022.

Dagenais, John, "Decolonizing the Medieval Page," in Stoicheff and Taylor, *The Future of the Page*, 37–70.

Daintith, John, ed., *A Dictionary of Chemistry*, 6th ed. (New York: Oxford University Press, 2008).

Dale, Robert, "GPT-3: What's It Good For?," *Natural Language Engineering*, 27.1 (2021), 113–18. https://doi.org/10.1017/S1351324920000601.

Dane, Joseph A., *Blind Impressions: Methods and Mythologies in Book History*, Material Texts (Philadelphia: University of Pennsylvania Press, 2013).

———, *Out of Sorts: On Typography and Print Culture*, Material Texts (Philadelphia: University of Pennsylvania Press, 2011).

Darnton, Robert, "What Is the History of Books?," *Daedalus*, 111.3 (1982), 65–83.

Da Rold, Orietta, *Paper in Medieval England: From Pulp to Fictions*, Cambridge Studies in Medieval Literature, 112 (Cambridge: Cambridge University Press, 2020).

David, Paul A., "Clio and the Economics of QWERTY," *American Economic Review*, 75.2 (1985), 332–37.

Davie, Bruce, "It's Time to Decentralize the Internet, Again: What Was Distributed Is Now Centralized by Google, Facebook, Etc," *Register*, 11 August 2021. https://www.theregister.com/2021/08/11/decentralized_internet/.

Davies, William, *The Limits of Neoliberalism: Authority, Sovereignty and the Logic of Competition* (Thousand Oaks, CA: SAGE, 2014).

Deazley, Ronan, "Commentary on the Statute of Anne 1710," Primary Sources on Copyright (1450–1900) (website), ed. by Lionel Bently and Martin Kretschmer, 2008. https://www.copyrighthistory.org/cam/tools/request/show Record.php?id=commentary_uk_1710.

———, "What's New about the Statute of Anne? Or Six Observations in Search of an Act," in Bently, Suthersanen, and Torremans, *Global Copyright*, 26–33.

De Bolla, Peter, *The Architecture of Concepts: The Historical Formation of Human Rights* (New York: Fordham University Press, 2013).

De Hamel, Christopher, *The Book: The History of the Bible* (London: Phaidon Press, 2005).

Demenchonok, Edward, "From Power Politics to the Ethics of Peace," in *Philosophy after Hiroshima*, ed. by Edward Demenchonok (Newcastle upon Tyne: Cambridge Scholars, 2010), 1–42.

DeNardis, Laura, *Protocol Politics: The Globalization of Internet Governance* (Cambridge, MA: MIT Press, 2009).

Derrida, Jacques, *Glas*, trans. by John P. Leavey Jr. and Richard Rand (Lincoln: University of Nebraska Press, 1986).

———, "The Law of Genre," trans. by Avital Ronell, *Critical Inquiry*, 7.1 (1980), 55–81.

———, *Paper Machine*, trans. by Rachel Bowlby, Cultural Memory in the Present (Stanford, CA: Stanford University Press, 2005).

———, *Writing and Difference*, trans. by Alan Bass, Routledge Classics (London: Routledge, 2005).

DeSantis, Rachel, "Inside the Real-Life Love Story That Inspired Microsoft's 'Bliss,' the Most Viewed Photo Ever," PEOPLE.Com, 14 April 2021. https://people.com/human-interest/how-an-unlikely-love-story-inspired-bliss-famous-microsoft-photo/.

"Desktop Metaphor," 2001. https://web.archive.org/web/20010222011552/http://www.csdl.tamu.edu/~lof0954/academic/cpsc610/hw2-3.htm. Accessed 14 December 2021.

Deville, Joe, Samuel Moore, and Tahani Nadim, eds., *The Commons and Care* (Birmingham: Post Office Press and Rope Press, 2018). https://hcommons.org/deposits/item/hc:19817/.

de Vries, Alex, "Renewable Energy Will Not Solve Bitcoin's Sustainability Problem," *Joule*, 3.4 (2019), 893–98. https://doi.org/10.1016/j.joule.2019.02.007.

de Vries, Alex, and Christian Stoll, "Bitcoin's Growing E-Waste Problem," *Resources, Conservation and Recycling*, 175 (2021), 105901. https://doi.org/10.1016/j.resconrec.2021.105901.

Dhaliwal, Ranjodh Singh, "On Addressability, or What Even Is Computation?," *Critical Inquiry*, 49.1 (2022), 1–27. https://doi.org/10.1086/721167.

Di Bitetti, Mario S., and Julián A. Ferreras, "Publish (in English) or Perish: The Effect on Citation Rate of Using Languages Other than English in Scientific Publications," *Ambio*, 46.1 (2017), 121–27. https://doi.org/10.1007/s13280-016-0820-7.

Diffie, Whitfield, and Susan Landau, "The Export of Cryptography in the 20th and the 21st Centuries," in *The History of Information Security*, ed. by Karl De Leeuw and Jan Bergstra (Amsterdam: Elsevier Science B.V., 2007), 725–36. https://doi.org/10.1016/B978-044451608-4/50027-4.

Digiconomist, "Bitcoin Energy Consumption Index." https://digiconomist.net/bitcoin-energy-consumption/. Accessed 26 October2021.

Digital Education Strategies, the Chang School, and Greg Gay, "The Evolution of Web Accessibility," in *Professional Web Accessibility Auditing Made Easy* (Toronto: Ryerson University Press, 2019). https://pressbooks.library.ryerson.ca/pwaa/chapter/the-evolution-of-web-accessibility/. Accessed 10 January 2022.

D'Ignazio, Catherine, and Lauren F. Klein, *Data Feminism*, Strong Ideas Series (Cambridge, MA: MIT Press, 2020).

Ding, Aaron Yi, Gianluca Limon De Jesus, and Marijn Janssen, "Ethical Hacking for Boosting IoT Vulnerability Management: A First Look into Bug Bounty Programs and Responsible Disclosure," in *Proceedings of the Eighth International Conference on Telecommunications and Remote Sensing*, ICTRS '19 (New York: Association for Computing Machinery, 2019), 49–55. https://doi.org/10.1145/3357767.3357774.

Diringer, David, *The Alphabet: A Key to the History of Mankind* (London: Hutchinson's Scientific and Technical Publications, 1948).

DiSalvo, Carl, *Design as Democratic Inquiry: Putting Experimental Civics into Practice* (Cambridge, MA: MIT Press, 2022).

Dobrusskin, Beate, and Kirsten Glaus, *Katalog der Schadensbilder Spuren und Phänomene an Kunst und Kulturgut Papier, Dobrusskin, Beate; Glaus, Kirsten (2012). Catalogue of Damage Terminology for Works of Art and Cultural Property Paper [Textbook]*, trans. by Jean F. Rosston (Bern: Schriftenreihe Konservierung und Restaurierung der Hochschule der Künste Bern, 2012). https://arbor.bfh.ch/10329/.

Dolgin, Elie, "The Secret Social Lives of Viruses," *Nature*, 570.7761 (2019), 290–92. https://doi.org/10.1038/d41586-019-01880-6.

Donahoo, Daniel, "Why the A Magazine Is an iPad That Does Not Work Video Is Ridiculous," *Wired*, 14 October 2011. https://www.wired.com/2011/10/why-the-a-magazine-is-an-ipad-that-does-not-work-video-is-ridiculous/.

Douglas, Mary, "The Idea of a Home: A Kind of Space," *Social Research*, 58.1 (1991), 287–307.

Drucker, Johanna, *The Century of Artists' Books* (New York: Granary Books, 1995).

——, "Graphesis," *Paj: The Journal of the Initiative for Digital Humanities, Media, and Culture*, 2.1 (2010). https://journals.tdl.org/paj/index.php/paj/article/view/4.

——, "Graphical Readings and the Visual Aesthetics of Textuality," *Text*, 16 (2006), 267–76.

——, *SpecLab: Digital Aesthetics and Projects in Speculative Computing* (Chicago: University of Chicago Press, 2009).

Du Bois, W. E. B., "Jefferson Davis as a Representative of Civilization," 1890, Special Collections and University Archives, University of Massachusetts Amherst Libraries, W. E. B. Du Bois Papers (MS 312). http://credo.library.umass.edu/view/full/mums312-b196-i029. Accessed 4 May 2021.

Duncan, Dennis, *Index, A History of the: A Bookish Adventure* (London: Allen Lane, 2021).

Duncan, Dennis, and Adam Smyth, "Introduction," in *Book Parts*, ed. by Dennis Duncan and Adam Smyth (Oxford: Oxford University Press, 2019), 3–10.

Dwork, Cynthia, and Moni Naor, "Pricing via Processing or Combatting Junk Mail," in *Advances in Cryptology—CRYPTO' 92*, ed. by Ernest F. Brickell, Lecture Notes in Computer Science (Berlin: Springer, 1993), 139–47. https://doi.org/10.1007/3-540-48071-4_10.

Dworkin, Craig, *No Medium* (Cambridge, MA: MIT Press, 2015).

Eire, Carlos M. N., *War against the Idols: The Reformation of Worship from Erasmus to Calvin* (Cambridge: Cambridge University Press, 1998).

Eisenstein, Elizabeth L, *The Printing Press as an Agent of Change: Communications and Cultural Transformations in Early-Modern Europe* (Cambridge: Cambridge University Press, 2009). https://doi.org/10.1017/CBO9781107049963.

Electronic Frontier Foundation, "Digital Rights Management: A Failure in the Developed World, a Danger to the Developing World," 23 March 2005. https://www.eff.org/wp/digital-rights-management-failure-developed-world-danger-developing-world.

Eliot, Simon, and Jonathan Rose, eds., *A Companion to the History of the Book*, Blackwell Companions to Literature and Culture, 48 (Malden, MA: Blackwell Publishers, 2007).

Elkins, Katherine, and Jon Chun, "Can GPT-3 Pass a Writer's Turing Test?," *Journal of Cultural Analytics*, 5.2 (2020), 17212. https://doi.org/10.22148/001c.17212.

Emens, Elizabeth F., "Framing Disability," *University of Illinois Law Review*, 5(2012), 1383–1442.

Emre, Merve, *Paraliterary: The Making of Bad Readers in Postwar America* (Chicago: University of Chicago Press, 2017).

Engelbart, D. C., "The Augmented Knowledge Workshop," in *A History of Personal Workstations*, ed. by A. Goldberg (New York: ACM Press, 1988), 187–232.

———, *Augmenting Human Intellect: A Conceptual Framework* (Menlo Park, CA: Air Force Office of Scientific Research, 1962).

Erickson, Thomas D., "Working with Interface Metaphors," in Laurel, *The Art of Human-Computer Interface Design*, 65–73.

Ermanen, "Is the Kanji/Kokuji 'Taito' (たいと) with 84 Strokes Legitimate and Ever Used?," Japanese Language Stack Exchange, 20 December 2014. https://japanese.stackexchange.com/q/20980.

Eve, Martin Paul, *The Digital Humanities and Literary Studies* (Oxford: Oxford University Press, 2022).

———, "The Great Automatic Grammatizator: Writing, Labour, Computers," *Critical Quarterly*, 59.3 (2017), 39–54. https://doi.org/10.1111/criq.12359.

———, "If We Choose to Align Open Access to Research with Geo-Political Borders We Negate the Moral Value of Open Access," *LSE Impact Blog*, 11

November 2019. https://blogs.lse.ac.uk/impactofsocialsciences/2019/11/11/
if-we-choose-to-align-open-access-to-research-with-geo-political-borders
-we-negate-the-moral-value-of-open-access/.

———, "Jennifer Egan," in *Dictionary of Literary Biography: Twenty-First-
Century American Novelists*, vol. 382, ed. by George P. Anderson (Columbia,
SC: Bruccoli Clark Layman, 2018), 75–86.

———, "Lessons from the Library: Extreme Minimalist Scaling at Pirate Ebook
Platforms," *Digital Humanities Quarterly*, 2022.

———, "On the Political Aesthetics of Metadata," *Alluvium*, 5.1 (2016). https://
doi.org/10.7766/alluvium.v5.1.04.

———, *Open Access and the Humanities: Contexts, Controversies and the Future*
(Cambridge: Cambridge University Press, 2014). https://doi.org/10.1017/
CBO9781316161012.

———, *Password* (New York: Bloomsbury, 2016).

———, "Review of Alan Liu, Local Transcendence: Essays on Postmodern Historicism and the Database," *Textual Practice*, 24.6 (2010), 1117–19. https://doi
.org/10.1080/0950236X.2010.521676.

———, "Scarcity and Abundance," in *The Bloomsbury Handbook of Electronic
Literature*, ed. by Joseph Tabbi (London: Bloomsbury, 2017), 385–98.

———, "Textual Scholarship and Contemporary Literary Studies: Jennifer
Egan's Editorial Processes and the Archival Edition of Emerald City," *Lit:
Literature Interpretation Theory*, 31.1 (2020), 25–41. https://doi.org/10.1080/
10436928.2020.1709713.

———, *Warez: The Infrastructure and Aesthetics of Piracy* (New York: Punctum
Books, 2021).

Eve, Martin Paul, and Jonathan Gray, eds., *Reassembling Scholarly Communications: Histories, Infrastructures, and Global Politics of Open Access* (Cambridge, MA: MIT Press, 2020).

Eve, Martin Paul, Cameron Neylon, Daniel O'Donnell, Samuel Moore, Robert
Gadie, Victoria Odeniyi, et al., *Reading Peer Review: PLOS ONE and Institutional Change in Academia* (Cambridge: Cambridge University Press,
2021).

Eyre-Walker, Adam, and Nina Stoletzki, "The Assessment of Science: The Relative Merits of Post-Publication Review, the Impact Factor, and the Number
of Citations," *PLOS Biology*, 11.10 (2013), e1001675. https://doi.org/10.1371/
journal.pbio.1001675.

"Facts and Figures of the British Library," The British Library (website). https:
//www.bl.uk/about-us/our-story/facts-and-figures-of-the-british-library.
Accessed 10 March 2020.

Fang, Ferric C, Anthony Bowen, and Arturo Casadevall, "NIH Peer Review

Percentile Scores Are Poorly Predictive of Grant Productivity," *ELife*, 5 (2016), e13323. https://doi.org/10.7554/eLife.13323.

Farbowitz, Jonathan, "More Than Digital Dirt: Preserving Malware in Archives, Museums, and Libraries" (New York University, 2016). http://archive .org/details/16sThesisFarbowitzFinal. Accessed 18 April 2022.

Febvre, Lucien, and Henri-Jean Martin, *The Coming of the Book: The Impact of Printing 1450—1800*, Verso Classics (London: Verso, 2000).

Fein, Susanna, "Somer Soneday: Kingship, Sainthood, and Fortune in Oxford, Bodleian Library, MS Laud Misc. 108," in *The Texts and Contexts of Oxford, Bodleian Library, MS Laud Misc. 108* (Amsterdam: Brill, 2011), 275–97. https://brill.com/view/book/edcoll/9789004192249/Bej.9789004192065.i-342_015 .xml.

Felski, Rita, *The Limits of Critique* (Chicago: University of Chicago Press, 2015).

Felt, Ulrike, "Sociotechnical Imaginaries of 'the Internet,' Digital Health Information and the Making of Citizen-Patients," in *Science and Democracy: Making Knowledge and Making Power in the Biosciences and Beyond*, ed. by Stephen Hilgartner, Clark Miller, and Rob Hagendijk (New York: Routledge, Taylor & Francis Group, 2015), 176–97.

Felten, Ed, "Taking Stevens Seriously," *Freedom to Tinker: Research and Expert Commentary on Digital Technologies in Public Life*(blog), 17 July 2006. https://freedom-to-tinker.com/2006/07/17/taking-stevens-seriously/.

Ferran, Bronač, *The Smell of Ink and Soil. The Story of (Edition) Hansjörg Mayer* (Cologne: Walther Koenig, 2017).

Fessenden, Therese, "Scrolling and Attention," Nielsen Norman Group, 2018. https://www.nngroup.com/articles/scrolling-and-attention/. Accessed 4 March 2021.

Fielder, Brigitte, and Jonathan Senchyne, eds., *Against a Sharp White Background: Infrastructures of African American Print* (Madison: University of Wisconsin Press, 2019).

Fieldhouse, Maggie, and Audrey Marshall, *Collection Development in the Digital Age* (London: Facet Publishing, 2011).

Finnegan, Kenneth, "Creating an Autonomous System for Fun and Profit," *The Life of Kenneth* (blog), 15 November 2017. https://blog.thelifeofkenneth.com /2017/11/creating-autonomous-system-for-fun-and.html.

Fiormonte, Domenico, "Digital Humanities and the Geopolitics of Knowledge," *Digital Studies/Le Champ Numérique*, 7.1 (2017), 5. https://doi.org/10 .16995/dscn.274.

———, "Towards a Cultural Critique of the Digital Humanities," *Historical Social Research / Historische Sozialforschung*, 37.3 (2012), 59–76.

Fitzpatrick, Elizabeth B., "The Public Library as Instrument of Colonialism:

The Case of the Netherlands East Indies," *Libraries & the Cultural Record*, 43.3 (2008), 270–85.

Fitzpatrick, Kathleen, *Planned Obsolescence: Publishing, Technology, and the Future of the Academy* (New York: New York University Press, 2011).

Floridi, Luciano, *The Philosophy of Information* (Oxford: Oxford University Press, 2011).

Foucault, Michel, "The Eye of Power," in *Power/Knowledge: Selected Interviews and Other Writings, 1972–1977*, ed. by Colin Gordon, trans. by Colin Gordon (Brighton: Harvester Press, 1980), 146–65.

——, "Of Other Spaces," trans. by Jay Miskowiec, *Diacritics*, 16.1 (1986), 22–27.

——, "What Is an Author?," in *The Essential Works of Michel Foucault, 1954–1984*, vol. 2 (London: Penguin, 2000), 205–22.

Fox, James, *The World According to Colour: A Cultural History* (London: Allen Lane, 2021).

Frutiger, A., "The IBM SELECTRIC Composer: The Evolution of Composition Technology," *IBM Journal of Research and Development*, 12.1 (1968), 9–14. https://doi.org/10.1147/rd.121.0009.

Gann, Kyle, *No Such Thing as Silence: John Cage's 4'33"* (New Haven, CT: Yale University Press, 2010).

Gardner, Eric, *Black Print Unbound: The Christian Recorder, African American Literature, and Periodical Culture* (New York: Oxford University Press, 2015).

Garland-Thomson, Rosemarie, *Extraordinary Bodies: Figuring Physical Disability in American Culture and Literature* (New York: Columbia University Press, 2017).

——, "Feminist Disability Studies," *Signs: Journal of Women in Culture and Society*, 30.2 (2005), 1557–87. https://doi.org/10.1086/423352.

Garner, Bryan A, *Black's Law Dictionary, Abridged*, 9th ed. (Toronto: West, 2010).

Gavin, Michael, *Literary Mathematics: Quantitative Theory for Textual Studies*, Stanford Text Technologies (Stanford, CA: Stanford University Press, 2023).

Geiger, John, *Chapel of Extreme Experience: A Short History of Stroboscopic Light and the Dream Machine* (Brooklyn, NY: Soft Skull Press 2003).

Genette, Gérard, *Paratexts*, trans. by Jane E. Lewin (Cambridge: Cambridge University Press, 1997).

Giesecke, Joan, "Finding the Right Metaphor: Restructuring, Realigning, and Repackaging Today's Research Libraries," *Journal of Library Administration*, 51.1 (2010), 54–65. https://doi.org/10.1080/01930826.2011.531641.

Gilchrist, Alan L., *Seeing Black and White* (Oxford: Oxford University Press, 2006).

Giles, Lionel, "Dated Chinese Manuscripts in the Stein Collection," *Bulletin of the School of Oriental Studies, University of London*, 7.4 (1935), 809–36.

Gillam, Richard, *Unicode Demystified: A Practical Programmer's Guide to the Encoding Standard* (Boston, MA: Addison-Wesley, 2003).

Gillespie, Alexandra, "The History of the Book," in *New Medieval Literatures*, vol. 9, ed. by David Lawton, Wendy Scase, and Rita Copeland (Turnhout, Belgium: Brepols, 2007), 245–86. https://www.brepolsonline.net/doi/10.14 84/J.NML.2.302743.

Gitelman, Lisa, "Media, Materiality, and the Measure of the Digital: Or, the Case of Sheet Music and the Problem of Piano Rolls," in *Memory Bytes: History, Technology, and Digital Culture*, ed. by Lauren Rabinovitz and Abraham Geil (Durham: Duke University Press, 2004), 199–217.

Godwin, Mike, "Meme, Counter-Meme," *Wired*, 1 October 1994. http://www.wired.com/wired/archive/2.10/godwin.if_pr.html.

Goldberg, Yoav, "A Criticism of 'On the Dangers of Stochastic Parrots: Can Language Models Be Too Big?,'" GitHub Gist, 23 January 2021. https://gist.github.com/yoavg/9fc9be2f98b47c189a513573d902fb27.

Gonsalves, Robert A., "Who Owns AI-Generated Art?," Medium, 1 March 2022. https://robgon.medium.com/who-owns-ai-generated-art-3b38626e8b33.

Gooding, Paul, and Melissa Terras, eds., *Electronic Legal Deposit: Shaping the Library Collections of the Future*, (London: Facet Publishing, 2020).

——, "Inheriting Library Cards to Babel and Alexandria: Contemporary Metaphors for the Digital Library," *International Journal on Digital Libraries*, 18.3 (2017), 207–22. https://doi.org/10.1007/s00799-016-0194-2.

——, "Introduction," in Gooding and Terras, *Electronic Legal Deposit*, xxiii–xxx.

Goodley, Dan, and Rebecca Lawthom, "Critical Disability Studies, Brexit and Trump: A Time of Neoliberal-Ableism," *Rethinking History*, 23.2 (2019), 233–51. https://doi.org/10.1080/13642529.2019.1607476.

Google, "About Google, Our Culture & Company News," 2020. https://about.google. Accessed 7 March 2020.

——, "KCTF," 2022. https://github.com/google/kctf. Accessed 19 April 2022.

Gozzi, Raymond, "The Power of Metaphor: In the Age of Electronic Media," *ETC: A Review of General Semantics*, 56.4 (2000), 380–404.

Gracyk, Theodore, and Andrew Kania, *The Routledge Companion to Philosophy and Music*, Routledge Philosophy Companions (London: Routledge, 2014).

Graziano, Valeria, Marcell Mars, and Tomislav Medak, "Introduction to Pirate Care," *Pirate Care Syllabus*, 2020. https://syllabus.pirate.care/topic/pirate careintroduction/. Accessed 18 September 2021.

Greetham, David, "The Philosophical Discourse of [Textuality]," in *Reimagining Textuality: Textual Studies in the Late Age of Print*, ed. by Elizabeth Bergmann Loizeaux and Neil Fraistat (Madison: University of Wisconsin Press, 2002), 31–47.

Greg, W. W., "On Certain False Dates in Shakespearian Quartos," *Library*, 34 (1908), 113–31.

Grindea, Miron, ed., *The London Library* (Ipswich: Boydell Press, 1978). http://archive.org/details/londonlibrary0000unse. Accessed 9 May 2022.

Grinfield, Edward William, *A Reply to Mr. Brougham's "Practical Observations upon the Education of the People; Addressed to the Working Classes and Their Employers"* (London: C. & J. Rivington, 1825).

Grosseteste, Robert, "De Iride Seu de Iride et Speculo," in *Beitrage Zur Geschichte Der Philosophie Des Mittelalters*, vol. 9, ed. by Ludwig Baur (Münster: Aschendorff, 1912), 72–78.

Grotke, Kelly L., and Stephen Hastings-King, "Historical Genesis of the Relation between Science, Numbers and Politics—Part I Introduction," in *Science, Numbers and Politics*, ed. by Markus J. Prutsch (New York: Springer Berlin Heidelberg, 2019), 21–27.

Guadamuz, Andrés, "The Monkey Selfie: Copyright Lessons for Originality in Photographs and Internet Jurisdiction," *Internet Policy Review*, 5.1 (2016). https://policyreview.info/articles/analysis/monkey-selfie-copyright-lessons-originality-photographs-and-internet-jurisdiction.

Guardian Staff and Agency, "Google Fires Software Engineer Who Claims AI Chatbot Is Sentient," *Guardian*, 23 July 2022. https://www.theguardian.com/technology/2022/jul/23/google-fires-software-engineer-who-claims-ai-chatbot-is-sentient.

Guillemin, Marilys, and Lynn Gillam, "Ethics, Reflexivity, and 'Ethically Important Moments' in Research," *Qualitative Inquiry*, 10.2 (2004), 261–80. https://doi.org/10.1177/1077800403262360.

Gullette, Margaret Morganroth, "Aged by Culture," in Twigg, *Routledge Handbook of Cultural Gerontology*, 21–28.

Hahn, Harlan, "The Politics of Physical Differences: Disability and Discrimination," *Journal of Social Issues*, 44.1 (1988), 39–47. https://doi.org/10.1111/j.1540-4560.1988.tb02047.x.

Hall, Jason David, "Popular Prosody: Spectacle and the Politics of Victorian Versification," *Nineteenth-Century Literature*, 62.2 (2007), 222–49. https://doi.org/10.1525/ncl.2007.62.2.222.

Hall, Richard, "On the University as Anxiety Machine," *Richard Hall's Space*, 19 March 2014. http://www.richard-hall.org/2014/03/19/on-the-university-as-anxiety-machine/.

Hall, Stuart, "Cultural Studies and Its Theoretical Legacies," in *Cultural Studies*, ed. by Lawrence Grossberg, Cary Nelson, and Paula A. Treichler (New York: Routledge, 1992), 277–94.

Hansen, David R., and Kyle K. Courtney, "A White Paper on Controlled Digital Lending of Library Books," Law Archive, 23 September 2018. https://doi.org/10.31228/osf.io/7fdyr.

Hardman, Phillipa, "Interpreting the Incomplete Scheme of Illustration in Cambridge, Corpus Christi College MS 61," *English Manuscript Studies 1100–1700*, 6 (1997), 52–69.

——, "Reading the Spaces: Pictorial Intentions in the Thornton MSS, Lincoln Cathedral MS 91, and BL MS Add. 31042," *Medium Aevum*, 63.2 (1994), 250–75.

——, "Windows into the Text: Unfilled Spaces in Some Fifteenth-Century English Manuscript," in *Texts and Their Contexts: Papers from the Early Book Society*, ed. by John Scattergood and Julia Boffey (Dublin: Four Courts Press, 1997), 44–70.

Harel, Naama, "De-Allegorizing Kafka's Ape: Two Animalistic Contexts," in *Kafka's Creatures: Animals, Hybrids, and Other Fantastic Beings*, ed. by Marc Lucht and Donna Yarri (Lanham, MD: Lexington Books, 2010), 53–66.

Harrison, K David, and Gregory Anderson, letter to Deborah Anderson, "Review of Proposal for Encoding Warang Chiti (Ho Orthography) in Unicode," 22 April 2007. https://www.unicode.org/L2/L2007/07137-warang-chiti-review.pdf.

Hartley, John, Jason Potts, Lucy Montgomery, Ellie Rennie, and Cameron Neylon, "Do We Need to Move from Communication Technology to User Community? A New Economic Model of the Journal as a Club," *Learned Publishing*, 32.1 (2019), 27–35. https://doi.org/10.1002/leap.1228.

Harvey, David, "The Geopolitics of Capitalism," in *Social Relations and Spatial Structures*, ed. by Derek Gregory and John Urry, Critical Human Geography (London: Macmillan Education UK, 1985), 128–63. https://doi.org/10.1007/978-1-349-27935-7_7.

Hayek, Friedrich, *The Constitution of Liberty* (Abingdon: Routledge, 2006).

——, *The Road to Serfdom* (Abingdon: Routledge, 2001).

Hayles, N. Katherine, *How We Became Posthuman: Virtual Bodies in Cybernetics, Literature, and Informatics* (Chicago: University Of Chicago Press, 1999).

——, *Writing Machines*, Mediawork Pamphlet (Cambridge, MA: MIT Press, 2002).

Heim, Michael, *Electric Language: A Philosophical Study of Word Processing* (New Haven, CT: Yale University Press, 1999).

Heisler, Yoni, "The Most Viewed Photo in the History of the World," BGR,

2015. https://bgr.com/general/most-viewed-photograph-windows-xp/. Accessed 15 December 2021.

Hemingway, Ernest, *The Old Man and the Sea* (New York: Scribner, 1996).

Hendricks, Perry, "The Axiology of Abortion: Should We Hope Pro-Choicers or Pro-Lifers Are Right?," *Ergo*, 7.29 (2021), 774–88. https://doi.org/10.3998 /ergo.1126.

Henley, Jon, "Chess Robot Grabs and Breaks Finger of Seven-Year-Old Opponent," *Guardian*, 24 July 2022. https://www.theguardian.com/sport/2022/jul /24/chess-robot-grabs-and-breaks-finger-of-seven-year-old-opponent-mos cow.

Henrickson, Leah, *Reading Computer-Generated Texts* (Cambridge: Cambridge University Press, 2021). https://doi.org/10.1017/9781108906463.

Hero of Alexandria, *The Pneumatics of Hero of Alexandria*, trans. by Bennet Woodcroft, History of Science Library Primary Sources (London: Taylor Walton and Maberly, 1971).

Hicks, Marie, *Programmed Inequality: How Britain Discarded Women Technologists and Lost Its Edge in Computing* (Cambridge, MA: MIT Press, 2018).

Hill, Will, *Space as Language: The Properties of Typographic Space* (Cambridge: Cambridge University Press, 2023). https://www.cambridge.org/core/ele ments/space-as-language/1BC7F7D5349DE22E88310CE06AB6F516.

Hills, Richard Leslie, *Papermaking in Britain 1488–1988* (London: Bloomsbury Academic, 2015).

Hinton, Charles Howard, *The Fourth Dimension* (New York: Arno Press, 1976).

Hollander, John, "It All Depends," *Social Research*, 58.1 (1991), 31–49.

Holley, Rose, "How Good Can It Get? Analysing and Improving OCR Accuracy in Large Scale Historic Newspaper Digitisation Programs," *D-Lib Magazine*, 15.3/4 (2009). https://doi.org/10.1045/march2009-holley.

Housman, Alfred Edward, "How Clear, How Lovely Bright," in *More Poems* (London: A. A. Knopf, 1936), 26–27.

Hu, Tung-Hui, *A Prehistory of the Cloud* (Cambridge, MA: MIT Press, 2015).

Hudson, Nicholas, "Challenging Eisenstein: Recent Studies in Print Culture," *Eighteenth-Century Life*, 26.2 (2002), 83–95.

Hufnagel, Silvia, Þórunn Sigurðardóttir, and Davíð Ólafsson, eds., *Paper Stories—Paper and Book History in Early Modern Europe* (Berlin: De Gruyter, 2023). https://doi.org/10.1515/9783111162768.

Hunt, Ray, "Transmission Control Protocol/Internet Protocol (TCP/IP)," in *Encyclopedia of Information Systems*, ed. by Hossein Bidgoli (New York: Elsevier, 2003), 489–510. https://doi.org/10.1016/B0-12-227240-4/00187-8.

Hunter, Dard, *Papermaking: The History and Technique of an Ancient Craft* (New York: Dover Publications, 1978).

Hurston, Zora Neale, "How It Feels to Be Colored Me," *World Tomorrow*, May 1928, 215–16.

Hutchinson, George, and John K. Young, "Introduction," in *Publishing Blackness: Textual Constructions of Race since 1850*, ed. by George Hutchinson and John K. Young, Editorial Theory and Literary Criticism (Ann Arbor: University of Michigan Press, 2013).

Huygens, Christiaan, *Correspondance*, vol. 4 (The Hague: Société Hollandaise des Sciences, 1888).

Ignatow, Gabe, "What Has Globalization Done to Developing Countries' Public Libraries?," *International Sociology*, 26.6 (2011), 746–68. https://doi.org/10.1177/0268580910393373.

Ihde, Don, *Embodied Technics* (Birkerød: Automatic Press/VIP, 2010).

IRG Meeting, "IRG Meeting No. 45 Website," 2015. https://appsrv.cse.cuhk.edu.hk/~irg/irg/irg45/IRG45.htm. Accessed 6 October 2021.

Isidore, Stephen A. Barney, W. J. Lewis, J. A. Beach, and Oliver Berghof, *The Etymologies of Isidore of Seville* (Cambridge: Cambridge University Press, 2006).

Islam, S. Nazrul, and John Winkel, "Climate Change and Social Inequality," *DESA Working Papers*, 152, 2017.

Jakobsson, Markus, and Ari Juels, "Proofs of Work and Bread Pudding Protocols," in *Secure Information Networks: Communications and Multimedia Security IFIP TC6/TC11 Joint Working Conference on Communications and Multimedia Security (CMS'99) September 20–21, 1999, Leuven, Belgium*, ed. by Bart Preneel, IFIP—The International Federation for Information Processing (Boston: Springer US, 1999), 258–72. https://doi.org/10.1007/978-0-387-35568-9_18.

Jarvis, Jeff, *The Gutenberg Parenthesis: The Age of Print and Its Lessons for the Age of the Internet* (New York: Bloomsbury Academic, 2023).

Jefferson, Thomas, *The Writings of Thomas Jefferson*, vol. 6, ed. by H. A. Washington (Washington, DC: The United States Congress, 1853).

Jenkins, Alice, *Space and the "March of Mind": Literature and the Physical Sciences in Britain, 1815–1850* (Oxford: Oxford University Press, 2007).

Johns, Adrian, *The Nature of the Book* (Chicago: University of Chicago Press, 1998).

Jones, Brad, "The Rise and Fall of Internet Explorer," Digital Trends, 2015. https://www.digitaltrends.com/computing/the-rise-and-fall-of-internet-explorer/. Accessed 12 November 2021.

Jorgensen, Kristine, *Gameworld Interfaces* (Cambridge, MA: MIT Press, 2013). http://ebookcentral.proquest.com/lib/bbk/detail.action?docID=3339717.

Jourdain, Anne, "Analysing the Symbolic Economy with Pierre Bourdieu: The

World of Crafts," *Forum for Social Economics*, 47.3–4 (2018), 342–61. https://doi.org/10.1080/07360932.2015.1075895.

Jung, Ena, "The Breath of Emily Dickinson's Dashes," *Emily Dickinson Journal*, 24.2 (2015), 1–23. https://doi.org/10.1353/edj.2015.0018.

Kahn, Douglas, "John Cage: Silence and Silencing," *Musical Quarterly*, 81.4 (1997), 556–98.

Karabacek, Josef, *Arab Paper*, trans. by Don Baker (London: Archetype, 2001).

Kaufmann, Eric, "The Dominant Ethnic Moment: Towards the Abolition of 'Whiteness'?," *Ethnicities*, 6.2 (2006), 231–53. https://doi.org/10.1177/1468796806063754.

Kay, A. C., "User Interface: A Personal View," in Laurel, *The Art of Human-Computer Interface Design*, 191–207.

Kay, Sarah, "Legible Skins: Animals and the Ethics of Medieval Reading," *Postmedieval: A Journal of Medieval Cultural Studies*, 2.1 (2011), 13–32. https://doi.org/10.1057/pmed.2010.48.

Kellner, Douglas, *Technology and Democracy: Toward a Critical Theory of Digital Technologies, Technopolitics, and Technocapitalism*, Medienkulturen im digitalen Zeitalter (Wiesbaden: Springer VS, 2021).

Kelly, Thomas, *History of Public Libraries in Great Britain, 1845–1975* (London: Library Association Publishing, 1977).

Kenlon, Seth, "Understanding Linus's Law for Open Source Security," Opensource.com, 21 February 2021. https://opensource.com/article/21/2/open-source-security.

Kennedy, Catherine, "Metaphor: Library" (unpublished master's thesis, University of Cape Town, 2007). https://open.uct.ac.za/handle/11427/8071. Accessed 4 October 2022.

Kern, Martin, "Ritual, Text, and the Formation of the Canon: Historical Transitions of 'Wen' in Early China," *T'oung Pao*, 87.1/3 (2001), 43–91.

Kessler, Gary, "File Signatures," GaryKessler.net, 2021. https://www.garykessler.net/library/file_sigs.html. Accessed 11 November 2021.

Kidd, Peter, "Nobody Cares about Your Blog!," *Medieval Manuscripts Provenance* (blog), 24 December 2022. https://mssprovenance.blogspot.com/2022/12/nobody-cares-about-your-blog.html.

——, "The RECEPTIO-Rossi Affair VI: The Backstory," *Medieval Manuscripts Provenance* (blog), 28 December 2022. https://mssprovenance.blogspot.com/2022/12/the-receptio-rossi-affair-vi-backstory.html.

Kihlstrom, John F., and Lillian Park, "Cognitive Psychology: Overview," in *Reference Module in Neuroscience and Biobehavioral Psychology* (Amsterdam: Elsevier, 2018), B9780128093245217000. https://doi.org/10.1016/B978-0-12-809324-5.21702-1.

Kincaid, Author Ellie, "University to Investigate Adjunct Professor after Alle-gations of Plagiarism—and Legal Threats," Retraction Watch, 30 Decem-ber 2022. https://retractionwatch.com/2022/12/30/university-to-investigate -adjunct-professor-after-allegations-of-plagiarism-and-legal-threats/.

Kington, Miles, *Le bumper book de franglais*(Brecon: Old Street, 2011). https:// archive.org/details/lebumperbookdefrooooking_h5x9.

Kinross, Robin, *A4 and Before: Towards a Long History of Paper Sizes*, KB Lec-ture, 6 (Wassenaar: NIAS, 2009).

Kirillova, Olga, "The Chemical Theory of Phlogiston in the Cultural Economy of Fire: From the Enlightenment to Contemporary Times," *Stasis*, 11.1 (2021), 75–111. https://doi.org/10.33280/2310-3817-21-11-1-75-111.

Kirschenbaum, Matthew G., *Bitstreams: The Future of Digital Literary Heritage* (Philadelphia: University of Pennsylvania Press, 2021).

———, "Extreme Inscription: Towards a Grammatology of the Hard Drive," *Text Technology*, 2 (2004), 91–125.

———, "Hello Worlds," *Chronicle of Higher Education*, 23 January 2009. https:/ /www.chronicle.com/article/Hello-Worlds/5476.

———, *Mechanisms: New Media and the Forensic Imagination* (Cambridge, MA: MIT Press, 2008).

———, "Prepare for the Textpocalypse," *Atlantic*, 8 March 2023. https://www .theatlantic.com/technology/archive/2023/03/ai-chatgpt-writing-language -models/673318/.

———, *Track Changes: A Literary History of Word Processing* (Cambridge, MA: The Belknap Press of Harvard University Press, 2016).

Kitch, Aaron, "Bastards and Broadsides in 'The Winter's Tale,'" *Renaissance Drama, New Series*, 30 (2001), 43–71.

Kittler, Friedrich A., *Discourse Networks 1800/1900*, trans. by Michael Metteer and Chris Cullens (Stanford, CA: Stanford University Press, 1990).

———, *Gramophone, Film, Typewriter*, trans. by Geoffrey Winthroup-Young and Michael Wutz (Stanford, CA: Stanford University Press, 1999).

———, "There Is No Software," in *Literature, Media, Information Systems: Essays*, ed. by John Johnston (Amsterdam: Overseas Publishers Association, 1997), 147–55.

Hachette Book Group, Inc. et al. v. Internet Archive, et al., 20-cv-4160 (JGK) (SDNY Mar. 24, 2023).

Koetsier, Teun, "On the Prehistory of Programmable Machines: Musical Au-tomata, Looms, Calculators," *Mechanism and Machine Theory*, 36.5 (2001), 589–603. https://doi.org/10.1016/S0094-114X(01)00005-2.

Komesaroff, Paul A., "From Bioethics to Microethics: Ethical Debate and Clin-ical Medicine," in *Troubled Bodies: Critical Perspectives on Postmodernism,*

Medical Ethics, and the Body, ed. by Paul A. Komesaroff (Durham, NC: Duke University Press, 1995), 62–86. https://doi.org/10.1515/9780822379782-004.

Kovač, Miha, Angus Phillips, Adriaan van der Weel, and Ruediger Wischenbart, "What Is a Book?," *Publishing Research Quarterly,* 35.3 (2019), 313–26. https://doi.org/10.1007/s12109-019-09665-5.

Kowalewski, Mark R., "Religious Constructions of the AIDS Crisis," *Sociological Analysis,* 51.1 (1990), 91–96. https://doi.org/10.2307/3711343.

Kozinets, Robert V., *Netnography: Ethnographic Research in the Age of the Internet,* 1st ed. (Thousand Oaks, CA: Sage Publications Ltd, 2010).

Krochmal, Mo, "Magaziner, Lessig Spar over Domain Name Plan," *TechN Web News,* 11 June 1998.

Kuhn, Thomas S., *The Structure of Scientific Revolutions,* 3rd ed. (Chicago: University of Chicago Press, 1996).

Kurlansky, Mark, *Paper: Paging through History* (New York: W. W. Norton & Company, 2016).

Kurzweil, Ray, "The Future of Machine-Human Intelligence," *Futurist,* 2006, 39–46.

Lakoff, George, and Mark Johnson, *Metaphors We Live By* (Chicago: University Of Chicago Press, 1980).

Lamb, Sarah, "Beyond the View of the West," in Twigg, *Routledge Handbook of Cultural Gerontology,* 37–44.

Landoni, Monica, and Forbes Gibb, "The Role of Visual Rhetoric in the Design and Production of Electronic Books: The Visual Book," *Electronic Library,* 18.3 (2000), 190–201. https://doi.org/10.1108/02640470010337490.

Langdale, Philip, "πfs: Never Worry about Data Again!," 2021. https://github.com/philipl/pifs. Accessed 16 November 2021.

Larivière, Jules, "Guidelines for Legal Deposit Legislation: A Revised, Enlarged and Updated Edition of the 1981 Publication by Dr. Jean LUNN IFLA Committee on Cataloguing" (UNESCO, 2000).

Larivière, Vincent, Stefanie Haustein, and Philippe Mongeon, "The Oligopoly of Academic Publishers in the Digital Era," *PLOS ONE,* 10.6 (2015), e0127502. https://doi.org/10.1371/journal.pone.0127502.

Larsen, Svend, "Preserving the Digital Heritage: New Legal Deposit Act in Denmark," *Alexandria: The Journal of National and International Library and Information Issues,* 17.2 (2005), 81–87. https://doi.org/10.1177/095574900501700204.

Laurel, Brenda, ed., *The Art of Human-Computer Interface Design* (Reading, MA: Addison-Wesley, 1990).

Lawson, Stuart, "Open Access Policy in the UK: From Neoliberalism to the

Commons" (unpublished doctoral thesis, Birkbeck, University of London, 2019). https://hcommons.org/deposits/item/hc:23661/. Accessed 1 June 2019.

———, "The Political Histories of UK Public Libraries and Access to Knowledge," in Eve and Grays, *Reassembling Scholarly Communications*, 161–72.

Lawton, Graham, "The Truth about the QWERTY Keyboard," *New Scientist*, 25 April 2019. https://www.newscientist.com/article/2200664-the-truth-about-the-qwerty-keyboard/.

Leach, R. H., C. Armstrong, J. F. Brown, M. J. Mackenzie, L. Randall, and H. G. Smith, *The Printing Ink Manual* (Boston: Springer US, 1988). https://doi.org/10.1007/978-1-4684-6906-6.

Leichtentritt, Hugo, "Mechanical Music in Olden Times," *Musical Quarterly*, 20.1 (1934), 15–26.

Leitch, Thomas M., *Wikipedia U: Knowledge, Authority, and Liberal Education in the Digital Age*, Tech.Edu: A Hopkins Series on Education and Technology (Baltimore, MD: Johns Hopkins University Press, 2014).

Leonardi, Paul M., "Digital Materiality? How Artifacts without Matter, Matter," *First Monday*, 15.6 (2010). http://firstmonday.org/ojs/index.php/fm/article/view/3036.

Leonelli, Sabina, *Philosophy of Open Science* (Cambridge: Cambridge University Press, 2023). https://doi.org/10.1017/9781009416368.

Lesser, Zachary, *Ghosts, Holes, Rips and Scrapes: Shakespeare in 1619, Bibliography in the Longue Durée* (Philadelphia: University of Pennsylvania Press, 2021).

Lessig, Lawrence, *Code: Version 2.0* (New York: Basic Books, 2006).

Leurs, Laurens, "The History of PDF," 2008. https://www.prepressure.com/pdf/basics/history. Accessed 13 November 2019.

Levey, Martin, "Some Black Inks in Early Mediaeval Jewish Literature," *Chymia*, 9 (1964), 27–31. https://doi.org/10.2307/27757229.

Levinson, Jerrold, and Philip Alperson, "What Is a Temporal Art?," in *Musical Concerns* (Oxford: Oxford University Press, 2015). https://doi.org/10.1093/acprof:oso/9780199669660.003.0013.

Lewontin, Richard C., *The Triple Helix: Gene, Organism, and Environment* (Cambridge, MA: Harvard University Press, 2001).

Li, Tiffany C., "Algorithmic Destruction," *SMU Law Review*, 75.3 (2022). https://doi.org/10.2139/ssrn.4066845.

Library of Congress, "Microsoft Office Word 97–2003 Binary File Format (.Doc)," Sustainability of Digital Formats: Planning for Library of Congress Collections (website), 2019. https://www.loc.gov/preservation/digital/formats/fdd/fdd000509.shtml. Accessed 11 November 2021.

Lichtenberg, Georg Christoph, *Briefwechsel*, vol. 3, *1785—1792* (München: Beck, 1990).

Licklider, J. C. R., *Libraries of the Future* (Cambridge, MA: MIT Press, 1965).

Lindner, Mark D., and Richard K. Nakamura, "Examining the Predictive Validity of NIH Peer Review Scores," ed. by Neil R. Smalheiser, *PLOS ONE*, 10.6 (2015), e0126938. https://doi.org/10.1371/journal.pone.0126938.

Lingel, Jessa, *The Gentrification of the Internet: How to Reclaim Our Digital Freedom* (Berkeley: University of California Press, 2021).

Lis-Green, Eva, and Göran Konstenius, "Electronic Legal Deposit in Sweden: The Evolution of Digital Publications and Legislative Systems," in Gooding and Terras, *Electronic Legal Deposit*, 99–118.

Litman, Elon, "Genesis," GitHub, 2022. https://github.com/elonlit/Genesis. Accessed 21 September 2022.

Liu, Alan, *Local Transcendence: Essays on Postmodern Historicism and the Database* (Chicago: University of Chicago Press, 2008).

Lloyd, Alan C., "Typewriters That Think," *Business Education World*, 27 (1947), 453-54.

Lobo, Gregory J., "A Critique of Searle's Linguistic Exceptionalism," *Philosophy of the Social Sciences*, 51.6 (2021), 555-73. https://doi.org/10.1177/004839 3121995581.

Locke, John, *An Essay Concerning Human Understanding*, ed. by P. H. Nidditch (Oxford: Clarendon, 1975). https://doi.org/10.1093/actrade/9780198243861 .book.1. Accessed 11 May 2021.

Loveday, Helen, *Islamic Paper: A Study of the Ancient Craft* (London: Archetype, 2001).

Lucht, Marc, and Donna Yarri, eds., *Kafka's Creatures: Animals, Hybrids, and Other Fantastic Beings* (Lanham, MD: Lexington Books, 2010).

Luckhurst, Roger, *The Invention of Telepathy, 1870-1901* (Oxford: Oxford University Press, 2002).

Lucy, "Inside the Mac OS X Kernel" (presented at the 24th Chaos Communication Congress 24C3, Berlin, 2007), 5.

Lucy, J. A., "Sapir–Whorf Hypothesis," in *International Encyclopedia of the Social & Behavioral Sciences* (Amsterdam: Elsevier, 2001), 13486-90. https://doi.org/10.1016/B0-08-043076-7/03042-4.

Lynch, Keith F., "Converting Pi to Binary: DON'T DO IT," Comp.Risks, 2001. https://www.netfunny.com/rhf/jokes/01/Jun/pi.html. Accessed 16 November 2021.

Lyne, Raphael, *Memory and Intertextuality in Renaissance Literature* (Cambridge: Cambridge University Press, 2016).

MacAskill, William, *What We Owe the Future*, 1st ed. (New York: Hachette Book Group, Inc, 2022).

Magee, Gary Bryan, "Competence or Omniscience? Assessing Entrepreneurship in the Victorian and Edwardian British Paper Industry," *Business History Review*, 71.2 (1997), 230–59. https://doi.org/10.2307/3116159.

———, *Productivity and Performance in the Paper Industry: Labour, Capital and Technology in Britain and America, 1860–1914* (Cambridge: Cambridge University Press, 2002).

Maguire, Laurie E., *The Rhetoric of the Page* (Oxford: Oxford University Press, 2020).

Maher, Jimmy, "Doing Windows, Part 2: From Interface Manager to Windows The Digital Antiquarian," *The Digital Antiquarian* (blog), 2018. https://www.filfre.net/2018/06/doing-windows-part-2-from-interface-manager-to-windows/. Accessed 12 December 2021.

Mak, Bonnie, *How the Page Matters*, Studies in Book and Print Culture Series (Toronto: University of Toronto Press, 2011).

Mallett, Shelley, "Understanding Home: A Critical Review of the Literature," *Sociological Review*, 52.1 (2004), 62–89. https://doi.org/10.1111/j.1467-954X.2004.00442.x.

Manguel, Alberto, *A Reader on Reading* (New Haven, CT: Yale University Press, 2010).

Mannoni, Laurent, *The Great Art of Light and Shadow: Archaeology of the Cinema* (Exeter: University of Exeter Press, 2000).

Manovich, Lev, *The Language of New Media*, Leonardo (Cambridge, MA: MIT Press, 2002).

Marache-Francisco, Cathie, and Eric Brangier, "Gamification and Human-Machine Interaction: A Synthesis," *Le travail humain*, 78.2 (2015), 165. https://doi.org/10.3917/th.782.0165.

Mari, Will, *A Short History of Disruptive Journalism Technologies 1960–1990* (Milton: Routledge, 2019). http://proxy.cm.umoncton.ca/login?url=https://ebookcentral.proquest.com/lib/umoncton-ebooks/detail.action?docID=5683704.

Markoff, John, "Computer Visionary Who Invented the Mouse," *New York Times*, 3 July 2013. https://www.nytimes.com/2013/07/04/technology/douglas-c-engelbart-inventor-of-the-computer-mouse-dies-at-88.html. Accessed 15 December 2021.

Marx, Karl, *Capital*, vol. 1 (London: Penguin, 1992).

Marx, Leo, *The Machine in the Garden: Technology and the Pastoral Ideal in America* (New York: Oxford University Press, 2000).

Massey, Doreen, "Double Articulation: A Place in the World," in *Displacements: Cultural Identities in Question*, ed. by Angelika Bammer (Bloomington: Indiana University Press, 1994), 112–20.

Masure-Williams, Monique, "In Defence of Henry de Montherlant's *Don Juan*," *CLA Journal*, 32.4 (1989), 466–83.

Mattern, Shannon, *A City Is Not a Computer: Other Urban Intelligences*, Places Books (Princeton, NJ: Princeton University Press, 2021).

Mauskop, Seymour, "Richard Kirwan's Phlogiston Theory: Its Success and Fate," *Ambix*, 49.3 (2002), 185–205. https://doi.org/10.1179/amb.2002.49.3.185.

Mauskopf, Seymour H., "Chemical Revolution," in *Reader's Guide to the History of Science*, ed. by Arne Hessenbruch (London: Fitzroy Dearborn, 2000), 127–29.

Mayor, Adrienne, *Greek Fire, Poison Arrows, and Scorpion Bombs: Biological and Chemical Warfare in the Ancient World* (Woodstock: Overlook, 2003).

Mazur, Lucas B., "The Epistemic Imperialism of Science. Reinvigorating Early Critiques of Scientism," *Frontiers in Psychology*, 11 (2021). https://www.frontiersin.org/articles/10.3389/fpsyg.2020.609823.

McArthur, J. A., "Digital Subculture: A Geek Meaning of Style," *Journal of Communication Inquiry*, 33.1 (2009), 58–70. https://doi.org/10.1177/0196859908325676.

McCabe, Michael, "AIDS and the God of Wrath," *Furrow*, 38.8 (1987), 512–21.

McGann, Jerome J., *The Textual Condition* (Princeton, NJ: Princeton University Press, 1991).

McGurl, Mark, *Everything and Less: The Novel in the Age of Amazon* (London: Verso, 2021).

McJones, Paul, and Liz Bond Crews, "The Advent of Digital Typography," *IEEE Annals of the History of Computing*, 42.1 (2020), 41–50. https://doi.org/10.1109/MAHC.2019.2929883.

McKenzie, D. F., *"What's Past Is Prologue": The Bibliographical Society and History of the Book* (London: Hearthstone Publications, 1993).

——, "Computers and the Humanities: A Personal Synthesis of Conference Issues," in *Scholarship and Technology in the Humanities*, ed. by May Katzen (London: British Library Research Series, 1991), pp. 157–69.

McKitterick, David, *Old Books, New Technologies: The Representation, Conservation And Transformation Of Books since 1700* (Cambridge: Cambridge University Press, 2014).

——, "What Is the Use of Books without Pictures? Empty Space in Some Early Printed Books," *La Bibliofilía*, 116.1–3 (2014), 67–82.

McLane, Maureen N., *Romanticism and the Human Sciences: Poetry, Population, and the Discourse of the Species*, Cambridge Studies in Romanticism, 41 (Cambridge: Cambridge University Press, 2000).

McLuhan, Marshall, *Understanding Media: The Extensions of Man* (Cambridge, MA: MIT Press, 1994).

McLuhan, Marshall, Quentin Fiore, and Jerome Agel, *The Medium Is the Massage* (Gingko Press, 1967). http://archive.org/details/pdfy-vNiFct6b-L5ucJEa.

Melville, Herman, *Moby-Dick: An Authoritative Text, Contexts, Criticism*, ed. by Hershel Parker, 3rd ed. (New York: W. W. Norton & Company, 2018)

Meng, Weishi, "Peer Review: Is NIH Rewarding Talent?," *Science Transparency*, 10 January 2016. https://scienceretractions.wordpress.com/2016/01/10/peer-review-is-nih-rewarding-talent/.

Mercado, Andrew, *Super Aussie Soaps—Behind the Scenes of Australia's Best Loved TV Shows* (Melbourne: Pluto Press Australia Limited, 2004).

Merton, Robert K., "The Matthew Effect in Science," *Science*, 159.3810 (1968), 56–63.

Microsoft, "Consumer Antivirus Software Providers for Windows," 2022. https://support.microsoft.com/en-gb/windows-antivirus-providers. Accessed 19 April 2022.

———, "[MS-DOC]: FibRgFcLcb2002," 2021. https://docs.microsoft.com/en-us/openspecs/office_file_formats/ms-doc/fce09f81-704b-460d-9bca-f7dc121aed66. Accessed 11 November 2021.

Mills, Elinor, "Security Researcher: I Keep Getting Detained by Feds," CNET, 18 November 2010. https://www.cnet.com/news/privacy/security-researcher-i-keep-getting-detained-by-feds/.

Mission, James, "Signifying Nothing: Following a Hole through Three Text Technologies," *Inscription: The Journal of Material Text—Theory, Practice, History*, 1.2 (2021), 60–70.

Mitchell, David T., and Sharon L. Snyder, *Narrative Prosthesis: Disability and the Dependencies of Discourse*, Corporealities (Ann Arbor: University of Michigan Press, 2001).

Mitnick, Kevin D., and William L. Simon, *Ghost in the Wires: My Adventures as the World's Most Wanted Hacker* (New York: Little, Brown and Company, 2011).

Mladenov, Teodor, "Neoliberalism, Postsocialism, Disability," *Disability & Society*, 30.3 (2015), 445–59. https://doi.org/10.1080/09687599.2015.1021758.

Mohrmann, Christine, "Observations sur la langue et le style de Saint Bernard," in *Sancti Bernardi opera*, vol. 2, ed. by Jean Leclercq and Henri Rochais (Rome: Editiones cistercienses, 1958), 9–33.

Monaco, James, *How to Read a Film: The World of Movies, Media, and Multimedia: Language, History, Theory*, 3rd ed. (New York: Oxford University Press, 2000).

Monique, Zerdoun Bat-Yehouda, *Les encres noires au Moyen Age* (Paris: CNRS Editions, 2003).

Monro, Alexander, *The Paper Trail: An Unexpected History of a Revolutionary Invention* (New York: Vintage Books, 2017).

Monroe, Randall, "Standards," *xkcd*, 2011. https://xkcd.com/927/. Accessed 10 September 2021.

Montfort, Nick, "Continuous Paper: The Early Materiality and Workings of Electronic Literature" (presented at the MLA Convention, Philadelphia, PA, 2004). https://nickm.com/writing/essays/continuous_paper_mla.html. Accessed 15 March 2021.

Montherlant, Henry de, *Don Juan* (Paris: Editions Gallimard, 1958).

Moody, Fred, *I Sing the Body Electronic: A Year with Microsoft on the Multimedia Frontier* (New York: Penguin Books, 1996).

Moore, Samuel, "The 'Care-Full' Commons: Open Access and the Care of Commoning," in Deville, Moore, and Nadim, *The Commons and Care*, 16–25.

———, "Common Struggles: Policy-Based vs. Scholar-Led Approaches to Open Access in the Humanities" (unpublished doctoral thesis, King's College London, 2019). https://hcommons.org/deposits/item/hc:24135/. Accessed 6 June 2019.

Moore, Samuel, Cameron Neylon, Martin Paul Eve, Daniel O'Donnell, and Damian Pattinson, "Excellence R Us: University Research and the Fetishisation of Excellence," *Palgrave Communications*, 3 (2017). https://doi.org/10.1057/palcomms.2016.105.

Morris, Sally, Ed Barnas, Douglas LaFrenier, and Margaret Reich, *The Handbook of Journal Publishing* (Cambridge: Cambridge University Press, 2013).

Morton, Dave, "Working Notes: 36.1 (Dead Medium: The Auto-Typist)," *The Dead Media Project*. http://www.deadmedia.org/notes/36/361.html. Accessed 26 August 2021.

Morton, Timothy, *Hyperobjects: Philosophy and Ecology for the End of the World* (Minneapolis: University of Minnesota Press, 2013).

Mountford, S. Joy, "Technique and Technology," in Laurel, *The Art of Human-Computer Interface Design*, 247–50.

Mountford, S. Joy, and William W. Gaver, "Talking and Listening to Computers," in Laurel, *The Art of Human-Computer Interface Design*, 319–34.

Moural, Josef, "Searle'S Theory of Institutional Facts: A Program of Critical Revision," in *Speech Acts, Mind, and Social Reality: Discussions with John R. Searle*, ed. by Günther Grewendorf and Georg Meggle, Studies in Linguistics and Philosophy (Dordrecht: Springer Netherlands, 2002), 271–86. https://doi.org/10.1007/978-94-010-0589-0_18.

Mozilla, "<blink>: The Blinking Text Element—HTML: HyperText Markup Language," MDN Web Docs. https://developer.mozilla.org/en-US/docs/Web/HTML/Element/blink. Accessed 9 January 2022.

Mueller, Milton, *Ruling the Root: Internet Governance and the Taming of Cyberspace* (Cambridge, MA: MIT Press, 2002).

Muggleton, David, and Rupert Weinzierl, *The Post-Subcultures Reader* (Oxford: Berg, 2003).

Mullaney, Thomas S., *The Chinese Typewriter: A History* (Cambridge, MA: MIT Press, 2017).

Müller, Lothar, *White Magic: The Age of Paper* (Cambridge: Polity Press, 2014).

Murray, Simone, *Introduction to Contemporary Print Culture: Books as Media* (London: Routledge, 2021).

Murray, Susan, *Bright Signals: A History of Color Television* (Durham, NC: Duke University Press, 2018).

Murray-Rust, Peter, "What Is TextAndData/ContentMining?," *Petermr's Blog*, 11 July 2017. https://blogs.ch.cam.ac.uk/pmr/2017/07/11/what-is-textanddatacontentmining/.

Nakamoto, Satoshi, "Bitcoin: A Peer-to-Peer Electronic Cash System," *Decentralized Business Review*, 2008.

Narayanan, Arvind, Joseph Bonneau, Edward Felten, Andrew Miller, and Steven Goldfeder, *Bitcoin and Cryptocurrency Technologies: A Comprehensive Introduction* (Princeton, NJ: Princeton University Press, 2016).

Nardini, Robert F., "A Search for Meaning: American Library Metaphors, 1876-1926," *Library Quarterly: Information, Community, Policy*, 71.2 (2001), 111–40.

Nash, Kate, "The Cultural Politics of Human Rights and Neoliberalism," *Journal of Human Rights*, 18.5 (2019), 490–505. https://doi.org/10.1080/14754835.2019.1653174.

Natale, Simone, *Deceitful Media: Artificial Intelligence and Social Life after the Turing Test* (Oxford: Oxford University Press, 2021).

National Health Service, "PDFs," *NHS Digital Service Manual*, 2019. https://beta.nhs.uk/service-manual. Accessed 20 November 2019.

Nature Portfolio, "Artificial Intelligence (AI)," 2023. https://www.nature.com/nature-portfolio/editorial-policies/ai. Accessed 30 June 2023.

Nelson, Theodor Holm, "The Right Way to Think about Software Design," in *The Art of Human-Computer Interface Design*, ed. by Brenda Laurel (Reading, MA: Addison-Wesley, 1990), 235–43.

Newell, Allen, "Metaphors for Mind, Theories of Mind: Should the Humanities

Mind?," in *The Boundaries of Humanity: Humans, Animals, Machines*, ed. by James J. Sheehan and Morton Sosna (Berkeley: University of California Press, 1991), 158–97.

Newton, Isaac, "Isaac Newton to Henry Oldenburg, 6 Feb, 1671/72," in *The Correspondence of Isaac Newton*, vol. 1, ed. by H. W. Turnbull, J. F. Scott, A. R. Hall, and Laura Tilling (Cambridge: Cambridge University Press, 1959).

Nguyen, Cong T., Dinh Thai Hoang, Diep N. Nguyen, Dusit Niyato, Huynh Tuong Nguyen, and Eryk Dutkiewicz, "Proof-of-Stake Consensus Mechanisms for Future Blockchain Networks: Fundamentals, Applications and Opportunities," *IEEE Access*, 7 (2019), 85727–45. https://doi.org/10.1109/ACCESS.2019.2925010.

Nielsen, Jakob, "Avoid PDF for On-Screen Reading," Nielsen Norman Group, 2001. https://www.nngroup.com/articles/avoid-pdf-onscreen-reading-original/. Accessed 20 November 2019.

———, "PDF: Unfit for Human Consumption," Nielsen Norman Group, 2003. https://www.nngroup.com/articles/pdf-unfit-for-human-consumption-original/. Accessed 20 November 2019.

Noble, Safiya Umoja, *Algorithms of Oppression: How Search Engines Reinforce Racism* (New York: New York University Press, 2018).

Nofre, David, Mark Priestley, and Gerard Alberts, "When Technology Became Language: The Origins of the Linguistic Conception of Computer Programming, 1950–1960," *Technology and Culture*, 55.1 (2014), 40–75. https://doi.org/10.1353/tech.2014.0031.

Norton, William B., *The 2014 Internet Peering Playbook: Connecting to the Core of the Internet* (Palo Alto, CA: DrPeering Press, 2014).

Nowviskie, Bethany, "Reconstitute the World: Machine-Reading Archives of Mass Extinction," Bethany Nowviskie (website), 12 June 2018. http://nowviskie.org/2018/reconstitute-the-world/.

Noyes, Jan, "The QWERTY Keyboard: A Review," *International Journal of Man-Machine Studies*, 18.3 (1983), 265–81. https://doi.org/10.1016/S0020-7373(83)80010-8.

Nudd, Tim, "Apple's 'Get a Mac,' the Complete Campaign," AdWeek, 2011. https://www.adweek.com/creativity/apples-get-mac-complete-campaign-130552/. Accessed 31 January 2022.

Oakland, William H., "Theory of Public Goods," in *Handbook of Public Economics*, vol. 2, ed. by Alan J. Auerbach and Martin S. Feldstein, Handbooks in Economics (Amsterdam: Elsevier, 1985), 485–535.

Ochai, Adakole, "The Purpose of the Library in Colonial Tropical Africa: An Historical Survey," *International Library Review*, 16.3 (1984), 309–15. https://doi.org/10.1016/0020-7837(84)90007-4.

O'Conor, John Francis Xavier, *Facts about Bookworms: Their History in Literature and Work in Libraries* (New York: F. P. Harper, 1898).

Odi, Amusi, "The Colonial Origins of Library Development in Africa: Some Reflections on Their Significance," *Libraries & Culture*, 26.4 (1991), 594–604.

Ong, Walter J., *Orality and Literacy: The Technologizing of the Word* (London: Routledge, 2002).

Oppenheim, Charles, Adrienne Muir, and Naomi Korn, *Information Law: Compliance for Librarians, Information Professionals and Knowledge Managers* (London: Facet Publishing, 2020). http://ebookcentral.proquest.com/lib/bbk/detail.action?docID=6235937.

Oren, Tim, "Designing a New Medium," in Laurel, *The Art of Human-Computer Interface Design*, 467–79.

Ortiz, Monica E., and Drew Endy, "Engineered Cell-Cell Communication via DNA Messaging," *Journal of Biological Engineering*, 6.1 (2012), 16. https://doi.org/10.1186/1754-1611-6-16.

Osborn, Don, *African Languages in a Digital Age: Challenges and Opportunities for Indigenous Language Computing* (Cape Town: HSRC Press, 2010).

Owen, Randall, and Sarah Parker Harris, "'No Rights without Responsibilities': Disability Rights and Neoliberal Reform under New Labour," *Disability Studies Quarterly*, 32.3 (2012). https://doi.org/10.18061/dsq.v32i3.3283.

Pagano, Michele, "American Idol and NIH Grant Review," *Cell*, 126.4 (2006), 637–38. https://doi.org/10.1016/j.cell.2006.08.004.

Parfit, Derek, "Personal Identity," *Philosophical Review*, 80.1 (1971), 3–27.

Parikka, Jussi, *Digital Contagions: A Media Archaeology of Computer Viruses* (New York: Peter Lang, 2016).

Parikka, Jussi, and Tony D. Sampson, eds., *The Spam Book: On Viruses, Porn, and Other Anomalies from the Dark Side of Digital Culture*, Hampton Press Communication Series: Communication Alternatives (Cresskill, NJ: Hampton Press, 2009).

Parry, Kate, "Libraries in Uganda: Not Just Linguistic Imperialism," *Libri*, 61.4 (2011), 328–37. https://doi.org/10.1515/libr.2011.027.

Pasanek, Brad, *Metaphors of Mind: An Eighteenth-Century Dictionary* (Baltimore, MD: Johns Hopkins University Press, 2015).

Pastoureau, Michel, *Black: The History of a Color* (Princeton, NJ: Princeton University Press, 2009).

———, "Les cisterciens et la couleur au XIIe siècle," in *L'Ordre cistercien et le Berry*, ed. by Pierre-Gilles Girault (Bourges: Conseil général du Cher, 1998), 21–30.

———, "L'incolore n'existe pas," in *Points de vue: Pour Philippe Junod*, ed. by Danielle Chaperon and Philippe Kaenel, Champs Visuels (Paris: L'Harmattan, 2003), 21–36.

———, *White: The History of a Color* (Princeton, NJ: Princeton University Press, 2023).

Patel, Jashu, and Krishan Kumar, *Libraries and Librarianship in India* (Westport, CT: Greenwood Press, 2001).

Patteson, Thomas W., "Player Piano," in *Oxford Handbooks Online: Scholarly Research Reviews* (Oxford: Oxford University Press, 2014). https://doi.org/10.1093/oxfordhb/9780199935321.013.16.

Pearson, Jennifer, George Buchanan, and Harold Thimbleby, "Designing for Digital Reading," *Synthesis Lectures on Information Concepts, Retrieval, and Services*, 5.4 (2013). https://doi.org/10.2200/S00539ED1V01Y201310ICR029.

Pecham, John, "De Iride," in *John Pecham and the Science of Optics*, ed. by David C. Lindberg, Perspectiva Communis (Madison: University of Wisconsin Press, 1970), 114–23.

Pellaschiar, Sofia, *A Hug in a Book: Everyday Self-Care and Comforting Rituals* (Pop Press, 2022).

Pérez, Gina M., *The Near Northwest Side Story: Migration, Displacement, and Puerto Rican Families* (Berkeley: University of California Press, 2004).

Piper, Andrew, "Deleafing: The History and Future of Losing Print," *Gramma: Journal of Theory and Criticism*, 21 (2013), 13–25. https://doi.org/10.26262/gramma.v21i0.6276.

Piper, Andrew, Chad Wellmon, and Mohamed Cheriet, "The Page Image: Towards a Visual History of Digital Documents," *Book History*, 23.1 (2020), 365–97. https://doi.org/10.1353/bh.2020.0010.

Plateau, Joseph, "Des illusions d'optique sur lesquelles se fonde le petit appareil appelé récemment Phénakistiscope," *Ann Chimie Phys*, 53 (1833), 304–8.

Plato, *Phaedrus*, trans. by Christopher Rowe (London: Penguin, 2005).

Plunkett, John, "Carphone Axes Big Brother Deal," *Guardian*, 18 January 2007. https://www.theguardian.com/media/2007/jan/18/business.marketingandpr.

Politzer-Ahles, Stephen, Teresa Girolamo, and Samantha Ghali, "Preliminary Evidence of Linguistic Bias in Academic Reviewing," *Journal of English for Academic Purposes*, 47 (2020), 100895. https://doi.org/10.1016/j.jeap.2020.100895.

Pomerantz, Jeffrey, *Metadata*, The MIT Press Essential Knowledge Series (Cambridge, MA: MIT Press, 2015).

Pomerantz, Jeffrey, and Gary Marchionini, "The Digital Library as Place," *Journal of Documentation*, 63.4 (2007), 505–33. https://doi.org/10.1108/00220410710758995.

Popper, Karl, *Conjectures and Refutations: The Growth of Scientific Knowledge,* Routledge Classics (London: Routledge, 2002).

———, *The Logic of Scientific Discovery* (London: Routledge, 2010).

———, *The Open Society and Its Enemies,* vol.1, *The Spell of Plato* (Abingdon: Routledge, 2003).

———, *The Open Society and Its Enemies,* vol.2, *Hegel and Marx* (Abingdon: Routledge, 2003).

Portela, Manuel, *Scripting Reading Motions: The Codex and the Computer as Self-Reflexive Machines* (Cambridge, MA: MIT Press, 2013).

Porter, Vincent, "The Three Phases of Film and Television," *Journal of Film and Video,* 36.1 (1984), 5–21.

Power, John, *A Handy-Book about Books, for Book-Lovers, Book-Buyers, and Book-Sellers* (London: John Wilson, 1870).

Priedhorsky, Reid, Jilin Chen, Shyong (Tony) K. Lam, Katherine Panciera, Loren Terveen, and John Riedl, "Creating, Destroying, and Restoring Value in Wikipedia," in *Proceedings of the 2007 International ACM Conference on Supporting Group Work—GROUP '07* (presented at the 2007 international ACM conference, Sanibel Island, Florida, USA: ACM Press, 2007), 259. https://doi.org/10.1145/1316624.1316663.

Purkinje, Jan E., *Beobachtungen und Versuche zur Physiologie der Sinne. Beiträge zur Kenntniss des Sehens in Subjectiver Hinsicht* (Prague: Calve, 1823).

Purohit, Ashwin, "How Many Chinese Characters and Words Are in Use?," Ashwin Purohit (website), 2014. https://puroh.it/how-many-chinese-characters-and-words-are-in-use/. Accessed 7 October 2021.

Quayson, Ato, *Aesthetic Nervousness: Disability and the Crisis of Representation* (New York: Columbia University Press, 2007).

Ralston, D. Christopher, and Justin Ho, "Introduction: Philosophical Reflections on Disability," in *Philosophical Reflections on Disability,* ed. by D. Christopher Ralston and Justin Ho, Philosophy and Medicine (Dordrecht: Springer Verlag, 2010), 1–16.

Ranganathan, S. R., *The Five Laws of Library Science* (Madras, London: The Madras Library Association, 1931). https://catalog.hathitrust.org/Record/001661182.

Rapport, Nigel, and Andrew Dawson, eds., *Migrants of Identity: Perceptions of Home in a World of Movement* (Oxford: Berg, 1998).

Raskin, Jef, "Viewpoint: Intuitive Equals Familiar," *Commun. ACM,* 37.9 (1994), 17–18. https://doi.org/10.1145/182987.584629.

Raykoff, Ivan, *Dreams of Love: Playing the Romantic Pianist* (Oxford: Oxford University Press, 2014).

Reardon, Sara, "'Forgotten' NIH Smallpox Virus Languishes on Death Row," *Nature*, 514.7524 (2014), 544. https://doi.org/10.1038/514544a.

Reimer, Jeremy, "A History of the GUI," *Ars Technica*, 5 May 2005. https://arstechnica.com/features/2005/05/gui/.

Reynolds, Paul, "A Glossary of Holes," *Inscription: The Journal of Material Text—Theory, Practice, History*, 1.2 (2021), 75–81.

Richter, Jean Paul, *The Literary Works of Leonardo Da Vinci* (London: Sampson Low, Marston, Searle, & Rivington, 1883).

Rieder, Bernhard, *Engines of Order: A Mechanology of Algorithmic Techniques* (Amsterdam: Amsterdam University Press, 2020).

Risam, Roopika, *New Digital Worlds: Postcolonial Digital Humanities in Theory, Praxis, and Pedagogy* (Evanston, IL: Northwestern University Press, 2018).

Roberts, Colin H., and Theodore C. Skeat, *The Birth of the Codex* (Oxford: Oxford University Press, 1987).

Robertson, Craig, and Deidre Lynch, "Pinning and Punching: A Provisional History of Holes, Paper, and Books," *Inscription: The Journal of Material Text—Theory, Practice, History*, 1.2 (2021), 13–23.

Rodgers Albro, Sylvia, *Fabriano: City of Medieval and Renaissance Papermaking* (New Castle, DE: Oak Knoll Press, 2016).

Roe, George, "Challenging the Control of Knowledge in Colonial India: Political Ideas in the Work of S. R. Ranganathan," *Library & Information History*, 26.1 (2010), 18–32. https://doi.org/10.1179/175834909X12593371068342.

Rogers, Everett M., *Diffusion of Innovations*, 3rd ed. (New York: Free Press, 1983).

Roget, Peter Mark, "V. Explanation of an Optical Deception in the Appearance of the Spokes of a Wheel Seen through Vertical Apertures," *Philosophical Transactions of the Royal Society of London*, 115 (1825), 131–40. https://doi.org/10.1098/rstl.1825.0007.

Romano, Frank J., and Miranda Mitrano, *History of Desktop Publishing* (New Castle, DE: Oak Knoll Press, 2019).

Rowberry, Simon Peter, "The Ebook Imagination," *Digital Humanities Quarterly*, 16.1 (2022).

Rubery, Matthew, *The Untold Story of the Talking Book* (Cambridge, MA: Harvard University Press, 2016).

Rucker, James J., Lindsey Marwood, Riikka-Liisa J. Ajantaival, Catherine Bird, Hans Eriksson, John Harrison, et al., "The Effects of Psilocybin on Cognitive and Emotional Functions in Healthy Participants: Results from a Phase 1, Randomised, Placebo-Controlled Trial Involving Simultaneous Psilocybin Administration and Preparation," *Journal of Psychopharmacology*, 36.1 (2022), 114–25. https://doi.org/10.1177/02698811211064720.

Running-Johnson, Cynthia, "Reading Life Signs in Jean Genet's 'Atelier d'Alberto Giacometti' and 'Ce qui est resté d'un Rembrandt . . .'," *L'Esprit Créateur*, 35.1 (1995), 20–29.

Ruscelli, Girolamo, *The Thyrde and Last Parte of the Secretes of the Reuerende Maister Alexis of Piemont*, trans. by William Ward (London: Rowland Hall for Nicholas England, 1562).

Russell, Isabel Galina, Jo Ana Morfin, and Ana Yuri Ramírez-Molina, "E-Legal Deposit at the Biblioteca Nacional de México (National Library of Mexico)," in Gooding and Terras, *Electronic Legal Deposit*, 57–76.

Russell, Matthew, "What Is Quartz (or Why Can't Windows Do That)," O'Reilly Media, 2013. https://web.archive.org/web/20130527151142/http://oreilly.com/pub/a/mac/2005/10/11/what-is-quartz.html. Accessed 13 January 2022.

Sakellariou, Dikaios, and Elena S. Rotarou, "The Effects of Neoliberal Policies on Access to Healthcare for People with Disabilities," *International Journal for Equity in Health*, 16.1 (2017), 1–8. https://doi.org/10.1186/s12939-017-0699-3.

Saleh, Ahmed S. M., Peng Wang, Na Wang, Liu Yang, and Zhigang Xiao, "Brown Rice versus White Rice: Nutritional Quality, Potential Health Benefits, Development of Food Products, and Preservation Technologies," *Comprehensive Reviews in Food Science and Food Safety*, 18.4 (2019), 1070–96. https://doi.org/10.1111/1541-4337.12449.

Salomon, Gitta, "New Uses for Color," in Laurel, *The Art of Human-Computer Interface Design*, 269–78.

Samaras, Evanthia, "Researching Malware at the British Library," Digital Preservation Coalition, last updated 4 October 2018. https://www.dpconline.org/blog/researching-malware-at-the-british-library.

Samuelson, Paul A., "The Pure Theory of Public Expenditure," *Review of Economics and Statistics*, 36.4 (1954), 387–89. https://doi.org/10.2307/1925895.

Santa Clara County v. Southern Pacific Railroad Co., 118 U.S. 394 (1886).

Sardoč, Mitja, "The Language of Neoliberalism in Education," in *The Impacts of Neoliberal Discourse and Language in Education: Critical Perspectives on a Rhetoric of Equality, Well-Being, and Justice*, ed. by Mitja Sardoč, Routledge Studies in Education, Neoliberalism, and Marxism (New York: Routledge, 2021), 1–13.

Särkkä, Timo, *Paper and the British Empire: The Quest for Imperial Raw Materials, 1861–1960*, Routledge Explorations in Economic History (Abingdon: Routledge, 2021).

Saussure, Ferdinand de, *Course in General Linguistics*, trans. by Roy Harris, reprint ed. (LaSalle, IL: Open Court, 1998).

Savage, Elizabeth, "Where Is the Colour in Book History?" (presented at the

Frederik Muller Lezing, online, 10 September 2021), YouTube video, 1:07:45. https://www.youtube.com/watch?v=NbDIpNQEVhU.

Savelyev, Alexander, *Contract Law 2.0: "Smart" Contracts as the Beginning of the End of Classic Contract Law* (Rochester, NY: Social Science Research Network, 14 December 2016). https://doi.org/10.2139/ssrn.2885241.

Schlick, Moritz, "Facts and Propositions," *Analysis*, 2.5 (1935), 65-70. https://doi.org/10.2307/3326403.

Schmitt, Jean-Claude, *Les revenants. Les vivants et les morts dans la société médiévale* (Paris: Gallimard, 1994).

Schneier, Bruce, "Essays: Did NSA Put a Secret Backdoor in New Encryption Standard?," *Schneier on Security*, 15 November 2007. https://www.schneier .com/essays/archives/2007/11/did_nsa_put_a_secret.html.

Schnell, Lisa J., "Muzzling the Competition: Rachel Speght and the Economics of Print," in *Debating Gender in Early Modern England, 1500-1700*, ed. by Cristina Malcolmson and Mihoko Suzuki, Early Modern Cultural Studies (New York: Palgrave Macmillan US, 2002), 57-77. https://doi.org/10.1057/9780230107540_4.

Schönberger, Daniel, "Deep Copyright: Up—And Downstream Questions Related to Artificial Intelligence (AI) and Machine Learning (ML)" (Rochester, NY, 9 January 2018). https://papers.ssrn.com/abstract=3098315.

Schonfeld, Roger C., Karin Wulf, Rick Anderson, Lisa Janicke Hinchliffe, Joseph Esposito, and Roy Kaufman, "The Internet Archive Loses on Controlled Digital Lending," *The Scholarly Kitchen*, 28 March 2023. https://scholarlykitchen.sspnet.org/2023/03/28/internet-archive-controlled-digital -lending/.

Scientific Data Systems, "SDS 940 Time-Sharing Computer System Manual," 1966.

Scott, Tom, "Data Ethics & Design Implications for Wellcome Collection's Digital Platform," Medium, 16 July 2020. https://stacks.wellcomecollection .org/data-ethics-design-implications-for-wellcome-collections-digital-plat form-64878cbe31d6.

Searle, John R., *The Construction of Social Reality* (New York: Free Press, 1997).

——, *Making the Social World: The Structure of Human Civilization* (Oxford: Oxford University Press, 2010).

——, "A Taxonomy of Illocutionary Acts," in *Language, Mind, and Knowledge*, ed. by K. Gunderson (Minneapolis: University of Minnesota Press, 1975), 344-69.

Secord, James A., *Victorian Sensation: The Extraordinary Publication, Reception, and Secret Authorship of Vestiges of the Natural History of Creation* (Chicago: University of Chicago Press, 2003).

Segal, Lynne, *Out of Time: The Pleasures and the Perils of Ageing* (London: Verso Books, 2013).

Seltzer, Mark, *Bodies and Machines* (New York: Routledge, 1992).

Semedo, Alvare de, *The History of That Great and Renowned Monarchy of China* (London: I. Crook, 1655).

Senchyne, Jonathan, *The Intimacy of Paper in Early and Nineteenth-Century American Literature*, Studies in Print Culture and the History of the Book (Amherst: University of Massachusetts Press, 2020).

Shailor, Barbara A., *The Medieval Book* (Toronto: University of Toronto Press, 1991).

Shakespeare, Tom, Jerome E. Bickenbach, David Pfeiffer, and Nicholas Watson, "Models," in *Encyclopedia of Disability*, ed. by Gary L. Albrecht (Thousand Oaks, CA: Sage Publications, 2006), 1101–8.

Shakespeare, William, *The Tragœdy of Othello, the Moore of Venice* (n.p.: Nicholas Okes for Thomas Walkley, 1622).

Shapiro, Alan E., "Artists' Colors and Newton's Colors," *Isis: A Journal of the History of Science Society*, 85.4 (1994), 600–630. https://doi.org/10.1086/356979.

Sharma, Anshula, Gaganjot Gupta, Tawseef Ahmad, Kewal Krishan, and Baljinder Kaur, "Next Generation Agents (Synthetic Agents): Emerging Threats and Challenges in Detection, Protection, and Decontamination," *Handbook on Biological Warfare Preparedness* (2020), 217–56. https://doi.org/10.1016/B978-0-12-812026-2.00012-8.

Sheldrake, Merlin, *Entangled Life: How Fungi Make Our Worlds, Change Our Minds, and Shape Our Futures* (London: Vintage, 2021).

Shep, Sydney J., "Digital Materiality," in *A New Companion to Digital Humanities* (Oxford: John Wiley & Sons, Ltd, 2015), 322–30. https://doi.org/10.1002/9781118680605.ch22.

Shneiderman, Ben, and Catherine Plaisant, *Designing the User Interface: Strategies for Effective Human-Computer Interaction*, 4th ed. (Boston: Pearson, 2004).

Siddiqui, Faiz, "Elon Musk Debuts Tesla Robot, Optimus, Calling It a 'Fundamental Transformation,'" *Washington Post*, 1 October 2022. https://www.washingtonpost.com/technology/2022/09/30/elon-musk-tesla-bot/.

Sigalos, MacKenzie, "'Squid Game' Crypto Token Cost One Shanghai Investor His Life Savings of $28,000 after Coin Plunged to Near Zero," *CNBC*, 2 November 2021. https://www.cnbc.com/2021/11/02/squid-game-token-cost-one-investor-28000-after-coin-plunged.html.

Silvast, Antti, and Markku Reunanen, "Multiple Users, Diverse Users: Appropriation of Personal Computers by Demoscene Hackers," in *Hacking Europe:*

From Computer Cultures to Demoscenes, ed. by Gerard Alberts (New York: Springer, 2014), 151–63.

Simondon, Gilbert, *On the Mode of Existence of Technical Objects* (Minneapolis, MN: Univocal Pub, 2016).

Sinclair, Ian, "Elements of Television," in *Electronics Simplified*, ed. by Ian Sinclair, 3rd ed. (Oxford: Newnes, 2011), 137–65. https://doi.org/10.1016/B978-0-08-097063-9.10008-1.

Slights, William W. E., *Managing Readers: Printed Marginalia in English Renaissance Books* (Ann Arbor: University of Michigan Press, 2001).

Smith, Helen, "'A Unique Instance of Art': The Proliferating Surfaces of Early Modern Paper," *Journal of the Northern Renaissance*, 10 July 2017. https://jnr2.hcommons.org/2017/4847/.

Smith, Helen, and Louise Wilson, eds., *Renaissance Paratexts* (Cambridge: Cambridge University Press, 2011).

Smith, Moira, and Paul Yachnes, "Scholar's Playground or Wisdom's Temple? Competing Metaphors in a Library Electronic Text Center," *Library Trends*, 46.4 (1998), 718–31.

Smits, Robert-Jan, and Rachael Pells, *Plan S for Shock: Science, Shock, Solution, Speed* (London: Ubiquity Press, 2022). https://doi.org/10.5334/bcq.

Smyth, Adam, *Material Texts in Early Modern England* (Cambridge: Cambridge University Press, 2018). https://doi.org/10.1017/9781108367868.

So, Richard Jean, "All Models Are Wrong," *PMLA*, 132.3 (2017), 668–73.

Sorensen, Roy A., *Seeing Dark Things: The Philosophy of Shadows* (New York: Oxford University Press, 2008).

Speight, Helen, "Rachel Speght's Polemical Life," *Huntington Library Quarterly*, 65.3/4 (2002), 449–63.

Spronk, Rachel, "The Disease Immorality: Narrating Aids as 'Sign of the Times' in Middle-Class Nairobi," *Etnofoor*, 13.1 (2000), 67–86.

Sproull, Robert F., "The Xerox Alto Publishing Platform," *IEEE Annals of the History of Computing*, 40.3 (2018), 38–54. https://doi.org/10.1109/MAHC.2018.033841110.

Stallman, Richard M., "Did You Say 'Intellectual Property'? It's a Seductive Mirage," Gnu.Org, 2015. https://www.gnu.org/philosophy/not-ipr.en.html. Accessed 2 August 2015.

Stampfer, Simon, *Die stroboscopischen Scheiben; oder, Optischen Zauberscheiben: Deren Theorie und wissenschaftliche Anwendung* (Vienna: Trentsensky & Vieweg, 1833).

Stankiewicz, Piotr, *Does Happiness Write Blank Pages? On Stoicism and Artistic Creativity* (Vernon Press, 2019).

Star, Susan Leigh, "The Ethnography of Infrastructure," *American Behavioral*

Scientist, 43.3 (1999), 377–91. https://doi.org/10.1177/00027649921955326.

———, "Power, Technology and the Phenomenology of Conventions: On Being Allergic to Onions," *Sociological Review*, 38 (1990), 26–56. https://doi.org/10.1111/j.1467-954X.1990.tb03347.x.

Stauffer, Andrew, and Kristin Jensen, "About," Book Traces, 2023. https://booktraces-public.lib.virginia.edu/about/.

Stefik, Mark, ed., *Internet Dreams: Archetypes, Myths, and Metaphors* (Cambridge, MA: MIT Press, 2001).

Steiner, Jennifer G., and Daniel E. Geer Jr., "Network Services in the Athena Environment," *Proceedings of the Winter 1988 Usenix Conference*, 1988.

Stewart, John, "The Reality of Phlogiston in Great Britain," *HYLE—International Journal for Philosophy of Chemistry*, 18.2 (2012), 175–94.

Stewart, Matthew, "The Most Important Supreme Court Decision for Data Science and Machine Learning," Medium, 31 October 2019. https://towardsdatascience.com/the-most-important-supreme-court-decision-for-data-science-and-machine-learning-44cfc1c1bcaf.

Sticchi, Francesco, "From Spinoza to Contemporary Linguistics: Pragmatic Ethics in Denis Villeneuve's *Arrival*," *Revue canadienne d'études cinématographiques / Canadian Journal of Film Studies*, 27.2 (2018), 48–65.

Stoicheff, Peter, and Andrew Taylor, "Introduction," in Stoicheff and Taylor, *The Future of the Page*, 3–25.

———, eds., *The Future of the Page* (Toronto: University of Toronto Press, 2004).

Stokes, Jon, "Please Stop Talking about The ELIZA Chatbot," Return, 23 February 2023. https://www.return.life/p/please-stop-talking-about-the-eliza-chatbot.

Stolfi, Jorge, "Bitcoin Is a Ponzi," State University of Campinas, 2 January 2021. https://ic.unicamp.br/~stolfi/bitcoin/2020-12-31-bitcoin-ponzi.html.

Stoll, Christian, Lena Klaaßen, and Ulrich Gallersdörfer, "The Carbon Footprint of Bitcoin," *Joule*, 3.7 (2019), 1647–61. https://doi.org/10.1016/j.joule.2019.05.012.

Suber, Peter, *Open Access*, Essential Knowledge Series (Cambridge, MA: MIT Press, 2012). http://bit.ly/oa-book.

Sugarbaker, Mike, "What Is a Geek?," *Gazebo (The Journal of Geek Culture)*, 1998. http://www.gibberish.com/gazebo/articles/geek3.html. Accessed 30 October 2020.

Suleman, Mehrunisha, "6 out of 10 People Who Have Died from COVID-19 Are Disabled," 11 February 2021. https://www.health.org.uk/news-and-comment/news/6-out-of-10-people-who-have-died-from-covid-19-are-disabled.

Sulistyo-Basuki, L., "The Rise and Growth of Libraries in Pre-War Indonesia," *Library History*, 14.1 (1998), 55–64. https://doi.org/10.1179/lib.1998.14.1.55.

Swartz, Aaron, "Jefferson: Nature Wants Information to Be Free," in *The Boy Who Could Change the World* (London: Verso, 2015), 23–25.

Sweeney, Cynthia, "Say Goodbye to 'Bliss,'" *Napa Valley Register*, 26 March 2014. https://napavalleyregister.com/star/lifestyles/say-goodbye-to-bliss/article_2c485132-b504-11e3-85ef-0019bb2963f4.html.

Tapscott, Don, and Alex Tapscott, *The Blockchain Revolution: How the Technology behind Bitcoin Is Changing Money, Business, and the World* (New York: Penguin, 2016).

Tarnoff, Ben, "Weizenbaum's Nightmares: How the Inventor of the First Chatbot Turned against AI," *Guardian*, 25 July 2023. https://www.theguardian.com/technology/2023/jul/25/joseph-weizenbaum-inventor-eliza-chatbot-turned-against-artificial-intelligence-ai.

Tay, Louis, and Ed Diener, "Needs and Subjective Well-Being around the World," *Journal of Personality and Social Psychology*, 101.2 (2011), 354–65. https://doi.org/10.1037/a0023779.

Taylor, J. D., "Spent? Capitalism's Growing Problem with Anxiety," *ROAR Magazine*, 14 March 2014. https://roarmag.org/essays/neoliberal-capitalism-anxiety-depression-insecurity/.

Taylor, Mike, "Heaven Protect Us from a 'UK National Licence,'" *Sauropod Vertebra Picture of the Week* (blog), 1 April 2015. https://svpow.com/2015/04/01/heaven-help-us-from-a-uk-national-licence/.

Temkin, Daniel, "Coding in Indigenous African Languages," *Esoteric.Codes* (blog), 18 August 2021. https://esoteric.codes/blog/african-programming-languages.

Tenen, Dennis, *Plain Text: The Poetics of Computation* (Stanford, CA: Stanford University Press, 2017).

Tenner, Edward, *Our Own Devices: The Past and Future of Body Technology* (New York: Alfred A. Knopf, 2003).

Thomas, David, "Policy Reform Required as Swedish Director Generals Look to Ban Proof-of-Work Mining," BeInCrypto, 7 November 2021. https://beincrypto.com/?p=166381. Accessed 8 November 2021.

Thompson, John B., *Books in the Digital Age: The Transformation of Academic and Higher Education Publishing in Britain and the United States* (Cambridge: Polity Press, 2005).

Tkacz, Nathaniel, *Wikipedia and the Politics of Openness* (Chicago: University of Chicago Press, 2014).

Tognazzini, Bruce, "Consistency," in Laurel, *The Art of Human-Computer Interface Design*, 75–77.

Treharne, Elaine, and Claude Willan, *Text Technologies: A History*, Stanford Text Technologies (Stanford, CA: Stanford University Press, 2020).

Tresch, John, *The Romantic Machine: Utopian Science and Technology after Napoleon* (Chicago: University of Chicago Press, 2012).

Tsien, Tsuen-hsuin, *Paper and Printing*, Science and Civilisation in China, ed. by Joseph Needham, vol. 5, part 1 (1985; repr., Cambridge: Cambridge University Press, 2001).

———, *Written on Bamboo and Silk: The Beginnings of Chinese Books and Inscriptions* (Chicago: University of Chicago Press, 1962).

Tucker, Aviezer, "In Search of Home," *Journal of Applied Philosophy*, 11.2 (1994), 181–87. https://doi.org/10.1111/j.1468-5930.1994.tb00107.x.

Turner, Eric G., *The Typology of the Early Codex* (Eugene, OR: Wipf & Stock, 2010).

Twigg, Julia, ed., *Routledge Handbook of Cultural Gerontology* (London: Routledge, 2015).

UK Web Archive, "About Us." https://www.webarchive.org.uk/en/ukwa/about. Accessed 10 February 2022.

———, "FAQ," https://www.webarchive.org.uk/en/ukwa/info/faq. Accessed 10 February 2022.

Underwood, Ted, "The Empirical Triumph of Theory," *Again Theory: A Forum on Language, Meaning, and Intent in a Time of Stochastic Parrots* (blog), 29 June 2023. https://critinq.wordpress.com/2023/06/29/the-empirical-triumph-of-theory/.

UNESCO, "Right to Participate in Cultural Life," 2019. https://en.unesco.org/human-rights/cultural-life. Accessed 11 December 2021.

Unicode, "Unicode 13.0 Versioned Charts Index," 2020. https://www.unicode.org/charts/PDF/Unicode-13.0/. Accessed 6 October 2021.

United States District Court, "Memorandum Order, in MPAA v. Reimerdes, Corley and Kazan," 2000. https://cyber.harvard.edu/openlaw/DVD/filings/NY/0202-mem-order.html. Accessed 21 September 2022.

Unsworth, John, "Scholarly Primitives: What Methods Do Humanities Researchers Have in Common, and How Might Our Tools Reflect This?" (presented at the Humanities Computing: formal methods, experimental practice, King's College London, 2000). http://www.people.virginia.edu/~jmu2m/Kings.5-00/primitives.html. Accessed 24 December 2016.

US Copyright Office Review Board, letter to Ryan Abbott, "Second Request for Reconsideration for Refusal to Register a Recent Entrance to Paradise (Correspondence ID 1-3ZPC6C3; SR # 1-7100387071)," 14 February 2022. https://www.copyright.gov/rulings-filings/review-board/docs/a-recent-entrance-to-paradise.pdf.

US Department of Justice Archives, "Overview of the Privacy Act of 1974," 2014. https://www.justice.gov/archives/opcl/definitions. Accessed 16 October 2021.

van Heertum, Cis, "A Hostile Annotation of Rachel Speght's *A Mouzell for Melastomus* (1617)," *English Studies*, 68.6 (1987), 490–96. https://doi.org/10.1080/00138388708598539.

van Mierlo, Wim, "Introduction," in *Textual Scholarship and the Material Book* (Amsterdam: Rodopi, 2007), 1–12. https://doi.org/10.1163/9789042028180_002.

Verhaert, "User Inyerface: A Worst-Practice UI Experiment," 2023. https://userinyerface.com/.

Vermeir, Koen, "The Magic of the Magic Lantern (1660–1700): On Analogical Demonstration and the Visualization of the Invisible," *British Journal for the History of Science*, 38.2 (2005), 127–59.

Veselovsky, Veniamin, Manoel Horta Ribeiro, and Robert West, "Artificial Artificial Artificial Intelligence: Crowd Workers Widely Use Large Language Models for Text Production Tasks" (arXiv, 2023). https://doi.org/10.48550/arXiv.2306.07899.

Videla, Alvaro, "Programming Languages Are Not Languages," Medium, 1 September 2018. https://old-sound.medium.com/programming-languages-are-not-languages-c6f161a78c44. Accessed 27 July 2022.

Wachowski, Lana (as Larry), and Lilly (as Andy) Wachowski, dirs., *The Matrix* (Warner Bros, 1999).

Wade, Nicholas J., "Toying with Science," *Perception*, 33.9 (2004), 1025–32. https://doi.org/10.1068/p3309ed.

Wade, Nicholas J., Josef Brožek, and Jiří Hoskovec, *Purkinje's Vision: The Dawning of Neuroscience* (Mahwah, NJ: Lawrence Erlbaum Associates, 2001).

Wahl, Robert S., "The History of Punched Cards: Using Paper to Store Information," in Wolf, *The Routledge Companion to Media Technology and Obsolescence*, 27–45.

Wakelin, Daniel, *Scribal Correction and Literary Craft: English Manuscripts 1375–1510*, Cambridge Studies in Medieval Literature (Cambridge: Cambridge University Press, 2014). https://doi.org/10.1017/CBO9781139923279.

———, "When Scribes Won't Write: Gaps in Middle English Books," *Studies in the Age of Chaucer*, 36.1 (2014), 249–78. https://doi.org/10.1353/sac.2014.0008.

Walker, John, "Through the Looking Glass," in Laurel, *The Art of Human-Computer Interface Design*, 439–47.

Wang, Jian, Reinhilde Veugelers, and Paula E. Stephan, *Bias against Novelty in Science: A Cautionary Tale for Users of Bibliometric Indicators* (Rochester, NY: Social Science Research Network, 1 December 2015). https://doi.org/10.2139/ssrn.2710572.

Warde, Beatrice, "The Crystal Goblet or Printing Should Be Invisible" (New York: The World Publishing Company, 1956), 11–17.

Warn, Colin, "Coding Is 90% Google Searching—A Brief Note for Beginners," *Medium*, 4 July 2019. https://medium.com/@DJVeaux/coding-is-90-google-searching-a-brief-note-for-beginners-f2f1161876b1.

Warnock, John E., "The Camelot Project," PlanetPDF, 1991. https://planetpdf.com/planetpdf/pdfs/warnock_camelot.pdf. Accessed 13 November 2019.

———, "The Origins of PostScript," *IEEE Annals of the History of Computing*, 40.3 (2018), 68–76. https://doi.org/10.1109/MAHC.2018.033841112.

———, "Simple Ideas That Changed Printing and Publishing," *Proceedings of the American Philosophical Society*, 156.4 (2012), 363–78.

Warnock, John E., and Charles Geschke, "Founding and Growing Adobe Systems, Inc.," *IEEE Annals of the History of Computing*, 41.3 (2019), 24–34. https://doi.org/10.1109/MAHC.2019.2923397.

Weinbren, Grahame String, "Mastery: Computer Games, Intuitive Interfaces, and Interactive Multimedia," *Leonardo*, 28.5 (1995), 403. https://doi.org/10.2307/1576225.

Weiner, Stacy, "The Growing Threat of Ransomware Attacks on Hospitals," AAMC, 20 July 2021. https://www.aamc.org/news-insights/growing-threat-ransomware-attacks-hospitals.

West, David, *Object Thinking* (Redmond, WA: Microsoft Press, 2004).

White, Thomas, "Potential Lives: The Matter of Late Medieval Manuscripts" (unpublished doctoral thesis, Birkbeck, University of London, 2016). http://vufind.lib.bbk.ac.uk/vufind/Record/560699. Accessed 9 September 2021.

Wiener, Ann Elizabeth, "What's That Smell You're Reading?," Science History Institute, 27 March 2018. https://www.sciencehistory.org/distillations/whats-that-smell-youre-reading.

Willinsky, John, *The Intellectual Properties of Learning: A Prehistory from Saint Jerome to John Locke* (Chicago, IL: University of Chicago Press, 2017).

Willinsky, John, Alex Garnett, and Angela Pan Wong, "Refurbishing the Camelot of Scholarship: How to Improve the Digital Contribution of the PDF Research Article," *Journal of Electronic Publishing*, 15.1 (2012). http://dx.doi.org/10.3998/3336451.0015.102.

Wilson, Georgina, "Surface Reading Paper as Feminist Bibliography," *Criticism*, 64.3 (2023), 369–83.

Wilson, Ruth, and Monica Landoni, "Evaluating the Usability of Portable Electronic Books," in *Proceedings of the 2003 ACM Symposium on Applied Computing—SAC '03* (presented at the 2003 ACM symposium, Melbourne, Florida: ACM Press, 2003), 564. https://doi.org/10.1145/952532.952644.

Winkler, Adam, "'Corporations Are People' Is Built on an Incredible 19th-Century Lie," *Atlantic*, 5 March 2018. https://www.theatlantic.com/business/archive/2018/03/corporations-people-adam-winkler/554852/.

Winograd, Terry, and Fernando Flores, *Understanding Computers and Cognition: A New Foundation for Design*, 24th printing (Boston: Addison-Wesley, 2008).

Wittgenstein, Ludwig, *Philosophical Investigations: The German Text, with a Revised English Translation* (Oxford: Blackwell, 2001).

Wolf, Mark J. P., "Farewell to the Phosphorescent Glow: The Long Life of the Cathode-Ray Tube," in Wolf, *The Routledge Companion to Media Technology and Obsolescence*, 118–35.

——, *The Routledge Companion to Media Technology and Obsolescence* (New York: Routledge, 2019).

Wolfe, Heather, "On Curating Filing Holes," *Inscription: The Journal of Material Text—Theory, Practice, History*, 1.2 (2021), 27–47.

Wolfram, Stephen, "What Is ChatGPT Doing . . . and Why Does It Work?," *Stephen Wolfram: Writings*, 14 February 2023. https://writings.stephenwolfram.com/2023/02/what-is-chatgpt-doing-and-why-does-it-work/.

WordPress Foundation, "About." https://wordpressfoundation.org/. Accessed 10 December 2021.

——, "Philosophy," 2010. https://wordpressfoundation.org/philosophy/. Accessed 10 December 2021.

Worstall, Tim, "'I'll Believe Corporations Are People When Texas Executes One': What Is This Foolishness From Robert Reich?" *Forbes*, 17 November 2012. https://www.forbes.com/sites/timworstall/2012/11/17/ill-believe-corporations-are-people-when-texas-executes-one-what-is-this-foolishness-from-robert-reich/.

Woudhuysen, Henry R., "Early Play Texts: Forms and Formes," in *In Arden: Editing Shakespeare: Essays in Honour of Richard Proudfoot*, ed. by Ann Thompson and Gordon McMullan (London: Arden Shakespeare, 2003), 48–61.

Wu, Jingfang, and Rong Chen, "Metaphors Ubiquitous in Computer and Internet Terminologies," *Journal of Arts and Humanities*, 10 (2013), 15.

Wu, Leon, "The Article about Paper Sizes You Didn't Know You Needed," *Medium*, 3 October 2019. https://modus.medium.com/a4-vs-letter-why-size-matters-5477a647b1c2.

Wu, Qiushi, and Kangjie Lu, "On the Feasibility of Stealthily Introducing Vulnerabilities in Open-Source Software via Hypocrite Commits," 2021. https://linuxreviews.org/images/d/d9/OpenSourceInsecurity.pdf.

Wyatt, Sally, "Metaphors in Critical Internet and Digital Media Studies," *New Media & Society*, 23.2 (2021), 406–16. https://doi.org/10.1177/1461444820929324.

Wylder, Edith, "Emily Dickinson's Punctuation: The Controversy Revisited," *American Literary Realism*, 36.3 (2004), 206–24.

Yanmaani, "Proof of Stake Is a Scam and the People Promoting It Are Scammers," *Yanmaani's Blog*, 9 November 2021. https://yanmaani.github.io/proof-of-stake-is-a-scam-and-the-people-promoting-it-are-scammers/.

Younger, Carolyn, "Windows XP Desktop Screen Is a Napa Image," *Napa Valley Register*, 18 January 2010. https://napavalleyregister.com/news/local/windows-xp-desktop-screen-is-a-napa-image/article_7703c8b2-03e9-11df-bb34-001cc4c03286.html.

Zanola, Maria Teresa, "Les anglicismes et le français du XXIe siècle : La fin du franglais ?," *Synergies*, 4, 2008, 87–96.

Zetter, Kim, "Another Hacker's Laptop, Cellphones Searched at Border," *Wired*, 18 November 2010. https://www.wired.com/2010/11/hacker-border-search/.

π, 2–4
πfs, 3–4, 220
ℒ symbol, 25, 102–3

accessibility, 201–6, 209–11, 219
Acid2 test, 148, 149
Ackerman, Mark S., 213
Adobe PDF. *See* PDF format
Alberti, Leon Battista, 68
algorithmic shadow, 228–30
Allen, Theodore W., 74
alphabets. *See* Unicode
Alvez, André Azevedo, 171
Amazon, 8
Anderson, Benedict, 115–16
Anderson, Gregory, 101
annotations (in books), 258–59, 264
anxiety, 248–49
Apple, 37, 62, 188–90, 197. *See also*
   macOS

Aqua interface system, 189–90
Aristotle, 262
Arrival, 90
artificial intelligence (AI), 8, 232;
   ethics of, 235–38, 240; singularity
   in, 235–37, 239. *See also* machine
   learning
artificial text generation. *See* natural
   language generation
ASCII (American Standard Code for
   Information Interchange), 84; art,
   99–100
Asimov's laws of robotics, 236
aspect ratio, 44–46
assessment (in higher education), 238
atomic bomb, development of, 237
Atwood, Jeff, 247, 248, 249
Austin, J. L., 85
autonomous systems (AS), 113–16,
   118, 138

Geoffrey Turnovsky
*Reading Typographically: Immersed in
Print in Early Modern France*

Collin Jennings
*Enlightenment Links: Theories of Mind and
Media in Eighteenth-Century Britain*

Bridget Whearty
Digital Codicology: Medieval Books and Modern Labor

Michael Gavin
*Literary Mathematics: Quantitative
Theory for Textual Studies*

Michelle Warren
Holy Digital Grail: A Medieval Book on the Internet

Blaine Greteman
*Networking Print in Shakespeare's England:
Influence, Agency, and Revolutionary Change*

Simon Reader
Notework: Victorian Literature and Nonlinear Style

Yohei Igarashi
*The Connected Condition: Romanticism
and the Dream of Communication*

Elaine Treharne and Claude Willan
Text Technologies: A History

The authorized representative in the EU for product safety and compliance is:
Mare Nostrum Group
B.V Doelen 72
4831 GR Breda
The Netherlands